Chica da Silva

Júnia Ferreira Furtado offers a fascinating study of the world of a freed woman of color in a small Brazilian town where itinerant merchants, former slaves, Portuguese administrators, and concubines interact across social and cultural lines. The child of an African slave from Costa da Mina and a Brazilian military nobleman of Portuguese descent, Chica da Silva won her freedom using social and matrimonial strategies. But the story of Chica da Silva is not merely the personal history of a woman nor the social history of a colonial Brazilian town. Rather, it provides a historical perspective on a woman's agency, the cultural universe she inhabited, and the myths that were created around her in subsequent centuries, as Chica de Silva came to symbolize both an example of racial democracy and the stereotype of licentiousness and sensuality always attributed to the black or mulatta female in the Brazilian popular imagination.

Júnia Ferreira Furtado holds a Ph.D. in social history from the Universidade de São Paulo, Brazil. She is currently a professor of history at the Universidade Federal de Minas Gerais. Her work on Chica da Silva has won awards from the Carlos Chagas Foundation for Women and Gender Research and the Ford Foundation. She has also contributed articles to *Cartografia da conquista das minas* and *History of Cartography*, volume 4. The Portuguese-language edition of this book was awarded honorable mention in 2004 by the Casa de las Américas Foundation of Cuba.

New Approaches to the Americas

Edited by Stuart Schwartz, *Yale University*

Also published in the series:

Arnold J. Bauer, *Goods, Power, History: Latin America's Material Culture*

Laird Bergad, *The Comparative Histories of Slavery in Brazil, Cuba, and the United States*

Noble David Cook, *Born to Die: Disease and New World Conquest, 1492–1650*

Sandra Lauderdale Graham, *Caetana Says No: Women's Stories from a Brazilian Slave Society*

Herbert S. Klein, *The Atlantic Slave Trade*

Robert M. Levine, *Father of the Poor? Vargas and His Era*

Shawn William Miller, *An Environmental History of Latin America*

Susan Socolow, *The Women of Colonial Latin America*

CHICA DA SILVA

A BRAZILIAN SLAVE OF THE EIGHTEENTH CENTURY

JÚNIA FERREIRA FURTADO
Universidade Federal de Minas Gerais, Brazil

CAMBRIDGE
UNIVERSITY PRESS

CAMBRIDGE
UNIVERSITY PRESS

32 Avenue of the Americas, New York NY 10013-2473, USA

Cambridge University Press is part of the University of Cambridge.

It furthers the University's mission by disseminating knowledge in the pursuit of education, learning, and research at the highest international levels of excellence.

www.cambridge.org
Information on this title: www.cambridge.org/9780521711555

© Júnia Ferreira Furtado 2009

First published 2009
Reprinted 2013

A catalog record for this publication is available from the British Library.

Library of Congress Cataloging in Publication data
Furtado, Júnia Ferreira.
Chica da Silva : a Brazilian slave of the eighteenth century / Júnia Ferreira Furtado.
    p.   cm. – (New approaches to the Americas)
Includes bibliographical references and index.
ISBN 978-0-521-88465-5 (hardback) – ISBN 978-0-521-71155-5 (pbk.)
1. Silva, Chica da, d. 1796.   2. Slaves – Brazil – Biography.   3. Slavery – Brazil – History – 18th century.   4. Brazil – Social conditions – 18th century.   I. Title.
HT869.S55F87   2005
306.3´62092–dc22   2007036949
[B]

ISBN   978-0-521-88465-5   Hardback
ISBN   978-0-521-71155-5   Paperback

It was there in the district of Tejuco,
where diamonds spilled forth from the stones.

– Cecília Meireles, *Romanceiro da Inconfidência**

---

* The epigraphs for each chapter were taken from *Romanceiro da Inconfidência*, by
Cecília Meireles. The term *Inconfidência* refers to a crime against the king's power, a
crime of lèse-majesté. In the second half of the eighteenth century, during the reign
of João I, a special criminal code was published prescribing severe punishments for
the crime of *Inconfidência*.

Contents

Acknowledgments

Before starting this book I had always believed that research work was, first and foremost, an essentially solitary undertaking that locked the researcher away in archives, libraries, or in an office in front of a computer screen. In reality, researching the life of Chica da Silva was a task shared with friends, historians, colleagues, students, family, staff, and many others who helped me reassemble the intricate web that was the life of this eighteenth-century woman. Thanking them all is a little like retracing the steps of the research that lies hidden behind this work.

First of all, I extend my gratitude to Virgínia dos Santos Mendes, whose friendship and academic companionship unwittingly set me on the course of this research. It was through her efforts to construct the Centro de Memória Cultural do Vale do Jequitinhonha (Jequitinhonha Valley Cultural Memory Center), and those of our colleagues and friends at the History Department of the Faculty of Philosophy of Diamantina (Fafidia)/Universidade Federal de Minas Gerais (UFMG), that this project began to take shape. It is to Virgínia, Neusa Fernandes, Mariuth Santos, Kiko (Paulo Francisco Flecha Alkimin), James William Goodwin Jr., Toninho (Antônio Carlos Fernandes), Marcos Lobato, and Dayse Lúcide Silva, companions on those lawless Diamantinian Mondays, that I dedicate this book. Our efforts to make the center a reality, a forum, and an instrument for historical research in the region would not have been possible without the support of the UFMG rector, Professor Aluísio Pimenta, and of the pro-rector of extended studies, Professor Eduardo Andrade Santa Cecília.

The establishment of the UFMG Extended Studies Center in the Jequitinhonha Valley, of which this project also came to be a part, furnished the interinstitutional partnerships, resources, and infrastructure that were indispensable in conducting this research. I would like to give special thanks to the research pro-rector, Professor Paulo Beirão, and the pro-rector for extended studies, Professor Evandro José Lemos da Cunha. To the tireless Marizinha Nogueira, without whom the center would be mere abstraction, I extend my special thanks, as well as to all of the colleagues who partake of this privileged space of academic integration at the UFMG.

At certain moments and stages I was able to draw upon financial assistance from research support agencies, which helped fund the hiring of scholarship students, the research trips, the purchase of material, and the reproduction of documents. I would like to thank Fapemig – Fundação de Amparo à Pesquisa do Estado de Minas Gerais (Research Support Foundation of Minas Gerais) – for being the first institution to concede funding through its support for the Jequitinhonha Valley Cultural Memory Center; the Ford Foundation/Carlos Chagas Foundation for selecting the project as one of the prize winners at the VIII Concurso de Dotações para a Pesquisa sobre Mulheres (VIII Prize Competition for the Funding of Research on Women) in 1999; Finep – Financiadora de Estudos e Projetos (Financer of Studies and Projects) – another institution whose funding came through the UFMG Jequitinhonha Valley Cultural Memory Center; and the Fundep – Fundação de Desenvolvimento da Pesquisa (Research Development Foundation) – Fund for Research and Integrated Projects for the support channeled to the project "A riqueza e a pobreza do vale do Jequitinhonha" (Wealth and poverty in the Jequitinhonha Valley) on its behalf by the UFMG Pro-Rectory for Post-Graduation. Coordinated by Professor Ralfo Matos, the research on Chica da Silva and the freedwomen of Tejuco came under this umbrella project as a subproject.

With the financial support of these institutions it was possible to recruit various scholarship holders to help me sift through records. I would especially like to thank Lígia Fátima de Carvalho, Maria

Angélica Alves Pereira, Renato de Carvalho Ribeiro, Maria José Ferro de Sousa, and Maria Eugênia Ribeiro Pinto.

The search for documents that could in some way reconstruct the life of Chica da Silva took me on a tireless tour of archives and libraries both in Brazil and abroad, institutions in which I always found helpful and attentive staff who made the distances, costs, and difficulties of the enormous task I had set myself that much smaller. In Diamantina, I thank Til Pestana, director of the region's Iphan – Instituto de Patrimônio Histórico e Artístico Nacional (Institute of National Historical and Artistic Heritage) – who gave me and my interns free run of the Antônio Torres Library and opened up the documentation on the House of the Ottoni at a time when it was undergoing restoration. I am also grateful to staff member Denise Alves Ferreira for all the attention she dispensed.

An important portion of this research was done at the Ecclesiastical Archive of the Archdiocese of Diamantina; I extend my sincerest thanks to the Bishops Geraldo Magela Reis and Paulo Lopes de Faria, who franchised my access to the archive, where, contrary to the rules of the house, I was providentially "forgotten" until late at night. I also thank staff member Débora Maria Braga Reis, who spared no effort to make the work of transcribing the documentation that much easier.

In Portugal, I would like to thank my good friend Tiago Pinto dos Reis Miranda, who volunteered to set up a visit to the former house of the contractor João Fernandes de Oliveira, and to the Fundação Luso-Americana para o Desenvolvimento (Luso-American Development Foundation), the current proprietor of the building, for granting access to the house and permission to photograph its interior. With Tiago I passed unforgettable afternoons wandering through the streets of Lisbon on veritable immersions in the history of this marvelous city. At the Arquivo Histórico Ultramarino (Overseas Historical Archive), Dr. José Sintra Martinheira made the institution's cartography of Diamantina and Tejuco promptly and swiftly available.

In Italy, I am grateful to the director of the Archivio Centrale dello Stato, Dr. Luigi Londei, for his prompt response to my research requests and to staff member Giuliana Adorni, who, despite the brief stay available to me in Rome, made an exception to the institution's norms in order to have the documentation released for my consultation.

At the convent of Macaúbas, where no direct access to the estate is allowed, I would like to thank Sister Maria Imaculada for so perfectly researching, photocopying, and transcribing the documents I requested.

In Belo Horizonte, I extend my gratitude to Assis Horta, who kindly introduced me to the rich collection of documents, photographs, and objects on the history of Diamantina she keeps in her private estate.

At Princeton University, New Jersey, USA, I found the environment and peace I needed to write the first full draft of this book. I also had the inestimable assistance of teachers and staff on the Latin American Studies Program there, who went on to become dear and much-missed friends. I would like to offer special thanks to Jeremy Adelman, Luiza Franco Moreira, David Myhre, Rose (Rosália Rivera), Stanley Stein, and Peter T. Johnson. I was able to avail of the stimulating and proficuous environment of debate at the history department, particularly through my contact with lecturers Robert Darnton, Kenneth Mills, Antony Grafton, Eileen Reeves, and Elizabeth Lunbeck. Amelia O'Neill, Andra Olívia Maciuceanu, Dean Antony Dent, Elizabeth Balthrop, Kathie Holtz, Kristina Allemany, and Nicolas Fintch, students in my course on Brazilian slavery, were also important interlocutors on my interpretations of Chica da Silva as both a theme and a figure.

Unexpected contributions from people I never actually got to meet in person enriched this text even further. In particular, I would like to say thanks for the generosity shown by Samuel da Cunha Pereira, who provided me with a copy of Jacinta da Siqueira's will; Valdina Oliveira Pinto, for her knowledge of the Banta religion; Tiche Puntoni and the group Klepsidra for recommending and transcribing the lyrics of the song "Xula carioca"; and Eneida Mercadante for her information on Carlos Julião.

(I can only lament the disappearance of the book of wills containing Chica da Silva's last will and testament. This important document went missing from the Archives of the Fórum do Serro, and its return, and that of its accompanying stands, would mean the recovery of part of the already dilapidated memory of the nation's history, the shared heritage of all of society.)

Many colleagues and friends joined me in the search for documents and collaborated with suggestions, readings, and comments on various chapters and drafts; among those to whom I would like to express my gratitude are Adriana Romeiro, Caio César Boschi, Renato Pinto Venâncio, Francis Dutra, Adalgisa Arantes Campos, Luciano Figueiredo, João José Reis, Stuart Schwartz, Thaïs Cougo Pimentel, Pedro Puntoni, and Íris Kantor.

I thank Maria Odila Leite da Silva Dias and Maria Luiza Mott, my readers on the project presented to the Ford Foundation/ Carlos Chagas Foundation, for their suggestions and critical readings, which enriched the research and pointed me in various directions pursued in the final draft. Amir Nadur Jr. took great care in photographing the sketches by Carlos Julião that illustrate the book, as did Maria Cristina Armendani Trivellato with those of the village of Milho Verde.

To my friends and colleagues at Aracne, António Manuel Hespanha, Federico Palomo, André Belo, Rui Tavares, Guiomar de Grammont, Neil Safier, and Angela Barreto Xavier, I extend my thanks for their suggestions, documents, and proficuous discussion on academic themes and on others less so but nonetheless just as enjoyable.

I also thank Professors Stuart Schwartz and Ana Lúcia Almeida Gazzola, the rector of UFMG, for all their support on the publication of the book in the USA. I extend my gratitude to Anthony Doyle for the English translation of the Portuguese originals; Fernanda Borges de Moraes, who allowed me to use her Minas Gerais maps; and Kris Lane, who made a generous and meticulous revision of the final proofs.

My hardest task is that of thanking my husband, Lucas Vanucci Lins; my parents, Ilda and Evaldo Furtado; my niece, Isabel Furtado Machado; and my daughters, Clara and Alice. My debt to them and love are boundless. Lucas was a keen reader of the infinite versions of each of the chapters and of the various forms the book took over the course of seven years. He spared no encouragement for me to go deeper into my research, even at the cost of long spells of absence or isolation in front of books and the computer. He was likewise a companion on those constant trips to Minas in search of the farms, towns, and convents through which Chica passed with her family and the routes they would have taken. I thank my parents, Ilda and Evaldo, for their encouragement; like all parents, they were my greatest fans. None of this would have been possible without them. Isabel, sweet as ever, read the original drafts and enriched them with her suggestions and criticism. My daughters, Clara and Alice, were brought up by a somewhat absent mother, which is why they "hate Chica da Silva," but their unconditional love has also been the reason for my deepest and truest happiness. It is to them, whom Chica robbed of their mother for countless hours, that I dedicate this book.

Preface

The day is still to come
When they shall turn to us and ask:
Who was this Chica da Silva,
That once lived in this place?

Sometime around the second quarter of the twentieth century, the journalist Antônio Torres gathered together items he found in various notebooks on figures and events from the history of Tejuco, then known by the name of Diamantina. On Chica da Silva he wrote: "It is said that her corpse was found many years after her death and that her skin was still dry and black."[1] At first glance, this affirmation might seem to suggest sainthood; after all, Chica would not have been the first or the last in the long line of Luso-Brazilian tradition to have been found in such a state, considered a triumph over deathly decay and a testament to the saintliness and purity of the deceased. An example of this phenomenon occurred in 1752, when the Portuguese newspaper *Gazeta de Lisboa* announced the death of Sister Isabel de Madre de Deus, a native of Bahia, attributing the fact that her body remained flexible and the presence of sweat in her coffin to the virtuous life she had led, "having lived abstracted from worldly things, conserving her memory and diligence for no other purpose than to serve God."[2]

[1]   BAT. Biblioteca Antônio Torres' Private Files, Box 7.
[2]   ANTT. Real Mesa Censória. Gazeta de Lisboa. Cx. 465, no. 39. Quinta-feira. 2 de novembro de 1752, pp. 562–3.

Chica da Silva was buried in the church of São Francisco de Assis in Tejuco, whose stone portal bore the carved image of Saint Margarida of Cortona. The undecayed body of the saint lay in repose in a church in Tuscany, where it worked miracles and cures.[3] The effect was deemed to be the result of her venerable life, as she had given all of her possessions to the poor after converting.[4]

The sight of Chica da Silva's still-intact body caused no such impression of purity in her fellow countrymen, much less the suggestion of sainthood. Below is how Antônio Torres described the reactions provoked by the discovery of her corpse:

> It was like a bag of bones, which rattled sinisterly with the slightest movement. The gravedigger had the scruples to store it in a sacred place and dispose of it in far off ravines, like the remains of a wild animal. Rolling in the wind, [the bones] produced strange and terrifying vibrations, seeming to snicker with scorn. The bravest amongst the passers-by blurted the customary insult: "Take it away, quingongo!" The rest scurried hurriedly past, blessing themselves at the sound of the rattling bones."[5]

Our interest in the description Antônio Torres provides about Chica's corpse, which was probably discovered during the restoration of the abovementioned church,[6] does not stem from a discussion of its veracity, but from the analysis of the impressions provoked by its unearthing. The reactions of repulsion and fear described by the author – very different from the sentiments Chica evokes today – expressed how the population of the time felt at the sight of her undecayed body, which conferred altogether different meanings upon the myth of this former Tejuco slave. The popular interjection of "Take it away, quingongo!" reflects the townsfolk's fear. Quingongo,

---

[3] Lúcia Machado de Almeida. *Passeio à Diamantina*. 1960, pp. 88–9.
[4] Luiz Mott. *Rosa Egipcíaca, uma santa africana no Brasil*. 1993, p. 70.
[5] BAT. Arquivo Particular de Antônio Torres. Caixa 7.
[6] In 1917, a grandiose restoration was carried out on the church, principally in the vault, which was in the process of caving in, thus exposing the pillars. The bodies buried there were transferred to ossuaries constructed outside the church. Iphan/BH archives. File on the Church of São Francisco de Assis in Diamantina.

a divinity of the Banta religion associated with the bowels of the earth – and thus also related to illness, death, and regeneration – was exhorted to remove her mortal remains.

However, in contradictory fashion, the figure of Chica da Silva always awoke and attracted curiosity. Her image, popularized first in history books and later in novels, cinema, and television, has stood the test of time.

From the mid-nineteenth century, when Joaquim Felício dos Santos, a native of Diamantina, wrote about Chica da Silva in his *Memórias do Distrito Diamantino* (*Memories of the Diamantine District*), she ceased to be just one of the many slave-girls living in Minas Gerais in the eighteenth century and became a myth, one that would over time, as demonstrated in Antônio Torres's account, undergo innumerable modifications, updates, and re-readings in accordance with the tastes of the day.

Witch, seductress, heroine, queen, or slave: who, after all, was Chica da Silva? After nearly three centuries, the lack of historical investigation into her life has meant that this question has effectively remained unanswered. This book aims to get to know her, not as a curiosity nor as an exception, but to use her as a medium through which to shed new light on the women of her period and therefore bring them into history. Only thus can they be freed from the stereotypes that have been imposed upon them over time. The path I chose was to search for records of Chica's passage through history in the available documents. What initially seemed impossible became a fruitful and productive task, as can be seen from the countless documents that speak of her and of the diamond contractor and his family found in various archives in Brazil and Portugal and listed at the end of this volume.

However, before the reader makes a foray into the pages that follow, it is necessary to give some indication of what should and should not be expected from this text, which is the fruit of historical reflection based on official documents stored in libraries and public and private archives in Portugal, Brazil, and the United States. These are not intimate records, which unfortunately have all been lost, registering the thoughts and desires of the men and women of the time; rather, they are baptismal records, brotherhood rosters, royal orders, lawsuits, petitions, and other such documents, which generally reveal facts, not opinions. That said, this does not prevent the historian from seeking the emotions, desires, and thoughts that motivated them; their re-reading can reveal a lot more than one would expect of the customary limited approach to this type of document.

Though based on painstaking documental and bibliographical research on Chica da Silva and her descendants, this book does not exhaust, nor was it ever intended to, the interpretations of this woman and of the time in which she lived. As such, various questions will remain unanswered. Furthermore, if the portrait that comes of this historical immersion cannot be compared to a Renaissance illuminated manuscript, replete with details, it is no less faithful to the original, albeit through brushstrokes more like those of an impressionist painter. All human lives are fathomless; it is impossible to know a life in full, but the Chica da Silva we have sought to describe herein tries to get as close as possible to the real woman who lived in Tejuco in the eighteenth century. By inserting her within her spatial and temporal context, I have tried to construct a historically credible character.[7]

It was also important to avoid the traps of biographical illusion.[8] One cannot pretend that biography and history are subordinate to a chronological rigidity in the manner of natural lives, nor expect them to be possessed of unique and linear sense and meanings ruled by rationality. Life and history are not always coherent and often take the least expected paths. Writing the history of a life requires paying due attention to the ruptures, to the disturbances, to the "tale told by an idiot, full of sound and fury, signifying nothing."[9]

---

[7] "Il m'a fallu me demander s'il était possible d'approcher un Saint Louis qu'on pourrait dire 'vrai', vraiment historique, à travers les sources." Jacques Le Goff. *Saint Louis*. 1996, p. 17.

[8] Pierre Bourdieu. "L'illusion biographique." *Actes de La Recherche*. 1986, pp. 69–72.

[9] William Shakespeare. *Macbeth*. Apud: Pierre Bourdieu, op. cit., p. 69.

This study sought to promote the intersection between the individual account and the historical context to which it belonged.[10] Only in this way does Chica cease to be a myth and become intelligible as a historical figure, both in the aspects she shared with other freedwomen of her time and in those in which she was unique. Biography is never intended to be capable of containing the multiplicity of meanings of a life. The time of biography is fragmented, like that of history, and therefore characterized by contradictions and paradoxes.[11]

If a novel is defined by the freedom with which the author constructs the histories of the characters, biography is limited by the life and real existence of its subject, which it pieces together by analyzing the material derived from the chosen sources. However, both genres are marked by narrative style, with biography being the best expression of the rebirth of the historical narrative.[12] The pleasure of narrating the life of Chica da Silva, of wrapping it in a web of words, was the guiding thread that led to the writing of this book. Even though I followed the guidelines of modern historical methodologies in writing the chapters and selecting the themes, it was the voices of the characters themselves, though indirect and filtered through the records, that determined the paths to be followed. As Borges reminds us: "There is something in the story, in narrative, that will always be with us. I do not believe that man will ever tire of telling stories."[13]

SLAVERY AND MANUMISSION IN MINAS

In the auriferous region, manumission was always more accessible to female slaves, although paid slaves or those employed in mining managed to save up enough money to buy their freedom, as few were ever released in return for the services rendered to their owners. As

---

[10] Michel Vovelle. "De la biographie à l'étude de cas." *Problèmes et méthodes de la biographie*. 1985, p. 191.
[11] Giovanni Levi. "Les usages de la biographie." *Annales*. 1989, pp. 1325–35.
[12] Ibidem.
[13] Jorge Luis Borges. *Esse ofício do verso*. 2000, p. 62.

the mining stations began to grow, women were in short supply (especially white women), concubinage became widespread, and many white landowners ended up freeing their slave mistresses. This was generally officially done on their deathbeds and a date was usually set for the concession of liberty, thus ensuring a few more years of service for their heirs. Rarely was manumission conceded during a gentleman's lifetime.[14]

In virtue of this, Minas Gerais presented much more diversity and a greater degree of miscegenation than the slave societies of the Brazilian coast, the Caribbean, and the southern United States.[15] In these regions, the generalization of monocultural exportation accentuated the gulf between the worlds of the free, dominated by the whites, and of the slaves, made up of blacks. As the eighteenth century wore on, a demographic of freed mulattos and blacks began to emerge, of which Chica da Silva was but a single example.[16]

In the diamond region, the role of women and the family has still not been studied with the depth the theme deserves; while in general terms we see the repetition of the same pattern as in the auriferous region, we can also detect certain particularities. The biography of Chica da Silva does shed some light on the worlds of the region's freedwomen, as the lives they actually led differed very little from those of other women. The historiography has tended to present their lifestyle from the perspective of a reconstructed stereotypical image of the black woman, whether free or slave. Recent studies have shown that once they had attained the condition of white man's concubine, something quite common at the time, the freedwomen sought to reinsert themselves within society, making the most of the advantages this condition conferred in terms of minimizing the stigma of their color and enslavement. However, the existence of this possibility should not be mistaken for a sign of tolerance or benignity

---

[14] Kathleen J. Higgins. *Licentious liberty.* 1999.

[15] Herbert S. Klein. *African slavery in Latin America and the Caribbean.* 1986.

[16] A. J. R. Russell-Wood. "Preconditions and precipitants of the independence movement in Portuguese America." In *From colony to nation: Essays on the independence of Brasil.* 1975, p. 11. Also A. J. R. Russell-Wood. *The black man in slavery and freedom in colonial Brazil.* 1982.

in racial relations in Brazil, as if stemming from some form of *racial democracy*.[17]

The myth of Chica da Silva has been used to support the thesis that, in Brazil, the bonds of affection between free whites and colored women that concubinage established somehow mitigated the exploitation inherent in the slave system.[18] However, we must not forget that, despite the economic benefit it brought to many of these women, this practice disguised a dual exploitation – both sexual and racial – as these women were never elevated to the condition of spouse. Furthermore, as we shall see, as they lived among the free, they tried to imitate their habits, customs, lifestyles, and dress, thus reproducing on a smaller scale the very world that had subjected them to slavery.

Therefore, rather than serving as a point of departure for the construction of a black identity, manumission all too often signaled the beginning of a process whereby former slave women embraced the values of the white elite with a view to finding a place in that society for themselves and their descendants. Far from revealing the democratic nature of race relations, this process of ethnic and cultural whitening really betrays the subtle traps though which racial oppression is hidden in Brazil. On the other hand, new studies on Brazilian slavery have shown that African customs and traditions were often maintained behind this innocuous front.[19]

In the hierarchical and exclusive society of the time, marriage was subject to stringent rules. The constant mobility of the men and the inequality of the spouses in terms of background, social standing, and race tended to complicate and even impede legal matrimony. The Portuguese state normally did not allow the union of individuals from different pedigrees and even went so far as to establish processes to verify the origins of the betrothed. In other words, black and mulatto women could only marry men of their ilk. The lack of

---

[17] Emília Viotti Costa. "The myth of racial democracy." In *Myths and histories*, 1985. This myth, formulated by Gilberto Freyre, found one of its most recent exponents in Darcy Ribeiro.

[18] Kathleen J. Higgins, op. cit., pp. 9–10.

[19] Robert W. Slenes. *Na senzala, uma flor.* 1999.

"suitable" consorts meant that consensual couplings between individuals from different conditions became common and widespread
among white men and colored women. Consequently, by not making these unions official, the white gentry could withhold from these
companions any right to their patrimony, as would otherwise have
been their due under Portuguese law, which meant that the position
of these women was clearly disadvantaged when compared to that of
a legal wife.[20] What was positive in this act was that it avoided the
stigmas of color and birthright inherited from former slave mothers
being perpetuated in official documents. In a society in which such
"marks" were handed down through the generations and in which
lineage was a fundamental element in social identification, having
this condition registered in as few official documents as possible was
the only way of minimizing what was clearly considered a handicap.
One lived in hope that time would erase these stains from memory.

This immersion in the past with a view to reconstructing the
influence of the family and women in the colony is a course that
still needs to be arduously pursued. Today, we can no longer accept
the traditional view of the patriarchal family in which the woman
was delegated a practically nullified role. Recent research on the
subject shows that there was a whole gamut of multiple and varied approaches and that countless possibilities opened up to these
women once freed, ranging from declassification to more positive
forms of social inclusion. Studying the life of Chica da Silva, among
other freedwomen, will allow us to understand the society in which
they lived and what they had to do to be accepted in it.

Chica da Silva lived a considerable part of her life at the side of the
High Court Judge João Fernandes. Her relationship with this important white man gave the course of that life altogether different meanings. Telling the tale of this woman's life will also require tracing the
history of the diamond contractor, as – though apart in their final
years, he in Portugal and she in Tejuco – their paths were otherwise
permanently entwined. This book tells the story of the lives of Chica
da Silva, João Fernandes de Oliveira, and their descendants; lives

[20]   Ibidem, p. 112.

that remained connected and whose meanings can only be under-stood if analyzed in conjunction.

The book begins with a treatment of the historical and geograph-ical context in which the lives of Chica da Silva and the High Court judge unfolded. Chapter 2 dissects the vastly different backgrounds of each; she the daughter of an African slave and he the son of a Portuguese with a descendant of the São Paulo gentry, whose father had sought social and economic ascension through business in the colonies. We will also seek to clarify how this slave-girl came to meet a noble diamond contractor in the mountains of the Diaman-tine District. Chapters 3 and 4 deal with the couple's relationship, which spanned fifteen years and produced thirteen children, and how this family came to hold a position at the heart of a society as dom-inated by the values of hierarchy and birthright as Minas Gerais. Chapters 5, 6, and 7 will analyze the lifestyle they led, the proper-ties they accumulated, the slaves they acquired, and the education they gave their children, and it will also glean something of the rela-tionships they established in the village through the examination of the godparents and wedding sponsors named in marriage and birth records. From Chapter 8 on, the book will describe the fates of Chica, João Fernandes, and their descendants after their separation, when he returned to the Court and she stayed on at Tejuco. Chapter 11 details the birth and metamorphosis of the myth of Tejuco's most famous slave.

One final forewarning: the Chica da Silva that emerges from these chapters bears little resemblance to the myth propagated by cinema and television; it is up to the reader, with an open mind, to find the answers to the question that has guided the production of this book: "After all, who was this Chica da Silva, that once lived in this place?"[21]

---

[21] Cecília Meireles. *Romanceiro da Inconfidência*, 1965, p. 51.

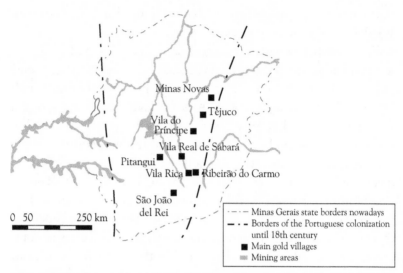

Map 1. Areas where gold and diamonds were produced in the first half of the eighteenth century.

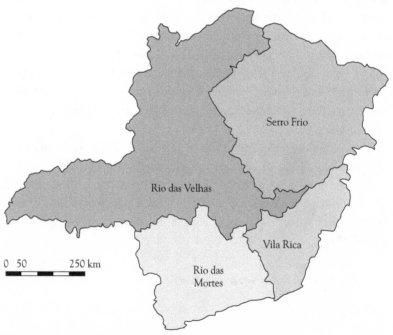

Map 2. Counties of the captaincy of Minas Gerais (1720–1815).
(Maps by Fernanda Borges de Moraes)

Introduction to the
English Edition

From the very beginning of the colonization of Brazil, in the sixteenth century, the Portuguese went to great lengths to find precious metals and stones on their American territory, following the example of the Spanish, who had located mines of silver and gold in their part situated west of the Tordesilhas[1] Meridian. This Portuguese quest was anchored in a firm conviction that such riches truly existed – a certainty that largely stemmed from the manner in which the Europeans understood universal cosmology and terrestrial geography. It was believed that the world was ordered according to the principles of sympathy and antipathy, setting in motion a chain of analogies and oppositions by which all living creatures and inanimate objects on earth either attracted or repelled each other.[2] Seen in this light, American geography, like that of the rest of the world, was expected to follow certain patterns, with similarities among regions on the same latitude or meridian, even if in different hemispheres. It was this belief that made the Portuguese so sure that there were enormous deposits of silver and gold to be found in the Brazilian midsouth. After all, this part of America was on the same latitude as the Potosi

---

[1] The Treaty of Tordesilhas, agreed between the Portuguese and the Spanish in 1494, divided the new world between the two empires via an imaginary meridian line 370 leagues west of an unspecified island in the Cape Verde archipelago.

[2] "Up to the end of the 16th Century, similarity played a constructive role in occidental cultural knowledge ... as it was [similarity] that organized the set of symbols, enabled the knowledge of visible and invisible things [and] guided the art of representing them." Michel Foucault. "A prosa do mundo." In *As palavras e as coisas*. 1985, p. 33.

mines, so the deposits would most likely be situated at roughly the same distance from the coast, near the captaincies of São Vicente, Santo Amaro, or Espírito Santo.[3]

The fact that the expanse and relief of the American interior were relatively unknown served to reinforce this certainty. Up to the mid-eighteenth century, it was believed that "this land [southeastern Brazil] and Peru is all one," as declared Tomé de Sousa, the first governor-general of Brazil, in 1550.[4] This view brought the auriferous riches of America into closer proximity and provided the premise for the intense search for mineral treasures that began to work its way inland from the Brazilian coast in the sixteenth century.

One of the first expeditions to set off toward the Andes from the coast of the captaincy of São Vicente was mounted by Martim Afonso de Sousa in 1531.[5] The expedition, led by Pero Lobo, never returned, as it was entirely decimated by Indians. This in no way cooled the Portuguese impetus to discover the coveted mines, as can be seen from the later expeditions, most of which left from Porto Seguro on the coast of Bahia or followed the Doce River inland from its estuary in the captaincy of Espírito Santo. Of these subsequent expeditions, the most important were those commanded by Francisco Bruza Espinosa (1553), Martim de Carvalho (1567), Sebastião Fernandes Tourinho (1572), Antônio Dias (1572), and Marcos de Azeredo (1596 and 1611). As many of these expeditions returned with the first mineral finds, they bolstered belief in the existence of untapped riches in the midlands and helped propagate various legends, such as those of a fabled golden lake or a mountain awash with emeralds, which further encouraged a continued search for the dreamt-of wealth deeper and deeper into the heartlands of Brazil.

The union of the two Iberian crowns between 1580 and 1640 removed, at least temporarily, the obstacles the Treaty of Tordesilhas

---

3   The captaincy of São Vicente gave rise to the captaincy of São Paulo, while that of Santo Amaro became Rio de Janeiro.

4   Cf. Sérgio Buarque de Holanda. *Visão do paraíso*, 1994, p. 41.

5   Martim Afonso de Sousa commanded the first full-scale expedition along the Brazilian coast, launched in 1530.

presented to further penetration into Portuguese America.[6] One of the most active pursuers of this goal was the twelfth governor-general, Francisco de Sousa, whose ambition was to earn the title of Marquis of the Mines, which the Spanish monarch Felipe II promised to whomever discovered gold in Brazil. After various attempts to find mineral deposits on expeditions leaving from Porto Seguro and Espírito Santo, Francisco de Sousa reached the conclusion that the legendary golden lake and resplendent mountain should be sought further south.

At this time, residents of the captaincy of São Vicente were making more frequent incursions inland from the town of São Paulo in search of indigenous manpower to work the fields and of pastureland for their cattle, but also in the hope of finding the fabled mineral treasures. The first gold deposits were finally discovered in São Vicente, and Francisco de Sousa set off for the captaincy in 1598. The following year he personally inspected the gold from the Jaraguá, Bitiruna, Monserrate, and Biroçoiaba (Araçoiaba) mines in the environs of São Paulo. While these discoveries were ephemeral and the production not particularly significant, they served to stimulate still further the search for gold in the region of São Vicente.

In 1602 Francisco de Sousa was replaced as governor-general. He not only managed to convince King Felipe II of the existence of the famous mines, but also to divide the governorship of Brazil in two, creating a Southern Partition that encompassed the promising lands around São Vicente. Francisco de Sousa was appointed governor of the new Southern Repartition and channeled most of his efforts into encouraging new expeditions in search of the mines of precious metals. Though his ambition remained frustrated upon his death and his

---

[6] The death of King Sebastião in 1578, who disappeared during the campaigns against the Moors in Africa, sparked a dynastic crisis in Portugal that resulted in the union of the two crowns under the Spanish scepter (Felipe II), thus beginning the so-called Iberian Union. It was only in 1640, with the Portuguese Restoration movement and ascension of the Bragança Dynasty, that Portugal reclaimed its autonomy.

task unfulfilled, his incentive proved fundamental to the discoveries that followed.[7]

In the second half of the seventeenth century, a new wave of expeditions ventured inland from the town of São Paulo. These expeditions came to be known as the *bandeiras* (flags) and their members as *Bandeirantes*. Central to the success of these expeditions was the command and participation of the *Paulistas*, the name given to people born in São Paulo, many of whom were of mixed Portuguese and Indian blood. Through their contact with the indians, the Paulistas not only learned the age-old routes through the heartlands, but also the knowledge they needed to survive in a harsh wilderness so often hostile to human passage.[8] The most important *Bandeiras* were those led by Agostinho Barbalho (1671), Matias Cardoso (1673), Fernão Dias Paes Leme (1674), Borba Gato (1681), and Antônio Rodrigues Arzão (1693).

The chronology in which these expeditions discovered gold in the region later known as Minas Gerais is uncertain and riddled with doubts. What is known is that they were made public between 1695 and 1698, attracting an influx of imigrants. The first considerable finds occurred in the beds of the rivers and streams that crisscrossed the area in large numbers, forming sedimentary alluvial deposits. Some years later, in or around 1720, diamonds were also discovered in the northeastern region of Minas Gerais. Tradition tells that, with the cessation of the armed conflict with Spain and the vast quantities of gold and diamonds that passed through the port of Lisbon each year offloaded from ships from Brazil, João V exclaimed: "My grandfather owed and feared, my father owed but feared no-one and I neither owe nor fear." Whether this sentence was actually spoken

---

[7] It would be no exaggeration to suggest that the first mining law, issued by Felipe II of Portugal (Felipe III of Spain) in 1603, to encourage the prospecting and mining of mineral assets in Brazil, and which remained in vigor throughout the entire seventeenth century, was the result of the obstinate efforts of Francisco de Sousa. This law permitted any individual to search for and discover mines, even on lands owned by third parties, with the sole condition that a fifth of all proceeds be paid to the Crown as tax.

[8] Sérgio Buarque de Holanda. *Caminhos e fronteiras*, 1994.

by the Portuguese monarch is of no real account, but it certainly symbolizes the jubilation of the Crown and the kingdom at the arrival of the mineral riches from the backwoods of America.

Such was the wealth proportioned by the gold and diamonds of Minas Gerais that it reconfigured the dynamic of the eighteenth-century Portuguese Empire, whose economic center shifted progressively toward Brazil. It is estimated that official gold production during the 1700s amounted to 650 tons, while diamond production reached a staggering sum of a little more than 3 million carats. Perfectly aware of this, in a letter of instruction to the new secretary of Portugal's Overseas Business, Marco Antônio de Azevedo Coutinho, Luís da Cunha, a Portuguese diplomat at various European courts in the first half of the 1700s and one of the greatest exponents of Portuguese politics in his day, predicted the future need to transfer the Portuguese Court to Brazil (which finally occurred in 1808 against the backdrop of the Napoleonic wars). Da Cunha argued that "in order to preserve Portugal, the prince has total need of the riches of Brazil and none whatsoever of those of Portugal . . . as it is cozier and safer to be where you have in abundance than to be where you must wait for what you lack."[9]

The first settlement in the area was established around the Tripuí stream and later gave rise to Vila Rica. Settlers branched out in all directions from this central base, and, by the beginning of the eighteenth century, there were already mining operations at Cataguazes, Sabará, Serro do Frio, Caeté, and Vila Rica, among other sites, which together constituted what came to be known as "Minas Gerais" (literally meaning "General Mines"). Word of the discoveries spread quickly and contingents began to flood into the region from Bahia, São Paulo, Pernambuco, and Portugal.

Colonial penetration into Minas Gerais was made possible by the interconnection of different routes opened almost simultaneously from São Paulo, Bahia and, from 1725 on, Rio de Janeiro.

---

[9] Luís da Cunha. Carta de Instrução a Marco Antônio de Azevedo Coutinho. Cf. Abílio Diniz Silva. (org.). *Instruções Políticas de Dom Luís da Cunha*. 2001, p. 371.

Throughout the eighteenth century, this triangle of routes was the main link between the coast and the Minas countryside. The first route was opened from São Paulo and became known as the *Caminho Paulista* (Paulista Road) or *Caminho Velho* (Old Road). Travelers coming into Minas from Bahia took the *Caminho da Bahia* (Bahia Road) or the *Currais do Sertão* (Corrals of the Hinterland), while those coming up from Rio de Janeiro took the *Caminho Novo* (New Road) or *Caminho do Garcia* (Garcia Road). Once they reached the captaincy, these roads spliced into countless trails interconnecting the older and more recent settlements.

In the early days, the mining communities were hit by two serious crises of supply and starvation, aggravated still further by the growing populations flooding the urban centers that sprang up around the riverside mines. In a bid to resolve this problem, the Crown adopted a policy of offering land concessions, known as *sesmarias*, to the free, slave-owning class, which began to produce some of the staple crops needed to sustain the population. Cassava, normally consumed as flour, and corn were the staple pillars of the foodstuffs locally produced. Trade between the coast and the central region was also vital to supply, as the diet was based around the meat that came from the hinterland cattle ranches between Minas and Bahia. Luxury goods and slave manpower were brought in from Salvador, in Bahia, from Rio de Janeiro, and by the Pernambucan horsemen.

Unlike in other regions, religious orders like the Company of Jesus, which had previously been fundamental in spreading the Catholic faith overseas, were prohibited from setting up in Minas Gerais. It therefore fell to the residents themselves, in partnership with the state, to organize their own religious practice by establishing brotherhoods, which built and maintained churches and chapels, ran church services, and took care of funerals and religious festivals.

The settlement of populations in the area did not occur without conflict or instability. During the *bandeirante* conquest, the Paulistas, as the discoverers of the precious metals, negotiated special privileges with the Crown, but as the outsiders began to arrive in droves, especially the Portuguese, they were forced to share the spoils and local administration.

The differences between the Paulistas and the Portugueses divided the population, and the mounting tensions resulted in a series of armed clashes between 1707 and 1709 for control of mines that came to be known as the War of the Emboabas. The war opposed the Paulistas on the one hand and the newly arrived immigrants on the other, who were generically dubbed *Emboabas*. The meaning of the term *Emboaba* is unclear and documents from the time reveal that its application was somewhat flexible. At times it was used exclusively in reference to the Portuguese, at others to designate all non-Paulistas, be they Portuguese or from the northeastern captaincies of Bahia and Pernambuco. It was also employed to differentiate those who had opened the mines, identified as Paulistas, from the new arrivals they accused of having contributed nothing to the exploration of the region and of merely exploiting its riches. On other occasions the term was used to refer to all travelers who arrived in Minas via the Bahia Road as opposed to those coming up from São Paulo. There were also distinct groups among the people from São Paulo who could be Paulistas, Taubateanos, or Santistas depending on the town from which they hailed (São Paulo, Taubaté, or Santos).[10]

The War of the Emboabas revealed the fragility of the Crown's control over the region and the need to install an administrative and fiscal apparatus closer to the mining area. Prior to the war, the governor of the Southern Repartition, who was therefore also responsible for the mines, resided some distance away in Rio de Janeiro. More direct control over Minas fell to a superintendent who handled the distribution of the mines and the collection of taxes. In 1709, as a result of the War of the Emboabas, the former Southern Repartition was dissolved with the creation of the captaincy of São Paulo e Minas do Ouro, entirely separate from the captaincy of Rio de Janeiro.

[10] Luciano Raposo de Almeida Figueiredo and Maria Verônica Campos. *Códice Costa Matoso*. 1999, pp. 198, 193, 230. Also see A. J. R. Russell-Wood. "Identidade, etnia e autoridade nas Minas Gerais do século XVIII: leituras do Códice Costa Matoso," 1999, pp. 100–18.

The first governor of the new captaincy of São Paulo e Minas do Ouro, Antônio de Albuquerque, the man responsible for brokering the peace, strove to impose some administrative order upon the region. His first step in this direction was to make towns of the largest existing urban settlements: Vila Rica, Vila de Nossa Senhora do Carmo, and Vila de Nossa Senhora do Sabará. The creation of these towns was essential to Portuguese institutional law and order, and pillories, normally of stone, were erected there as symbols of submission to the Portuguese Crown. Each town also received its own municipal chamber, an organ that was fundamental in maintaining control, ensuring the participation of the elite in the local government,[11] and regulating the urban supply chain. The administrative posts, including those responsible for tax collection, were also based in the towns.

With time, it became necessary to create new territorial divisions, and Minas was subdivided into three counties, namely Ouro Preto (run from Vila Rica), Rio das Velhas (run from Sabará), and Rio das Mortes (run from Vila de São João del Rei). By 1720, the population of Minas de Ouro had reached 250,000 inhabitants, including whites, slaves, and freed slaves. Gold production was growing at extraordinary rates at this time, and the Crown perceived that the amount of taxes collected always seemed to be well out of proportion with levels of production. In order to avoid such discrepancies, a law was passed prohibiting the circulation of gold dust and stipulating that all of the metal produced had to be smelted into bars, the only form in which it would be allowed to circulate from that time on. To enforce the law, it was decided that smelting houses would be set up in each county to smelt the metal and collect taxes. This measure was met by public opposition and stirred an uprising in Vila Rica, known as the Vila Rica Revolt.

If the revolt delayed the installation of the melting houses, as the measure required a more favorable climate in order to be implemented, it also accelerated the decision to give Minas administrative

---

[11] A. J. R. Russell-Wood. "O governo local na América portuguesa: um estudo de divergência cultural." 1977, pp. 25–80.

autonomy in a bid to bridge the distance between the seat of government and the population of the region. To this end, in late 1720, João V created the captaincy of Minas Gerais, wholly distinct from the captaincy of São Paulo. It also led to the creation of another county, Serro do Frio (run from Vila do Príncipe), designed to bring greater administrative control to the northeast of the captaincy, which was fast becoming more densely populated as newcomers were enticed by the gold and diamond finds. The first governor of the new captaincy of Minas Gerais, Lourenço de Almeida, was sworn in on August 18, 1721, at Vila do Carmo. One of his first administrative actions was to install the government headquarters in Vila Rica, where he could keep a closer watch over his subjects.

Throughout the eighteenth century the Crown grappled with the thorny issue of raising taxes in Minas. The contributions charged included the traditional royal tributes, like the *dizimo* (tithe) – 10 percent on all productive activity, especially agriculture; the *entrada* (entrance) – tax on incoming merchandise for resale inside the captaincy, including slaves; and the ferry tax – payable upon the crossing of any of the region's swollen rivers. There were also temporary charges, such as the Voluntary Subsidy – a tax originally established for a ten-year period to help finance the reconstruction of Lisbon, devastated by an earthquake in 1755; and the Literary Subsidy – to help fund schooling, laicized in the second half of the eighteenth century with the expulsion of the Jesuits from the Portuguese Empire, who had previously practically monopolized the teaching institutions. Most important of all, however, was the *quinto*, a special royal tax on metals, in this case gold, equivalent to one-fifth of production, though it was not always so precise.

The charging of the *quinto* was marked by various particularities and the sums and means of deduction varied throughout the eighteenth century. There were two main issues to be faced. First, there were the difficulties inherent in controlling or even estimating total production, upon which the *quinto* was supposed to be paid. The second was that the subjects were not always willing to pay what the Crown desired. The result was that the authorities often had to negotiate the contributions and the county councils had a fundamental role in these talks. The *quinto*, therefore, oscillated until a final value of 20 percent on official production was established in 1750, though even then the tax could not always be collected in full. Diamond taxation was even more complicated and generally took the form of a manpower tax for as long as production was in the hands of private individuals. The manpower tax was an annual charge (whose value varied throughout the century) on the slave manpower employed at the mines. In 1772, the Crown assumed total control over diamond production, with the creation of a state-run company, the Royal Diamond Extractor, for precisely this end.

Minas saw a form of occupation altogether different to that on the coast where the economy was based on crop production – mainly sugarcane – and gave rise to a rural society with large monocultural farms producing for export and run on slave labor.[12] In its own diverse manner, the mining economy created an urbanized, highly miscegenated society with a more robust urban middle class, which was nonetheless firmly rooted in slave labor just like the sugarcane region.[13] In an emblematic phrase from the beginning of the eighteenth century, Father Antonil foretold the symbiosis between the cane-based economy and slave labor when he said, "Slaves are the hands and feet of the sugar miller."[14] The same could just as easily have been said of the miner, as a popular saying from the time went: "Without them [slaves] in Brazil it is impossible to make, conserve or increase revenues."[15]

One of the most striking characteristics of Minas Gerais in the eighteenth century was the emergence of a significant class of freed slaves who gained their liberty through letters of manumission. This class, which congregated in the mining towns, did not enjoy the

---

[12] Stuart Schwartz. *Slaves, peasants, and rebels: Reconsidering Brazilian slavery.* 1992; Kátia Queirós Mattoso. *To be a slave in Brazil, 1550–1888.* 1986.

[13] Laird W. Bergad. *Slavery and demographic and economic history of Minas Gerais, Brazil, 1720–1888.* 1999.

[14] André João Antonil. *Cultura e opulência no Brasil, por suas drogas e minas.* 1982, p. 89.

[15] Ibidem.

same status as the freeborn, which generally meant the white, mostly Portuguese population.[16] The freed, on the other hand, were mostly black, Indian, or racially mixed, the so-called men and women of color. All over the captaincy and throughout the eighteenth century there was a proliferation of freed slaves, such that "Minas Gerais not only had the largest slave stock, but also the largest freed population in the Colony."[17]

SLAVES AND FORMER SLAVES

In 1930, in his work *The Masters and the Slaves*,[18] Gilberto Freyre immortalized the notion that Brazilian society, unlike in the United States, was characterized by a harmonious relationship between the races. For Freyre, while colonial society was largely based around the model of the patriarchal family, the domain of the *pater famílias*, the size and space of the Brazilian manor and the licentious relations that went on between landowners and their slave women in the colonial sugar mill had brought the worlds of master and slave into a more harmonious proximity. Working from this observation, Freyre went on to argue that *racial democracy* was the dominant feature of contemporary Brazilian social relations, an idea that would, with time, come to configure the social self-image of Brazilian society itself, an image it continues to export to this day.

As time went by, the figure of the former slave Chica da Silva came to symbolize for the majority of Brazilians one of the mythical examples of the real existence of this racial democracy in the country. With the publication of Joaquim Felício dos Santos' *Memórias do Distrito Diamantino* in 1868, which dedicates two chapters to her life in the village of Tejuco, now the city of Diamantina, the center of diamond production during the colonial period, her story became a well-known and integral part of the history of the mining region

---

[16] A. J. R. Russell-Wood. "The other slavery: Gold mining and the 'peculiar institution.'" In *The black man in slavery and freedom in colonial Brazil*. 1982, pp. 104–27.
[17] Eduardo França Paiva. *Escravos e libertos nas Minas Gerais do século XVIII*, p. 106.
[18] Gilberto Freyre. *The masters and the slaves*. 1946.

in the eighteenth century. Unthinkable during the nineteenth century, when slaves and freed slaves were the butt of prejudice, the book scandalized its readers with the story of an ex-slave in Minas Gerais in the previous century, Chica da Silva, who had lived a long-standing and stable love affair with one of the richest and most powerful men in the Diamantine District. Her lover was Chief Judge João Fernandes de Oliveira, a man who enjoyed successive monopolies over the region's diamond extraction. From 1739, this monopoly was conceded through four-year tenders and sealed in a contract that stipulated the rules for the extraction, taxation, and sale of the diamonds. It was because of this contract that the leaseholders were commonly known as *diamond contractors*.

However, it was not literature that transformed Chica da Silva into a national figure, but cinema. Cacá Diegues's 1975 movie titled *Xica da Silva* reinforced, propagated, and amplified the myth. Released during a time of popularization and renewal in Brazilian cinema known as the *Cinema Novo* movement, Cacá Diegues's film was the vehicle by which Chica da Silva definitively embodied the stereotype of licentiousness and sensuality always attributed to the black or mulatta female in the Brazilian popular imagination. The art of seduction, so natural to these women, enabled them to invert the logic of the system and three-tiered discrimination of race, color, and gender to which they were customarily submitted. And once turned on its head, it was they who became the dominators. As was the case with Chica da Silva, through her relationship with the white contractor, this inversion of the order revealed one of the facets of the Brazilian racial democracy, that which allowed some individuals of color, particularly women, to climb the social ladder and even "dominate" those who were once their masters.

However, over the course of the twentieth century the image of a racial democracy that Brazil endeavored to promote for itself began to detach from the reality of racial and social contradictions that more recent sociological, anthropological, and historical studies sought to reveal. Particularly striking was the work of the São Paulo sociologist Florestan Fernandes, who spent the 1960s and 1970s drawing attention to the perversion of the race system in Brazil, which, as capitalism took hold, pushed large swathes of the black population to the margins of the class system.[19]

Prior to the 1970s, a Marxist historiography rebelled against that conformist vision of Brazilian society, accentuating the exploitative character of slavery;[20] but these studies usually limited interpretations regarding the subject to the so-called *Thing* or *Zumbi* binomial.[21] That is, either the slave submitted to the violent coercion of the master (as a *thing*) or he escaped to the runaway slave *quilombos* and established a rebellion (as *Zumbi*). From 1980 on, under the influence of the new social history methodologies, several researchers began to criticize these rooted analyses, both those that accentuated the conformist character of the process of enslavement and those that underscored its exploitative character alone and the slave revolts and resistance it sparked. Such research revealed the multiplicity and diversity of slave society in Brazil.[22]

By suggesting new themes, new interpretations, and new approaches, recent research on women and slavery in eighteenth-century Minas Gerais has contributed significantly to transforming the traditional historiographical notions about the slave society in Brazil. Supported by vast documentary research and asking new questions of the sources, historians studying Minas Gerais have helped transform the view that prevailed about social relations in the colonial period, especially in relation to the captaincy's slave and colored population,

---

[19] Florestan Fernandes. *The negro in Brazilian society.* 1969.

[20] Emília Viotti Da Costa. "The myth of racial democracy." In *The Brazilian empire: Myths and histories.* 1985, pp. 234–46; Richard Graham. "Brazilian slavery re-examined: A review article." *Journal of Social History*, vol. 3, 1970, pp. 431–53.

[21] Zumbi was the leader of the Palmares quilombo, a large runaway slave colony that emerged in the seventeenth century in the captaincy of Alagoas and resisted decimation into the following century. The black movement in Brazil adopted Zumbi as a symbol of resistance against slavery.

[22] The approaching commemorations of the centenary of the abolition of slavery, celebrated in 1988, prompted new studies on the theme of slavery from a revisionist perspective. See Stuart Schwartz. "Recent trends in the study of Brazilian slavery." In *Slaves, peasants, and rebels: Reconsidering Brazilian slavery.* 1992, pp. 1–38.

and their analyses have provided fresh orientation for more recent studies on slavery in Brazil.

Most of these research projects have relied on the use of data in series, systematically consulting censuses, inventories, wills, birth, death and marriage records, and tax registers, among other sources. These consultations, whether conducted for the entire captaincy, for specific counties, or for a town and its surroundings, have enabled historians to unveil the composition of the mining society, with its immense layer of slaves and growing population of freedmen and women.

These studies afforded a new perspective on the droves of slaves and freed slaves that amassed in the captaincy. The study of the behavior of this significant captive and freed population revealed that while they occasionally created previously unheard of behavioral norms, they also largely remained within the behavioral limits imposed by white society. It was possible to observe how their practices contradicted two of the most deep-rooted beliefs of the traditional historiography: that captivity generated an aversion to slavery within the black and mixed population and that reducing slaves to animal conditions prevented them from establishing stable relationship bonds. Studies showed that marriage among captives was common, albeit to a lesser degree than in free, white society, and that the high costs of matrimony did little to discourage them from forming legitimate families, consecrated by Catholic sacrament.[23] Some captives and many freed slaves managed to accumulate a patrimony of their own, which they passed on to heirs, be they children, spouses, or close relatives, thus revealing similar care for the welfare of their descendants as that shown by whites. The slaves also

[23] As an example, see A. J. R. Russell-Wood. "The other slavery: Gold mining and the 'peculiar institution.'" In *The black man in slavery and freedom in colonial Brazil*. pp. 104–27; Donald Ramos. "The slave." In *A social history of Ouro Preto – 1695/1726*. 1972, pp. 189–225; Kathleen J. Higgins. "Patterns of living and working among slaves, ex-slaves." In *Licentious liberty in a Brazilian gold-mining region*, pp. 43–88; Júnia Ferreira Furtado. "A sociedade diamantina." In *O Livro da Capa Verde*, pp. 37–72; Laird W. Bergad. *Slavery and demographic and economic history of Minas Gerais, Brazil, 1720–1888*.

nurtured religious concerns, not solely expressed in rituals of African origin, but also through Catholicism. Like their free white counterparts, the captives also attended official Catholic services and left instructions for their funerals and the masses to be said posthumously for the salvation of their souls, all of which indicates that they were often in line with the strategies for conversion to the Christian faith orchestrated by the church and implemented by their masters.

However, various studies have shown that the cultural universe of the colored population was not restricted to a mere imitation of white values. The slaves brought with them from Africa many of their own customs, beliefs, and objects, which, in a circular movement, they incorporated into the local culture, albeit often invested with new meanings.[24] More specific and focused studies on the captive population have recently sought to identify cultural nuances among the various African nations and ethnicities that were brought to the captaincy and understand their cultural, ethnic, and linguistic diversity, which undoubtedly served "as criteria in organizing African slaves and freed slaves towards varied ends, from devotion to the saints to slave revolts."[25]

Censuses carried out in Minas Gerais in the eighteenth century show that men outnumbered women in the captaincy, both among the gentry and the slaves. The latter comprised the bulk of the population and were generally, though not exclusively, engaged in the mining operations. However, the opposite was true of the freed population in which women were the majority. The proliferation of manumission throughout the captaincy over the course of the century and the growth of a class of freed slaves in Minas Gerais was caused by various factors and subject to certain gender conditions. Concubinage, for example, was one of the most common ways a female slave could earn her liberty. The scarcity of women, especially white women, in the demographic composition of the mining settlements meant

[24] Eduardo França Paiva. "Fortuna, poder e objetos mágicos." In *Escravos e libertos nas Minas Gerais do século XVIII*, pp. 217–38.

[25] Mariza de Carvalho Soares. "Os *mina* em Minas: tráfico atlântico, redes de comércio e etnicidade." 1999, p. 693.

that illegitimate relationships became widespread, generating many couples involving white gentlemen and black or mixed-race slave women. A slave concubine was generally granted manumission upon her master's death, though usually only after buying her liberty at a price stipulated in the will of the deceased or after providing a certain number of extra years of service to his heirs, who were sometimes the slave's own children. There were some cases, however rare, in which no compensation, whether in specie or service, was demanded of the slave. Rarer still was for manumission to be granted during the master's lifetime. The generalization of concubinage between whites (mostly men) and coloreds (mostly female) had a significant impact on the mining society, which became considerably diverse and miscegenated. It was thus, as the eighteenth century wore on, that a growing class of freedmen and women emerged in the captaincy.[26] The fact that this social segment was predominantly female indicates that the mining society afforded slave women more opportunities to earn their freedom than it did their male counterparts.

The most common way for slaves to obtain their freedom, even for slave concubines, was to buy their way out of slavery. This was possible because many slave men and women received payment for providing services and doing odd jobs around the mining towns and villages. Part of this payment (*os jornais* – the daily rate) was handed over to the master, while the captive kept the rest. These were the so-called slave earners – those who managed to save up a certain reserve by selling services or products on the streets so that they could buy their freedom. As women provided most of these services and tasks, manumission was especially frequent among adult female slaves.

It was also common practice for landowners to free the illegitimate offspring of their relationships with slaves, and this usually occurred at the baptismal urn. In this case, the preference was to manumit illegitimate sons. While it was much harder for slaves working the mines to save a financial reserve and buy their freedom, it was not impossible. Not infrequently they were able to lay their hands on some gold or a diamond during the extraction process, which they would

[26] A. J. R. Russell-Wood. *The black man in slavery and freedom in colonial Brazil.*

put aside for the purpose of buying their liberty, and some masters even let their slaves mine for their own account on Sundays, which enabled them to accumulate some funds.

Although women were the majority among freed slaves, many ended up living on the margins of society as prostitutes, *tabuleiro* women,[27] or *vendeiras*.[28] Nevertheless, even if many lived on the brink of poverty, the concession of manumission generally led to some degree of ascension, if not social, at least financial, for a good portion of these women. Many freedwomen directly or indirectly found an open door to enrichment in gold and diamond exploration and ended up owning houses, jewelry, and slaves. Closer examination of the funeral rites these women received gives a clear indication of this social ascension. At the threshold of death, they normally took pains to organize a host of final ostentations – such as the profusion of candles to be lit for their souls, the best possible localization of the tomb inside the church, an exaggerated number of mourners in attendance at the open casket vigil, the sumptuousness of the funeral cortege or burial shroud, among other details – with which to show the local society how they had risen from slavery and found their place at the heart of free, white society.[29]

Among the assets freedmen and women could accumulate in Minas, the most common and most valuable was a stock of slaves. In the colonial society, owning slaves had various functions and meanings. First and foremost, slaves were essential to the livelihoods of their masters and therefore played an important economic role. They were also an important means of keeping their owners out of the workforce, as to work and live off one's own graft in a slave society

---

[27] *Negras de tabuleiro* (black tray women) – a term used to designate the colored women who roamed the streets of the urban centers selling foodstuffs carried on trays.

[28] In the mining region, the vendas were establishments that mainly sold food and cachaça rum to the blacks employed at the mines. They were usually situated on the hills near the mining operations and were disliked by the population, as they were meeting places for blacks, drumming bands, and prostitutes. These establishments were often run by slave or freed women – the *vendeiras*.

[29] Júnia F. Furtado. "Transitoriedade da vida, eternidade da morte: ritos fúnebres de forros e livres nas Minas setecentistas." 2001, pp. 397–416.

amounted to serious social dishonor. Owning slaves was therefore a fundamental means toward social distinction, separating and hierarchizing owners and nonowners, masters and slaves. And so, contrary to what one would expect today, both freedmen and freedwomen were often slave owners themselves, which enabled them to make a living and even sometimes become rich, but, most important, brought them closer to the world of the free.[30]

Another characteristic of the mining region was the level of autonomy enjoyed by freedwomen and even many slave women who often lived away from their masters and were free to roam the villages and towns with their food trays balanced on their heads, peddling their services and products. These slave women were known as *escravas de tabueiro*, after the food trays (*tabuleiros*) they carried. This relative autonomy also meant that they occasionally engaged in practices considered scandalous by the misogynistic and moralist standards of the church and Portuguese state. In Minas, concubinage was rife amongst these women and the liberty in which they lived was a constant source of tension with the traditional family model, always organized in accordance with the social standards of the state and underscored in sacrament by the Catholic Church.[31] Immersed in trades that ensured their livelihoods, the freedwomen had an ethic of their own when it came to building family and emotional bonds. In contrast to how we tend to think today, the mining society of the eighteenth century was by no means traditional, even if it still idealized the Christian model of the patriarchal family and monogamous marriage. The auriferous society of the 1700s was marked for its social mobility and the fluidity of its social structures, despite the continued dominance of notions of rigidity, respect for hierarchies,

[30] Mariana Libânio de Rezende Dantas. *Black townsmen: A comparative study of the lives of persons of African origin and descent in slavery and freedom in Baltimore, Maryland, and Sabará, Minas Gerais, 1750–1810.* 2003; Kathleen J. Higgins. *Licentious liberty in a Brazilian gold-mining region.*

[31] Donald Ramos. "Marriage and family in colonial Vila Rica." 1975, pp. 200–25. Donald Ramos. "Single and married women in Vila Rica, Brazil, 1754–1838," 1991, pp. 261–81.

and fixed social classes considered so desirable throughout the Portuguese world.

Studies based on serial sources of information on the captive population are not alone in their capacity to elucidate the world of the freedwomen of eighteenth-century Minas Gerais and their descendants; the analysis of individual lives also sheds a great deal of light.[32] The famous mulatta Chica da Silva – Francisca da Silva de Oliveira – is a case in point, as her life reveals many of the possibilities and limitations freedwomen faced in their pursuit of inclusion within the white mining society. Taking a historical approach, this book on the life of Chica da Silva seeks to eschew the stereotypes commonly attributed to her, be it the notion that she was an exception or that she was an example of the sensuality of the Brazilian mulatta or even of cordial conviviality between the races in Brazil. The aim of this book has been to use primary sources consulted in various archives in Brazil and Portugal to reconstruct the history of Chica da Silva by reinserting her within her own time. More than this, by taking that life as its guide, this book hopes to delve into the quotidian of eighteenth-century mining society and especially into the world of the freedwomen of the day.

[32] Luiz Mott. *Rosa Egipcíaca, uma santa africana no Brasil.* 1993.

CHAPTER ONE

LAND OF STARS

Weeping and fallen diamonds made all a sea of stars.

THE DIAMANTINE DEMARCATION

The stage upon which the course of Chica da Silva's life played out was the village of Tejuco, now the town of Diamantina, and its surroundings in the captaincy of Minas Gerais, an outpost of the Portuguese Empire. Though remote, the village was a kaleidoscope of the world around it, and the life that unfolded there was a mirror to the age.

Throughout the entire Western world, the eighteenth century was a period of enormous transformation. Discontent reigned in all corners, and revolts brimmed over into what came to be known as the "age of revolutions."At either end of a period of just less than a hundred years, the power of kings was to reach its peak in the figure of Louis XIV, the Sun King, as France was to become the stage for the most important revolutionary movement of the modern age. Meanwhile, in the gold-rich backwoods of Minas Gerais, the partisans of the Inconfidência Mineira[1] met to draft seditious plans for the independence of the richest region in Portuguese America.

---

[1]   The Inconfidência Mineira was a conspiracy aimed at creating independence for the captaincy of Minas Gerais that was discovered in 1789 and brutally repressed before it even began. For an interpretation of the movement, see Kenneth Maxwell. *Conflicts and conspiracies: Brazil and Portugal, 1750–1808.* 1973.

Not even the heavens could resist the thirst for change. As a premonition of the turbulent century to come, the English astronomer Edmund Halley called the world's attention to the fact that three important stars, Sirius, Procyon, and Arcturus, had changed their angular distances – immutable since the age of the Greeks.[2] In 1759, the passing of the comet sparked more attention than the apprehension usually provoked by such baleful omens. Its arrival proved Halley's theory that comets were not aimlessly wandering bodies, but followed fixed elliptical orbits that caused them to visit the earth at regular intervals.[3]

In Portugal, the 1700s were marked by the splendorous wealth derived from the Brazilian mines. If Louis XIV was the Sun King, João V was the Emperor of the Sun, his transoceanic empire positively shining with Brazilian gold. Crowned in 1706, his power and glory were immortalized in the construction of the Mafra palace – "great in every sense of the word"[4] – which included a convent and a basilica. During its thirteen-year construction, the palace consumed much of the gold shipped in from Brazil, which was incorporated into Belgian chimes, Carrara marble, Italian statues, and French images. The wealth that emerged from the gold and diamond-bearing riverbeds of the captaincy of Minas Gerais was nothing short of stupendous. In Lisbon, the discovery of these much-coveted gems was cause for parties and processions that brought the Portuguese people out into the streets. Congratulations poured in from all over Europe. In Rome, Pope Clement XI ordered a mass of solemn thanksgiving: "The Holy Pope and his Cardinals wish to congratulate the King of Portugal, as do all the Monarchs of Europe. The peoples of this Earth speak of no other matter or news. I would say that what has been found shall regenerate and bring great joy to the universe."[5]

---

[2] Arthur Berry. *A short history of astronomy.* 1961, p. 225.
[3] Ibidem, pp. 251, 252, 255.
[4] Jacome Ratton. *Recordações de Jacome Ratton sobre ocorrências do seu tempo em Portugal.* 1992, p. 145.
[5] J. M. Pereira da Silva. "História da fundação do Império Brasileiro." In Joaquim Felício dos Santos. *Memórias do Distrito Diamantino.* 1976, p. 50.

In the eighteenth century, the first migrations to the diamantine region were sparked by the discovery of gold in the vicinity
of Vila do Príncipe. As for the diamonds, these were found later in
the 1720s by prospectors working the streams near Tejuco, including
the Caeté-Mirim, the Santo Antônio, and the Inferno among other
tributaries of the Jequitinhonha River where the search for gold was
already under way. One observer, a merchant named Francisco da
Cruz, relates how Vila de Sabará was fast becoming a ghost town, as
the population rushed off to the diamantine region. The diamond
fever that gripped the town was so strong that people were swapping
their houses for a horse bit, while others sold off all their belongings
to buy slaves with whom to explore the precious diamond fields.[6]

In Brazil, the gold and diamond rush brought about the exploration and occupation of Minas Gerais. Production reached its peak
during the eighteenth century, a period in which many made their
fortunes, before gradually trailing off. The village of Tejuco was situated in the northeast of Minas Gerais, a region that basically corresponded to the county of Serro do Frio, one of the administrative units into which the captaincy was divided. The county capital,
established at Vila do Príncipe, now the town of Serro, was home
to the Town Council, the Magistracy – with full judicial powers –
and the Gold Intendancy, which was in charge of organizing the distribution of the gold mines and of collecting the *quinto*, the main
tax upon mining proceeds, roughly equivalent to a fifth of yields on
production.

The county limits of Serro do Frio began close to the 19th degree
of south latitude and, from the center of the captaincy, could be
reached by two routes running parallel to the so-called Grande
mountain range, nowadays known as the Espinhaço. The first of
these, on the eastern slopes of the range and known as the "Mato
Dentro" (Forestside road), was more frequently used by travelers
coming up from Vila Rica in the county of Ouro Preto and passed
through Conceição do Mato Dentro. The other, "do Campo" (the

---

[6]   HSJ/TFP. Letter 166, March 29, fls. 257, 258, 259, 271. In Luís Lisanti Filho.
      Negócios coloniais. 1973.

Field road), which ran along the western side, started out from Sabará county. Entering Serro do Frio, the traveler would have noted the various alterations in the landscape. The forest was no longer quite so tall or dense, the vegetation was more open and a lighter shade of green, and the land was rockier and more sandy, though still beautiful all the same. Once past the first ridges of mountain, which had stood black against the distance, the traveler would have beheld "a new sky, a new climate, felt the air colder and more bothersome winds."[7]

The first expeditions to reach the region during the sixteenth and seventeenth centuries followed the Doce River from the captaincies of Porto Seguro and Espírito Santo. Nonetheless, even the discovery of precious stones did not lead to lasting settlements. The area was only really populated later on when gold prospecting took hold at the centre of Minas Gerais, though even then it remained more sparsely populated[8] than the central region.

While the discovery of the diamonds officially dates to 1729, the exploitation of diamond fields had already been under way for some time. It was only in this year, however, that the governor, Lourenço de Almeida, dispatched his communiqué of the fact to Lisbon, apparently feeling the pressure of the notoriety of the clandestine mining of the stones, which he was rumored to have had a hand in himself. Brother to the Lisbon patriarch and brother-in-law to the secretary of state, governor of Minas from 1721 to 1731, Lourenço de Almeida returned to court with some 18 million cruzados, a sum considered a fortune at the time, amassed through his involvement in various businesses in the colony – diamonds included.

Once the diamonds had been "officially" discovered, it was necessary to organize the mining and the collection of taxes. In principle, the Gold Intendancy was responsible for the distribution and concession of the mines. Between 1729 and 1734, exploration was open to everyone who owned slaves and had capital to invest; though a tax was charged on each slave employed – the so-called head

---

[7] José Vieira Couto. *Memória sobre a capitania de Minas Gerais, seu território, clima e produções metálicas.* 1994, p. 54.

[8] Júnia Ferreira Furtado. *O livro da capa verde.* 1996, pp. 45–6.

tax – which was often fixed at a high rate so as to restrict access to the diamond fields and to raise more taxes.

The first stage of the mining process involved using a sieve to pan the alluvial beds of rivers where diamonds could be found more easily and in greater quantities. The simplest methods were employed and mining was preferably done during the dry season. Once the silt was exhausted, work shifted to the banks or terraces (which came to be the banks or elevated riverside ground). As this stage required more sophisticated techniques, such as the removal of rubble dredged up from the riverbed and accumulated on the banks, operating costs were high. Once the process was complete, the gravel was panned a second time in search of stones that had not made the grade the first time round.

The richness of the mines made production soar, and the Portuguese authorities soon realized that diamond prices were sensitive and directly related to the gem's rarity. With excess supply, the price per carat on the global market plummeted.[9]

In a bid to reduce and control production, head taxes were raised considerably and remained high until 1734, when the Crown sent Martinho de Mendonça Pina e Proença to Minas Gerais to assess the situation. A military engineer named Rafael Pires Pardinho was also assigned to mark out the diamondiferous region, hence the Diamantine Demarcation, a quadrangle drawn around the village of Tejuco encapsulating the villages and settlements of Gouveia, Milho Verde, São Gonçalo, Chapada, Rio Manso, Picada, and Pé do Morro. The limits of this quadrangle could be shifted to incorporate any other regions in which new discoveries were made.[10]

The Diamantine Demarcation impressed travelers with its natural exuberance. The Frenchman Alcide D'Orbigny affirmed that its soil was almost sacred for all the riches it concealed and each stone privileged.[11] The naturalist José Vieira Couto described it as a "black, hispid and jagged" sight, composed of "a thousand uneven

[9] Júnia F. Furtado. *O livro da capa verde.* 1996, p. 25.
[10] Ibidem, p. 26.
[11] Alcide D'Orbigny. *Viagem pitoresca através do Brasil.* 1976, p. 135.

mountain peaks, . . . vaulted shanks of individual, perpendicularly shaped stone [that] reached into the clouds." Scrub and brown moss covered the near-barren land, and yet, to refresh the travelers, criss-crossing the trails ran a "thousand brooks of crystalline waters," some of which "flowed vertiginously from the highest mountains," while others broke and split "upon the rocks all the way to the foot of the mountain," emptying into larger rivers after endless twists and turns. On calmer stretches, the creeks would open onto sweeping white sandy beaches or disappear from view as they wound their way among the closely packed mountains, only to reemerge in the distance, restored to full fury. On all sides, nature put on an unforgettable spectacle.[12]

The climate was moderate, with temperatures ranging between 14 and 27 degrees Celsius, with slightly chillier weather only in June and July. The seasons were not rigorously distinct, though two blocks stood out: a dry period stretching from April to September and a rainy season lasting from October through to March. When the rains came, they were "far from meek and mild," but heavy and loud, dragging on for days or even weeks. The clamour of the thunder rolling above the mountains made the earth tremble, frightening the inhabitants, though when the sun reappeared in a clear blue sky, life was renewed and nature reemerged in all her beauty and joy. In January the temperature rose a little and the people could enjoy an Indian summer. In the two months that followed, the rains became increasingly sparse until they ceased altogether in April, when the mining work could begin on the fast-drying riverbeds.[13]

In 1734, only a few years after the official discovery of the dia-monds, exploration was suspended in the area so that prices could return to normal on the international market. All mining con-cessions were revoked, and the only new licenses granted were those exclusively for gold. Diamonds already mined were to be reg-istered and stockpiled in safes. These measures caused enormous

---

[12] José Vieira Couto. *Memória sobre a capitania de Minas Gerais, seu território, clima e produções metálicas*. 1994, p. 54.
[13] Ibidem, pp. 56–7.

commotion among the hordes that had migrated there in search of riches.

A specific administration was also set up for the demarcation – the Diamond Intendancy – with headquarters in Tejuco. The first intendant was none other than Rafael Pires Pardinho. However, in administrative terms, the region remained under the jurisdiction of the council and magistracy of Vila do Príncipe.

The end of the 1730s was a significant time for Tejuco and, in particular, for the protagonists of this story. In the small village of Milho Verde, lost in the Diamantine Demarcation halfway between Tejuco and Vila do Príncipe, in a slave quarters in one of the region's crudely built houses, almost all thatched huts, a woman gave birth to one of the individuals whose destiny it is our aim to trace: a little slave girl whom she named Francisca.[14]

Some years later, in 1739, with all the pomp befitting his position, the governor Gomes Freire de Andrade set off toward Tejuco. His coming was to trigger a series of changes in the region that would also have a deep impact upon little Chica's life. The governor was under the king's orders to reopen the diamond mines, as prices on the international market had risen and stabilized.

Since January of that year, edicts posted throughout the captaincy and in Rio de Janeiro invited traders interested in bidding for diamond concessions to present themselves at Tejuco that coming April. The Crown had decided to implement a new system of operations: it would now use concession contracts renewable every four years, whether by a single individual or a partnership, which it believed would give it more control and make it easier to avoid a brusque slump in prices. Furthermore, the payment of the concession bid was to be made in advance and, it was hoped, at a high price.

Traveling with the entourage was one Sergeant Major João Fernandes de Oliveira, then an unknown Portuguese businessman intent on moving up in the world at all costs and on lining his pockets with the wealth glistening in the captaincy's streams. Events did not go as planned and, to his great displeasure, the governor had

[14] ANTT. Habilitações da Ordem de Cristo. Letra s. Maço 5, doc. 5.

to stay on at the village until August. While the area near the port in Lisbon smouldered in flames in 1739, Gomes Freire de Andrade used all his skill to close a deal which was considered vital to the royal interests.[15] Satisfied with the results he had obtained, he could finally leave Tejuco and his entourage along with him.

From 1740 on, six contracts were celebrated, some of which were renewed, thus extending beyond the four-year period originally agreed. Sergeant Major João Fernandes de Oliveira, in partnership with Francisco Ferreira da Silva, was the first contractor. He extended the enterprise for another four years in 1744, though financial setbacks meant he did not renew the contract upon expiry in 1747 and returned to the Realm.[16] The following year, a third contract was celebrated with Felisberto Caldeira Brant, in partnership with Alberto Luís Pereira and Conrado Caldeira Brant.[17] Swimming in debt and accused of diamond smuggling, Felisberto Caldeira Brant was forced to leave Tejuco and was escorted back to Portugal in custody. The fourth contract, valid from 1753 to 1758, and the fifth, valid from 1759 to 1761, were once again signed with João Fernandes de Oliveira, this time in partnership with Antônio dos Santos Pinto and Domingos de Basto Viana. Now living in Lisbon, the contractor decided to send his son – his namesake, High Court Judge João Fernandes de Oliveira – to administrate the business in Tejuco. On the sixth contract, the longest of them all, valid from 1762 to 1771, the Sergeant Major and his son became partners on the undertaking.

---

[15] The closing of this contract will be discussed in more detail in Chapter 3.

[16] In the Portuguese Empire there was a territorial hierarchy that distinguished between the Reino (Realm), meaning Portugal itself, and the Conquistas Ultramarinas (Overseas Conquests), referring to the colonies. From 1815 on, after the arrival of the royal family in 1808, Brazil's status was raised to part of the United Kingdom of Portugal, Algarve, and Brazil.

[17] Although the fourth contract was signed in December 1751 to the value of 240 million reis for the following six years, João Fernandes only assumed control over the mining operations in mid-1753, with the accounts pushed back to the beginning of that year. AHU, MAMG. Box 60, doc. 7. See Chapter 5. The letter "quitação do contrato dos diamantes nos anos de 1756, 1757, 1758 e 1760," reads: "the fourth contract, which came into vigour in January 1753 and expired in December 1759..."ANTT. Ministério do Reino. Book 208, fls. 227 and 227v.

The contractors enjoyed enormous wealth and prestige and were able to secure the complaisance of the local authorities and even of the governors of the captaincy through political and economic alliances that made them even more powerful. Though the management of the contracts was somewhat haphazard, the sheer abundance of the minerals extracted from the diamondiferous rivers was enough to bathe the Portuguese monarch in a scintillating glow.

The system contained a series of strictly binding clauses that regulated the rights and obligations of the contracted party. These articles sought to control production (and therefore also supply and prices), limit the area open for mining and the number of slaves employed therein, and repress smuggling.

The diamonds were sent annually in small boxes to Lisbon where they were deposited at the Royal Mint. Up to the end of the third contract, in 1752, all diamonds greater than twenty carats were royal property, while the remainder was sold by the contractor's agents. As the accounts were settled on a yearly basis, the contractors could issue credit letters in Lisbon and Rio de Janeiro in order to raise the capital they needed to cover their high production costs. An advertisement in the *Gazeta de Lisboa* of March 1754 read as follows: "Whomsoever should wish to purchase raw diamonds for the consumption of this realm and its conquered lands may speak with the cashiers under the present contract, who shall be available to sell as many as necessary."[18]

From the fourth contract on, celebrated once again with Sergeant Major João Fernandes de Oliveira, the Crown began to monopolize the sale of the stones on the international market, leaving only the mining rights to the contractor. However, this contract also contained a clause permitting the latter to delegate the onsite management of the operations to a third party. It was via this expedient that the Sergeant Major was able to send his namesake to Tejuco in his stead. A year after arriving in the village in 1753, the High

[18] ANTT. Real Mesa Censória. *Gazeta de Lisboa*. Caixa 465, n. 12. Quinta feira, 21 de março de 1754, p. 96.

Court Judge João Fernandes de Oliveira began what was to become a long-standing relationship with the mulatta Francisca, who, once freed, assumed the name Francisca da Silva de Oliveira – Chica da Silva.

From 1745 on, the Portuguese started to control entry into the demarcation, which was only permitted at specific locations, the so-called registration points – Caeté-Mirim, Rabelo, Palheiro, Pé do Morro, Inhacica, and Paraúna. Each registration point was staffed by an inspector who was responsible for charging taxes on all merchandise destined for the demarcation and a military detachment whose function was to prevent travelers from straying from the established routes and to block the entry of unauthorized individuals or merchandise. By implementing this measure the Crown believed it could control the production of the gems.

The second half of the eighteenth century saw changes in the Realm that would have significant repercussions on the diamantine region. With the death of João V in 1750, the throne was filled by his son José I, whose reign was marked by the political ascension of Sebastião José de Carvalho e Melo, the future Count Oeiras and later Marquis of Pombal. The economic policy orchestrated by this minister gave rise to a merchant class strongly allied with the interests of the state, of which João Fernandes de Oliveira, both father and son, were typical examples. This was also a period in which the Crown established various monopolies through which it hoped to exercise greater control over the riches of the empire.

At the end of 1771, a royal decree abolishing the contract system made mining another monopoly of the Crown and led to the establishment of the Royal Diamond Extraction Company, an imperial organ directed by the diamond intendant.[19] This signaled the end of the age of the contractors in the colony and, principally, in Tejuco. Meanwhile in the Metropole, the fall of the minister Pombal, which would finally come in 1777 with the death of José I, was drawing near.

---

[19] Júnia F. Furtado. O livro da capa verde. 1996, p. 26.

For some time to come, the High Court Judge João Fernandes would continue to enjoy the enormous wealth he had amassed and which had made him one of the richest men in Portugal. His rise symbolized the era in which, under Pombal's banner, the merchant class, having joined its interests with those of the Empire and with the proceeds from its business overseas, ascended both economically and socially, mingling with the noble bloodlines.

The Village of Tejuco

At the center of the Diamantine Demarcation, nine leagues from Vila do Príncipe, was the village of Tejuco, home to the diamond contractor and intendant. The village first emerged before the diamonds were discovered, during the exploration of the Piruruca and Grande Rivers, both panned exclusively for gold. Where these two rivers met, on the hillside of Santo Antônio, work began on the construction of a cluster of houses that would become the village's first and somewhat haphazard street, Burgalhau. Around the year 1730, the still wild environs of Tejuco were overrun with gypsies, vagrants, and runaway slaves who terrorized the residents.

There were three routes of access to the town, approaching as if from the points of a triangle. Leaving Tejuco and climbing the Santo Antônio hillside, you would pass through the village objectively called Cima (upper), from where you could take the trail heading north toward the bushlands of Bahia, whence came the large herds of cattle that supplied Tejuco and the surrounding area with meat. On the eastern rim of the village, setting off from Rosário Square, was the trail leading to Vila do Príncipe, which also passed through the village "de Baixo" (lower). However, by far the best view was to be had by travelers coming from Minas Novas, who would come down from the São Francisco Mountain and see the entire serpentine village nestled on the slopes of the Santo Antônio, the mountain directly facing it on the other side of the valley. From high on the São Francisco, a narrow trail wound its way down the mountainside and onto the valley floor where it crossed the river from which the mountain took its name, bypassed the small village of Rio Grande, and, climbing a little way up the other side, reached Tejuco via Burgalhau street.[20]

Between 1720 and 1750, as more and more diamond fields were discovered in nearby rivers, the small village began to grow, with new roads creeping crosswise up the slope. The village center was established around the Santo Antônio church, built in a square described as "quadrangular, concentrated and reticulated," unlike most town centers in Minas Gerais, which tended to be more sprawling and disordered.[21] By the mid-eighteenth century, the format of the village had already been defined, with most of its buildings concentrated around the main square. This was where the largest houses and mansions were situated, with pride of place for the imposing manor of the contractor Felisberto Caldeira Brant.

Rua Direita, the main street, was where the most important men in the village chose to construct their residences. In 1774, this street was home to both the diamond intendant, Bento Joaquim de Siqueira Aiala, and Sergeant Major José da Silva de Oliveira, who lived with his wife and four children – one of whom, José da Silva de Oliveira Rolim, would later be ordained a priest and become a member of the Inconfidência movement.[22] During the time of the mining contracts and even afterward during the royal monopoly, Sergeant Major José da Silva de Oliveira was involved in the diamond business. He was a personal friend of Sergeant Major João Fernandes de Oliveira and even came to hold the position of inspector for the Royal Extractor. Various freedwomen also lived on Rua Direita, including Maria Carvalha and Josefa Maria de Freitas, both black, and Inês Maria de Azevedo and Mariana Pereira, both mulatto,[23] which gives an indication of the fluid frontiers established between the different social segments in mining towns. Although households headed by freedwomen were spread throughout the village, their distribution was by no means heterogeneous. Whites were the majority

---

[20] Sílvio de Vasconcelos. "A formação urbana do arraial do Tejuco." *Revista do Patrimônio Histórico e Artístico Nacional*, 1959, p. 127.

[21] Ibidem, p. 121.

[22] AHU, MAMG. Caixa 108, doc. 9, f. 1.

[23] Ibidem.

on Rua Direita and Rua Quitanda, streets where most of the traders
lived, and on Cavalhada Nova and Rua do Amparo, both in the
town center, while the freedwomen were the majority on less central streets like Macau, Macau de Baixo, Campo, and Burgalhau, and
on such lanes as Gomes de Aquino, Intendência, Cadeia, Padre José
Guedes, and Mandioca.[24]

From a distance, the village looked like a little crib, given the
rusticity of its houses and chapels, which were all built in loam and
stone. The white-painted buildings rose snakelike up the hillside,
speckled among the orchards, flower gardens, and vegetable patches,
like an oasis in the middle of an inhospitable and stony landscape.
The houses, with their whitewashed outer walls, were capped with
tiled roofs.[25] The mansions also differed to the constructions of other
places in Minas in virtue of the use of muxarabi, an architectural style
brought over from the Orient most likely by the diamond traders and
lapidaries, which consisted of a trellised balcony in the Moorish style
that ensured the privacy of those inside the house. A remnant of this
type of balcony can still be seen in Diamantina today on Rua Francisco Sá in the building that now houses the Antônio Torres Library.

Up to the second half of the eighteenth century there was no
jail in Tejuco, only a pillory to which errant slaves were chained
pending punishment or execution, while prisoners were sent to Vila
do Príncipe.[26] When the contracts were established, a hospital was
built to tend to the infirmities of the captives working the diamond
mines. At this time, the upkeep of the hospital fell to the contractors,
though this responsibility passed to the Diamond Intendant upon the
establishment of the royal monopoly.

The source of the Tejuco stream, which supplied the locals with
ample, clean water for consumption, was located on the slopes of
Rua Santo Antônio. A ditch was opened to allow water to flow into
the center of the village where an ornate fountain was built, lending
its name to the street on which it was erected – Rua do Chafariz.

[24] Ibidem, fls. 1–9.
[25] Alcide D'Orbigny, op. cit., p. 135.
[26] ACO. *Livro de autos de arrematações e termos de fianças.* 1722–1742, p. 62.

Toward the end of the century, with the increase in population and expansion of the village, Tejuco received its second drinking fountain, built near the Rosário church.[27]

As the town grew, building proliferated. The installation of religious orders was prohibited in Minas Gerais; all clergy and their affiliates were barred from the region because, according to the imperial authorities, they were responsible for much of the contraband and so were only allowed entry when on pilgrimage to collect donations – though even then only with a royal permit. The construction of the churches and the holding of mass and other Christian rites, for which parish priests were hired, fell to the lay brotherhoods, which were generally formed in devotion to some particular saint. In Tejuco, the brotherhoods were initially based in the Santo Antônio parish church where there were four lateral altars. The most important brotherhoods were Our Lady of the Steps, Our Lady of the Rosary, Our Lady of the Souls, and Our Lady of the Most Holy Sacrament, all of which were mostly composed of free whites. The churches of The Rosary, Our Lady of Carmo, Saint Francis, The Mercies, Amparo, and Bonfim were all built in the second half of the eighteenth century.

Up to the end of the eighteenth century, the administrative headquarters was housed in the Casa do Contrato (Contract House), later called the Intendancy, on Rua do Contrato, where the Bishopric of Diamantina is based today. The weekly weighing of the diamonds, which was done in the presence of the intendant, contractor, and treasurer, took place in the parlor on the first floor, and the amounts were recorded in a ledger so they could be settled later.[28] Once weighed, the diamonds were stowed in a chest and closed with three locks, with each authority holding the key to one. Every year a specific detachment, the Diamantine Guard, escorted the diamond hoard from Tejuco to the port of Rio de Janeiro.

By the standards of the day, Tejuco was no small settlement. In 1732, Lourenço de Almeida recognized that the population of the

---

[27] Sílvio de Vasconcelos, op. cit., p. 127.
[28] AHU, MAMG. Caixa 63, doc. 1.

village had already far surpassed that of Vila do Príncipe, though the latter remained the provincial "head." According to the governor, the villa was far from the rivers and sparsely populated, while the village was closer to the watercourses and more populous, which was why the businessmen and miners had congregated there.[29]

In the third quarter of the eighteenth century there were some 510 houses in the village, home to a total of 884 free residents.[30] By the beginning of the following century, when the French traveler Saint-Hilare visited the region, Tejuco already had a population of 6,000 and some 800 houses. The traveler not only marveled at the environment of luxury and abundance that reigned in the village, but also at the vibrancy of the local commerce whose shops were replete with imported goods, such as English and Indian crockery, all of which had been brought there on donkey-back. In 1774, the shop of the freed mulatto Manuel da Encarnação, which was located on Rua da Quitanda, specialized in the sale of Indian crockery and beverages.[31] In August 1800, on behalf of the residents of Tejuco who wished to have the status of the village upgraded to that of a villa, the naturalist José Vieira Couto is recorded as saying that it was the largest urban center in the county, home to a flourishing and wealthy society.[32]

It was in Tejuco that Saint-Hilare found the most fertile intellectual environment in the captaincy, one in which the educated elite could speak to him fluently in French, his native tongue.[33] From the 1750s, the village had its own opera house where the most popular pieces of the time were performed.[34] The churches commissioned musicians to write new pieces for the annual celebrations – Holy Week, Ash Wednesday, the Stations of the Cross, and Corpus Christi, as well as the various funeral and other sung masses. The

[29] *Revista do Arquivo Público Mineiro*, vol. 7, p. 279. Apud: Sílvio de Vasconcelos, op. cit., p. 126.
[30] AHU, MAMG. Caixa 108, doc. 9, fls. 1–9.
[31] Ibidem, f. 5.
[32] APM. Seção Colonial, 268, fls. 277–80.
[33] Auguste de Saint-Hilare. *Viagem pelo Distrito dos Diamantes e litoral do Brasil.* 1974, pp. 29–33.
[34] APM. Seção Colonial, 176, p. 24.

mulatto José Joaquim Emerico Lobo de Mesquita stood out among the 120 or so musicians working in Tejuco during the eighteenth century and became a renowned composer.

A Te Deum was frequently offered in thanks for a divine blessing bestowed upon the Portuguese people, and the one sung in Tejuco on November 9, 1751, to celebrate the ascension of José I is a good example. Organized on the order of the captain of the Dragoons, Simão da Cunha Pereira, the commemorations stretched over three days of dance, masked balls, illuminations, sung masses, and a sermon at the Rosário church. The entire event was accompanied by the diamond intendant and the most illustrious residents of the village and was brought to a close with a banquet thrown by the former.[35]

Fourteen inventories in the Antônio Torres Library register the possession of books, revealing a level of instruction that could be considered high for the time. Twelve of these inventories belonged to Portuguese residents, with that of Manuel Pires de Figueiredo warranting special attention for its 140 works in some 360 volumes, covering a range of subjects in Latin and French. His bookshelves contained Montesquieu's *The Spirit of Laws* and a copy of *Portable Encyclopaedia*, Diderot and D'Alembert's compendium of the greatest work of the French Enlightenment.[36]

No less significant was the library of the naturalist José Vieira Couto, one of the largest in Minas Gerais. Nonconformity reigned supreme in this collection, with many works betraying the owner's familiarity with new and radical ideas. Vieira Couto possessed six volumes of Montesquieu; Cervantes' classic *Don Quixote*, in which the author satirized chivalry and the notions of honor inherent in it; both critical volumes of Luís Antônio Verney's *Verdadeiro método de estudar para ser útil à República e à Igreja*; and an English edition of Volney's *The Ruins, A Meditation on the Revolutions of Empires*, which, among other controversial themes, radically criticized the Catholic faith. Elected to the States General and later to the National Assembly,

---

[35] "Notícias históricas de Portugal e do Brasil (1751–1964)." *Gazeta de Lisboa*, 1964, p. 13.
[36] Júnia Furtado. *O livro da capa verde*. 1996, pp. 54–5.

Volney advocated the expropriation and sale of Church assets during the French Revolution.[37]

A decisive factor in this cultural exchange was the significant presence of students from Tejuco in universities abroad, which resulted in a high level of local instruction that increased over the course of the eighteenth century. In the last two decades of the 1700s, a good number of the Brazilian students at the University of Coimbra came from the diamantine region. "Such that, in the year of 1782, almost half of the candidates from Minas Gerais came from the village of Tejuco or from Serro do Frio; four out of a total of nine students admitted."[38]

Diamantine society followed the same pyramid as the rest of the captaincy, with a considerable slave base, a smaller layer of freedmen and women (largely mulatto), and a small white ruling class (mostly Portuguese), which held the main administrative posts and monopolized the higher military ranks and other honors. And yet, though its principal values were grounded on criteria of birth and honor, there was some upward mobility, enabling freed mulatto men and women to seek social ascension. For the women, this usually came in the form of concubinage to a white man, or through the running of stalls in the village or the provision of such services as sewing, laundry, delivery, or even prostitution.

The household census carried out in Tejuco in 1774 revealed that of the 511 household heads there was rough equivalence between the number of freed blacks and mulattos and free whites. Of this total, 282 were men and 229 were women.[39] With the exception of

---

[37] Idem. "Estudo crítico." In José Vieira Couto. *Memória sobre a capitania de Minas Gerais.* 1994, p. 19.

[38] Sérgio Buarque de Holanda. "Metais e pedras preciosas." 1985, p. 306.

[39] AHU, MAMG. Caixa 108, doc.9, fls. 1–9. Given the information it provides, this is an extremely interesting document in terms of reconstructing the local society, listing the heads of each household in the village by street, color, occupation, civil status, and number of free residents in the house. There were 510 listed houses and 511 household heads, as two captive slaves shared the position of household head in the same dwelling. Five lodgers (four men and one woman) originally counted in the census were omitted from the final household total.

Vitoriano and Anacleto, two "coartado" (self-purchased)[40] slaves, all were either free or freed[41] and thus made up what one could call the village elite. There were 286 nonwhite men and women, the equivalent of 56 percent of the population, though it must be remembered that the mining society was known for its fluidity and rapid turnover.

What calls most attention about the profile of the household heads is the proximity in number between free white men and freed women of color; proof that these women did ascend socially and economically. However, their ascension sometimes revealed itself to be somewhat paradoxical. On the one hand there were women like the freed black Josefa Maria de Freitas who lived in a house of her own on Rua Direita, near the residence of Colonel Luís de Mendonça Cabral, the secretary of the Royal Diamond Extractor;[42] on the other hand were people like the freed mulatta Arcângela who was found one night repeatedly slamming her back against the doors of the Santo Antônio church while mumbling blasphemies and superstitions, a good illustration of the difficulties some of these women had in controlling their behavior.[43]

There was room in the diamantine society for men and women of color to gain their freedom. Once inserted in the free world, many accumulated assets and mingled with the free white society of the village. Regardless of how prominent it may have been, the presence of these people has been all but forgotten. Whenever their existence is sporadically mentioned in the history books, it is almost always portrayed as an exception. Chica da Silva and the composer Lobo de Mesquita are good examples[44]; while the former used all her mulatta sensuality to win the heart of a powerful diamond contractor, the latter used his artistic gifts, immortalized in works of musical genius.

---

[40] *Coartação* was a manumission process through which a slave could shoulder the costs of his liberty, whether through services rendered or in cash. As this payment was generally made over a long period of time, the slaves often lived far from their former owners.

[41] AHU, MAMG. Caixa 108, doc. 9, f. 5.

[42] AHU, MAMG. Caixa 108, doc. 9, f. 1.

[43] AEAM. Livro de devassas. 1750–1753, fls. 40–41v.

[44] Joaquim Felício dos Santos, op. cit., 1976, pp. 123–30.

However, their liberty was the culmination of two very different life courses.

However forgotten this population of freed blacks and mulattos might have been, the history of the mining region was atavistically linked with its presence. Antonil, one of its first chroniclers, remarked that the sacrileges committed in the region were largely the result of the social disorganization provoked by the Minas gold rush. One of these "sacrileges" was the exorbitant and superfluous spending of the miners who would buy "a Negro trumpeter for a thousand cruzados and a two-bit mulatta for twice the price, with whom to engage in continuous and scandalous sin." Moreover, the vast quantities of gold extracted were converted into "necklaces, earrings and other trinkets today more often seen adorning mulattas and blacks of ill-repute than ladies of society."[45]

Many former slave women maintained long-standing or short-lived affairs with white men. However, the trajectories and accumulation of wealth of many of these women cannot be explained by these relationships alone. Rita Pais de Gouveia, a creole from Sabará, was typical of this circumstance, claiming to have made her living "by her own agency and business," which in the parlance of the day meant she had made her own fortune. In 1774, a single woman, she lived alone in a house she owned on Rua do Rosário in the village center. As she was childless, she left her patrimony of a set of houses, eight slaves, and household items of nonspecified uses to her nephew. Upon her death in 1796, she was given an open funeral at the Rosário church, with a congregation of fifty to pray for her soul. She was also a sister in the Brotherhood of the Souls and Mercies.[46]

The census of 1774 revealed that the women of Tejuco were predominantly colored and lived alone at the head of their own households, in which they were the sole residents of free status. The slaves they possessed were excluded from the count and therefore also from the document. Of the 197 women of color, 166 were single – an

[45] André João Antonil, op. cit., 1974, pp. 194–5.
[46] AEAD. Óbito e testamento de Rita Pais de Gouveia. Livro de óbitos do Tejuco. Caixa 521, fls. 35–35v.

expressive majority of 84.2 percent. Of the 31 that lived in shared households along with other free or freed residents, none was married and all lived with relatives (children, sisters, or mothers), friends, or lodgers. On Rua Direita, a single black woman named Ana Maria lived in her own house along with her mother and a sister, while the mulatta Felipa Antônia, also single, shared a rented house on the same street with her sister. On Rua Padre Manuel da Costa, two single mulattas, Juliana Francisca and Maria Angélica, lived in rented houses they each shared with a lodger, though Juliana also had the company of a sister and a daughter. Vitória da Costa, a single creole, owned a house on Rua do Bomfin where she lived with her three children.

Though the census registered these women as single homeowners, they were not really single at all. The Episcopal inquests conducted in Tejuco in 1750 and 1753 reveal the bonds of affection, albeit split into different houses, that kept those living in sin from the eyes of the Catholic Church. This explains the high number of illegitimate children living in houses owned by freedwomen that the census had registered as single. It was in this society, plural, heterogeneous, and multiple, controlled and governed with such difficulty by the authorities that Chica da Silva lived her days, first as a slave, later as a free mulatta and companion to the most important man in the region – the diamond contractor – and finally as the matriarch of many offspring whom she sought to protect and give a positive standing in the local society. It was in this manner that she proceeded in her bid to erase the stigma of color and enslavement that was hers to leave to her descendants.

CHAPTER TWO

CHICA DA SILVA

Face the colour of night,
eyes the colour of stars.

SLAVE, MULATTA

Chica da Silva, born between 1731 and 1735,[1] was the daughter of
Maria da Costa, a black slave, and Antônio Caetano de Sá, a white
man. Although various documents have helped shed light on her
origins, some questions remain unanswered. A slave from birth, this
condition and her later status of freedwoman were always associated
with her name on the known records.

Born in the village of Milho Verde at a time when her mother was
still a slave to Domingues da Costa, Chica da Silva declared herself
to be, in her own words, "the daughter of Maria da Costa and an
unknown father, born and baptised at the chapel of Nossa Senhora
dos Prazeres (Our Lady of the Pleasures) . . . in the parish of Vila do
Príncipe."[2] Many years later, her grandson Lourenço João de Oliveira

---

[1] AEAM. *Auto de genere et moribus de Simão Pires Sardinha.* 1768. Cabinet 10, file
    1782. On Simão's letter of request for entry into the Lower Orders, the witnesses
    mention that Chica da Silva was somewhere between thirty-four and thirty-
    seven years of age in 1768, which meant she must have been born between 1731
    and 1735. It was not unusual for people to know only each other's approximate
    rather than exact ages, as documents were rare and subject to error. There were
    no birth certificates, only baptismal records, and the date of one did not always
    coincide with that of the other.
[2] AEAM. *Auto de genere et moribus de Simão Pires Sardinha.* 1768. Armário 10, pasta
    1782. Auto de batismo de Francisca da Silva de Oliveira.

Grijó affirmed in more general terms that she had been born in Vila do Príncipe, under whose administrative jurisdiction the previously mentioned village fell.[3]

The village of Milho Verde was a small urban cluster on the banks of Fundo Creek, some six kilometers from Tejuco on the road to Vila do Príncipe. The village was built upon a small plateau perched between two steep slopes along which the stream flowed almost level, though winding in and out among the rocks, earning it the local name *lajeado*, a term for a creek on a rocky bed. Almost entirely composed of thatched huts organized around a small church dedicated to Our Lady of the Pleasures,[4] the people of the village made a living from gold and diamond mining or from subsistence agriculture. As much can be inferred from the will of Ana da Glória dos Santos, a Mina black woman who owned a ranch in Bicas, near the village, on the land of a certain Donna Teotônia. Among the assets she left behind were a cotton gin and a spinning wheel, indications that she planted cotton and produced homespun fabrics (a throwback to African tradition, as the weaving of homemade fabrics was a common practice for women in Africa).[5]

A slave-girl's baptism was a simple and concise affair, and Chica's took place in or around 1734, celebrated by one Reverend Mateus de Sá Cavalcanti, "then chaplain of said chapel."[6] Her sponsors were Alexandre Rodrigues de Fontoura and Luís de Barros Nogueira. If the parish priest followed the ecclesiastical norms, he would have

---

[3]   ANTT. Leitura de bacharéis. Letra L. Maço A, doc. 24.

[4]   The Milho Verde church was dedicated to Our Lady of the Pleasures, though Canon Raimundo Trindade informs that a church affiliated to the parish of Vila do Príncipe and dedicated to Saint Joseph was consecrated in the place on October 8, 1781, on the orders of Captain José de Moura e Oliveira. However, it would seem that the devotion to Our Lady of the Pleasures abided for some time afterward, as records from 1799 show that a creole named Inês Fernandes Neves was buried at the "chapel of Our Lady of the Pleasures in the village of Milho Verde." BAT. Cartório do Primeiro Ofício, maço 26. Inês Fernandes Neves.

[5]   BAT. Testamento de Ana da Glória dos Santos. Cartório do Primeiro Ofício, maço 4.

[6]   AEAM. *Auto de genere et moribus* de Simão Pires Sardinha. 1768. Armário 10, pasta 1782. Testemunho de Silvestre de Reis Drago.

been wearing an alb with a purple amice and would have started the
ceremony by washing his hands. Next, he would have taken Chica
in his arms and, holding the child facedown, immersed her in the
baptismal urn very briefly so as not to endanger her life. The chapel
was practically empty, but the surgeon Silvestre de Reis Drago was
still able to describe the ceremony some thirty-five years later.[7]

The infant mortality rate was very high in those days, and the risk
of death was ever-present from the moment of birth. Hygiene conditions during childbirth were minimal, and the child, exposed to
all manner of microorganisms, was washed and wrapped as soon as it
came into the world. Tetanus among newborn babies, known as the
seven-day sickness, was rife and its causes unknown. At the beginning of the nineteenth century, the traveler John Luccock noted in
his diary that there was a great deal of negligence with the welfare
of children. One can see from the death records for Tejuco for the
year 1817 that the main illnesses to which children succumbed were
fever, diarrhoea, typhoid, and tuberculosis.

Between 1791 and 1792, when Vila do Príncipe was assailed by
an outbreak of flu, the children, being more susceptible to epidemics,
suffered the heaviest losses. Twenty-eight infants and eleven abandoned children were registered among the deceased in the first year,
with a further forty-eight deaths in the second year, respectively
accounting for 38.2 percent and 44 percent of total deaths for those
years. Luckily, Chica survived this childhood stage of life.

Slave children were generally not dispensed any special care.
Treated as "small adults," their childhood was somewhat truncated
and, given the amount of time they spent around adults, it was common for them to have already mastered a trade by the age of seven.
Among the whites, on the other hand, there was no fixed deadline
for childhood, which could end at anywhere from seven to fourteen
years of age. It was common practice for slave mothers to take their
children to work with them from a very early age, usually carried
on their backs wrapped in shawls improvised from lengths of cloth.
Maria da Costa must have done the same with little Chica.

[7] Ibidem.

Various documents refer to Chica da Silva as mestizo, others as "parda," (brown) still others as mulatta,[8] the child of black and white parents. While the Africans were called after their place of origin or embarkation in Africa, the slaves born in Brazil were classified by color rather than place of birth. Such designations included *creoles*, who tended to be the dark-skinned (children of black parents, almost always Africans), *mulattos*, and *pardos*. Those born of a more diversified racial mix, often with Indian blood, were branded *cabras* and considered inferior to all the rest.[9]

Having inherited her mother's Mina traits, Chica had a fair complexion and a physique that attracted the interest of the newly arrived Portuguese. As she had been born a slave, this condition and her later status as a freedwoman were always registered in the official documents of Tejuco. Nevertheless, having never met Chica and unaware of the terms used overseas to distinguish between slaves, the Portuguese priest, Nuno Henriques de Orta, executor of João Fernandes de Oliveira's will in Lisbon, affirmed that all of the latter's descendants were mulattos "born to a black woman."[10] The terms *mulatto* and *black*, employed in a general manner, were intended to denigrate the inferior origin of the powerful judge's companion and offspring.

The first document registering the presence of Chica da Silva in the village of Tejuco dates to 1749. In November of that year, the "mulatta Francisca" godmothered by Ana, the daughter of Rita, slave to Antônio Vieira Balverde, with Sergeant Major Antônio de Araújo de Freitas as godfather.[11] She was at this time a slave to the Portuguese physician Manuel Pires Sardinha, born in the Villa of

---

8   AEAD. Baptismal records of the village of Tejuco. 1745–1765. Box 297, f. 2; livro de termos do Serro do Frio. 1750–1753. Box 557, f. 102v.

9   Mary C. Karasch, Slave life in Rio de Janeiro, 1987, pp. 36–7. See also Stuart B. Schwartz. "The manumission of slaves in colonial Brazil: Bahia, 1684–1745." *Hispanic American Historical Review*, vol. 54, 1974, pp. 603–35.

10 ANTT. Chancellery of Donna Maria I. Book 20, f. 11.

11 AEAD. Baptismal records of the village of Tejuco. 1745–1765. Box 297, f. 22. Comparison between this document and others proves that the parda slave named Francisca, property of Manuel Pires Sardinha, was indeed Chica da Silva.

Estremoz, near Évora, in Alentejo. He emigrated to Minas Gerais upon completing his studies in medicine and settled permanently in Tejuco. He lived off the proceeds from his gold mine, the rent he charged on slaves working the contract, and the fees he charged for his medical practice. Though he was nearly sixty by this time, he had never married.[12] In 1750, Manuel Pires Sardinha held the important position of judge at the court in Vila do Príncipe, an honor reserved for members of the region's old-boy elite, those considered honorable and worthy of such representation.[13] He prepared his will in 1755, five years before his death. He was buried in a Franciscan habit at the Santo Antônio church in Tejuco, which he declared was "the church with the best funeral pomp in the area." His corpse was carried up the carpeted aisle to its tomb in the main chapel by a procession of mendicants and paid slaves, a privilege only bestowed upon the benefactors to the Brotherhood of the Most Holy Sacrament.[14] He left alms for each of the masses to be said for his soul between then and the seventh-day anniversary of his death.[15]

After her sale to the doctor Manuel Pires Sardinha, Chica spent the early years of her adolescence in Tejuco as a domestic slave in his house. She shared the chores of the household with fellow slaves Antônia and Francisca, both creole.[16] By the age of seven, like any other slave, she was already able to execute the tasks reserved for the adults, such as serving at the table, preparing the meals, airing

---

[12] AHU, MAMG. Caixa 60, doc. 29. On June 30, 1752, Dr. Manuel Pires Sardinha gave testimony at a judicial inquiry at which he stated that he was white, made his living from his mine and medical practice in the village of Tejuco, and that he was sixty years of age.

[13] ACO. Livro de registro de patentes da Câmara da Vila do Príncipe, fls. 6v–9.

[14] AEAD. Livro de óbitos do arraial do Tejuco. 1752–1895. Caixa 350, fls. 70v–71v.

[15] AEAD. Livro de óbitos do arraial do Tejuco. 1752–1895. Caixa 350, fls. 70v–71v.

[16] Slaves did not have surnames, as they were considered mere things, the property of a master, and thus lacked any official status. Whenever they were featured in documents they were referred to by their first names followed by an indication of origin, which could be the name of a tribe or place of birth or embarkation, in the case of the Africans, or the terms creole, mulatto, pardo, or cabra for those born in Brazil.

the laundry, and cleaning the house. Her range of mobility was not restricted to the interior of the residence, as slave women were also required to wash clothes in the Santo Antônio River, deliver messages, run errands, and fetch pails of water from the public fountain on Rua do Chafariz. They would go out in groups, barefoot and colorfully dressed, wearing headcloths and a shawl over their shoulders, carrying the baskets of fruit, foods, and dainties to be sold each day on the streets or to the slaves working the diamond mines, though this was prohibited by the administration.[17] On Sundays, it was customary for the slaves to follow their master in rank and file to mass at the Santo Antônio church.

Manuel Pires Sardinha was owner of a sizable slave stock, and two of his captives formed a family that provided him with a steady supply over the years. Manuel Gonçalves and his wife Maria "creole" had three daughters, Teresa, Gertrude, and Maria, as well as the twin boys, José and Francisco.[18] He is also known to have possessed other slaves by the names of José, Paulo, Ventura, Felipa, João, and João mina.[19] He was a conventional master who did not grant manumission to any of his slaves in his will, nor at the baptismal urn, unless the child was his own. However, all of his so-called godchildren – children born to other owners' slaves – were presented with two eighths[20] of gold, which means that he paid for the liberty of these children. Such was the case with Rosa, the daughter of Maria parda, who belonged to the licentiate José Gomes Ferreira.[21]

---

[17]   The slave women of Tejuco were drawn by Carlos Julião between 1776 and 1799. "Julião was born in Turin in 1740 and served the Portuguese army, gradually climbing to the rank of Colonel. He was a military engineer and watercolour painter." His sketches of slaves from Serro do Frio and Rio de Janeiro are rare examples of pictures of slaves in the eighteenth century. Carlos Julião. *Riscos iluminados de figurinhos de broncos e negros dos usos do Rio de Janeiro e Serro do Frio*, 1960.

[18]   AEAD. Livro de batizados do arraial do Tejuco. 1745–1765. Caixa 297, fls. 14, 34, 53.

[19]   Ibidem, fls. 6v, 48, 52v, 57, 109.

[20]   An eighth was a gold measure equivalent to 350 reis during the eighteenth century.

[21]   Ibidem, f. 49.

On December 1, 1750, on the orders of Bishop Manuel da Cruz, the Reverend Inquisitor Miguel de Carvalho Almeida e Matos arrived in Tejuco to conduct an ecclesiastical visit.[22] The intention was to use this imposing and threatening mechanism to sweep the bedrooms and beds of the village clean and impose vigilance upon the bodies and intimate lives of its townsfolk.[23] During his brief weeklong stay, as the highest ecclesiastical authority in the place, the inquisitor had the powers to summon the presence of any priest, civil authority, or resident and impose whatever punishments he deemed necessary to reestablish discipline and banish "vices, sins, abuses and scandals." The customary edict was posted throughout the entire town demanding that all present themselves before the tribunal within the period of twenty-four hours to confess their sins and denounce any villager whose wrongdoings were "public and scandalous."[24]

Among the avalanche of denunciations of witchery, disorder, African dancing, and concubinage, the Portuguese Manuel Vieira Couto, forty-two years of age, who lived off his gold mine, came before the visitor to denounce "Manuel Pires Sardinha, judge, [who] makes illicit treatment of one of his female slaves, who he bought for this express purpose, named Francisca."[25] As this accusation stood alone, it was not enough to incriminate the accused parties and the investigation went no further.

In 1751, Chica da Silva bore her first son, Simão, fruit of her relationship with her owner, Manuel Pires Sardinha. Contrary to the affirmation on Simão's *de genere* papers, his father did not assume paternity in his will, nor on the baptismal certificate, though manumission had been granted to Simão at the baptismal urn. His first name was taken in honor of his godfather, Captain Simão da Cunha Pereira.[26] In his will of 1755, Manuel Pires Sardinha named Simão as one of his heirs[27] alongside two other sons, neither officially

---

[22] AEAM. Livro de devassas. 1750–1753, f. 40.
[23] Gilberto Freyre. The Master and the Slaves. 1946, p. 16.
[24] Kathleen J. Higgins. *Licentious liberty*. 1999, pp. 109–10.
[25] AEAM. Livro de devassas. 1750–1753, fls. 43v–45v.
[26] AEAD. Livro de batizados do arraial do Tejuco. 1745–1765. Caixa 297, f. 29.
[27] AEAD. Livro de óbitos do arraial do Tejuco. 1752–1895. Caixa 350, f. 27.

recognized as such: Plácido, son of the slave Antônia, and Cipriano, born of the slave Francisca creole.[28]

In July 1753, Tejuco received a second visit from the Inquisition, this time from Reverend Vicar Manuel Ribeiro Taborda. On this occasion, the fact that children had been born of his unofficial relationships was enough to have Manuel Pires Sardinha and his slaves Francisca parda and Francisca creole convicted of the crime of concubinage in the first instance.[29] All three presented themselves at the tribunal to sign the confession. The document, signed by the owner and marked with an X by the two slaves, stood out among other crimes of the same nature insofar as it was the only case in which a single man had been maintaining relations with two women at the same time.[30]

In the case of Manuel Pires Sardinha and his two slaves, the ecclesiastical visit of 1753 condemned and "admonished them paternally ... so that all would desist of such illicit communication ... avoiding, by so doing, any offence to God, scandal to others and the danger to which they had exposed their souls."[31] Slaves did not have surnames, as they were considered mere things, the property of a master, and thus lacked any official status. Whenever they were featured in documents they were referred to by their first names followed by an indication of origin, which could be the name of a tribe or place of birth or embarkation, in the case of the Africans, or the terms creole, mulatto, pardo, or cabra for those born in Brazil. The designations used for Manuel Pires Sardinha's slaves in the terms of confession – Francisca parda and Francisca creole – reveal that the former was a light-skinned mulatta while the latter, a daughter born to African parents in Brazil, was black.

---

[28] AEAD. Livro de batizados do arraial do Tejuco. 1745–1765. Caixa 297, f. 11. AFS. Livro avulso de testamentos. AEAD. Livro de óbitos do arraial do Tejuco. Caixa 350, f. 71.

[29] AEAM. Livro de devassas. 1750–1753, f. 102.

[30] Manuel Pires Sardinha had three children with different slave women, but at the time in question he was only maintaining relations with the two Franciscas. AEAD. Livro de termos do Serro do Frio. 1750. Caixa 557, f. 102v.

[31] Ibidem.

Comparison with other documents dispels any doubt there may be as to the maternity of Cipriano and Simão. The baptismal records for the children prove that Francisca parda was the mother of Simão[32] and Francisca creole the mother of Cipriano.[33] The historiography was unanimously wrong in affirming that Chica da Silva was the mother of both.

The baptismal records, the ecclesiastical visit of 1753, and the will Manuel Pires Sardinha left behind upon his death in 1755 leave no doubt as to the existence of two Franciscas. By the time the will was drafted, both had already received manumission and now had their own surnames, and it is from this document that we can see that Francisca parda became Francisca da Silva. The will contains the former master's clarification that the children he was nominating as his heirs were "three freed mulatto children born to my household, for the love I bear them, and that I raised them as sons, one by the name of Plácido, the son of Antônia Xavier, a freedwoman; another by the name of Cipriano, the son of Francisca, a freed creole; and another by the name of Simão, son of Francisca da Silva, a freed parda. These three little mulattos I institute as my universal and legitimate heirs."[34] There can therefore be no doubt that Chica da Silva was parda and the mother of little Simão.

Cipriano's birth certificate identifies his mother as Francisca Pires, black.[35] Unlike his father, Manuel Pires Sardinha, who does not mention her surname in the passage from his will cited previously, Cipriano was incisive about his maternal identity, referring to his mother as "Francisca Pires, freedwoman and creole, from Vila da Cachoeira in the archdiocese of Bahia, maternal granddaughter of Luísa Pires, born and baptised in the Kingdom of Angola."[36] In 1785, now a recently ordained priest, Cipriano requested that he be allocated to a church in Tejuco, his hometown. There were two impediments to this ordination: the fact that he was mulatto and also

---

[32] AEAD. Livro de batizados do arraial do Tejuco. 1745–1765. Caixa 297, f. 29.
[33] Ibidem, f. 11.
[34] AEAD. Livro de óbitos do arraial do Tejuco. 1752–1895. Caixa 350, f. 27.
[35] AEAD. Livro de batizados do arraial do Tejuco. 1745–1765. Caixa 297, f. 21.
[36] AEAM. Auto de gênese de Cipriano Pires Sardinha. 1785. Gaveta 34.

Table 2.1. *Crimes of Concubinage Listed at the Episcopal*
Hearings in Tejuco (1750 and 1753)

Sex	Condition	Number	Percentage
Men	Free	54	94.7
	Freed	3	5.3
	TOTAL	57	100
Women	Free	3	5.1
	Slave	15	25.9
	Freed	39	67.3
	Unknown	1	1.7
	TOTAL	58*	100

* The higher number given for women involved in these crimes is due to
the case of Manuel Pires Sardinha and his two slaves. *Source:* Ecclesiastical Archives of the Archdiocese of Diamantina. *Livro de Termos do*
Serro do Frio. 1750/1753, box 557.

illegitimate. In Brazil, a blind eye was generally turned so that being
mulatto did not present any real impediment to the ecclesiastical
vocation. What this document shows is that the son of Francisca
Pires managed to secure dispensation for his so-called defects, but
also chose to erase his paternal descent, which would have given him
legitimacy – his father is not mentioned even once throughout the
entire process – insisting that all deponents accentuate his maternal
origin, of which he had inherited only the color.[37]

As Table 2.1 shows, the only difference about Chica's concubinage to her master is that it was the only case of bigamy. Licentious
couplings had proliferated throughout the Diamantine Demarcation
to such degree that they constituted the absolute majority of the
crimes cited.

Almost all of these relationships involved free white men and
freedwomen, followed by free white men and female slaves. On Rua
do Contrato, the official goldsmith, Caetano Francisco Guimarães,
had "a slave woman under his roof named Teresa, with whom he had
illicit relations and who, having already borne him a son, now found

[37] Ibidem, fls. 13–17v.

herself once more pregnant by that same gentleman."[38] Though the couple was sentenced in 1750, they were still living together at the time of the next inquest. They were penalized again, though this time more severely for being reoffenders, receiving twice the customary fine.[39]

Though in smaller number, there was also concubinage between freedmen and freedwomen, like that of a pardo slave-hunter, a resident of the same street, who "lives illicitly with a freed black woman named Rose, from the nation of Angola, ... over whom he keeps a zealous eye, beating her constantly, [and] treating her like his concubine."[40]

Some rare cases also involved white men and women. Joana Leite, for example, who was married to Francisco José de Menezes, lived illicitly with a certain Tomé, a resident of Rua Direita, the village's main street. The husband tried to force her to come back and live with him, but Joana refused and managed to have Francisco José arrested on the orders of the county magistrate. After a brief stay at the house of Manuel Fernandes de Carvalho, she returned to Tomé, with whom she had a son.[41] The inquisitor found the accused guilty and ordered her to return to her husband within the period of three months or face excommunication.[42]

When he denounced Manuel Pires Sardinha for practicing concubinage with his slave Francisca, Manuel Vieira Couto declared "that [he] had bought her for that express purpose."[43] As previously shown, this proves that the doctor purchased Chica and that she had not belonged to him from birth. Furthermore, there is not one document connecting Chica to the slave stock of José da Silva de Oliveira, the father of Rolim, or that would suggest that her choice of surname had anything to do with him, as Joaquim Felício dos Santos

[38] AEAM. Livro de devassas. 1750–1753, f. 41.
[39] AEAD. Livro de termos do Serro do Frio. 1750. Caixa 557, fls. 99–100.
[40] AEAM. Livro de devassas. 1750–1753, f. 41.
[41] Ibidem, f. 41v.
[42] AEAD. Livro de termos do Serro do Frio. 1750. Caixa 557, fls. 34v–35.
[43] AEAM. Livro de devassas. 1750–1753, fls. 43v–45v.

affirmed.[44] Her first owner was Domingos da Costa, from the village of Milho Verde, followed by Manuel Pires Sardinha, who sold her to João Fernandes de Oliveira.[45]

The practice of freed blacks adopting the surnames of their former owners became widespread from the end of the eighteenth century. It was probably this custom, disseminated a century later, that led Joaquim Felício dos Santos to believe that the surname Silva de Oliveira, which Chica was to later adopt, indicated that she had once belonged to José da Silva de Oliveira.

Even José da Silva de Oliveira's will reveals no connection with Chica da Silva, though it does express the desire that a lass named Dalida, abandoned on his doorstep while still a child, receive as inheritance a slave woman he had already given to her on loan, plus fifty eighths of gold in cash. This decision was justified in the following terms: "as I raised her as her father... as she never gave me cause for displeasure and for the love I bear her."[46] He also expressed his gratitude for the services rendered by Mother Luísa, a freed black woman who was once his slave, and Custódio, a freed cabra in his service, leaving some gold to both.[47] According to the historiography, Chica's case was supposed to be somewhat similar to that of the child he had raised as a daughter, though there is no evidence to reveal the existence of any special bond between them, nor does José da Silva de Oliveira make any mention of her in his will.[48]

The taking of a new name postmanumission and the transformation of Francisca parda into Francisca da Silva do suggest some interesting considerations. The first document to mention Chica after manumission and to refer to her as "Francisca da Silva, freed parda" dates to 1754.[49] At that time, the name Silva, as generally adopted

---

[44] Joaquim Felício dos Santos, op. cit., 1976, p. 124.

[45] AFS. Livro de notas. 1754, fls. 55–55v.

[46] AEAD. Livro de óbitos do arraial do Tejuco. Caixa 521, f. 69. BAT. Inventário de José da Silva de Oliveira. 1796–1797. Cartório do Primeiro Ofício, maço 28.

[47] AEAD. Livro de óbitos do arraial do Tejuco. Caixa 521, f. 70.

[48] BAT. Inventário de José da Silva de Oliveira. 1796–1797. Cartório do Primeiro Ofício, maço 28, fls. 23, 73v.

[49] AEAD. Livro de batizados do arraial do Tejuco. 1745–1765. Caixa 297, f. 32.

throughout the Portuguese world, signified an individual of indefinite origin or lineage. What we can conclude is that the former slave entered the world of the free on her own steam, without connections or sponsors.

The surname Oliveira, a clear reference to the chief judge João Fernandes de Oliveira, only appeared in an official context after the birth of the couple's first child, on whose baptismal records Chica features as Francisca da Silva de Oliveira,[50] which, given the inappropriateness of legalizing the relationship, would indicate some form of informal pact between the consorts. Indeed, the production of official documents linking a white and honored father to a mestizo freedwoman would have been considered a disadvantage to their offspring, as their parentage would certainly have been investigated in the case of candidature for an important position or honor. The fewer documents that made mention of Chica and the more informational lacunas there were about her, the more easily the memory of her inferior status could be erased.

The adoption of a different name was also common practice when an individual converted to the cult of some particular saint. In these cases, the change of name, which occurred by celestial ordination and was equivalent to an initiation rite in the Christian–Judaic tradition, signified a change of life.[51] In Minas Gerais in the year 1751, a black woman named Rose, slave to one Donna Ana in the village of Infeccionado, took the name of Rosa Maria Egipcíaca da Vera Cruz as her rites of passage symbolizing her new life as a convert, made holy in God.[52] Like Rosa, though for different reasons, Chica too sought to construct a new identity that could at once definitively sever all ties to her slave past and announce her entrance into village society. Francisca da Silva de Oliveira – it was under this name that Chica began this new phase in her life, one in which she would consolidate her standing in the world of the free by her own means, albeit with connections to a man with whom she would remain entwined for the rest of her days.

[50] Ibidem, f. 42v.
[51] Luiz Mott. *Rosa Egipcíaca, uma santa africana no Brasil.* 1993, p. 162.
[52] Ibidem, p. 161.

ANCESTRY

The process of admission of Chica da Silva's eldest son, Simão Pires Sardinha, fathered by her second owner, Manuel Pires Sardinha, into the Order of Christ cast a great deal of light on his maternal descent but also caused some misunderstandings.[53] In the eighteenth century, reaching the condition of knight of the Order of Christ was the highest honor to which any nonnoble could aspire in the Portuguese Kingdom.[54] For centuries, admission to this order had been restricted to those of noble birth, though as time passed its statutes relaxed enough to allow the entrance of members of the higher echelons of the commercial and financial classes, which had amassed great wealth with maritime expansion.

Under the Old Regime, the place someone held in society was based on lineage; as such, honors and titles were birthrights handed down from generation to generation. In Portugal, in order to gain access to any position or honor, whether civil or ecclesiastical, the candidate had to be submitted to a process of *de genere*. The Order of Christ not only investigated the applicant but also his line of descent in a bid to ascertain if there was any "stain" that could render him ineligible. A *de genere* process was installed to this end, and the commissaries appointed by the order would be dispatched to the places of birth of the candidate for the investigation of his lineage – his parents and all four grandparents – to interview individuals of spotless reputation who might have known them. In *de genere* investigations, indispensable in the granting of habits, great store was placed on everything "public and notorious," that is, "on hearsay." However, once admitted, any blemish upon the honored member or his line that had failed to surface during the process was erased forever and the bearer subsequently immortalized.

---

[53] José Teixeira Neves wrongly attributed the paternity of Chica's firstborn to Rafael Pires Pardinho, the first diamond intendant, who he confused with Simão Pires Sardinha. Apud: Joaquim Felício dos Santos, op. cit., 1956, note 26, p. 162.

[54] On the meaning, development, and admission into the order, see Francis A. Dutra. "Membership in the Order of Christ in the seventeenth century: Its rights, privileges and obligations." 1970.

Before admitting someone to the order it was necessary to investigate "if [the applicant], his parents and grandparents were of noble
birth" and "if [he] was born of legitimate marriage."[55] Clearly, Simão
Pires Sardinha could meet none of these requirements: not only was
he not a noble, but he was also the illegitimate son of a slave with
her master. His only recourse was therefore to manipulate the process, taking advantage of the elasticity the concept of nobility had
acquired in order to accommodate the bourgeoisie. After all, following the standards of the day, in addition to lineage, "living in nobility" could also be construed as having beasts of burden, servants,
and slaves at one's beck and call, all of which could confer a certain
nobility upon an applicant. In an earlier process dating to 1768, in
which he requested admittance to the Lower Orders,[56] Simão Pires
Sardinha had fabricated an alternative history and genealogy that
revealed how manipulable these processes were.[57]

The near insurmountable obstacle to the concession of a habit was
his descent from a line of slaves, as being illegitimate and mulatto
were, in themselves, "defects" subject to royal dispensation. In his
process, Simão declined to avail of a half-truth that could have
ensured his knightly status but also obscured information about his
maternal lineage. His strategy was as follows: In 1779, when he was
granted the habit of the Order of Christ, Simão Pires Sardinho was
living in Lisbon under the patronage of chief judge João Fernandes
de Oliveira, at his mansion in the borough of Lapa.[58] His mother still

---

[55] ANTT. Habilitações da Ordem de Cristo. Letra s. Maço 5, doc. 5. Interro-
gatórios.

[56] There were seven degrees to the sacramental orders: the first four were considered the Lower Orders and the pinnacle three, the Sacred Orders. The Lower
Orders were Porter, Lector, Exorcist, and Acolyte, and the Sacred Orders were
Subdeacon, Deacon, and Priest. All were consecrated and devoted to God
through the vow of celibacy and impediment from holding any secular office.
Constituições primeiras do arcebispado da Bahia. Livro Primeiro, 1853, capítulo 209,
p. 86.

[57] AEAM. *Auto de genere et moribus* de Simão Pires Sardinha. 1768. Armário 10,
pasta 1782.

[58] ANTT. Habilitações da Ordem de Cristo. Letra s. Maço 5, doc. 5. Interro-
gatórios, fls. 2, 9.

lived in Tejuco, and a brief investigation in the village would have readily brought to light her former condition of slavery.

The first step toward reducing or even concealing his stigmas of color and slavery, not to mention his illegitimacy, was to recruit deponents who could testify to his maternal descent in Lisbon instead of in Tejuco, as would have been the custom. In the middle of 1779, Queen Maria I released him from the impediment of his illegitimacy, which removed one of the obstacles to the concession of the title. She also forgave the "lack of certificates of conduct of his native land"; thus authorizing that the investigation into his parents and grandparents could be conducted in Lisbon alone.[59] This was the chance Simão had been waiting for to rewrite the history of his ascendancy and diminish its inherent "defects." With this royal dispensation, the commissary knight in charge of the process, Francisco Joaquim da Silveira, could recruit witnesses offering a distorted version of Simão's family history. In this, he no doubt counted on the patronage of the powerful stepfather.

Fourteen deponents were recruited to give information about Simão Pires Sardinha and his lineage; two for Simão himself, six to speak on his paternal line, and six on his maternal line. The first of these, José Matias Frantsen, a resident of the borough of Lapa, said that he did know Simão and gave no further information.[60] However, Manuel Luís Esteves, his neighbor on Rua Buenos Aires, confirmed that he was a bright presence at court and, while he had not met his parents personally, had "always heard said" that they were reputable people.[61]

As Manuel Pires Sardinha, his father, had been born in the Villa of Estremoz, the commissary sought out some fellow townsmen who would have known him and his antecedents. They found six deponents, all of whom confirmed that Manuel and his parents, Dionísio Lopes Sardinha and Paula do Espírito Santo Sardinha, were "people of sound repute in both blood and habit, living with

---

[59] ANTT. Ministério do Reino. Livro 215, fls. 207, 208.
[60] ANTT. Habilitações da Ordem de Cristo. Letra s. Maço 5, doc. 5, f. 3.
[61] Ibidem, fls. 3–3v.

distinction and gravity, without crime or infamy."[62] Manuel had left for Brazil after graduating in medicine from Coimbra,[63] so Simão's paternal line really posed no greater problem than the threatened reminder of his illegitimacy.

The commissary then proceeded to investigate his maternal line of descent, upon which he located another six deponents. The first of these, Antônio Borges de Freitas, a native of Rio de Janeiro, revealed that he knew the applicant personally and confirmed all of the information he had provided. His deposition unveiled for the first time the story Chica's son had spun about his past and that of his family. Borges de Freitas affirmed that Simão Pires Sardinha was the "natural son"[64] of Manuel Pires Sardinha, who had nevertheless "affiliated him and made him heir to the assets under his direct possession," somewhat mitigating the negative impact of his illegitimacy. According to the deponent, Manuel Pires Sardinha had recognized his son on his deathbed and left him an inheritance, which made him "almost" legitimate.[65] The fact that Chica da Silva's father had been captain of the auxiliaries in Minas Gerais also contributed to the positive outcome, as it was an indication of nobility. Simão also alleged that all of his antecedents on his mother's side were dead, but that they had "always lived in the light of nobility, in a fine mansion often visited by the cream of the continent."[66]

Only three deponents actually knew Tejuco and the people under examination, and all three appeared to have had some connection

---

[62] Ibidem, f. 4v.

[63] Ibidem, f. 6.

[64] In Portuguese legislation there are various types of illegitimacy, and "natural child" – which denotes an illegitimate child born of single parents – is one category. Illegitimate children could also be adulterine, incestuous, spurious, or sacrilegious depending on the conditions of the parents.

[65] What we have here is a certain manipulation of Manuel Pires Sardinha's will, as he did not go so far as to actually recognize the children in this document, although he did bequeath them his patrimony. The text reads that these three little mulatto boys had been born to his household and that he bore them affection. AEAD. Livro de óbitos do Arraial do Tejuco. Box 350. 1752–1895, f. 27.

[66] ANTT. Habilitações da Ordem de Cristo. Letter s. Box 5, doc. 5, f. 3v.

with the Chief Judge João Fernandes. Evasive in their testimony, they helped Simão Pires Sardinha to consolidate his version that all of his family in Minas Gerais had been nobles, omitting his mother and grandmother's condition as former slaves. The Reverend Domingos Caldas Barbosa, at the time a guest of the Count of Calheta,[67] without going into the details claimed to be unsure as to whether Simão's parents had been married or not. However, he could confirm that Chica da Silva was the legitimate daughter of Maria da Costa and that the entire family was "equally opulent, possessed of a copious slave stock and lived in the light of nobility," despite the grandmother's pardo complexion.[68]

Francisco Xavier de Oliveira, who had lived in Tejuco for three years and held the position of diamond inspector, told the commissary that Simão Pires Sardinha was the son of "Francisca da Silva, who lived and still lives in the greatest ostentation, the lady of a large house."[69] Notice that the surname Oliveira, which Chica would have been using at this time, was omitted from this and all other depositions, thus concealing her connection with João Fernandes de Oliveira and further obscuring her past before the inquisitor.[70] There were two reasons for hiding his mother's relationship with the chief judge. The first was that the inquisitors would have easily discovered that the relationship was consensual rather than legitimate. The second was that, in the light of this concubinage, it would have been extremely difficult to make Chica's relationship with Manuel Pires

---

[67] The sixth Count of Calheta, a title conferred by a royal letter of January 3, 1766, was Antônio de Vasconcelos e Sousa, the grandson of Afonso de Vasconcelos e Sousa, third Count of Castelo Melhor and fifth Count of Calheta.

[68] ANTT. Habilitações da Ordem de Cristo. Letter s. Box 5, doc. 5, f. 8.

[69] Ibidem, f. 10.

[70] This strategy reveals how he behaved differently in relation to his paternal descent in both instances. During the first process, while living in Tejuco under the protection of Chica and the judge, he insisted that "no-one knew who his father was" and that he was an illegitimate son "whose father was unknown to anyone in the village." In the second process, he invoked the paternity of Manuel Pires Sardinha, an indispensable artifice in the concession of the habit of the order, while entirely erasing his mother's relationship with João Fernandes de Oliveira.

Sardinha look like a stable involvement, thus adding two further blemishes to Chica's past.

How the relationship was broached seemed to change depending on the requirements of the situation. At another moment, Lourenço João de Oliveira Grijó, Chica da Silva's grandson, had no qualms about not only recovering the surname Oliveira, but actually referring to his grandmother as *Donna*, a term reserved for the married lady of a household. When he was admitted to the Judiciary of the Paço, he declared himself to be "the paternal grandson of João Fernandes de Oliveira, of Tejuco in Minas Gerais, and *Donna* Francisca da Silva Oliveira, of Vila do Príncipe."[71] With time, this latter approach came to prevail in the paperwork in Tejuco, indicating the distinction Chica had achieved during her life, which permitted her to lay claim to such an identity in the society of the free whites.

The deponents omitted the slave pasts of both mother and grandmother and lied about Chica da Silva's legitimacy in order to dilute the presence of Negro blood coursing through Simão Pires Sardinha's veins and those of his maternal antecedents. The deposition of Baltazar Gonçalves de Carvalho, a gardener by trade who had lived in Brazil for fifty years, was exemplary in revealing Simão's strategy of "whitening" his way to legitimacy, affirming that Chica was

> the legitimate child of Captain of the Auxiliaries Antônio Caetano de Sá and Maria da Costa, owners of a large estate and copious slave stock, she being parda and thus, consequently, also her daughter, the applicant's mother. In her case [the daughter], this was only in the third or fourth degree, and all enjoyed most excellent reputations and lived in the light of nobility, with a great deal of wealth and cutting the first figure on the continent, visited by [sic] people of the highest order.[72]

Only two deponents mentioned that Chica was still alive, though they omitted her condition of former slave. As for her house, they

---

71 ANTT. Índice de leitura de bacharéis. Letter l. Box a, doc. 24.
72 ANTT. Habilitações da Ordem de Cristo Letter s. Box 5, doc. 5, f. 11.

affirmed that it was the best on the continent, visited by "people of the highest order, of both government and the judiciary."[73] Supported by Chica and her vast fortune, Simão would receive "at Court considerable sums from his mother," enabling him to live ostentatiously, "as a noble, living off his farms and incomes."[74]

From Sardinha's process, regardless of the evasive responses and inconsistent affirmations, not to mention the distortion of certain evidence – reproduced uncritically by many who have written about Chica da Silva – we can extract some shreds of information about his mother's parentage. According to the deponents, Chica's father, captain Antônio Caetano de Sá, a white man, was born and baptized in Candelária in Rio de Janeiro and that her mother, Maria da Costa, hailed from the parish of Conceição da Praia in the city of Salvador, Bahia.[75] This last piece of information was a distortion designed to suggest that Maria da Costa was Brazilian and mulatta, thus whitening her blood and consequently also that of Chica and Simão.

In 1726, Antônio Caetano de Sá held the post of captain of the squadrons of Bocaina, Três Cruzes, and Itatiaia, all districts of Vila Rica.[76] Little is known about him, but the rank of captain would denote honor, distinction, and the fact that he was white, rendering invalid the argument put forward by various authors that he was the slave master of José da Silva de Oliveira, the father of Father Rolim. It was in honor of her father that Chica's fourth son, the third with João Fernandes de Oliveira, was named Antônio. Chica was not his legitimate daughter, as relationships between white men and black women had to remain informal.

More information could be garnered about Maria da Costa. The information that she was baptized in Bahia is false, and even if it were true, this would not necessarily be an indication that she had been born there, as Simão Pires Sardinha and his deponents sought

[73] Ibidem, f. 9.
[74] Ibidem, fls. 9 and 11.
[75] Ibidem, fls. 8–14.
[76] AHU, MAMG. Caixa 9, doc. 53.

to imply. The reference to the parish of Conceição da Praia was just part of a strategy to minimize the stigma of her color.

While still a child, Maria da Costa arrived at the village of Milho Verde, one of the urban centers near Tejuco in the Diamantine Demarcation, sometime around 1720 as part of a slave caravan escorted by the freed black Domingos da Costa, her owner.[77]

In truth, it was there, at the church of Nossa Senhora dos Prazeres, that Maria da Costa was baptized along with the rest of the slaves brought in by Domingos da Costa, as "there is also no doubt [that] the masters, when they bring black slaves to this land, if they are not already baptised, have them baptised straight away, as everyone knows, because it's commonplace."[78] In order to receive the sacrament, the adults in the group had to have rudimentary Portuguese so that they could be given basic instruction in the Catholic faith and be able to answer the six questions the parish priest would ask them at the baptismal urn. Children up to the age of seven, like Maria da Costa, were baptized without parental consent, unlike the free whose parents could give or withhold consent to conferral of the sacrament.[79] While many, like her, were baptized only after their arrival in Brazil, some slave ships had priests on board to administer the sacrament before the slaves embarked.[80]

Many freedwomen in Tejuco lived something similar to Maria da Costa. The analysis of the wills of twenty-four women who lived in the village during the eighteenth century reveals that of the fifteen Africans, the majority was baptized in Brazil. An example of this practice is Maria da Encarnação, a native of the Coast of Mina, who was brought over on a slave ship that landed initially in Bahia,

---

[77] AEAM. *Auto de genere et moribus de Simão Pires Sardinha.* 1768. Armário 10, pasta 1782.

[78] AEAM. *Auto de genere et moribus de Simão Pires Sardinha.* 1768. Armário 10, pasta 1782. Testemunha Maria Furtado de Mendonça.

[79] *Constituições primeiras do arcebispado da Bahia.* Livro Primeiro, título 14, 1853, pp. 20–1.

[80] Coimbra University Library. Brazil manuscripts, f. 140. Letter of law referring to the chaplains that all ships sailing from the port of Bahia to Angola, the Gold Coast of Mina, and so forth had to have on board.

where she was baptized.[81] The black freedwoman Rosa Fernandes[82] received the sacrament in Paracatu, while the previously mentioned Ana da Glória dos Santos,[83] brought to Brazil while still a child, was also baptized in Bahia.

Simão Pires Sardinha's *de genere* process for admittance into the Lower Orders effectively yielded much more precise information about his maternal line of descent than did the later process. The fact that the inquiries were made in Tejuco on this occasion, in 1768, when almost all those involved were still alive, meant the deponents could not hide information, though attempts to do so were on a much smaller scale.[84] Unlike in the *de genere* process for the Order of Christ, Simão sought to erase his parental descent, with his deponents insisting that he was the son of an unknown father ("no-one in the village knows who he is"[85]) and that his maternal grandfather was likewise unknown, thus omitting the name of Antônio Caetano de Sá. His mother's name, on this occasion, was given as Francisca da Silva de Oliveira, as she was generally known in Tejuco.

The document reveals that Maria da Costa requested that she be given dispensation from presenting her baptismal certificate, as the papers had disappeared and, as she had been baptized in Milho Verde some forty-six years earlier, the priest who had conducted the ceremony had passed away and few individuals in the village would have been old enough to remember the event, as she, Maria da Costa, was already one of its most elderly residents.[86] She affirmed that she was a native of the "Coast of Mina," thus confirming what Simão Pires Sardinha and other deponents had attested concerning his maternal lineage. Some witnesses were rather less precise

---

[81] AEAD. Livro de óbitos do arraial do Tejuco. 1752–1895. Caixa 350, fls. 34–35.
[82] AEAD. Livro de óbitos do arraial do Tejuco. Caixa 521, fls. 102–102v.
[83] Ibidem, fls. 379v–380.
[84] Only Manuel Pires Sardinha was dead in 1760. AEAD. Livro de óbitos do arraial do Tejuco. 1752–1895. Caixa 350, f. 27.
[85] AEAM. *Auto de genere et moribus* de Simão Pires Sardinha. 1768. Armário 10, pasta 1782. Depositions of the witness Custódio Vieira da Costa.
[86] Ibidem. "She was so old that it was no easy task finding someone still alive who had seen her baptised."

in stating that she was "a black woman from the Coast of Guinea" or, as informed in 1768, "a black freedwoman from the heathens of Guinea."[87]

At the time, the expression "heathens of Guinea" was used generically to describe all blacks from Greater West Africa, a region that stretched from Guinea Bissau along the so-called Gold Coast of Mina to Equatorial Guinea, combining the Portuguese toponymy and African geography. When the slaves reached Brazil they were generally identified on the registers by their tribe of origin, though as such designations were very imprecise, they usually ended up being registered under whatever African port they had sailed from.[88]

The expression *da Costa* (from the Coast) associated with countless slaves is a reference to the Slave Coast, a region of Africa that corresponds to the Benin and Nigeria of today, and which was inhabited by Sudanese blacks, generally referred to as *Minas*. The term derived from the castle of São Jorge da Mina, also called Elmina, which was the point of departure for slave ships leaving from the northwestern coast of Africa, better known as the Coast of Guinea. The most important region of the Coast of Guinea was the Gold Coast of Mina,[89] where gold mining was a major activity, so its people were already skilled in extraction techniques. The slaves rounded up in this region were exported en masse to Minas Gerais, where they formed the majority of slaves up to the mid-eighteenth century. These expressions and terms were used indiscriminately and so did not designate any single tribe or ethnicity, but rather lumped together the different groups that were shipped to Brazil via the same point of embarkation: the castle of São Jorge in northeastern Africa.

The Minas were generally considered more efficient workers, more resistant to illness and stronger than slaves from other regions.[90]

---

[87] Ibidem. Depositions of the witnesses Captain Luís Lopes da Costa and Captain Luís de Mendonça Cabral. Captain Major Francisco Malheiros de Araújo said the grandmother was "Maria da Costa, a freed black woman, native of the Guinea Coast."

[88] Mary C. Karasch. Op. cit., pp. 36–7.

[89] Mary C. Karasch, op. cit., p. 64.

[90] A. J. R. Russell-Wood, op. cit., 1982, p. 113.

They were feared by their masters for their indomitable spirit, prone-
ness to revolt, and intellectual superiority (many were Muslim and
able to read and write in Arabic).[91] The Mina women were known
for their beauty, so frequently praised by the foreign travelers visiting Brazil in the nineteenth century: lighter in color and with long
slender bodies they were always the first to be chosen by the white
men as concubines.[92] "From 1711 to 1720, approximately 60.2% of
slaves imported into the Captaincy were Minas. This figure dropped
to 54.1% between 1721 and 1730 and later to 34.2%, when the
Bantus and Angolans started coming over in greater quantities to
work the fields."[93]

In 1725, the governor of Rio de Janeiro, Luís Vaia Monteiro,
described the miners' dependence upon Mina slaves:

> The mines, of course, could not be worked if not by blacks . . . the
> Minas blacks have the best reputation for this work . . . but I under-
> stand they have acquired that reputation for being considered
> magicians and witches, for having introduced the devil, as they
> alone find gold, and so for this reason every miner must have a
> Mina black, claiming that only with these is there any fortune to
> be had.

Maria da Costa, like many women in Minas Gerais, succeeded in
being manumitted. She probably took the name da Costa either in
reference to the surname of her former owner or to her origins on
the Gold Coast of Mina. The reverend Leonardo da Costa Almeida
revealed that no sooner had she obtained manumission than she
left the village of Milho Verde with her children and settled in
Tejuco.[94] It is only through this account that we learn that she

[91] Mary C. Karasch, op. cit., p. 64.
[92] Ibidem.
[93] Maria Odila L. S. Dias. "Nos sertões do Rio das Velhas e das Gerais: vida
      social numa frente de povoamento,1710–1733." In Erário Mineral, vol. 1, 2002,
      pp. 45–105. Calculations based on inventories from Minas Gerais show that
      the majority of African slaves during the period 1720 to 1888 were Benguela
      (28.3%), Angolan (23.9%), Congan (10.7%), and Mina (10.5%). Laird W.
      Bergad, op. cit., p. 151.
[94] AEAM. Auto de genere et moribus de Simão Pires Sardinha. 1768. Armário 10, pasta
      1782.

had other children besides Chica da Silva. There is also a reference to a baptism: in 1740, the chaplain João de Souza Lemos baptized Anastácio, son of Maria of the Mina nation, slave to Domingos da Costa, who granted him manumission at the baptismal urn.[95]

Does the fact that Maria obtained manumission and adopted the surname Costa once freed indicate that she had had an illicit relationship with her owner, as was so common in Minas Gerais? Domingos da Costa was married to Ana da Costa, both freed blacks, and the couple had at least one daughter, named Catarina, who was baptized in Tejuco in 1743.[96] It is not known exactly how Chica's mother secured her liberty, but, whatever her mechanisms might have been, it was the first time women like Maria da Costa could take their own decisions and point their lives in whatever directions they saw fit.

It is possible to follow the life paths of many ex-slaves who, like Chica and her mother, were manumitted and became the mistresses of their own destinies. In her will, which was written in Tejuco, the freedwoman Ana da Glória offered a glimpse of how she interpreted her own life, using verbs in the passive voice when describing her coming to Brazil, her marriage, and conversion to Catholicism, then switching to active voice when treating of her manumission, demonstrating that by securing her freedom she had also seized control of her own life.[97]

In 1737, a freed black woman named Maria da Costa had a daughter named Rita.[98] There is no way we can be sure that this Maria da Costa was Chica da Silva's mother, as many freedwomen adopted this surname, but the fact does suggest a possible connection with Chica, who had the habit of naming her children after members of hers and João Fernandes' families: Rita was the first name of one of her daughters and the second of another. This Maria da Costa, now in the condition of freedwoman, moved to Conceição do Mato Dentro, midway between Tejuco and Sabará, where she lived a far from conventional life.

---

[95] AEAD. Livro de batizados do arraial do Tejuco. 1740–1754. Caixa 297, f. 33.
[96] Ibidem, f. 48.
[97] AEAD. Livro de óbitos do arraial do Tejuco. Caixa 521, fls. 397v–398.
[98] AEAD. Documentos sem identificação. Caixa 230.

During the eighteenth century, the captaincy of Minas Gerais was mobilized by the Catholic Church in search of sinners. In terms of morals and good habits, the most common sin was concubinage, usually between white men and mulatto or black women. The instability of these relationships was due in large part to the transitory nature of the mining business and the very composition of the population – in the newly inhabited diamantine region, for example, there was a striking disproportion between the number of men and women. An examination of the census conducted in Serro do Frio in 1738, which included the Diamantine District, reveals that, of the total of 9,681 inhabitants, 83.5 percent were men and 16.5 percent women. Among the slave population, only 3.1 percent were women, as mining was basically work for men.

However, the proportion is reversed when it comes to freed slaves, with women constituting the grand majority. The same document tells us that 63 percent of the 387 former slaves reintroduced to the census were female and 37 percent male, a clear indication that women were the greatest beneficiaries of manumission and far more likely to accumulate assets. Once freed, they oscillated between social exclusion and inclusion, however precarious, in the universe formerly restricted exclusively to the free whites of Minas Gerais.

As a result, concubinage proliferated not only in the Diamantine Demarcation, but throughout the entire captaincy, and the main mechanism the Catholic Church had at its disposal in endeavoring to shape the morals and customs of its sinful flock was the ecclesiastical visit. From time to time the bishops patroled the villages and villas to root out crimes against morality and the faith. A board of inquisition would be installed and the residents shamed into confessing their own sins and denouncing those of others. All matters "public and notorious" were investigated, and many moral stains seeped from the local streets. While some confessed to what they could not hide, others took the chance to re-ignite old tensions and grudges between neighbors and rivals. The denunciations, verdicts of guilt, and corresponding sentences were registered in well-kept books in which the inquisitors, by their zeal, have bequeathed to the researcher an invaluable source of information from which to reconstruct the daily colonial routine of that region.

In 1748, in Conceição do Mato Dentro, the Maria da Costa previously mentioned was indicted during one such visit. While it cannot
be affirmed in all certainty that we are dealing with the same person here, it must be remembered that she did move to Conceição
after her manumission. Though already an ironmonger's mistress,
Maria da Costa was accused of sleeping with "every man who offered
himself."[99] Various witnesses testified to the fact that it was general
knowledge in the village that her jealous companion beat her frequently. On one of these occasions "they abused each other with
jealous curses and blows and [it was said] that the way of life of [the
accused] had resulted in a great deal of ruin and death."[100]

It appears that Maria da Costa was involved in a lot of strife in
Conceição do Mato Dentro and that the kind of life she led was an
example of the tensions caused by the influx of freedwomen of low
social station. If she really was involved with various men, she must
have provoked the ire of various women. One such woman threatened physical aggression, claiming to be "capable of levelling a blow
against Our Lady of the Pillar."[101] It was not unusual for the settlers
to confer meanings upon the cults of saints that were markedly different to those officially recommended by the Catholic Church, thus
popularizing them to the point that women would sometimes bring
religion into their daily disputes and tensions. Accused of being a
harlot, the defendant retorted that if she was a sinful woman, she
was no different than Saint Mary Magdalene, a riposte that promptly
scandalized the society and clergy alike.[102]

Despite the censure of the church, Maria da Costa did not change
her ways. A few years later she was denounced yet again by one Francisco de Brito Bittencourt who revealed that "with her tongue"[103]
she was a public and scandalous woman and that her nickname in
the village was "the broomstick." In 1753, the inquisitor Miguel de
Carvalho Almeida Neves noted that, though she had promised to

---

[99] AEAM. Devassas. Fevereiro de 1748, f. 33.
[100] AEAM. Devassas. Fevereiro de 1748, f. 33.
[101] AEAM. Devassas. Fevereiro de 1748, fls. 31v–32.
[102] Ibidem.
[103] AEAM. Devassa de 1750–1753, fls. 16–16v.

mend her ways, Maria da Costa continued "to insult both men and women with slanderous and indecent names."[104] In addition to this, she was found guilty of concubinage in the first instance, that is, for the first time, with one Bartolomeu Martins da Rocha, who lived on the outskirts of the village. Condemned on both counts, she was ordered to pay two eighths of gold to the tribunal and was threatened with more rigorous punishment unless she changed her behavior. As she was illiterate, she signed her terms of guilt with an X.

However, if this Maria da Costa really was Chica da Silva's mother, with her fierce tongue and less than orthodox religiosity, in other moments we see her observing Catholic rites, especially those based on relationships of favor, friendship, or cronyism. In 1753 she turned up at the Santo Antônio church in Tejuco to fulfill the role of godmother at the baptism of the daughter of a slave named Silvéria. Her condition is noted as freedwoman in the baptismal records.[105]

In Simão Pires Sardinha's *de genere* process for entry into the Lower Orders, the witnesses describe her as a good Christian. Captain Luís Lopes da Costa, a white Portuguese who had been living in Tejuco for some fourteen years by that time, affirmed that

> Maria da Costa is a Christian and has lived her life in the creed and teachings of the Holy Mother Church, as a Christian woman of old, observing all the requirements of the Laws of God and the Holy Mother Church and all of the functions and pious acts..., with great devotion [and] special zeal, giving alms and contributing with all she can to the divine cult.[106]

Reverend José Ribeiro Aldonço was yet more specific, declaring that she attended mass every day and took communion on various occasions per year.[107] In 1774, Maria da Costa was living in a house of her own on Rua Macau in Tejuco, where her neighbors included Silvestre de Almeida, a pardo painter, and Manuel do Nascimento, a

---

[104] AEAD. Livro de termos do Serro do Frio. 1750. Caixa 557, f. 10.
[105] AEAD. Livro de batizados do arraial do Tejuco. 1745–1765. Caixa 297, f. 6v.
[106] AEAM. *Auto de genere et moribus de Simão Pires Sardinha.* 1768. Armário 10, pasta 1782. Inquirição de costumes. Witness capitão Luís Lopes da Costa.
[107] Ibidem. Inquirição de costumes. Witness priest José Ribeiro Allonço.

white man who lived in the company of his wife, four sons, and four daughters.[108]

The governor of Minas Gerais, the Count of Galveias, was horrified by the laxity of customs and subversion of order he beheld on his arrival in the village in 1733 and issued the following order for the repression of

> the public sins that run so loose and free in the village of Tejuco, due to the high number of dishonest women in the same village living a life so dissolute and scandalous that, not content to parade about in sedan-chairs and pole couches accompanied by slaves, they have the irreverence to dare enter the house of God in rich and pompous garments totally unbefitting and inappropriate to their station.[109]

Maria da Costa was not alone. In the diamantine society, the trappings that were the exclusive prerogative of the white ladies back in the Realm – the access to the outward signs of distinction – had to be shared with black and mulatto freedwomen, clouding the social hierarchy and giving it fluidity, even if many of these freedwomen behaved in a less than conventional manner.

[108] AHU, MAMG. Caixa 108, doc. 9, f. 8.
[109] Bando do governador de 2 de dezembro de 1933.

CHAPTER THREE

The Diamond Contractors

Ah, those that owned the riches
that gush from the District
without descending from their horses ...
without setting foot in the rivers ...

The Old Sergeant Major

In August 1753 the young chief judge João Fernandes de Oliveira arrived in Tejuco to represent his father, who had managed to secure his fourth diamond contract with the Realm. He was a young man basking in glory whose career, carefully planned by Sergeant Major João Fernandes de Oliveira, was a reflection of the rise to notability and social standing the elderly diamond contractor had sought to establish for his family as he grew steadily richer. João Fernandes de Oliveira the elder, despite the fortune he had accumulated since sealing his first diamond contract in 1740, had never risen beyond the rank of sergeant major, a title that always accompanied his name to distinguish father from homonymous son.[1]

Born in Santa Maria de Oliveira, a village belonging to Vila de Barcelos in the Archdiocese of Braga in the captaincy of Minho in northern Portugal, it was in the first decade of the eighteenth century

---

[1] ANTT. Cartórios notariais. 5B. Box 15, book 75. Notes. Current 12, fls. 75–78v. For a short biography of the Chief Judge João Fernandes de Oliveira, see Manoel da Silveira Cardozo. "O desembargador João Fernandes de Oliveira." *Separata da Revista da Universidade de Coimbra*, vol. 27, 1979.

that the elder João Fernandes de Oliveira, already of age, left the small village and embarked for Brazil.[2] His saga was one shared with countless others from the region whose predominantly agriculture-based economy was in crisis. The eighteenth century saw the emigration of a significant parcel of the young male population of the captaincies of Minho and Douro. Mostly single, few left wives and children behind as they set off in search of El Dorado.

Upon arriving in Brazil, João Fernandes de Oliveira had a brief stay in Rio de Janeiro before continuing into Minas Gerais after the promise of the region's gold wealth. His first base in Minas was in Vila Rica (now Ouro Preto), though he quickly moved on to Vila do Riberão do Carmo (now Mariana), where he initially engaged in mining.[3] When a fortune began to appear on the horizon, he bought Vargem farm, near Itacolomi peak. Lost in a rugged and inhospitable region, close to the village of Passagem, on the other side of the Itacolomi ridge, the property was a mixture of rural and mineral land.

A frequent visitor to the farm was the surgeon Luís Gomes Ferreira, owner of a farm on the banks of the same river that flowed through the Vargem property[4] and author of a treatise on practical medicine titled *Erário mineral* (*Mineral Exchequer*), in which he described his curing of a slave that João Fernandes valued highly. The patient, who complained of a cough so severe that his companions in the slave quarters could not sleep, had been receiving treatment from a doctor in the region, but without any visible improvement. Lung complaints were common among those who spent days on end mining for gold, forever wet, inappropriately dressed, and undernourished. The surgeon cured the slave with a medicine prepared from a saffron base.[5] In 1725 the Vargem farm was home to thirty-nine slaves, all of whom, with the exception of three mulattos, were from

[2]   AEAM. Processo matrimonial de João Fernandes de Oliveira e Maria de São José, no. 3608. 1726, fls. 4, 10v.
[3]   Deposition of the priest Melquior dos Reis, vigário da Vila do Carmo. AEAM. Processo matrimonial no. 3608. 1726, f. 5v.
[4]   Luís Gomes Ferreira. *Erário mineral*, vol. 1, 2002, pp. 275–7.
[5]   Ibidem, p. 276.

the various African "nations": Benguela, Mina, Nago, Cape Verde, and so on.[6]

João Fernandes de Oliveira invested in various sectors, and it was this diversification that had enabled him to amass wealth and acquire a reputation as a man of business by the 1750s. This designation – *man of business* – was used for the holders of ample capital in the wholesale sector, people who dealt in bulk, lent money at interest, and were licensed by the Crown to collect taxes, among other activities that required heavy investment.

The enormous population that flocked into the urban centers of the captaincy of Minas Gerais was an attractive consumer market that expanded the commercial sector and made it highly profitable, as a great deal of the wealth of the miners and farmers ended up in the hands of the merchants. In 1732 the state government secretary attested to the importance and strength of the commercial sector, claiming that "the country of Minas is and always has been the captaincy of all business."[7]

In the beginning, with only modest sums at his disposal, João Fernandes de Oliveira set about associating himself with the Realm's most renowned businessmen with a view to representing them. He organized a partnership to lease the rights to collect the region's tithes, one of the Crown's main sources of income.[8] Originally an ecclesiastical tax, these moneys were redirected by papal bull to the Portuguese king in his capacity as grand master of the Order of Christ. The Crown, in turn, outsourced its collection in the general form of four-yearly contracts. In Minas Gerais, the tithe was payable on all internal production with the exception of gold.

The first partnership was formed with Manuel Mateus Tinoco, who negotiated the contract in Lisbon, Manuel de Bastos Viana, and Francisco Xavier Braga. João Fernandes's role was to represent the firm in Minas Gerais and serve as cashier.[9] It must have been a

---

6 AHCMM. Códice 150. Lista de escravos, lojas e vendas dadas em capitação no ano de 1725, f. 72v.
7 APM. Seção Colonial. 35. Representação do secretário das Minas ao rei. 1732.
8 ACS. Justificações. Códice 300. Auto 6118. Primeiro Ofício, f. 18v.
9 ANTT. Cartórios notariais. Testamentos. Livro 300, fls. 30v–31.

lucrative business, as he stayed on to represent the incoming contractor in Lisbon, Jorge Pinto de Azevedo, with whom he formed a
new partnership after the expiry of the first contract.[10]

As was common at the time, he took one of his slaves, a mulatta
named Lourença Batista, as a mistress during the first years. When
Lourença became pregnant, João Fernandes forced her to marry
another, most likely a slave from his property. The child, who was
given the name Teodósio, was baptized by the Sergeant Major and
given manumission at the baptismal urn. Under João Fernandes'
patronage, the lad was sent to study surgery in France, despite the
fact that he could never actually be sure he was the father, as the
mother, in his own words, "had always been a harlot."[11]

As his business progressed, the Sergeant Major started to bring
members of his extended family over to Brazil so they could seek
their own enrichment. It was by no means uncommon for bonds of
blood and friendship in the private sphere to spill over into the world
of business. The first to arrive was his cousin Ventura Fernandes de
Oliveira, who provided various services to the Sergeant Major. Following in João Fernandes' footsteps, he took a lease on the collection of tithes at Vila do Carmo,[12] prospered, and received the title of
lieutenant colonel of the Cavalry of Mariana.[13] Three more cousins
arrived, one of whom was Miguel Fernandes de Oliveira who went
to work on a cattle ranch, which the Sergeant Major had acquired
in Formiga.[14] Many family members moved to Brazil to do business

[10] Ibidem, f. 31; Ministério do Reino. Livro 208, fls. 74v–75v.
[11] Ibidem, f. 30.
[12] AHCMM. Livro 189, f. 124v. "Warrant for the arrest Captain Paulo Moreira da
      Silva as requested by the tithe collector Ventura Fernandes de Oliveira, 1784."
      AHU, MAMG. Box 95, doc. 18. "Solicitation of Ventura Fernandes de Oliveira,
      cashier of the tithe contract for Minas Gerais during the three-year period 1759
      to 1762." See also AHU, MAMG. Box 90, doc. 43, and box 119, doc. 67.
[13] ANTT. Chancellery of José I. Book 9, f. 19. AHU, MAMG. Box 96, doc. 24.
      "Solicitation of Ventura Fernandes de Oliveira, requesting official letter of confir-
      mation of the post of Lieutenant Colonel of the Auxiliary Cavalry [of Mariana]."
      Pedindo carta patente de confirmação do posto de tenente-coronel do Regimento
      da Cavalaria Auxiliar da Nobreza, termo da cidade de Mariana.
[14] ANTT. Cartórios notariais. Last wills and testament. Book 300, f. 30.

with the Sergeant Major and later with his son, the chief judge. Some of these relatives received loans or advances, like the cousin Manuel Fernandes de Oliveira, whose debts João Fernandes forgave in his will. In thanks for the favors received, Manuel baptized his son under the name of João and invited his successful cousin to godfather the child.[15] Brazil afforded João Fernandes de Oliveira and his relatives such opportunities for enrichment that he even left fifty thousand reis in his will to ten lads who had shown themselves to be cousins in the third degree and willing to leave the homeland to "prosper and settle in Brazil."[16]

The Sergeant Major formed alliances with important figures in the region, piecing together the sort of networks of friendship and cronyism with which he had sought to surround himself since he was a youth back in the Realm. The Sunday masses said at the chapel of Our Lady of the Conception, which he had built on the Vargem farm, were social events for forging ties with the important neighbors constantly invited to attend. On the head altar of the chapel, which was painted blue and had white flowers decorating its columns, rested the image of the saint from which it took its name, the patron of Portugal, to whom João Fernandes had a special devotion.

Important mechanisms of identification and sociability in the Portuguese kingdom, clientele networks reached overseas, and the exchange of favors on which they were based made the connections between the participants impossible to erase. João Fernandes de Oliveira never missed an opportunity to extend his power by swelling the ranks of those under his protection. He became the executor of the wills of various individuals with whom he had business dealings, which was not only lucrative but also ensured that the ties established in life endured beyond death. For example, after the death of his neighbor Domingos Pinto Machado, he became the executor of his will and tutor to his daughter, Rita, fathered with his slave

---

[15] Ibidem.
[16] Ibidem. Manuel settled in Vila do Carmo, married a woman from Rio de Janeiro named Bárbara do Rosário and had two more children, José and Pedro Francisco. AEAM. *Auto de genere.* 1778. Cabinet 7, file 1135.

Joana Pinta. He assumed responsibility for the orphan's education and treated her with "honesty and care inside his house, in the company of his own wife and children."[17] When Rita reached marrying age, João Fernandes arranged her betrothal to Domingos Gonçalves Rodrigues and used part of the inheritance left to the young lady in her father's will as a dowry, thus enabling her to marry a white man, the only way she could erase the vestiges of the less than favorable conditions of her birth. By acting in this manner he not only protected the orphan but also kept the patrimony of the deceased at his disposal by delaying the end of his executorship for as long as he could.[18]

Once the prosperous owner of stable businesses and seeing that his stay in Minas Gerais would be somewhat prolonged, João Fernandes de Oliveira decided it was time to lay down some roots. In August 1726, at the age of 29, he married Maria de São José, daughter of a merchant in Rio de Janeiro with whom he probably had business dealings.[19]

His wife was born in Rio de Janeiro,[20] where her parents, Pedro do Reis Pimentel and Maria Inês de Sousa, had initially settled in the parish of São José, hence the name Maria de São José, before moving to the vicinity of Cathedral Church. Her father, a former farmer, was from Ilha das Flores[21] in the Azores and, like many of his fellow islanders, had come to Brazil in search of a better life. He worked as a merchant in Taubaté in the captaincy of São Paulo, where he married Maria Inês, a local girl from Vila dos Santos. After a brief stint on Ilha Grande in the captaincy of Rio de Janeiro, they decided to move to the capital.[22] While waiting for a suitable consort, Maria de

---

[17] ACS. Justificações. Códice 301. Auto 6130. Primeiro Ofício.
[18] ANTT. Cartórios notariais. Testamentos. Livro 300, f. 30v.
[19] AEAM. Processo matrimonial no. 3608. 1726, f. 5v.
[20] "Termo de depoimento de Maria de São José: disse ser natural e batizada na freguesia de São José, da cidade do Rio de Janeiro." AEAM. Processo matrimonial no. 3608. 1726, f. 9v. ANTT. Índice de leitura de bacharéis. João Fernandes de Oliveira. Maço 22, doc. 37, f. 1.
[21] ANTT. Santo Ofício. Habilitações incompletas. Maço 3, doc. 87.
[22] Ibidem, Maço 3, doc. 87; Maço 1, doc. 46.

José, the youngest of five children – the two sons had taken religious vocations[23] and the elder sisters were both married[24] – was sent to a finishing school in Guarapiranga where she received a formal education and led a virtuous life. She most likely only met her betrothed on the eve of their wedding. As she had learned to read and write at the institution – something rare for women of the day – she was able to sign her own name on the wedding papers to Sergeant Major João Fernandes de Oliveira.[25]

The religious ceremony, celebrated by father José Simões at the church of Nossa Senhora da Conceição in Vila do Carmo, was surrounded by a great deal of pomp and followed by three days of festivities.[26] As bigamy was considered an extremely serious crime, punishable by death under the Filipine Code, wedding procedures involved lengthy investigations to ascertain the marital status of the betrothed. This made the proclamations, certificates, and investigations very costly, especially as the geographic territory colonized by the Portuguese Empire expanded and mobility between the Realm and the various colonies increased. As João Fernandes was late submitting the papers from the inquests conducted in his homeland proving that there was no impediment to matrimony on his part, the wedding had to be held on trust. The process was only concluded in 1736, when he finally got round to submitting the documents, which had arrived from Portugal some six years earlier.[27]

One year after the wedding, in the middle of 1727, the couple bore their first child, who, like his father and grandfather before him, received the name João Fernandes de Oliveira. He was christened at the baptismal urn installed at the Chapel of Nossa Senhora da Conceição on the Vargem farm in a ceremony celebrated by father Antônio Sanches Chaves. The godparents were Francisco

---

23 One of them was the priest José de Sousa Pimentel. AEAM. Armário 5, pasta 806. *Auto de genere de João Fernandes de Oliveira*, f. 2. ANTT. Índice de leitura de bacharéis. João Fernandes de Oliveira. Maço 22, doc. 37.
24 ANTT. Santo Ofício. Habilitações incompletas. Maço 1, doc. 46.
25 AEAM. Processo matrimonial no. 3608. 1726, f. 8.
26 Ibidem, f. 2.
27 Ibidem, fls. 13–15.

da Cunha Macedo and Josefa Rodrigues da Silva, wife of Sergeant Major Domingos Pinto Machado, their neighbor.[28] Five daughters followed: Ana Quitéria de São José, Maria Margarida Angélica de Belém, Rita Isabel de Jesus, Helena Leocádia da Cruz, and Francisca Joaquina do Pilar. Later, all five were to withdraw to the Convent of Madre de Deus de Monchique in the city of Porto where they took their vows as nuns.[29]

In 1739, João Fernandes de Oliveira prepared to embark on a riskier line of business, one that involved a lot of money. It was in this year that the Crown opened the process of periodically leasing the exploration of diamonds in the Diamantine Demarcation. Gomes Freire de Andrade, governor of the captaincies of Rio de Janeiro and Minas Gerais, departed for Tejuco, where he would remain from April to August of that year in an attempt to convince the local miners to offer a bid. The first negotiations involved only the businessmen from Rio de Janeiro and took place at Vila Rica, where João Fernandes de Oliveira and Francisco Ferreira da Silva joined the governor's entourage, though they later came to include the miners of Tejuco. The businessmen took a hard line against the miners who were trying to force greater flexibility in the operating conditions. The negotiations were tense and almost ended in violence amid accusations of favoritism.[30] The best bid the miners of Tejuco were prepared to place, offered in public auction,[31] envisaged a thousand slaves working the mines over a period of ten years, with the option of extending exploration throughout the district, a term the governor considered unacceptable.[32] As far as the Crown was concerned, João Fernandes and Francisco Ferreira presented an

[28] AEAM. *Auto de genere de João Fernandes de Oliveira.* Armário 5, pasta 806.
[29] ANTT. Cartórios notariais. Testamentos. Livro 300, fls. 29–30; Desembargo do Paço. Minho e Trás-os-Montes. Maço 41, doc. 16; Cartórios notariais. 5B. Livro 75, caixa 15. Notas. Atual 12, f. 77.
[30] AHU, MAMG. Caixa 37, doc. 69.
[31] BNL. Notícias das minas dos diamantes. Seção de Reservados. Avulsos. Cód. 7167.
[32] AHU, MAMG. Caixa 37, doc. 69. "Carta de Gomes Freire de Andrade . . . dando conta das diligências por ele feitas para a arrematação do contrato dos diamantes."

altogether better proposal, one that not only limited the number of slaves to six hundred and the exploration period to four years, but also accepted the Realm's restrictions on the rivers to be mined.[33] As the miners made no counter bid, the two businessmen had no choice but to honor those terms and settled the contract with the Crown. Francisco Ferreira, a converted Jew and renowned businessman, put up the capital and left for Lisbon soon afterward, while the Sergeant Major stayed on to run the business in return for a 3 percent share of the profits.[34] The sum paid on this contract was 230,000 reis, which established a four-year timeframe, limited the range of exploration to a handful of rivers, and put a cap on the number of slaves employed.[35]

According to Friar Gaspar da Encarnação, the king's minister, the real interests behind the partnership were those of the governor, Gomes Freire de Andrade. João Fernandes was only a front and the bid was nothing more than a farce put together to convince the local miners that they would have to vie against heavy businessmen from outside Tejuco. João Fernandes de Oliveira's second wife revealed some years later that her husband became involved in the business as the governor's intermediary, that the two were close friends, and that it was common knowledge in Minas that "[the contract] served the interests of Gomes Freire de Andrade, who [everyone] blindly respected and obeyed."[36] Despite the assurances of the diamond intendant, Rafael Pires Pardinho, that the bidding had been fair, talk of Gomes Freire de Andrade's involvement would not seem to have been unfounded, as the governor did express his friendship for João Fernandes on various occasions and even went so far as to

---

[33] From the point of view of the Crown, the range of exploration could not be unlimited, as this could lead to an excess supply of stones and another slump in prices on the world diamond market. For the miners, however, the limits imposed on extraction risked making the business barely profitable or even a losing proposition.

[34] ANTT. Cartórios notariais. Testamentos. Book 300, f. 31v.

[35] Ibidem. AHU, MAMG. Box 37, doc. 64. "Certidão do auto de arrematação do contrato de extração dos diamantes, realizado entre Gomes Freire de Andrade, governador das Minas, e João Fernandes de Oliveira."

[36] ANTT. Desembargo do Paço. Ilhas. Maço 1342, doc. 7, fls. 32, 37.

bail him out of financial difficulty, thus preventing the financial ruin of the contract.[37]

As the terms of the contract required the Sergeant Major's presence in Tejuco, he sublet his tithe collection contract in 1740 to Jorge Pinto,[38] who assumed the functions of cashier and representative of the business,[39] and moved to the village from Vila do Carmo. When the diamond contract expired in 1743, Francisco Ferreira da Silva and João Fernandes de Oliveira joined forces once again on a second contract valid from 1744 to 1748. This time, however, the Sergeant Major negotiated more favorable terms for himself, and his share in return for his services was increased to 4 percent on total profits.[40]

However, matters did not proceed as expected. As the experienced miners of Tejuco had predicted, the conditions offered by the Metropole were unfavorable, especially those limiting the number of slaves to six hundred. The best lands, those easier to mine, had already been exhausted, so a higher number of slaves was needed just to keep production stable. João Fernandes went to Gomes Freire de Andrade in the hope that these clauses could be changed, particularly those limiting manpower, but there was nothing the governor could do. The investment made was considerable, as extracting diamonds from *grupiara* (unused riverbeds) involved displacing much more water and soil. By the end of the second contract, expenses had superseded those for the first contract by some 1 million reis.[41]

With such punishing expenses, debts on the endeavor reached 700,000 cruzados,[42] a fortune in those days, thus threatening the health of one of the Crown's most lucrative businesses, not to mention its credibility. As the diamonds were only sold upon arrival in

---

[37] ANTT. Desembargo do Paço. Ilhas. Maço 1342. doc. 7.
[38] ANTT. Cartórios notariais. Testamentos. Livro 300, f. 31.
[39] ANTT. Ministério do Reino. Livro 208, fls. 74v a 75v.
[40] ANTT. Cartórios notariais. Testamentos. Livro 300, f. 31v.
[41] BNL. Notícias das minas dos diamantes. Seção de Reservados. Avulsos. Cód. 7167.
[42] ANTT. Ministério do Reino. Decretos. Maço 10, doc. 41.

Lisbon – with only one shipment leaving per year – the contractors had to run into debt in order to cover their running costs, selling promissory notes on the markets of Lisbon and Rio de Janeiro issued by cashiers nominated by the contractor and guaranteed by the Crown. At the end of each contract, these notes were honored from the profits, as were the fees on the leasing contract. Insolvency therefore threatened not only the Portuguese financial market, but also those of Holland and England, the sources of much of the capital employed by the Portuguese businessmen.

João Fernandes de Oliveira was experiencing trying times that were exacerbated in April 1746 with the death of Maria de São José, who had been seriously ill since the previous year.[43] Her funeral was held at Santo Antônio church in Tejuco.[44] Adding to his financial difficulties, the death of his wife deprived him of almost half of his fortune, as according to Portuguese inheritance law, as set down in the Filipine Code, when one spouse died, the children automatically inherited two-thirds of the half belonging to the deceased, while the final third was dispensed in accordance with the last will and testament. The soul of the deceased was frequently nominated as heir to this remaining third, which basically meant it was used to pay for the funeral, the celebration of masses, offering of alms, and other practices advocated by the Catholic Church for the salvation of the soul of the departed.[45] Though he did have some masses said for his dead wife, João Fernandes de Oliveira, who Maria de São José had nominated as the executor of this third, aggregated the sum to his own fortune, carefully putting off reading the will until after 1750.[46] After the Sergeant Major's death, it fell to his son, the chief judge, to administrate the assets of his mother's third.[47]

43 AHU, MAMG. Caixa 45, doc. 8. "Requerimento de João Fernandes de Oliveira, solicitando licença para passar ao Reino com sua mulher."
44 AEAD. Livro de batizados do arraial do Tejuco. 1745–1765. Caixa 297.
45 Ordenações filipinas. Livro Quarto, título 12. Ver também Kathleen J. Higgins, op. cit., p. 112.
46 ANTT. Cartórios notariais. Testamentos. Livro 300, f. 32v. ANTT. Desembargo do Paço. Ilhas. Maço 1342, doc. 7.
47 ANTT. Cartórios notariais 5B. Livro 75, caixa 15. Notas. Atual 12, f. 76.

At the end of 1747, when all seemed lost and the demise of the contract imminent, João Fernandes de Oliveira sought the protection of the governor one more time. The solution proffered by his friend Gomes Freire was that he persuade the wealthy widow of Captain Major Luís Siqueira Brandão to marry him. Given the revulsion she felt for her suitor, Isabel Pires Monteiro resisted for as long as she could, but the pressure was coming from all sides. Not only was the governor sending constant letters, but her father and son-in-law, Colonel Alexandre Luís de Sousa, also supported the union, the latter claiming "there was no remedy but to accept the intended matrimony, as that was the will of the powers that be."[48] In December of that year, now married and living in Tejuco, Isabel and João Fernandes baptized an infant, the son of their friend José da Silva de Oliveira and Ana Joaquina Rosa Batista, who would grow up to become none other than Father Rolim[49] of the Inconfidência Mineira.[50]

In 1748, in an attempt to gain access to the properties still pending to his second wife in the inventory of her first husband's will, with which he hoped to resolve his financial problems, João Fernandes and Isabel made a pact to incorporate their assets, witnessed by her daughter and son-in-law Alexandre.[51] This pact established that Isabel would nominally "sell" her immense patrimony to her husband, upon whose death, should no children come of the new marriage, a sum corresponding to the six farms, thirty-six slaves, five and a half thousand head of cattle, and six hundred and ten horses and mares she currently possessed would be returned to her from his estate. Once the pact was signed, the control of all of these assets came into the hands of the Sergeant Major.[52]

---

[48] ANTT. Desembargo do Paço. Ilhas. Maço 1342, doc. 7, fls. 31v–32.

[49] AEAD. Livro de batizados do arraial do Tejuco. 1745–1765. Caixa 297, f. 11v.

[50] The Inconfidência Mineira was a rebellion in the state of Minas Gerais in 1789 that sought the independence of the mines from the Portuguese Empire. In the twentieth century this movement came to be considered a milestone in the formation of the Brazilian nationality.

[51] While the son affirms that this pact was made before the wedding, Isabel insists that it occurred only after they were married. ANTT. Desembargo do Paço. Ilhas. Maço 1342, doc. 7.

[52] Ibidem. The farms were later inherited by his son, the Chief Judge João Fernandes de Oliveira.

With this patrimony behind him he could now offer credibility and reliability to his creditors,[53] especially as his debts from the contract would not be called in immediately, as they involved negotiations that would drag on for years.[54] Only in 1760 did the Crown issue a letter of quittance on the first two contracts.[55] However, at the same time, João Fernandes and his cashiers in Portugal were involved in litigation to postpone payment to holders of their promissory notes, such as the Brotherhood of the Most Holy of the parish of the Martyrs in Lisbon.[56]

As he was heavily in debt, João Fernandes had no interest in directly managing the new contract under negotiation and no diamond exploration was made in 1748.[57] Gomes Freire de Andrade's presence was once more required in Tejuco. He traveled to the village where he closed a third contract at the end of that year with one Felisberto Caldeira Brant, who had experience with this type

---

[53] Isabel states that João Fernandes told her that her assets would be "applied in the payment of his debts." ANTT. Desembargo do Paço. Ilhas. Maço 1342, doc. 7.

[54] The High Court Judge João Fernandes remarked that his father, the Sergeant Major, was "a businessman who found himself financially embarrassed not only by the accounts of the two diamond contracts, but also with the Royal Revenue Service, with which he was still not quits." ANTT. Desembargo do Paço. Ilhas. Maço 1342, doc.7

[55] ANTT. Ministério do Reino. Decretos. Maço 6, doc.109. In the same archive, book 208, fls. 226 and 226v, "Quittance of the diamond contract for the years 1744 to 1747.... The sum of 995 contos, 875 thousand, 726 reis ... money I sent to finance and enliven the contract and the washing of the gravel ... 18th of December 1760." In the same book, we read "Quittance of the diamond contract for the years 1740 to 1743 ... [On] the sum of 575 contos, 864 thousand 864 reis, an importance owed to my Royal Revenue through said contract ... I hereby issue the letter of quittance ... 18th of December 1760."

[56] ANTT. Ministério do Reino. Book 208, fls. 137v and 138. "In the petition of João Fernandes de Oliveira, José and Domingos Ferreira da Veiga and Manuel Gomes de Campos[,] in which they request the suspension of the action taken against them by the Irmandade do Santíssimo Sacramento da Freguesia de Nossa Senhora dos Mártires for the sum of 32 contos, ... Nossa Senhora da Ajuda, 5 de março de 1760."

[57] ANTT. Ministério do Reino. Box 10, doc. 41. Reproduces a petition from Sergeant Major João Fernandes de Oliveira in which he complains of delays in closing the accounts of the second contract and of his running debts.

of mining in the Claro River in Goiás.[58] Brant was the administrator and representative of a partnership that included the brothers Conrad and Sebastião, his friend Luís Alberto Pereira, and various businessmen from Tejuco.[59] The Sergeant Major sold him all of the works and tools at his disposal that he might need for the mining operations for the sum of 80,000 cruzados – payable from the profits on the contract[60] – and bought credit letters to the value of 136,000 reis to capitalize the new contractor.[61] The Sergeant Major was helpful to the point of writing to a merchant in Rio de Janeiro by the name of Lourenço Antunes Viana asking him to continue his supply under the same conditions of sale, which meant giving the new contractor credit to acquire everything he needed for the venture.[62]

The conditions established for the third contract were even less favorable than those for the previous ones. The incorporation of the Claro River region led the Crown to limit the number of slaves that could be used in the Diamantine Demarcation to four hundred. Caldeira Brant soon realized that the profitability of the business depended on his capacity to circumvent the authorities. There were no major problems in the first years, as Chief Judge Plácido de Almeida Moutoso, who was very ill and died in Tejuco in 1750, held the position of diamond intendant. Such was Moutoso's total confidence in the contractor Caldeira Brant that he named him

---

[58] ANTT. Manuscritos do Brasil. Conditions to be observed on the third contract..., vol. 31.

[59] "Do descobrimento dos diamantes e diferentes métodos que se têm praticado na sua extração." *Anais da Biblioteca Nacional*, vol. 80, 1960, p. 175.

[60] ANTT. Cartórios notariais. Testamentos. Livro 300, f. 33.

[61] "Do descobrimento dos diamantes...," op. cit., p. 171. ANTT. Desembargo do Paço. Ilhas. Box 1342, doc. 7. A document in which Chief Judge João Fernandes de Oliveira provides an account of events in Tejuco and tells that his father had been a partner on Felisberto Caldeira Brant's contract.

[62] ANTT. Ministério do Reino. Box 17, doc. 36. Attached to this document is a rendering of accounts by Luís Alberto Pereira, one of the partners on the third contract, which contains the following statements: "On his arrival at Serro, his brother Francisco Xavier Feliz left for Rio de Janeiro with letters from João Fernandes de Oliveira requesting Lourenço Antunes Viana to give whatever assistance necessary in the purchases of said provisions.

executor of his will.[63] Moutoso's interim successor was the magistrate from Serro do Frio, Francisco Moreira de Matos, who rarely appeared in Tejuco. However, in 1751, this all changed with the appointment of Sancho de Andrade Castro e Lanções as the new intendant. Unlike his predecessors, Lanções was prepared to investigate Caldeira Brant's procedures and began to pressure him to provide the exact number of slaves employed at the mines – which had reached the absurd number of five thousand. The tension between the two mounted day by day and conflict grew imminent.

In 1750, João Fernandes de Oliveira decided to return to the Realm to settle his accounts with the Crown and his partners on the diamond contracts.[64] He went first to Vila Rica where he and Isabel were godparents at the baptism of Álvaro, the legitimate son of Sergeant Major Gregório de Matos Lobo and Vitoriana Pais de Queirós, thus ensuring the bonds that governed the conviviality of the day. It was there in that August that the Sergeant Major, perhaps ill or fearful of the long voyage ahead, decided to make his will. As he was involved in so many business dealings in Minas Gerais, Rio de Janeiro, and Lisbon, and believing that "his assets were greatly embarrassed by a series of debts and payments to be made,"[65] he resolved not to stipulate any timeframe for his executors to settle his accounts.

He left with the fleet sailing from Rio de Janeiro on May 31, 1751, and arrived in Lisbon on August 24.[66] This was no longer the youth who had arrived in Brazil decades earlier with little but the clothes

---

[63] AEAD. Livro de batizados do arraial do Tejuco. 1745–1765. Caixa 297, f. 127.

[64] The chief judge affirmed that his father decided to "visit the Realm to settle the accounts on his contracts and negotiations." ANTT. Desembargo do Paço. Ilhas. Box 1342, doc. 7

[65] ANTT. Cartórios notariais. Testamentos. Livro 300, f. 33.

[66] "Lisbon, 24th of August. This morning a fleet from Rio de Janeiro, composed of fourteen merchant ships escorted by two warships, arrived at port. Lisbon, 26th of August. The fleet of fourteen merchant ships we mentioned made port the day before yesterday left Rio de Janeiro on the last day of May this year and sailed under the escort of two warships, *Nossa Senhora da Piedade* (Our Lady of Piety) and *Nossa Senhora do Livramento* (Our Lady of Release)." *Gazeta de Lisboa*, Notícias históricas de Portugal e do Brasil (1751–1964), 1964, p. 9.

on his back. João Fernandes de Oliveira could now leave Brazil in a privileged position, with a new wife, the owner of a vast patrimony consisting of various farms (counting the rural properties of Isabel Pires Monteiro, which had been incorporated, the Vargem farm in Itacolomi, an allotment awarded by Gomes Freire de Andrade in 1744,[67] and the Canastra farm, which he had bought on the banks of the Araçuaí River[68]), and seven houses in Vila Rica and another in Rio de Janeiro. With such a patrimony, he could live comfortably at court and enjoy the social circle he had begun to weave for himself in Minas Gerais, particularly through his friendship with the governor.

Once back in the Realm, João Fernandes was expected to act in the defense of the new contractor in his dispute with the intendant, as he was, after all, a guarantor and partner in the business and enjoyed the sponsorship of Gomes Freire de Andrade, who had taken Caldeira Brant's side in the dispute. Effectively, João Fernandes de Oliveira was still involved in the third contract, as he had rescued and paid several promissory notes that the contractor had failed to honor.[69]

At the end of the contract, the partnership found itself swimming in debt once again. Doubts hung over the quittance of the credit letters and the situation in Tejuco was about to spin out of control. Calderia Brant, who obviously expected João Fernandes to intercede on his behalf at court, had spent the period 1751 to 1752 trying to renew the contract, but rather than defend his friend, the Sergeant Major negotiated a fourth diamond contract for himself, this time as a businessman in the confidence of Sebastião José de Carvalho e Melo, the future Marquis of Pombal.[70]

The new contract came into force on January 1, 1752, though Caldeira Brant continued to run the operations in Tejuco for this entire year. João Fernandes only assumed charge of the fourth

[67] "Concessão de sesmarias." *Revista do Arquivo Público Mineiro*, ano 10, 1905, pp. 224–5.
[68] Manoel da Silveira Cardozo, op. cit., pp. 313–14.
[69] ANTT. Manuscritos do Brasil, no. 31. s.f.
[70] The contract was closed in December 1751 for 240 million reis over a period of six years AHU, MAMG. Box 60, doc. 7.

contract in January 1753 through his local representative José Álvares Maciel.[71] The previously friendly relations between the two contractors deteriorated, and João Fernandes did not hesitate to protest the promissory notes he had purchased in Brant's name when the third contract effectively broke.[72] The enmity between the two families was perpetuated in Joaquim Felício dos Santos' *Memórias do Distrito Diamantino*, with the author taking the side of Caldeira Brant, who is presented as a paragon of virtue, against João Fernandes de Oliveira, who he paints in an exaggeratedly negative light.[73]

THE YOUNG CHIEF JUDGE

The young João Fernandes de Oliveira left the family home in Minas Gerais at around the age of thirteen, leaving behind him his mother, whom he would never see again, and his younger sisters. He set off for Rio de Janeiro, where he would remain for a time under the hospitality of his maternal grandparents before finally embarking for Portugal.[74] It is almost certain that he separated from his family at

---

[71] AHU, MAMG. Box 63, doc. 80. The magistrate of Serro do Frio county gave a detailed description of how the exploration was done during this period: "The work [on the third contract] began on January 1st, 1749 and ended on the last day of December 1752. Work in this county began in January of 1749 and in Goiás . . . on July 28th, the two hundred from Goiás left those mines in December 1751 and arrived at the mines here in early March 1752, so four hundred slaves came to mine in this county between January 1749 and the beginning of 1752, or six hundred from then up to the end of that same year." AHU, MAMG. Box 63, doc. 29. In a letter dated the 8th of August 1754, the new diamond intendant, Tomás Robi de Barros Barreto, tells that, up to the end of 1753, the fourth contract was managed in Tejuco by José Álvares Maciel. AHU, MAMG. Box 66, doc. 6

[72] ANTT. Ministério do Reino. Decrees. Box 17, doc. 36. Attached to this document is a rendering of accounts by Luís Alberto Pereira, one of the partners on the third contract, which contains information about the promissory notes that João Fernandes bought, being partner of the third contract.

[73] Joaquim Felício dos Santos. *Memórias do Distrito Diamantino*. 1976.

[74] AEAM. *Auto de genere* of João Fernandes de Oliveira. Cabinet 5, file 806, fls. 5v–6. In June 1742, "Manuel Ribeiro Pereira, married, native of Setúbal, apothecary . . . , resident of this city [of Rio de Janeiro], who makes a living from his business, seventy years of age . . . said that he met [João Fernandes de Oliveira] in this city, where he saw him embark for Coimbra."

around the time his father moved to Tejuco to take care of his diamond business.

Among the wealthier classes, formal learning began at this age,
and the Sergeant Major resolved to offer his only son the best possible education, a prerequisite for the social ascension he sought more
intensely the richer he became. He was therefore sent to Portugal
to take a university degree, which was not only fundamental for
those wishing to occupy any bureaucratic or ecclesiastical position
in the Portuguese Empire, but also comprised an indispensable stage
in earning the prestige and influence businessmen invariably wanted
for their sons.[75] In Minas Gerais, the first secondary-level institution – the Boa Morte seminary in Mariana – would only be founded
in 1748 and the creation of universities was prohibited throughout
the colony.[76] In the villages of Minas, responsibility for teaching fell
to the local priests who taught the boys how to read and write and
taught Latin to those seeking an ecclesiastical career.

As seen in Chapter 2, unlike slave children, the youth of the
wealthier classes spent their childhoods – which could stretch to
the age of fourteen – at home in the care of "indoor" slaves and wet
nurses. Prior to leaving home, João Fernandes probably received first
communion, the rite that marked the onset of adulthood and the
adolescent's entry into the social networks of the community.

Leaving his boyhood life on the Vargem farm behind him, the
young João Fernandes, whose final destination was Rio de Janeiro,
set off for Vila Rica, the as yet rustic capital of Minas Gerais, a town

---

[75] "A university degree not only elevated the recipient, upon whom it conferred
certain privileges and access to the ruling class in the colony, but was also a
means of social ascension for his entire family." According to Russell-Wood, from
the eighteenth century on, the sons of the merchants in full financial ascension
joined those of the landed elite at the universities of the Realm. A. J. R. Russell-
Wood. "Relato de um caso luso-brasileiro do século dezessete." *Stvdia*, no. 36,
June 1973, p. 20.

[76] AHU, MAMG. Box 63, doc. 49. "Representation of officals of the Council
Chamber of Mariana, informing Dom José I of the erection of a seminary in said
city." Mariana, 24th of October 1753. Caio Boschi. "Ordens religiosas, clero secular e missionário no Brasil." In: Francisco Bethencourt et al. *História da expansão
portuguesa*, vol. 3, 1998, p. 314.

"almost always ... shrouded in fog [that] generally plagued the inhabitants with head colds."[77] He also left behind him the promise of
marriage his father had made to a friend's niece, a girl named Rita; a
promise that would never be fulfilled.[78] He took the Caminho Novo
(New Road) – later known as the Estrada Real (Royal Highway) –
built by Garcia Rodrigues Pais between 1698 and 1725, which cut
through the Minas Forest Zone and the Mantiqueira Mountains,
shortening a journey that once took two months to just forty-five
days. The old route, known as the Caminho Velho, passed through
the captaincy of São Paulo.

In the interests of safety, the journey, which was both long and
dangerous, was always taken in well-armed traveling parties, as bands
of runaway blacks and mulattos, just as well armed as the travelers, often attacked along the route. Upon completing the stretch
that went from the coast to Vila Rica, the merchant Francisco da
Cruz described the route as "long and diabolical."[79] In 1719, in a
bid to protect the travelers, Pedro Miguel de Almeida, the Count of
Assumar and captain general of São Paulo and Minas Gerais since
1717, passed an order prohibiting any Negro, "be it in the Villas or on
the highways ... to bear firearms, whether long or short, knives, dag-
gers, swords, cudgels [or] spiked clubs." Such weapons could only be
worn "to accompany [their masters] when travelling in person."[80] As
journeys were made on foot, donkey-back, or in hammocks carried by
slaves, there was no option but to make occasional stops or dismount
in places generally considered dangerous.

77 José Joaquim da Rocha. *Geografia histórica da capitania de Minas Gerais*. 1995,
    p. 162.
78 In the will of Caetano Soares Barreto, a lawyer, Álvaro Antunes encoun-
    tered the promise of an inheritance of "four hundred thousand reis ... to my
    niece, Donna Rita, should her marriage to the Chief Judge João Fernandes de
    Oliveira proceed, or five thousand cruzados should it not." Arquivo Histórico
    da Casa do Pilar. 1°. Ofício, códice 88, auto 1.065. Apud: Álvaro Antunes. *Fiat
    Justitia*: os advogados e a prática da justiça em Minas Gerais (1750–1808), 2005,
    p. 44.
79 Hospital São José. Testamentaria de Francisco Pinheiro. Carta 150, maço 29, f.
    166.
80 APM. Câmara Municipal de Ouro Preto. Códice 6, fls. 12v–14.

The last stretch of the itinerary involved a slow crossing of the coastal mountains (Serra do Mar) along roads lined by steep cliff sides, which demanded extra care from the traveler. Despite the dangers, João Fernandes witnessed some magnificent scenery, with "altitudes [reaching] seven or eight hundred feet."[81] His eyes must certainly have widened before the lush green of the forests, in which a multitude of unknown species of plant and animal abounded, as if preparing him for the new phase of life he was about to begin. All around him would have been vine-covered trunks and flocks of toucans, parakeets, and parrots, and abundant game. At dawn, a thick mist would have veiled the surrounding landscape, but he would have heard the birdsong and the varied sounds of animals. As day broke, a gentle light would have flooded the impressive scenery as it slowly emerged into view.

João Fernandes arrived in the city of São Sebastião do Rio de Janeiro through the port, having come down from the mountains at Guanabara Bay and crossed by boat. The sight must have been grandiose in comparison with the red-roofed, whitewashed houses of the gold-mining villages of Minas. When the Sergeant Major's son made port, Rio de Janeiro was already the second largest urban center in the colony with a population of twenty-four thousand, second only to Salvador. The Castelo, São Bento, and Santo Antônio hills could be seen from the port enclosing the city in a ring. On Castelo were the Jesuit fort and church, both dedicated to Saint Sebastian, the patron and guardian of the city, while the other two hills were home to the Benedictine and Franciscan monasteries, respectively.[82] In the urban nucleus enframed by these three hills, the population devoted its time to God and to business, which was booming from the lucrative mineral market.

He lodged at the house of his maternal grandmother, Maria Inês de Sousa, in Rosário Square[83] in the borough of cathedral parish, where

---

[81] John Luccock. *Notas sobre o Rio de Janeiro e partes meridionais do Brasil*. 1975, p. 274.

[82] Luiz Mott. *Rosa Egipcíaca, uma santa africana no Brasil*. 1993, p. 196.

[83] Years later, in 1789, Simão Pires Sardinha, Chica da Silva's eldest son, also stayed at the house. In one of the depositions appended to the minutes of the hearings

he stayed only as long as it took for the fleet to set sail for Portugal.[84] He was introduced to the acquaintances, friends, and neighbors that frequented his grandparents' house, such as the merchants João Carneiro da Silva and Lourenço Antunes Viana, who had business dealings with his grandfather, and the lawyer José Carlos Pereira. In the mid-1730s, while the new cathedral was still under construction, the see was transferred to the Rosário church, situated in the central lea, nestled against the wall the governor Vaia Monteiro had built around the land-facing rim of the town to protect against foreign invasions and to mark out the city limits. Rosário Square was on Vala street, which took its name from the dike (*vala*) that ran along it, draining the waters of the Santo Antônio Lake and making it possible for the adjacent terrain to be occupied.[85] In the mid-eighteenth century, the previously sparsely populated cathedral square experienced a boom due to the expansion of the lower city beyond the walls erected by the military engineer Jean Massé. At the time João Fernandes would have known it, the area was a hive of construction, as the São Francisco de Paula and new cathedral[86] churches were in the process of being built, while the old city walls were being pulled down. The new role the region would come to fulfill in the lower city attracted a lot of commercial houses to the area.

on the Inconfidência Mineira, Squadron Leader Pedro de Oliveira Silva declares that Simão said to him: "Come to my house on Rosário this afternoon." *Autos da devassa da Inconfidência Mineira*, vol. 2, 1978, p. 75.

[84] AEAM. *Auto de genere* de João Fernandes de Oliveira. Cabinet 5, file 806.

[85] Latter named Uruguaiana street.

[86] "In 1740–1750, the site of the Our Lady of the Rosary church of the Brotherhood of Our Lady of the Rosary and Saint Benedict of the Blacks had already been occupied, since 1708, by the brotherhood's chapel. After the French invasion of 1711, the military engineer Jean Massé (a Frenchman in the service of Portugal) came to Rio de Janeiro and projected a wall around the city passing just behind the Rosário chapel. The area was not considered urban at the time, given its low population density and scarcity of buildings, even though, at the same time, the land beyond the walls was already starting to be occupied in virtue of the construction of the Saint Francis de Paul church and the beginning of the construction of the new Sé cathedral of Rio de Janeiro. Construction of the wall was never completed and the ruins were donated by Don João to the Military Academy." Nireu Oliveira Cavalcanti. *A cidade de São Sebastião do Rio de Janeiro: as muralhas, sua gente, os construtores* (1710–1810). 1997.

The sea crossing between Rio de Janeiro and Portugal, considered just as dangerous as the descent from Minas, took from eighty to ninety days. The ships made stops at Bahia and Pernambuco before a twenty-day stretch up to the much-feared equatorial line – the "world's belt" – whose crossing the sailors celebrated with drinking and a dip in the sea.[87] A month after sailing past the Atlantic islands the ships would make port in Lisbon.[88] The average fleet consisted of a hundred ships. The convoy system had been adopted to make the crossings safer, as the seas were crawling with pirates. The merchant vessels, which were heavier and larger, carried merchandise and passengers and were escorted by smaller and more agile warships. In general, the convoys set sail from the Realm in the first semester and returned in the second, thus taking advantage of the monsoons.

Despite the best precautions, shipwrecks were a constant, almost always caused by the age, unseaworthiness, or overcrowding of the ships.[89] João Fernandes's crossing can not have been much different than that endured by Antônio Álvares Pereira, native of Bahia, in 1694 when he left Brazil to study the Canon at Coimbra. In his letters to his father, the young student remarks that once past the Atlantic Islands it seemed they had sailed into the Final Judgment itself, as "every day there was thunder and lightning, storms and tempests

---

[87] "On this day, the 4th of February, on which we crossed the world's belt, the sailors practiced the habitual ceremonies proper to this most dangerous passage. Namely, those who have not before ever crossed the Equator are tied with ropes and dipped into the sea or have their faces smeared with the slop from the boiler dregs. Though the victim can save himself, as I did, by buying a round of wine." Jean Léry. *Viagem à Terra do Brasil.* 1960, p. 69.

[88] Letter of Antônio Álvares Pereira to his father, written at Coimbra on March 3, 1695. Apud: A. J. R. Russell-Wood, "Relato de um caso luso-brasileiro....", p. 33.

[89] For example, the ship *Nossa Senhora da Natividade* (Our Lady of the Nativity), which set sail with the fleet from Rio de Janeiro in November 1753, almost capsized for being overloaded with passengers. On the stop at Bahia the captain sent the slave entourages ashore, which caused great discomfort on board. ANTT. Feitos findos. Juízo da Índia e Mina. Justificações ultramarinas. Brasil. Box 60. Package 4, doc. 3.

and I feared that ours was the unluckiest fleet ever to set sail from Bahia."[90]

Life on board was not easy. For the entire duration of the crossing the passengers were submitted to a frugal diet, consisting mainly of biscuits and, to a lesser degree, salted meats, onions, vinegar, and olive oil. Water and wine were stored in barrels. Fish and cheese was reserved for holy days. Sugar, honey, butter, and plums were also to be had. Even though all aboard ship had the right to exactly the same rations, there were some differences that reflected the social hierarchy, as the ships were organized to mirror the social structure that existed on dry land. Captains and officers could bring chickens and sheep aboard to provide eggs and milk. The scarcity of food was constant and a permanent cause of tension: the larder was kept under lock and guard. The most fortunate travelers enjoyed the recommendation of the ship's captain, which often meant privileged treatment.

João Fernandes de Oliveira, like the other passengers who dared challenge the great ocean, celebrated the end of the voyage. Soon after rounding the bar of the tagus, now free from the danger of the waves and tides, he would have caught a glimpse of Lisbon in the distance – its forts, palaces, and mansions dotted across the hill face, "decked out as in a window display above the wide estuary."[91]

As was customary,[92] once ashore, the young traveler went to recover at the house of José Ferreira da Veiga, a friend of his father and the man who would be responsible for providing the monthly allowance to cover his expenses while studying.[93] The Sergeant Major reimbursed these moneys annually through one of

---

[90] Letter of Antônio Álvares Pereira to his father, written at Coimbra on March 3, 1695. Apud: A. J. R. Russell-Wood, "Relato de um caso luso-brasileiro....", pp. 33–4.

[91] José Sarmento Matos. *Uma casa na Lapa.* 1994, p. 17.

[92] Letter from Antônio Álvares Pereira a seu pai, escrita em Coimbra a 3 de março de 1695. Apud: A. J. R. Russell-Wood, "Relato de um caso luso-brasileiro...," op. cit., p. 34.

[93] ANTT. Cartórios notariais. Testamentos. Livro 300, f. 31v.

the diamond contract cashiers in Lisbon, who deducted the sum from the profits on the sale of the diamonds.[94]

Soon, the young João Fernandes de Oliveira was enrolled as a boarder at the São Patrício Seminary in the city of Lisbon.[95] Founded by the Irish in 1593, the institution belonged to the Jesuits and was located close to the steps of São Crispim, in the parish of São Mamede, near the church of the same name. The construction had once been the residence of the viceroy Garcia de Noronha, though was later acquired by Antônio Fernandes Ximenes, a nobleman of the Royal House and founder of the convent under the direction of the Jesuits.

Though famous for the quality of the education they provided, the main mission of institutions like this was to form clergy, as their curriculum was basically an extension of the catechesis. The Jesuit method was based on repetition and respect for authority, which was not to be questioned. Their rules determined that "new thinking, even when it posed no immediate threat to the faith," was to be avoided.

In Brazil and in the Realm the Jesuits had a monopoly over the education of the sons of the elite, as they were the owners of the majority of secondary institutions and seminaries and had great influence over the universities of Évora and Coimbra. In the first half of the eighteenth century, when João Fernandes arrived in Portugal, they ran "twenty colleges, four seminaries, two novitiates, two monasteries, [and] eighteen residences," with a total of 716 members.[96]

Their doctrine was laid down in the summula *Ratio studiorum*, promulgated in 1599 by Company of Jesus and based on the notes on education left by Ignatius of Loyola, who unified the teaching of all of the colleges and seminaries that comprised the Company and laid the foundations for a Christian pedagogy.[97] With rigorous

[94] Ibidem.
[95] AEAM. *Auto de genere* de João Fernandes de Oliveira. Armário 5, pasta 806.
[96] Francisco Rodrigues. *História da Companhia de Jesus*, t. 4, vol. 1, 1950, pp. 4–5.
[97] George Ganss. "Ignatius' constitutions of education is the spirit of the *Ratio Studiorum*." In: *Saint Ignatius, idea of a jesuit university*. 1954, pp. 194–207.

discipline and by dispensing a humanist education, the Jesuits hoped to conjugate academic excellence and the observance of the morals and virtues with religious formation. The seminaries taught grammar, spelling, Latin, Greek, oratory, rhetoric, philosophy, morals, and writing, with emphasis given to the study of such classical authors as Aristotle, Cicero, Ovid, Horace, Plato, Homer, and Saint Thomas Aquinas. Jerônimo Ximenes de Aragão, then director of the institution, introduced the study of theology at the São Patrício seminary in the seventeenth century.

The seminarists dedicated much of their time to perfecting spiritual life, mainly through meditation and contemplation structured by mental prayer and the spiritual exercises developed by Saint Ignatius to introduce the novices into the mysteries of Christ's life and bring them closer to God.

In June 1742, at the age of fifteen, João Fernandes de Oliveira requested permission to pursue an ecclesiastical vocation and promotion to the Lower Orders where he could "serve the Lord as a cleric." Thus began his *de genere* process, part of which would require the verification of his line of descent on the side of his maternal grandparents, which took place in Rio de Janeiro in 1742 and 1745. Despite various requests for the process be taken to its conclusion, it remained incomplete, and the youth never received the dispatch required in order to take the habit.

In October 1743, wishing to improve his religious formation, João Fernandes de Oliveira left the seminary and enrolled on the canonical course at Coimbra. São Patrício had afforded him the requisites for entry into this university, namely a mastery of rhetoric, Latin, logic, metaphysics, ethics, and Greek.

Completing a university course – especially one in canonical law – conferred both honor and prestige upon the bearer. According to the Portuguese jurists of the eighteenth century, the study of law meant ennoblement[98] and for this reason attracted the sons of so many men of business who, lacking noble birth, sought more bureaucratic

---

[98] Stuart B. Schwartz. "Magistracy and society in colonial Brazil," *Hispanic American Historical Review*, 1970, p. 724.

channels of social ascension.[99] The canon course chosen by João Fernandes entitled the graduate to practice canonical and civil law, which was indispensable for anyone aspiring to an ecclesiastical career or magistracy.[100]

Though Coimbra was only a five-day journey from Lisbon, the student's life was not an easy one. The cold and shortage of food provoked by high prices were particularly difficult for the Brazilian youngsters who had only their allowances to sustain them.[101] Often discriminated against by the students from the Realm, a species of camaraderie developed among the Brazilian pupils, with the elder students taking it upon themselves to introduce the younger boys to the teachers and peers. In order to break into the institution's social circles, in which merit counted for much less than networks of cronyism and friendship, letters of recommendation brought from home were essential for new arrivals, as they would continue to be later in life for admittance to civil or ecclesiastical posts.[102]

In 1743, along with the Sergeant Major's son, twenty-seven Brazilian students enrolled at the university of Coimbra, including Tomás de Aquino Belo, from Ribeirão do Carmo, and José Gomes do Rego, from Vila do Príncipe, both of whom were João Fernandes' classmates on the canon course.[103]

The students stayed in dorms of two or three beds where they were served by a housemaid or, if they had enough money, by servants or even slaves.[104] Throughout the first year, the novices suffered a series of hazings that often ended in violence, ranging from floggings to being thrown into the icy waters of the city fountain. The university administration's attempts to control these excesses

---

[99] Ibidem.
[100] A. J. R. Russell-Wood. "Relato de um caso luso-brasileiro...," op. cit., p. 21.
[101] Ibidem, p. 30.
[102] A. J. R. Russell-Wood. "Relato de um caso luso-brasileiro...," op. cit., pp. 30, 34–35.
[103] "Estudantes da Universidade de Coimbra nascidos no Brasil." Brasília, 1949, pp. 174–9.
[104] Theóphilo Braga. História da Universidade de Coimbra, vol. 3, 1898, p. 181.

included prohibiting freshmen from leaving home unaccompanied by a veteran or from speaking before being spoken to first.[105] Such was the threat of violence that the students walked around armed, accompanied by bulldogs and not unusually disguised under heavy cloaks.

During the school year students had to be well dressed at all times, as it was one of the ways in which they could publicly display social distinction. According to the university's statues, the students "should be honestly dressed and not bring any garment, cassock, mantle, waistcoat or trousers in any of the following colours: yellow, red, green, orange or scarlet."[106] Despite these prohibitions, the pamphlet "Feição à moderna" ("Modern Dress") advised the students to cut a fine figure in the academic circles of Coimbra by

Arming yourselves with the best attire and accessories required to make the appearance of a scholastic figure, with a green coif for the hair, a lace cap, silk neck-scarf, short English vest, scarlet suede riding boots for daily use; black-buckled overshoes for races; metal spurs, gold braided cape, French-style shoulder belt; pocket knife; short broadsword; crêpe undercoat, fine black woollen bonnet, pocket watch, worn outside the pocket, and with this apparel you shall be the very model of a Coimbra student, a noble rogue."[107]

The teaching was bookish and repetitive, with the students doing little beyond transcribing the teachers' heavy lessons into their notebooks. In the first year they studied Justinian's *Institutions*, the kernel of juridical knowledge; moving on to civil law in the second year and to canonical law in the third and fourth.[108]

Having completed the four compulsory years between 1743 and 1746, João Fernandes de Oliveira earned his bachelor's degree in 1747 and graduated in June 1748.[109] The climax came in the last year, when the students had to sit for their final exams, an

[105] Ibidem, pp. 167, 173–4.
[106] Estatutos da Universidade de Coimbra (1559). 1965, p. 230.
[107] "Feição à moderna." Apud: Theóphilo Braga, op. cit., p. 172.
[108] Theóphilo Braga, op. cit., p. 234.
[109] AUC. Actos e graus de estudantes da Universidade por faculdade.

event accompanied by fanfare designed to heighten the honor and distinction of the university degree being bestowed. At these public solemnities and closing ceremonies the graduates were expected to appear wearing a well-starched crepe cassock with frills and cambric cuffs topped off with a baize cap.[110]

João Fernandes de Oliveira took his first final exam, an oral test, on June 23, 1748, at the school chapel where he arrived in the company of his sponsor. After the celebration of a mass, the young student entered the examination room to the sound of trumpets, where he spoke for about an hour on a randomly selected theme with three teachers, or lecturers, to probe him.[111] On the eve of the second exam, or repetition, which took place on July 4, the bells of the university rang out and the examinee, following the custom, was successively received at the main entrance, the rector's door, those of the two colleges of the canonical faculty, and finally by the head teacher of the course – all to the sound of trumpet call. Circled by the rector and the senior teachers, the candidate had to speak on another randomly selected theme. The atmosphere in the examination hall was one of austerity, with the walls draped in red and yellow taffeta.

His private exam, another oral test, was conducted on July 14 at the university chapel in the company of the head teacher of the canon. The following day, the bells rang out once again in salutation, and on July 16 João Fernandes de Oliveira attended mass at the university royal chapel alongside the general assembly of Santa Cruz and other graduates. After the service, he left the chapel without his beret, once more accompanied by trumpets and shawms.[112]

The doctoral ceremony was the apogee of academic life. After the older doctors of the canon had spoken on the proposed theme, João Fernandes rose from his high-backed chair, always placed below the

---

[110] Theóphilo Braga, op. cit., p. 185.
[111] Estatutos da Universidade de Coimbra (1559). 1965, pp. 261–3.
[112] ver Theóphilo Braga. *História da Universidade de Coimbra*, vol. 2, 1895, pp. 720–3.

rector, and addressed the chancellor,[113] the clergyman responsible for conferring academic degrees. Upon receiving his request for the degree of doctor, the chancellor, who sat surrounded by the beadles, exalted his merits in the form of a concise oration. The young doctor then repeated his oath and was presented with his doctoral insignia by his sponsor, who then made a brief speech. Finally, João Fernandes offered a prayer of thanks to Our Lady and went home.[114]

In July 1748 the young bachelor of law received the title of knight of the Order of Christ and a pension of twelve thousand reis.[115] The commandery had been bought for him by his father as part of his strategy of promoting his family before the nobles of the Realm. The initiation took place with full pomp and ceremony at the Nossa Senhora da Conceição church in Lisbon.[116] Built in a Manueline style, this church, situated between the Palace Court-yard and the Lisbon See, belonged to the Order of Christ, as did the chaplains in the choir that accompanied the services administered therein and whose singing was much appreciated in the city.[117] At João Fernandes's side were two sponsors chosen from the ranks of the knights of the order, all wearing the white habit.[118] The cere-mony unfolded as follows: the chaplain blessed the sword, helmet, and spurs of the new member of the order, who was then armed by his sponsors, who placed the helmet on his head, the spurs on his heels, and slid the sword into its sheath. One of the sponsors held

---

[113] The chancellor of the University of Coimbra was always the prior of the monastery of Santa Cruz. "Said Chancellor has faculty and power to confer all degres upon the licentiates, doctors and masters and the scores obtained for the lessons that had to do in the provate exams." Rafael Bluteau. *Dicionário da língua portuguesa*. Ampliado por Antônio de Morais. 1739, p. 5.

[114] Estatutos da Universidade de Coimbra (1559). 1965, pp. 293–5.

[115] ANTT. Chancelaria antiga da Ordem de Cristo. Livro 235, f. 319; livro 237, f. 318. No mesmo arquivo, Mercês de dom João V. Livro 38, f. 283.

[116] ANTT. Mercês de dom João V. Livro 38, f. 283.

[117] This church was almost entirely destroyed in the earthquake of 1755, with only the southern façade of the transept left standing.

[118] Definitions and statutes of the knights and friars of the Order of Our Lord Jesus Christ, 1628.

the sheathed sword of the beknighted in his hands and asked if this was what he desired. The affirmative answer was followed by the taking of the vows of chastity,[119] poverty, and obedience, which everyone knew where rarely observed.[120] The priest then offered a final prayer, and the sponsors disarmed and embraced the new member, a gesture repeated by all those in attendance.[121] After another ceremony, this time under the direction of the prior of the order at the monastery of Tomar, to the northeast of Lisbon, João Fernandes was granted the right to wear the white habit and mantle, as well as the scapular and cross of the Order of Christ, the public symbols of his distinction.

It seemed the young João Fernandes intended to establish himself in the Realm and make a quick and brilliant career in law or the magistracy. However, the following year he launched his candidature to dispute one of the chairs on the Canonical course at Coimbra but was not approved.[122] On March 16, 1750, armed with his letters of graduation from the university of Coimbra, he presented himself before the legal bar in Lisbon seeking a license to practice law, as, as we have already seen, the canonical course entitled the graduate to exercise this profession. His father's strategy had thus ended in success: João Fernandes's university degree had effectively opened the doors to a palace judgeship, to the administrative posts in the judiciary, and to the military ranks. The process of admittance was completed two years later, after all the customary investigations.[123] The papers submitted as the results of the investigative

---

[119] From 1496, by papal decree, the knights were allowed to marry, though there were strict orders against concubinage, which was punishable by confinement at the order's monastery in Tomar. Francis A. Dutra. "Membership in the Order of Christ in the seventeenth century: its rights, privileges and obligations." *The Americas*, 1970, p. 13.

[120] Ibidem, pp. 12–13.

[121] Definições e estatutos dos cavaleiros e freires da Ordem de Nosso Senhor Jesus Christo, 1628.

[122] APM. Seção Colonial.131, fls. 53v–54.

[123] ANTT. Índice de leitura de bacharéis. João Fernandes de Oliveira. Maço 22, doc. 37.

process registered João Fernandes as being thirty years of age, which was untrue, as he was not yet even twenty-five and therefore not old enough to receive such an investiture.[124]

When the Sergeant Major arrived in Lisbon in 1751, the youth went to live in the family home beside the Horta Seca, facing the residence of Count Vila Nova.[125] In 1752, adding to the honors he had already accumulated, he was appointed to the Porto Court of Appeal and thus assumed the title of chief judge.[126] However, some facts concerning this appointment run counter to the unwritten rules that guided careers in the Portuguese magistracy of the seventeenth and eighteenth centuries.[127] Particularly suspect are his direct access to such an important post as a first appointment, his young age at the time of conferral, the absence of any chief judges in his family, and his Brazilian origins. The contractor's power and the support of high-ranking local authorities would have been fundamental in bringing about this meteoric rise to notoriety that the Sergeant Major had so desperately sought for his son.

The fourth diamond contract came into force in January 1753. João Fernandes de Oliveira, the father, wanted to stay in Portugal and decided to send his son to take direct care of the diamond exploration in Tejuco. Thus the young chief judge, leaving behind him the unfinished ecclesiastical career for which he had prepared himself, sailed from the port of Lisbon to represent his father at the head of the new contract. The fleet that left for Rio de Janeiro on June 7, 1753, composed of twenty-three ships escorted by the warship *Nossa Senhora do Livramento*, also carried with it the warrant for the arrest of Felisberto Caldeira Brant, accused of illegally extracting an enormous quantity of diamonds.[128] The ships made port in Rio de Janeiro on

---

[124] Ibidem.
[125] Ibidem. Certidões de José Carlos Castelo e Antônio Velho da Costa.
[126] ANTT. Desembargo do Paço. Ilhas. Maço 1342, doc. 7.
[127] Stuart B. Schwartz. "Magistracy and society in colonial Brazil." *Hispanic American Historical Review*, pp. 715–30, 1970.
[128] AHU, MAMG. Caixa 58, doc. 110.

August 4,[129] where, exhausted from his long voyage, João was reunited with his maternal grandparents.

Meanwhile in Tejuco, events were unraveling at full steam. With the prison order from the Realm in hand, the interim governor of Minas Gerais, José Antônio Freire de Andrade, and the magistrate of Serro do Frio, José Pinto de Morais Bacelar, proceeded immediately to the village and on August 31 of that year remanded Caldeira Brant and his associates into custody. In addition to the arrests, they also relieved the diamond intendant, Sancho de Andrade Castro e Lanções, of his position.

Duly cautious, Chief Judge João Fernandes de Oliveira spent some days in Rio de Janeiro to let the dust settle in Tejuco. He took the Caminho Novo toward Minas Gerais, as this road could now offer a reasonable number of ranches, halfway houses, clearings, inns, and villages to provide shelter to the traveler and herbage for the animals on this long journey. In no particular hurry, his retinue took various stops for rest, covering the same distance each day with a São Paulo-style "march until mid-day or one or two in the afternoon at most, so they could make a spurt and have time to rest or [either] hunt or fish [later in the day]."[130]

At the banks of the swollen Paraibuna River, which marked the border between Minas Gerais and Rio de Janeiro, the retinue passed the first highway inspection point – called registers – where "there were boats ready to ferry the travellers and their business cargo."[131] The registers charged the Royal Crossing Tax, which was payable on the crossing of any of the captaincy's major rivers. Once in Minas Gerais, the traveling party passed through all the main urban centers along the way, such as Matias Barbosa, Juiz de Fora, Borda do Campo, Registro Velho, Carandaí, and Carijós, until finally reaching its destination – Vila Rica where João Fernandes would certainly have met with his relatives, especially his cousin Ventura Fernandes

---

[129] AHU, MAMG. Caixa 58, doc. 110, e caixa 63, docs. 28, 36.
[130] André João Antonil. Op cit., 1982, p. 182.
[131] José Joaquim da Rocha, op. cit., p. 162.

de Oliveira, who would have brought him up to speed on the events and situation of the region.

Continuing along the Caminho do Campo (Field Road) and trekking along dirt roads through the Espinhaço Mountains, João Fernandes left the villages of Camargos, Catas Altas, Santa Bárbara, Morro do Pilar, Nossa Senhora da Conceição do Mato Dentro, and Córregos in his wake before finally entering Vila do Príncipe, the main center of Serra do Frio county. From there, it was only a few hours walk past the villages of São Gonçalo do Rio das Pedras and Milho Verde into the Diamantine Demarcation. Along the way he would have come upon the well-armed troops of the traders heading back to Tejuco after selling their wares, which included valuable slaves. He would also have seen the first signs of the mining operations, digging in the riverbeds and smaller streams.

João Fernandes arrived at the village in early September. On the fifth of that month the new diamond intendant, Tomás Robi de Barros Barreto,[132] took office under royal orders to get along with the new diamond contractor, as the discord between the former holders of these posts had caused the Crown enormous losses. Hardly had he assumed his position than Robi made a point of meeting Chief Judge João Fernandes and his partners[133] in order to discuss the situation in Tejuco and establish their points of common interest. Two cultured men, both had been appointed to the post of chief judge: João Fernandes at the Porto Court of Appeals and Robi at the same courts in Rio de Janeiro.[134] The new intendant was a poet who belonged to the Academia dos Seletos (Academy of the Select), which in 1752 gathered together various writers to celebrate the appointment of Gomes Freire de Andrade – whose circle of friendship and protection therefore included both men – as the official responsible for demarcating the southern border of Brazil

---

[132] AHU, MAMG. Caixa 63, doc. 38.
[133] Ibidem.
[134] AMU. Documentos relativos ao Brasil – Bahia, no. 2585. In Eduardo de Castro Almeida. "Inventário dos existentes...." Anais da Biblioteca Nacional, vol. 31, 1909, p. 172.

as negotiated with the Spanish in the 1750 Treaty of Madrid.[135] These two men certainly belonged to the same clientele networks and must have shared similar interests.

Since January of 1753, the diamond contract had been run by the representative José Álvares Maciel, an old friend and ally of the Sergeant Major in Tejuco. However, backed by his partner Manuel Tinoco and armed with the signed powers of attorney from his father, the chief judge was undoubtedly the rightful incumbent to the post. Following royal orders, Robi suspended the contract and obliged José Álvares Maciel to turn the position over to João Fernandes de Oliveira. On September 15, Maciel was expelled from the Diamantine Demarcation under the accusation of bad administration.[136]

As soon as he was apprised of the diamond mining situation in the region, the chief judge sent petitions to the viceroy, Count Atouguia, in Rio de Janeiro requesting that the Pardo and Jequitinhonha Rivers be opened for exploration. He alleged that the mines at the Caeté-Mirim and Calhambolas Rivers, which the recently signed contract established as the rivers he was supposed to work, were already exhausted, a fact corroborated by the intendant Robi, who conducted analyses at the locale throughout the month of January.[137] Proof of the state of the two streams further incriminated Felisberto Caldeira Brant, who had not been authorized to explore them, as legally they were, in terms established under the prevailing contract, off limits for mining.

---

[135] The set of poems written to mark the occasion were published under the title *Júbilos da América*.

[136] AHU, MAMG. Caixa 66, doc. 6.

[137] AHU. Manuscritos Avulsos do Rio de Janeiro. Box 75, doc. 17 353. APM. Colonial section 33, fls. 129–144v. On November 15, 1753, in Rio de Janeiro, João Fernandes filed a request to open the Pardo River mines for exploration, as those of the Caeté-Mirim River had been exhausted. The viceroy ordered an inspection, which was carried out by the Intendant Robi and other authorities on January 2, 1754. Once the depletion of the mines was confirmed, the Pardo River sites were opened for operations. In July of this same year João Fernandes requested the opening of the Jequitinhonha River. Robi's response to this second request was obstinate, suggesting that the exploration of the rivers be alternated during the dry season.

Without doubt, the young João Fernandes, "single and of good life and habits,"[138] basking in nobility and the representative of his father's considerable wealth, was certainly what one could call a good catch. However, defying all expectations, shortly after his arrival in Tejuco he began his involvement with Chica da Silva, a mulatta slave, with whom he would remain linked until death.

[138] ANTT. Índice de leitura de bacharéis. João Fernandes de Oliveira. Maço 22, doc. 37. Deposition of Dr. José Antônio Cobeiro de Azevedo, corregedor civil.

CHAPTER FOUR

BLACK DIAMOND

Here is my palace
and here my table wines
my gold-framed mirrors
and silk-covered bed
the fragrance of my farmhouse
with my lighted chapel

PROFANE LOVE

In the second semester of 1753, shortly before arriving in Tejuco to assume his post, João Fernandes de Oliveira bought a parda slave named Chica from Manuel Pires Sardinha for 800,000 reis.[1] It is not known exactly what led Pires Sardinha to sell her, though it is worth remembering that in August of that same year, during the ecclesiastical visit,[2] the physician had signed a commitment to "break off [sic] all illicit communication" he had maintained with two slaves from his estate. Selling these women, such that all three would come to live in different houses, was an essential condition for the fulfilment of the terms of this commitment.[3]

At another ecclesiastical visit held in Tejuco in 1750, one Alexandre Gama de Sá, accused of concubinage in the first instance with

---

[1]   AFS. Livro de notas. 1754, fls. 55–55v.
[2]   The ecclesiastical visits were carried out by the bishops, whose duty it was to visit their diocese to punish crimes of a moral or religious order, such as bigamy, adultery, usury, and perjury, among others. The jurisdiction of these visits was different than that of the Inquisition.
[3]   AEAD. Livro de termos do Serro do Frio. 1750–1753, caixa 557, f. 102v.

his slave Ana, in addition to the customary fine, was ordered to "rid himself of the slave woman who lives in his house so that he can no longer meddle with her."[4] In 1753, in the village of Itambé, Manuel Rodrigues da Costa was admonished to expel from his house a slave woman named Lucrécia de Sá, his concubine, despite the fact that she was already married to the freed black Domingos de Sá. In the terms signed by the slave, the visiting inquisitor stipulated a fifteen-day timeframe within which she was to have parted company with her master and left his house. She was also reminded "that if he tried to prevent her from leaving, she was to return to His Excellency so that he could have him ordered to sell her and issued with a letter of manumission."[5]

Did João Fernandes buy Chica with the intention of making her his companion? It is highly probable that he did, especially as their relationship flowered within a matter of months and given that the young chief judge registered Chica's manumission papers at the registry office in Vila do Príncipe as early as that December, so soon after buying her.[6]

The date chosen for her manumission, December 25 – Christmas Day – was charged with meaning. João Fernandes, like his father, was extremely religious[7] – as the fact that he had trained for an ecclesiastical career would attest. According to the customs of the day, the seven days leading up to Christmas were devoted to prayer,[8] and as a former student of the seminary of São Patrício and later of the canon at Coimbra, he would have been accustomed to the Jesuit festivities for celebrating this date. At the university, the determinations set down in the will of the infant Henry were followed to the

---

[4] Ibidem, f. 25.

[5] Ibidem, fls. 61v–62.

[6] AFS. Livro de notas. 1754, fls. 55–55v. Everything would indicate that the slave in question was Chica da Silva, as in the letter registered in Vila do Príncipe João Fernandes, who had just arrived from Portugal, was already manumitting a slave named Francisca, whom he had bought for 800,000 reis. It is highly unlikely that this could be referring to another slave of the same name.

[7] ANTT. Desembargo do Paço. Ilhas. Maço 1342, doc. 7.

[8] ANTT. Real Mesa Censória. *Gazeta de Lisboa*. Caixa 465. Suplemento ao no. 8, 26 de fevereiro de 1752, p. 160.

letter: students and teachers would gather at one o'clock in the afternoon on Christmas Eve and make their way in procession to the
chapel where they attended a religious service. At the head of the
procession was the rector, clad in a rich cape and carrying the sacred
relics, followed by the chaplains in white vestments. On Christmas
Day, a solemn mass was said in the same chapel and an Our Father
and a Hail Mary were offered up for the infant's soul and for the
knights of the Order of Christ.[9] While in Lisbon, the young João
Fernandes would certainly have joined his father at the palace where
the ring-kissing of the sovereigns took place, as it was there, amid full
pomp and ceremony, that "all of the grandest and most important figures in the Kingdom, the ministers of the Courts and all other men
of distinction" commemorated such important dates.[10]

As a member of the Order of Christ, the chief judge was obliged
to confess and receive communion four times per year, especially on
the most important religious dates – Christmas, Easter, the Penta-
cost, and the day of the Holy Cross. While the knights of the Order
in Lisbon donned their white mantles and gathered for mass at the
Nossa Senhora da Conceição church,[11] João Fernandes chose to celebrate his first Christmas in Tejuco with the concession of manumission to his future companion.

Manumitting a slave soon after purchase was not common practice among the slave owners of Minas. Liberty was usually granted to
concubines or trusted slaves through the process of *coartation*, or self-
purchase through installments. In general, emancipation was only
granted in the owner's will and only became effective one year after
his death. Under these conditions, slaves were rarely freed without having to give something in return, whether services or cash.
Manumitting slaves on the deathbed was doubly advantageous: not
only did it constitute an act of Christian charity, always necessary to
help the soul on its way to heaven, but it was also good business, as by

[9] Estatutos da Universidade de Coimbra (1559). 1965, pp. 20–1.
[10] ANTT. Real Mesa Censória. *Gazeta de Lisboa*. Caixa 465, no. 52, 27 de dezembro
de 1753, p. 416.
[11] Francis A. Dutra. "Membership in the Order of Christ in the seventeenth
century: its rights, privileges and obligations." *The Americas*, 1970, pp. 14–15.

setting the price at which the slave was to buy his or her liberty, the owners avoided the risk of their fetching much lower sums at public auctions.

Analyzing the histories of the various freedwomen of Tejuco during the eighteenth century enables us to identify the particularities and similarities among them and therefore unveil part of the universe in which they and Chica lived. Of the twenty-three freedwomen who registered their wills in the village over the course of that century, only one was freed in the same manner as Chica. Maria de Sousa da Encarnação, a freed black woman born on the Gold Coast of Mina, reveals that she was the mistress of one Domingos Alves Maciel, a white man, who bought her from her owner, Pedro Mendes, for 150 eighths of gold, only to manumit her soon afterward. In 1756, the year she died, she was the owner of four houses in the village, three of which she rented out, while she had a private oratory built at her own residence.[12] All the other freedwomen make a point of stating that they had paid for their own liberty.

The number of women who availed of this recourse was considerable, as a concubine had no access to the patrimony of the white man with whom she lived. As for the children born of these consensual relationships, the fortunes of the white fathers could become attainable through inheritance – as was the case with Manuel Pires Sardinha's three sons, all born from concubinage with his slaves and all emancipated at the baptismal urn.[13]

The process of slave manumission in the region of Sabará and Tejuco was not much different. The emancipation of natural sons and daughters was quite common at baptism, but the freeing of concubines generally occurred only in the owner's will. Countless cases illustrate this type of behavior. Lourenço de Melo e Madureira freed his five natural daughters and named them all his heiresses while their mother remained enslaved so that she could look after

[12] AEAD. Livros de óbitos do arraial do Tejuco. 1752–1895, caixa 350, fls. 34–34v.
[13] AEAD. Livro de batizados do arraial do Tejuco. 1745–1765, caixa 297, f. 29. No mesmo arquivo, Livro de óbitos do arraial do Tejuco. 1752–1895, caixa 350, f. 27.

the progeny. Antônio da Rocha Flores did something similar, setting the manumission date for his slave, Rosa, for six years after his death, during which time she was to continue caring for their children, who were all immediately freed and named as heirs. Francisco Roiz Neto set a period of twelve years for the freeing of his slave Antônia, who in the meantime tended to the three mulatto children she had borne him.[14] In his will, Bonifácio Antunes, Portuguese, married and the father of six children, manumitted his slave Antônia, who ran a stall and with whom he had fathered one child, on the condition that she continue to look after his children for the period of six years following his death.

According to the magistrate Caetano Costa Matoso, the history of the region had always been connected with powerful freed black and mulatto women who subjected the white men to their every whim. The magistrate revealed that Vila do Príncipe itself had been founded on the caprice of one such woman. The pillory[15] had originally been erected at a place only two leagues away from Tejuco by order of Luís Botelho de Queirós, the magistrate for Sabará, but soon afterward the judge Antônio Quaresma had the settlement moved to another site, where it remains to this day, at a distance of nine leagues from the village of Tejuco – and all at "the behest of a Negro lady-friend named Jacinta, still alive today, who lived and owned some mines there."[16]

The Jacinta referred to here was Jacinta de Siqueira, one of the first inhabitants of Vila do Príncipe, who lived in the first half of the eighteenth century (dying in 1751). Her will reveals how she owed her social ascension to her access to the mines and to her concubinage to some white men. Though Jacinta claimed to have never married,

---

[14] Kathleen J. Higgins. "Manumissions in Sabará." In *Licentious liberty*. 1999, p. 39.

[15] The pillory was an important symbol of a city's political submission to the Portuguese Crown. Made of stone or wood, it was usually erected in the main square in front of the municipal chamber. The pillory was commonly used as place of slaves' punishment.

[16] "História da Vila do Príncipe e do modo de lavar os diamantes e de extrair o cascalho." Documento 129. In Caetano Costa Matoso. *Códice Costa Matoso*, vol. 1, 2000, pp. 845–50.

she had five mulatto daughters: Bernarda, Quitéria, Rita, Josefa, and Vitória. Her main achievement, not merely in financial terms but also socially, was to have all five legally married off to white men, thus ensuring their entry into the society of the day and erasing forever the stigma of color and slavery that they bore. As she lived in a society where more store was put on the status of a person's antecedents than on how he or she actually chose to live, Jacinta omitted her own background from her will, preferring to name in detail only the descent and ties she had established with white society through marriage. These bonds were reaffirmed as she neared death, as the dying – as we shall see – always remembered to leave money for a mass to be said to help the souls of their loved ones seek salvation.

In addition to owning slaves, which would have placed her among the villa's elite, various other assets, real estate and otherwise, were also listed in her will. In order to reaffirm her religiosity she left alms of gold – like the thirty-four eighths of gold bequeathed to the Brotherhood of the Rosary – in an act that also publicly flaunted her power, as only the rich could afford to give charity. Indispensable for the ascension of the soul, she also arranged for masses to be said at the village church. In addition to those to be said in her own name, not counting her funeral mass itself, she commissioned a further fifty-five services: fifteen for Saint Anthony, twenty for the souls in Purgatory, ten for the soul of Antônio Quaresma, and ten for the soul of Vitória Pereira, her deceased daughter – and all with the concession of the customary alms. The dedications made to Antônio Quaresma would confirm Costa Matoso's intimation about the nature of their relationship in life.

On one hand, concubinage with white men certainly held some advantages for these women. Once freed, the stigma of color and slavery would be diminished, not only for themselves but more importantly for their children and descendants. Many of Chica da Silva's daughters with João Fernandes, like those of Jacinta de Siqueira, were legally married to white men, despite being mulatto and the daughters of a former slave. On the other hand, however, concubinage denied them the legal privileges reserved for wives. Matrimony, regardless of the color of the spouses, granted the wife access to her husband's estate, whatever its value, or vice versa, as we shall see.

Marriage between men and women of color, for example, rarely increased either party's patrimony or status. Nor was marriage generally the guarantee of a more secure life. In fact, it could often give rise to rather paradoxical situations. The analysis of the cases of ten freedwomen who married in Tejuco and registered their wills there actually pointed to less stability in postmarriage life. Seven of these women – and thus an expressive majority of 70 percent – were either widows or abandoned wives; situations just as precarious as being single.

Maria Vaz da Conceição, a black woman from the Coast of Mina and widow of Antônio da Costa, also black, is a case in point. She claimed to have bought her liberty and all the assets she possessed prior to marriage "of her own agency." She was more grateful to her former owner than to her husband, for whose soul she did not so much as leave a mass, though she did name a pardo son fathered by her former master among her heirs. She also sought her own salvation by having masses said in her name and by leaving charity.[17] In 1774, Maria Vaz was living in a house she owned on Rua do Macau in Tejuco, the same street as Maria da Costa.[18]

Many married freedwomen stress in their wills that their husbands in no way contributed to the patrimony they had managed to accumulate "by the agency of their own labours." In this respect, Portuguese law was disadvantageous to women, as the assets they acquired became the patrimony of the couple, over which the husband, legally the head of the family, had total control. The freedwomen Maria Martins Castanheira and Bernardina Maria da Conceição, both abandoned wives, experienced the full vigour of this disadvantage. The former, a *Benguela*, was married to a black man named Francisco Pereira Lima who spent all her money and "was always absent." The latter, a cabra, was married to a freed pardo named Gonçalo, "who left after [she] had fallen into his disfavour."

---

[17] AEAD. Livro de de óbitos do arraial do Tejuco. Caixa 521, fls. 49v–50.
[18] AHU, MAMG. Caixa 108, doc. 9, f. 8v.

Both tried to prevent their husbands from having total access to their money by taking provisions to have the third of it set aside exclusively for use as they saw fit.

Gender and race relations were intrinsically interconnected in Minas Gerais. The lives of Chica da Silva and other freedwomen of Tejuco and the surrounding areas are proof of this. Sex was a determining factor in access to manumission: the majority of freed women achieved manumission in adulthood, while the reverse is true of freed males, most of whom were sons born of mixed relationships who were given their liberty at baptism.[19] The economic and social makeup of the region thus explains why wage-earning black women who could put together some savings, and slave women who lived as concubines to white men stood a much better chance of being manumitted than other slaves. For men of color who were almost always put to work in the fields or mines, the chances of being able to earn some money on the side with which to buy their liberty were extremely low.

It is therefore no accident that only one of the black freedwomen classified as household heads in the Tejuco census of 1774 registered any kind of profession: one Joana Gertrudes, a parda freedwoman, who lived in her own house on Rua do Amparo where she practiced the profession of innkeeper. Most freedwomen largely lived off the income from the slaves they owned, which, though low, was enough to keep them out of the working world.[20] However, the opposite was true of the freedmen. The census revealed that there were eighty-nine freedmen in the village, sixty of whom exercised some trade or craft: fifteen were tailors, eleven shoemakers, six ironmongers, four sellers of dry goods, three carpenters, three barbers, two teachers, one painter, one miner, and one slave hunter, among other activities.[21] Mastering a craft was fundamental for a man to earn his freedom and keep his head above water in the world of the free.

Rosa Correia, married to a Mina called Inácio, a slave of Captain Francisco Lima, was one of the freedwomen who actually managed

---

[19] Kathleen J. Higgins, "Manumissions in …," op. cit., pp. 145–74.
[20] AHU, MAMG. Caixa 108, doc. 9, f. 5.
[21] AHU, MAMG. Caixa 108, doc. 9, fls. 1–9.

to amass a patrimony. At the time of her death, she owned one slave, the house in which she lived, and had a lot of incoming debts. The wealth she had accumulated enabled her to work in wholesaling, an activity generally monopolized by white men, so she also had some outstanding accounts to settle on cargo received from the Realm. Given her financial endowments, Rosa was able to ensure the alms-giving needed to commend her soul to heaven,[22] thus giving herself the luxury of a good death, while also publicly parading the social standing she had achieved in life. At the time, the expression "a good death" meant having the opportunity to prepare the passage of one's soul toward salvation. This former slave woman, whose corpse was accompanied to the grave by four clergymen, was buried at the parish church in Sabará.

In Mariana, the will of a beverage seller named Maria das Candeias showed that she was the wife of José de Lima and that she owned a corn and bean partnership, five slaves, and a farm with a flour mill. Her will leaves some casks for storing corn, flour, and beans, as well as two yokes and stocks and products to her descendants.

The last will and testament of Antônia Nunes dos Anjos, born in Bahia and freed on the road to Minas, registers a lot of credit from the sale of slaves and gold buttons and chains. She belonged to the Brotherhood of the Rosary and upon her death left three slaves, vari-ous items in gold and diamonds, including jewelery, clasps, padlocks, chains, and buttons, as well as an image of Saint Brás and a relic of Saint Benedict. She died single and heirless, though the assets she accumulated would indicate that she had lived a much better life than that of her parents, both slaves from the Coast of Mina.[23]

An equally salient point about manumission is that obtaining free-dom did not always result in a better life for the former slave, espe-cially for those without a craft. After gaining their liberty, the women saw the stigma of sex incremented to that of color and condition. The marginal situation to which they were relegated was worse than that endured by some types of slaves, such as the domestics, for example.

[22]   MO/CBG.Testamento. Livro 5(11), fls. 7v–11.
[23]   MO/CBG. Testamento de Antônia Nunes dos Anjos. Livro 7(13), fls. 15v–18.

The life of Rosa Tibães, a freed black woman, was typical of the difficulties these women faced in their attempt to find a place for themselves in the world of the free. Sergeant Major José da Silva de Oliveira, taking pity on her poverty and prizing charity as one of the virtues of the good Christian, allowed her to build a small shack on one of his properties in Tejuco, near the Bonfim church.[24]

In 1780, in the captaincy of Pará, a half-black, half-Indian named Joana Batista presented herself before the public notary and, by public office, had herself sold to Pedro da Costa, a resident of the same town and Spanish citizen. Joana left no doubts as to the fact that she was a freewoman voluntarily relinquishing her liberty, claiming "she had been free and exempt from captivity since birth." Her parents, both deceased, were "a black man named Ventura, once slave of Father José de Melo" and the "Indian Ana Maria, formerly in the service of the same priest."[25]

Moving against the tide, she renounced her own liberty in favor of a sheltered, secure, and honorable old age. For Joana, her actions were justified by the wish to be able to "live in peace," which basically meant that living in captivity exempted her from the daily uncertainty of a life without guarantees. As an active party to the contract, entered into by her own free will, she underlines the condition that "the sale includes herself alone and all she may possess," but that "if someday [she had] children, these [would] be free and exempt from captivity." Now, could this woman be reduced to a mere instrument in the hands of historiography? By giving up her own freedom and submitting herself to slavery, Joana Batista was also giving herself the chance of a dignified life denied her as a woman. The most interesting point is that, as the fruit of her sale as a slave, she would have finally been able to accumulate some peculium in the form of clothes, jewelery, and money.

The lives of these women in all their similarities and peculiarities afford us a better understanding of the world of slavery in which they and Chica were immersed. It also helps us comprehend the

[24] APM. Seção Colonial. 260, fls. 3v–4.
[25] ANTT. Papéis do Brasil. Avulso 7, no. 1.

alternatives marriage, concubinage, and manumission either offered
or denied in the context of the Tejucan society in which they lived.

Donna Francisca

According to the information provided by the deponents in Simão
Pires Sardinha's *de genere* process, Chica da Silva was somewhere
between eighteen and twenty-two years of age when she met João
Fernandes, then twenty-six. This young woman, the mother of a two-
year-old child – the sex life of a slave began early, generally between
twelve or fourteen years of age[26] – possessed all the beauty of the
women from the Coast of Mina so frequently praised by the Europeans. Documents from the time describe her as parda, the term used
to denote the lightest tone of skin found among mestizos. While we
cannot know what effect Chica da Silva had on João Fernandes,
something of the attraction these women wielded can be gleaned
from this account by a European chronicler:

> twelve is the age at which the African girls flower, [in whom]
> from time to time there is such enchantment that one forgets
> their colour. ... The little black girls are usually strong and solid,
> with features denoting agreeable amiability and movements full
> of natural grace, with artfully beautiful feet and hands. Their eyes
> irradiate a fire so particular and their chests heave with such ardent
> desire that it is difficult to resist such seductions.[27]

In his song *Xula carioca* (*Onde vás, linda negrinha*), the Rio de Janeiro–
born composer Antônio da Silva Leite immortalized the play of
seduction between the white men and the colored women that cir-
culated so freely and boldly through the streets of Brazilian towns
and cities:

> With all your disaffection
> Don't rush by in such a hurry;

---

[26] Luiz Mott. *Rosa Egipcíaca*, 1993, pp. 18–20.
[27] Carl Schlichthorst. *O Rio de Janeiro como é* (1825–26). Apud: Maria Lúcia Mott.
      A criança escrava na literatura de viajantes. 1979, p. 64.

have pity, have compassion

…

Beautiful perfection
Don't you want to give wings
To my heart

…

Don't make off in such a hurry
No need to be so ill-mannered
I'm a master of the realm
Not some swaggering braggard

…

Don't flee, cruel enchantment,
Lay down the pail and come to me
Else I may well lose my cool
And go running after thee.[28]

Though we do not have a precise description of Chica, the information that comes down to us about the mestizo descendants of
slaves from the Coast of Mina gives us some idea of what she
would have been like. On the same continent, though in rather
distant lands, the Englishman John Gabriel Stedman recorded the
strong impression made upon him by "the marvellous mulatta, the
slave Joana," the only mestizo he had the chance to see in Suri-
name. Though his account was about the slave revolt that occurred
there from 1772 to 1777, the sight of Joana pushed the insurrec-
tion from his mind long enough to jot down this enraptured description:

> Rather more than middle-sized, she was perfectly strait, with the
> most elegant shapes that can be viewed in nature, moving her
> well-formed limbs as when a goddess walked. Her face was full of
> native modesty and the most distinguished sweetness. Her eyes, as
> black as ebony, were large and full of expression, bespeaking the
> goodness of her heart.... her nose was perfectly well-formed and
> rather small; her lips a little prominent which, when she spoke,

[28] Antônio da Silva Leite. *Xula carioca* (*Onde vás, linda negrinha*).

discovered two regular rows of pearls as white as mountain snow. Her hair was a dark brown, next to black, forming a beauteous globe of small ringlets, ornamed with flowers and gold spangles.[29]

What we can be sure of is that João Fernandes was ardently impressed by Chica da Silva whose physical characteristics, at once exotic and familiar, fully corresponded to the European notion of beauty. In the eighteenth century, beauty was considered "just proportion amongst the parts of the body, accompanied by grace and pleasant colour."[30] Chica must have possessed all the attributes capable of underlining a woman's beauty, such as:

> just proportion amongst the features; in the union of one with the others; in the elegance of each in itself; in the vividness of the colours, imperceptibly embellished with white and flesh-tones, which form the facial complexion; in the brilliant fire of the eyes; in the quantity, length and colour of the hair; in the whiteness and regularity of the teeth; in the exact symmetry of all other parts; but also in the grace, stature and *donayre* [sic] of the body and the majesty of the walk.[31]

In Chica's day, love was a sphere of two halves: the divine and the profane. The former was understood, above all, as the love God nurtured for mankind and vice versa.[32] For the Catholic Church, the love of God was the most perfect and sublime form this sentiment could attain, and chastity was a necessary means toward it. But there were also profane forms of love, such as that between parents and children, men and their homelands, and between men and women. The latter was considered "a movement of the appetite through

---

[29] J. G. Stedman. "Narrative of a five year expedition." In Richard Price et al. (org.). *Stedman's Surinam*, 1992, p. 40.

[30] Rafael Bluteau. *Dicionário da língua portuguesa*. Ampliado por Antônio de Morais, 1739, p. 91. Entry: beauty.

[31] Ibidem.

[32] Ibidem, p. 346. Entry: love.

which the soul seeks unity what it deems good or beautiful," with the adjunct that the love "men have for women is often unruly."[33]

Not only was love not a condition of marriage, but the sentiment was totally disassociated from the institution, which was not considered a forum in which to satisfy the passions. Matrimony was a family matter and a means toward constructing alliances that brought social and economic promotion for those involved, considering "motives other than the personal interests of the participants"[34] – hence the designation "marriage of reason." The feelings that were supposed to unite spouses were basically friendship and respect, the main values of conjugal love. Sergeant Major João Fernandes' second marriage, to Isabel Monteiro Pires, was exemplary in this sense, having been orchestrated entirely as a solution to the financial problems pending from his second diamond contract. His son most certainly had no doubts that marriage was a social convention between equals and a key part of family strategy. It was precisely because of this that he determined that none of his heirs "would assume marital status and wed by their own free will and choice before the age of thirty, when they would be old enough to appreciate the civil state they were entering, without worrying about passions, which all too often blind the young, . . . and that none could marry below his station."[35]

In Portugal, it was not only family that sought to consolidate marital unions between parties of equal birth and social status. The church and state were only supposed to concede marriage licenses based on the principle of equality. Matrimony was always preceded by processes that carefully examined not only the present situation of the betrothed, but also that of their maternal and paternal lines of descent. In Brazil, in line with the laws of the realm, marriage was regulated by the "First Constitutions of the Archbishopric of Bahia."

---

[33] Rafael Bluteau. *Dicionário da língua portuguesa.* 1739, p. 346. Entry: love.

[34] Morton Hunt. *The natural history of love*, 1960.

[35] ANTT. Cartórios notariais. (C-5B). Caixa 15, livro 78. Notas. Atual 12, fls. 48v–49.

The sphere of passion, of illicit love, of consensual relationships was quite another. "Love was a game, a source of fun. Seduction and adultery were pastimes."[36] In Minas Gerais, with the huge dispro-portion between men and women and with the growing influx of black and mulatto women, both slaves and freedwomen, licentious relationships multiplied exponentially resulting in countless and var-ied forms of family arrangement. In the village of Tejuco, for exam-ple, the licentiate José Gomes Ferreira, the godfather of Simão Pires Sardinha,[37] lived with his slave Maria. Likewise, Caetano Francisco Guimarães lived with Teresa ladá, a fact severely reprimanded by the visiting inquisitor, who warned him "[of the] spiritual ruin he wrought upon his neighbour,[38] . . . to whom he by rights should seek to give good doctrine, in the interests of the good of his salvation and that of the aforesaid slave, with commination [sic] that by doing the contrary he would be more gravely punished with the full force of justice,"[39] as by his acts "he risked offending God and provoking guilt."

According to the dominant view of the day, women "were courted, deceived, manipulated like toys, but never taken seriously"[40]; their wishes simply did not matter. This was especially true of slave women whose lot was to be used to their masters' liking. Considered inca-pable and deprived of reason, all that was left for women was sub-jugation by men, so for the visiting inquisitors, the owners were the main culprits for the adultery practiced with the slaves – the mere objects of their desire.

Contrary to this image, a great many women, whether free, freed, or slaves, were clearly active participants in these illicit relationships from which they certainly reaped some benefit. In Tejuco, a woman named Joana, despite the fact that she was already married, lived with one Antônio de Azevedo Correia of her own free will. In the nearby village of Tapera, Teresa de Sousa Lobo allowed one Sebastião

[36] Nathaniel Branden, op. cit., p. 41.
[37] AEAD. Livro de batizados do arraial do Tejuco. 1745–1765, caixa 297, f. 21.
[38] Ibidem, f. 99.
[39] Ibidem, f. 61v.
[40] Nathaniel Branden, op. cit., p. 41.

Ferreira into her house, while the slave Catarina Teixeira, who did not live at the same property as her owner, a resident of Paracatu, lived in sin with the farrier José Ribeiro da Silva. A creole slave named Micaela Pereira, who likewise lived off her owner's premises, not only maintained illicit relations with the pardo Simão Pereira but also allowed her house to be used as a place for "women to converse with men." Francisca Leite Batista had a relationship with Francisco Borges de Sousa with the consent of her own husband who probably could do little to oppose her wishes.[41]

The desire to have their love reciprocated – *amor mutuus* – without submission to the masculine will led many women from the colony to resort to the magic love potions prepared with the help of reputable witches.[42] In Bahia in 1591, the witch Antônia Fernandes, also known as Nóbrega, possessed a failsafe recipe for keeping a man's passions aflame. [She was known to] recommend to her acquaintances that they drink special concoctions.

Although they were illicit according to the prevailing behavioral norms, these relationships gave the appearance of legality and stability, albeit informally and without the blessing of the church – in fact, "profane love" consolidated itself in the guise of "conjugal love." The tendency toward stability was a striking factor in various consensual relationships in the mining region, many of which were more lasting than legal marriages. Though it was not unusual for the lovers to live in separate abodes, the bonds of affection were nonetheless preserved. This can be seen from the number of couples first caught during the Inquisition of 1750 found to be still together by the Inquisition of 1753, such as Domingos José Coutinho, who had been living with the freed parda Micaela Maria da Conceição for many years; Romana Teresa, another freed parda, who was the concubine of Antônio José; and Alexandre da Gama, who had been

---

[41] AEAD. Livro de batizados do arraial do Tejuco. 1745–1765, caixa 297, fls. 98, 15 e 14.

[42] "... as with witchcraft in Portugal, spellbinding in Brazil, as it was later called by the Negros, continued to revolve around amorous concerns." Gilberto Freyre. Op cit., 1946, p. 324.

having an affair with his slave Ana, as had José Coutinho with Rosa parda.[43]

Like Chica and João Fernandes, the surgeon José Gomes Ferreira had a long-standing affair with his slave Maria parda, who he later manumitted. Maria and Chica da Silva were acquaintances and their lives crossed paths on various occasions. José Gomes Ferreira worked as a surgeon at the hospital originally maintained by the diamond contractors and incorporated by the intendancy after the royal diamond monopoly was established by decree. He probably secured this post through his uncle, Luís Gomes Ferreira, the author of *Erário mineral*, who had developed close connections with his neighbor, the future contractor Sergeant Major João Fernandes de Oliveira, at Itacolomi.[44] Despite being caught by the Inquisition of 1753,[45] José and Maria were still living together five years later, now with three daughters – Rosa, Matilde, and Francisca[46] – and one son. In 1774, Maria Gomes was living in a rented house on Rua Padre de Manoel da Costa, while José Gomes resided on Rua Luís Gomes in the company of his son,[47] who would later join the clergy after inheriting a patrimony from his great uncle João Gomes Ferreira, the former abbot of Prondas,[48] which guaranteed him the income so indispensable for the pursuit of an ecclesiastical career. João Gomes was acting landlord of some houses in a hamlet near Vila da Freira in Portugal that belonged to the firstborn of Salvador da Rocha Tavares. As these assets were indefeasible, the only way he could provide his nephew with some endowment was by filing for disassociation to Her Majesty Maria I, who accepted his request.[49]

[43] AEAD. Livro de termos do Serro do Frio. 1750–1753, caixa 557, fls. 96v, 98v, 96 e 102.
[44] At this time, both Sergeant Major João Fernandes de Oliveira and the doctor Luís Gomes Ferreira were back in Lisbon where they certainly would have met up.
[45] AEAD. Livro de termos do Serro do Frio. 1750–1753. Caixa 557, f. 96v.
[46] AEAD. Livro de batizados do arraial do Tejuco. 1745–1765. Caixa 297, fls. 49, 76v e 96v.
[47] Ibidem.
[48] Luís Gomes Ferreira. *Erário mineral*, vol. 2, 2002, p. 665.
[49] ANTT. Chancelaria de dom João V. "Provisão de licença para o padre João Gomes fazer patrimônio ao dito sobrinho," 17 de março de 1716.

Some of João Fernandes's actions reveal an intention to confer an air of stability but not legality upon his relationship with Chica da Silva (after all, legal matrimony was only permitted between individuals of equal status), such as her abnormally early manumission, which enabled her to acquire patrimony, the use Chica made of the surname Oliveira, the high number of children they had together (all named after members of the parents' families), and the longevity of their relationship.

Some months after manumission, in 1754, Chica became pregnant by João Fernandes. Little was known back then about the workings of the human body, and the causes of pregnancy were still shrouded in mystery. The limits between life and death were tenuous, and countless dangers surrounded mother and child. Mortality among newborns was high, and an idea of the death rate can be gleaned from the obituary records, on which these infants, who normally died before baptism, are registered as "little angels." In Tejuco in 1753, for example, eight newborns died, the equivalent of 11.3 percent of total deaths for that year. Four infants – an abandoned child, a legitimate son of Dr. José Pinheiro, a son of Manuel Alves Maia, and the son of a slave of Manuel Soares[50] – passed away in the month of September alone.

Pregnancy unfolded amid fears of bearing a disabled or deformed child. Among the many superstitions that abounded were the beliefs that women who kept cats at home risked giving birth to children with hairy backs; that necklaces and other jewels left marks on the skin; and that carrying keys about the waist or neck, as was the custom at the time, resulted in cleft palate. In order to protect the newborn from illness and the evil eye, Chica, like the other pregnant and recent mothers of her day, would have taken such special precautions as wearing a little bag around the neck filled with stones chipped from an altar.[51] Alimentation was hearty, and all effort was made to cater to the desires of the new mother, especially during the puerperal phase, which could last for months. In Sergeant Major José da Silva Oliveira's inventory, among other expenses related to

[50] AEAD. Livro de óbitos do arraial do Tejuco. 1752–1895, caixa 350.
[51] Gilberto Freyre, op. cit., 1940, p. 326.

the sick and the infirm, we find sums for the purchase of chicken and beef for the creole slaves Maria and Rita, both recent mothers, as these foods were believed to have curative effects.[52]

Mothers, fathers, and other family members prayed for divine protection at the hour of childbirth, beseeching Our Lady of the Graces, also known as Our Lady of the Blessed Birth, among other saints. In Tejuco, on December 22, 1781, after eight days of labor, Rita Angélica da Costa, with her unborn dead inside her womb, finally gave birth. Throughout her ordeal she had prayed to Our Lady of Matosinho to save her, and when her request was fulfilled, she gave thanks for the miracle by making an ex-voto immortalizing the fact and pledging devotion to the miracle-working saint.[53]

In line with the standards of the day, the birth of Chica and João Fernandes's baby would have been a public affair, accompanied by the midwife, the family of the parturient, and various elderly women and slaves. Whenever complications arose and there was still time, a priest was called to administer the last rites. Midwives had to be licensed by the town council, which issued *letters of usance* that entitled them to exercise their craft. They were, in general, poor black elderly freedwomen with a special air about them. Experts in the art of childbirth, they were entrusted with all of the village's births, though they were also deeply feared for the power of life or death they wielded over the mother and her infant. The fear they inspired fueled the popular imagination with tales of witchery worked upon newborns with a simple breath or touch. During the period Chica da Silva had her children, the midwives working in Tejuco were Maria da Silva Tomé and Antônia de Sousa,[54] one of whom would certainly have accompanied her labors.

For sixteen years, from 1754 to 1770, the year João Fernandes returned to Portugal, he and Chica maintained a stable relationship

---

[52] BAT. Inventário de José da Silva de Oliveira. 1796–1797. Cartório do Primeiro Ofício, maço 28, f. 39.

[53] Ex-voto of the "Milagre que fez o Senhor do Matosinho a Rita Angélica da Costa". Property of Museu do Diamante, Diamantina.

[54] AEAD. Livro de batizados do arraial do Tejuco. 1745–1765, caixa 297, fls. 10, 14 e 24v.

that would bear thirteen children: nine girls and four boys. This average of a birth every thirteen months puts to rest the myth of the sensual and lascivious man-eater that has always lingered around Chica. João Fernandes obviously never had any doubt as to the paternity of his progeny, as he legitimized them all and made them his heirs, though his will does reveal a lingering wish to have a legitimate son to succeed him.[55] While the baptismal records of eleven of these children can be found in Tejuco and Macaúbas, the dismal condition of the records from Tejuco for the period 1769 to 1780 unfortunately makes consultation impossible. Despite the high infant and child mortality rates of the day, Chica and João Fernandes's children all lived up to adolescence at least, with few failing to reach adulthood.

As death from puerperal fever was common,[56] the period of convalescence for free women lasted about three months, during which time they did not leave the house and received few visitors. In May 1762, Chica was unable to attend the baptismal ceremony of her goddaughter, the daughter of Luís Antônio da Silva and Micaela Arcângela da Silva, because she was in convalescence after the birth of her own daughter, Ana.[57]

The eldest daughter of the chief judge and his ex-slave was born on April 7, 1755. She was registered as Francisca de Paula, mulatta,

[55] ANTT. Cartórios notariais. (C-5B). Caixa 15, livro 75. Notas. Atual 12, f. 77v.

[56] ANTT. Real Mesa Censória. *Gazeta de Lisboa.* Caixa 465, no. 10. Tuesday, May 7th, 1752, p. 192. "In the early morning of the 13th of February, at her manor in Marialva, the illustrious and most excellent Marchioness de Marialva, Donna Eugênia Mascarenhas, successfully gave birth to a son. After only a few days she began to experience pains and high fever. The remedy of bloodletting was applied along with all other recommended treatments, which conferred a certain relief. However, as the illness aggravated and the symptoms were recognised as mortal, with the constancy of a truly catholic animus and totally resigned to the Divine will, the sacraments were requested on the 26th of the month and, with many other predestined signs, she passed away the following morning, to the universal sentiment of the court, at the age of 29." This passage speaks of the birth of the future governor of Minas Gerais, Rodrigo José de Meneses, whose mother died soon after childbirth. The funeral rites were conducted on February 28, 1752.

[57] AEAD. Livro de batizados do arraial do Tejuco. 1745–1765, caixa 291, f. 86.

father unknown.[58] The name chosen for her was a clear reference to both Chica and Saint Francis de Paul, one of the saints to which João Fernandes's family was most devoted, according to declarations made by the Sergeant Major in his will.[59] It was at this christening that Chica made ostensive use of her new surname for the first time, with Francisca da Silva de Oliveira replacing "Francisca, parda, slave of...," as she was commonly described in earlier documents.

After the birth of Francisca de Paula in 1755 came João in 1756, the chief heir of his homonymous father.[60] In 1757, Chica gave birth to Rita,[61] and then to Joaquim two years later.[62] Antônio Caetano was born in 1761, with Ana,[63] Helena,[64] and Luísa[65] all following in sequence. Maria was born on January 22, 1766, though she was baptized in February, and Quitéria Rita arrived in 1767,[66] followed by Mariana in 1769,[67] though Antônia had likely preceded her in 1768, while José Agostinho followed a year after Mariana, in 1770, as we know that he was still living in Tejuco with his mother in 1774, being far too young to study abroad like his elder brothers.[68]

As soon as a baby was born, it was washed, swaddled – a habit that all too often resulted in suffocation or atrophy – and wrapped in cloth (normally lacework and ribbon if the family was wealthy). Other common accessories were swathes and bonnets, which protected the child from the cold and draughts. Wet nurses recruited from puerperal slave women helped breastfeed and take care of the newborns. From what can be gathered, the first slave Chica purchased was a wet nurse for her firstborn daughter Francisca de Paula, who was suckled by Ana, whose son Manuel had been born toward the end of 1754.[69]

---

[58] AEAD. Livro de batizados do arraial do Tejuco. 1745–1765, caixa 297, f. 42v.
[59] ANTT. Cartórios notariais. Livro 300, fls. 28v–34v.
[60] AEAD. Livro de batizados do arraial do Tejuco. 1745–1765, caixa 297, f. 47v.
[61] Ibidem, f. 55.
[62] Ibidem, f. 74.
[63] Ibidem, f. 85v.
[64] Ibidem, f. 89v.
[65] Ibidem, f. 98v. ARM. Livro de registros de saídas do recolhimento. 1781, s.n.
[66] ARM. Livro de registros de saídas do recolhimento. 1781, s.n.
[67] AEAD. Livro de batizados do arraial do Tejuco. 1769–1780, caixa 297, f. 84.
[68] AHU, MAMG. Caixa 108, doc. 9, f. 2.
[69] AEAD. Livro de batizados do arraial do Tejuco. 1745–1765. Caixa 297, f. 42v.

By the time Rita Quitéria was born, Chica had three slaves to feed her: Rita parda, who had just given birth to Maria, goddaughter of the little Simão Pires Sardinha[70]; Ana Mina, mother of Sotério, godson of Maria da Costa, Chica's mother[71]; and Catarina, who had given birth to a little girl she named Francisca.[72] In 1759, when Joaquim was born, the slave who had breastfed Francisca de Paula had just given birth to a little boy named Antônio.[73]

The close sequence in which she had her children and the fact that she gave birth at regular intervals throughout the sixteen years she lived with the chief judge indicate that Chica, like the white ladies of her time, did not breastfeed her other children as she had her first child, Simão, born while she was still a slave. Indeed, Chica was not to become pregnant again for another three years after his birth. The fact that newborns were breastfed by wet nurses should not be interpreted as a lack of care on the part of the mothers, but as a way of fulfilling the role reserved for ladies of the upper classes – that of generating numerous offspring in order to guarantee the perpetuation of the family line.

The name chosen for a child was normally based on religious and family traditions and was intended either as a sign of devotion to a saint or as a tribute to a relative or godparent. The name was also what introduced the child into the family, the source of his or her identity until adult life. The first names chosen by Chica and João Fernandes – Francisca de Paula, João, Rita Quitéria, Joaquim, Antônio Caetano, Ana Quitéria, Helena, Luísa Maria, Maria, Quitéria Rita, Antônia Maria, Mariana de Jesus, and José Agostinho – reaffirm family ties and suggest an attempt to establish an authentic family, albeit one not consecrated in the official rites of matrimony. The records show that the chief judge's sisters were named Ana Quitéria, Maria Margarida, Rita Isabel, Helena Leocádia, and Francisca Joaquina.[74] He himself was named after both his father and grandfather, while his mother's name was Maria de São

[70] Ibidem, f. 53v.
[71] Ibidem, f. 53.
[72] Ibidem, f. 53v.
[73] Ibidem, f. 76.
[74] ANTT. Cartórios notariais. Livro 300, fls. 28v–34v.

José. On Chica's side, her father was Antônio Caetano, her mother Maria, and her (probable) sister, Rita.

The saints featured prominently in popular Portuguese tradition. It was believed that they were part of the family and many were treated with intimate devotion.[75] In his will, Sergeant Major João Fernandes de Oliveira claimed to be a devotee of Saint John the Baptist, Saint Anne, the Virgin Mary, Saint Rita, Saint Francis de Paul, Saint Joachim, and Saint Anthony.[76] For his part, in honor of his grandmother, a devotee of Saint Joseph, the chief judge added São José (Saint Joseph) to the names of some of his nine daughters[77] – just like his mother and some aunts (all nuns) before them.

All of Chica's children were baptized at Santo Antônio church, the parish church of Tejuco, situated in the central square on Rua Direita. Baptism, the sacrament that marks a child's entrance into the Catholic religion, was preferably conferred within eight days of birth. As with all public ceremonies at the time, it was a moment in which to flaunt one's social status through pomp and ceremony and the pedigree of the guests in attendance.

Wrapped in new and elaborate shawls, like "the damask baptismal mantle with three silver hems … and baptismal sprays" the Inquisition confiscated from the merchant Belquior Mendes Correia in Bahia,[78] the infant was immersed in the baptismal font by the celebrant who then summoned the godparents to lay their hands upon the child as he issued the customary warning: "As guarantors before God of the preservation of this infant in the faith … as his spiritual parents, it is your obligation to instruct [the child] in Christian doctrine and good conduct."[79] The godparent's function was not, however, exclusively spiritual; bonds of godparentage were another way

---

[75] Gilberto Freyre, op. cit., pp. viii–ix. Ver também Laura de Mello e Souza. *The devil and the land of the holy cross*, 2003.

[76] ANTT. Cartórios notariais. Livro 300, fls. 28v–34v.

[77] Ibidem.

[78] Anita Novinsky. *Inquisição; inventários de bens conquistados a cristãos-novos*, 1976, p. 65.

[79] *Constituições primeiras do arcebispado da Bahia*.Livro Primeiro, título 18, 1853, p. 26.

of establishing or strengthening social alliances that were important in times of difficulty, as illustrated by the relationship between João Fernandes and the governor Gomes Freire de Andrade.

During the third diamond contract, won by Felisberto Caldeira Brant and his partner Alberto Luís Pereira, the baptism of their children was a clear pretext for establishing ties with the key figures of Minas Gerais. Alberto's daughters Ana and Teresa, baptized in Tejuco in 1750 and 1752 respectively, were both godchildren of Gomes Freire de Andrade, who sent representatives to the ceremonies rather than attend in person. However, he did make an appearance at the baptism of Teresa, one of Felisberto's daughters, as whose godfather he was also chosen.[80] Later, during the disputes between the contract partners and the intendant Sancho de Andrade e Lanções, Gomes Freire de Andrade proved a loyal ally, positioning himself in favor of the contractors and thus repaying their demonstrations of friendship and honoring the bonds established through their children. When he left for the south in 1752, the ex-governor installed his brother José Antonio Freire de Andrade as interim governor and, siding with Caldeira Brant once again, warned him to be careful with the intendant who he described as "a minister very badly thought of at the ministry."[81]

The baptismal records of Tejuco show that this amicable relationship was not only long-standing but extended beyond the deaths of those involved. A curious fact in terms of the morals of the day is that Manuel Pires Sardinha was chosen as Francisca de Paula's godfather. Chica's former owner had been the attorney on the second diamond contract, on which he served as Sergeant Major João Fernandes de Oliveira's guarantor, which would indicate that they had a relationship of trust and belonged to the same circle of friends.[82] The bonds of godparentage soon sealed the reciprocal commitments inherent in this relationship. In 1756, in another

---

[80] Ibidem, f. 29v.
[81] "Instruções que o governador Gomes Freire de Andrade...." *Revista do Arquivo Público Mineiro*, vol. 4, 1899, p. 374.
[82] AHU, MAMG. Caixa 60, maço 29.

manifestation of this friendship, Chica and the physician were chosen as the godparents of Rosa, the daughter of the slave Maria parda
and the surgeon José Gomes Ferreira.[83] We can be sure that Chica
inherited assets from her former owner, as the inventory of Sergeant
Major José da Silva de Oliveira of 1796 reveals that she was called
upon to settle outstanding debts to the tune of 28,856 reis that
Manuel Pires Sardinha had with the sergeant major, of which 3,000
was registered as having been paid.[84]

Analysis of the names of those chosen to baptize Chica da Silva
and João Fernandes's children reveals the absence of authorities from
either the captaincy or the district. We could expect someone in his
position to have at least chosen the diamond intendant, an expedient the contractors often used to win the grace of the most important local representative of Portugal. The godparents chosen for little
João were José da Silva de Oliveira and his wife, Rosa, both long-
standing friends of the judge's father. Sergeant Major João Fernandes himself had been a sponsor at the couple's wedding[85] and was the
godfather of their son José,[86] demonstrating once again how personal
ties so frequently extended into business.

In a bid to strengthen family bonds, the chief judge chose Ventura Fernandes de Oliveira, a cousin on his father's side who had
settled in Vila Rica, to be Joaquim's godfather, while Colonel José
Velho Barreto, a farm owner and wholesaler from Tejuco, was chosen to godfather Rita.[87] All the others were local low-ranking military officers: Sergeant Major Antônio Araújo de Freitas baptized
Antônio Caetano, whose name was at once a tribute to himself and
to Chica's father, while Captain Luís Lopes da Costa was godfather
to Ana, Helena, and Luísa (the latter's godmother was Donna Mariana Lemes de Assunção). Lastly, Captains Francisco Malheiros and
Luís de Mendonça Cabral were chosen to sponsor Mariana.

---

[83] AEAD. Livro de batizados do arraial do Tejuco. 1745–1765, caixa 297, f. 49.
[84] BAT. Testamento de José da Silva de Oliveira. 1796–1797. Cartório do Primeiro
Ofício, maço 28.
[85] AEAD. Livro de casamentos do arraial do Tejuco. 1746–1811, caixa 335, f. 5v.
[86] This would be the priest Rolim, who was involved in the Inconfidência Mineira.
[87] AEAD. Livro de batizados do arraial do Tejuco. 1745–1765, caixa 297, f. 55.

While the choice of names was anchored in the past and in family traditions, the baptismal records point toward the future and show that the choice of godparents was a way of honoring the bonds a couple had formed in the village society and which could be relied upon whenever necessary, as they constituted reciprocal commitments. If, on the one hand, these ties of godparentage prove that the illicit relationship between Chica and João Fernandes was accepted by the local society, they also show that the chief judge was barred from using these family ceremonies to establish relationships that extended beyond the village or to forge connections with the most important authorities of the captaincy and mining society, most notably with the governor. They also reveal the paradoxical forms in which this family, like so many others, was to insert itself within the mining society elite during the eighteenth and nineteenth centuries.

CHAPTER FIVE

THE LADY OF TEJUCO

Not even Saint Ifigênia,
in full feast day gleam,
outshines the negress
in all her riches.

THE HOUSE AND THE STREET

In 1754, now free and bearing the surname Silva, Chica was the owner of a house and slaves. According to the village baptismal records, the birth of the daughter of her slave Ana took place at her house.[1] During the *de genere* process for Simão Pires Sardinha's admittance into the Order of Christ, the deponents in Lisbon affirmed that the subject's mother was an important person who lived "in the greatest ostentation, the lady of a large house,"[2] basking "in the light of nobility and great wealth."

The house of Chica da Silva, visited "by people of the highest order, from the government and the judiciary,"[3] was on Ópera Street,[4] now Lalau Pires Street, on which the free and the freed, white and black, lived side by side, blurring the hierarchical boundaries by which the mining society sought to order itself. The street took its name from the opera house constructed on it, the oldest in

---

[1]   AEAD. Livro de batizados do arraial do Tejuco. 1745–1765, caixa 297, f. 42v.
[2]   ANTT. Habilitações da Ordem de Cristo. Letra s. Maço 5, doc.5, f. 10 e ss.
[3]   Ibidem, f. 9.
[4]   AHU, MAMG. Caixa 108, doc. 9, f. 2.

Minas Gerais.[5] In 1774 Chica's neighbors were João Antônio Maria Versiane and João Machado Pena, the bookkeeper and notary of the Royal Diamond Extractor. The former, white and married, lived as a tenant, though he later purchased two houses on Rua Direita, near the parish church. In addition to these houses, his will also lists a farm, a tile-roofed house in Bananal, eight slaves, various valuables such as gold, stones, and china, and large sums of money to be received from the Royal Diamond Extractor.[6] Rua da Ópera was also home to Antônia Xavier, an ex-slave of Manuel Pires Sardinha, like Chica; a black woman called Ana Maria de Jesus; the creole tailor Vicente Ferreira; and the carpenter Antônio Pinto Guimarães.[7]

There is no doubt that this house belonged to Chica and not to the chief judge. Among other documents, the residential census of Tejuco conducted in 1774 registers Chica as the owner of the property where she lived in the company of one son.[8]

Chica da Silva was not the only ex-slave who owned urban property in Tejuco. In Chapter 1, in which we approached the socioeconomic context in the Diamantine Demarcation, we spoke of the residential census of 1774, which registered a total of 510 residences, 229 of which were headed by free or freed women.[9] Of the 282 male family heads, only 89 were black; that is, a mere 31.5 percent. The situation was reversed when it came to women, who accounted for 197 of the abovementioned total, an overwhelming 86 percent. Of the 32 white female family heads, 9 were widows and thus only held that position in virtue of their husbands' deaths, while one, Ana Perpétua Marcelina da Fonseca, assumed charge of her household after her husband, the physician Luís José de Figueiredo, was expelled

---

[5] In 1770, Count Valadares lamented some disorder that occurred at the Tejuco Opera House, which shows the opera house already existed at this time. Belo Horizonte, APM. Seção Colonial. 176, f. 24.

[6] Júnia Furtado. O livro da capa verde, 1996, p. 49.

[7] AHU, MAMG. Caixa 108, doc. 9, f. 2.

[8] Ibidem.

[9] Ibidem, fls. 1–9.

from the Diamantine Demarcation under accusations of diamond smuggling.[10]

One fact that stands out in an analysis of the profile of the Tejuco family head is the numerical balance between white men (193, or 37.7 percent) and freed black women (197, or 38.5 percent), a factor that reveals the latter's paradoxical economic ascension and status.

The distribution of properties belonging to whites, blacks, and mestizos was not homogeneous. The whites were the majority on Rua Direita, Rua Quitanda (where the merchants congregated), Caval-hada Nova, and Amparo, all of which were more central streets. That said, Rua Direita, the main street of the village, was home to Maria Carvalha and Josefa Maria de Freitas, both black; Inês Maria de Azevedo and Mariana Pereira, both parda;[11] and Teresa Feliz, another black woman, who owned one of the tile-roofed houses.[12]

The mansion of wood and adobe in which Chica da Silva lived was a solid, ample, and airy construction that consisted of a two-story square-shaped main building with lath and plaster partitions and a backyard. It was entirely whitewashed except for its tiled roof and balconies, windows, and colored wooden slats. The three jalousie windows and doorway that led into the entrance hall comprised the façade of the first floor, which functioned as the service area and slave quarters. From the ground floor entrance hall, a stairway led to the upper floor where the main rooms were located.

This second floor contained a large living room with four doors and balconies facing onto the street, allowing in light and air. At one of the far ends, a door opened onto a lateral veranda, which meant it could receive natural light and ventilation without having to leave the street-facing balcony doors open. The veranda was encased in a delicate Moorish-style trellis that protected the interior from outside view, thus preserving domestic privacy while also ensuring the comfort of the social spaces.[13] The more private enclosures of the house

---

[10] Junia Furtado. *O livro da capa verde*. 1996, p. 98.
[11] AHU, MAMG. Caixa 108, doc. 9, f. 1.
[12] AEAD. Livro de óbitos do arraial do Tejuco. Caixa 521, f. 48.
[13] http://www.iphan.gov.br/bancodados/mostrabenstombados.asp?CodBem=1297.

opened onto a rear balcony overlooking a garden patio with its own entrance.

In 1784, the location at which this house was built was still somewhat on the outer rim of the central urban nucleus of the village. A street plan of Tejuco produced at the time shows Chica's house and gardens, with an orchard at the back. The green of the village's gardens contrasted against the darker tones of the moss-green lawns and dark browns of the craggy rock that surrounded the buildings.[14] Oranges, bananas, peaches, jaboticaba, figs, and quince were grown in the orchard and used to complement the residents' diet, especially in the form of desserts. The vegetable garden abounded with cabbage, lettuce, chicory, potato, and medicinal herbs. The garden, which was laid out symmetrically, was mostly used to plant carnations.[15] Seasonal plants were interspersed, with violets predominating in August, followed by windflowers in September, and yellow-eyed grass, scabiosa, daisies, and pansies in October and November. Asparagus was also grown in the garden, its leaves mixed in among the flower stalks, which were picked to adorn the tables of the house.[16]

The residence also had its own chapel, dedicated to Saint Quitéria, in which two of Chica's daughters were to marry. Having a private chapel was a rare privilege in the village, one Chica shared with only Bernardo da Fonseca Lobo, credited by the Crown as the official discoverer of the diamonds, and Maria de Sousa da Encarnação, a black lady from the Coast of Mina. The chapel was almost entirely destroyed, and all that remains of it today is the façade. The altar is believed to have been transferred to the church of Nossa Senhora das Dores in Gouveia. In 1774, the priest responsible for celebrating mass there was Father Manuel da Costa Dantas.[17]

Saint Quitéria was one of the saints to which Sergeant Major João Fernandes de Oliveira was devoted, and he named one of his

[14] A. de Saint-Hilare. *Viagem pelo Distrito dos Diamantes e litoral do Brasil.* 1974, p. 27.
[15] Ibidem, p. 28.
[16] Ibidem, pp. 31–3.
[17] AHU, MAMG. Caixa 108, doc. 9, f. 1.

daughters, Ana Quitéria de São José, in her honor, as was common practice at the time. The chief judge and Chica da Silva professed the same devotion, which they manifested not only by building and con-secrating the chapel to this saint, but also by giving her name to three of their daughters: Quitéria Rita, Ana Quitéria (cited previously), and Rita Quitéria. Saint Quitéria lived in what is modern-day Por-tugal during the expansion of the Roman Empire. She converted to Christianity against her parents' wishes and swore herself to the Lord and to preserve her virginity after being visited by an angel. Intent on making her go through with their proposed marriage, she was fol-lowed to her place of retreat and contemplation by her betrothed, Germano, who martyred her when she refused to seal their union. Saint Quitéria was venerated in the eighteenth century in virtue of the many miracles accredited to her.[18] On the decorative tile façade of the Fernandes de Oliveira family manor in Lisbon, the saint was represented by the palm of a hand, the symbol of her martyrdom.

The interior of the two-story house on Rua da Ópera would have been furnished much like the other residences of Tejuco. While there is no list of Chica's furnishings and belongings, some information about the tastes and objects with which the houses of the day were adorned can be found in the wills and inventories of her descen-dants and other inhabitants of the village. Furniture was generally sparse, as it was acquired more by practical necessity than for any decorative effect. There would have been tables of various sizes, some with drawers; chairs, benches, and tabourets covered in leather or canvas; chests and trunks; bottle racks; and, occasionally, wardrobes for storing clothes and other personal objects.

The interiors were lit with candle lamps spread throughout the house. There would have been poster beds made from rosewood, adorned with canopies and curtains and with a hair-stuffed mattress as a base, though there would also have been truckle beds and even canvas foldup beds, or so-called wind beds. A small number of houses

---

[18]   Vida y leyenda de santa Quitéria: wysiwg://316/htp://www.fortunecity.es/felices/ lapaz/78/vida.htm; santa Quiteria: http://www.terravista.pt/Enseada/2362/ Santa%20Quitéria.html.

would also have had divanlike "stretchers," large bathtubs, mirrors, chests of drawers, couches, and bookshelves.[19] Captain João Azevedo Pereira, a resident on Rua do Rosário, possessed various tables with tabourets, a cotton-curtained cot bed and a door curtain.[20] In 1797 Colonel Paulo José Velho, an important local figure and godfather of Chica's daughter Rita, owned ten slaves and a select library. His inventory lists five tables, including one dining rosewood table, six tabourets upholstered in sole leather, twelve chairs, a wardrobe, a large rosewood cot bed, bookstands, and a closet.[21]

At the Buriti farmhouse, João Fernandes's rural property in the vicinity of São Gonçalo do Rio Preto, there were three leather cot beds, one divan, a carved rosewood bed, rosewood chairs and mocho stools,[22] three tables, and six tabourets in carved wood and leather. Curiously, the list of furnishings and items at the farmhouse also includes "eyeglasses for seeing into the distance," a novelty recently brought over from Europe.[23] The furniture at another of his farms, located close to Buriti at Pé do Morro in the Diamantine Demarcation, was likewise simple, consisting of a canopy bed with silk bedspread, three cotton covers, three hair-stuffed mattresses, four tables with drawers, a box of gold-tinted glassware, a crockery stand, and a wardrobe.[24] When Ana Quitéria inherited Chica's house on the Rua Bonfim junction, there was a bunk and a carved rosewood table, eight high-backed chairs, another three chairs covered in sole leather, a white wood chest of drawers, and such wooden items as a

---

[19] Inventories from the late eighteenth century and the early nineteenth century from the Antônio Torres Library mention wall clocks, which would have been a recent invention at the time.

[20] BAT. Inventário de João de Azevedo Pereira (capitão). Cartório do Primeiro Ofício, maço 27.

[21] BAT. Inventário de Paulo José Velho Barreto (coronel). Cartório do Primeiro Ofício, maço 63.

[22] Bench with no arms to be seated only by one person.

[23] BAT. Inventário de Rita Quitéria de São José. Cartório do Primeiro Ofício, maço 63, f. 4; inventário de Bento Dias Chaves. Cartório do Primeiro Ofício, maço 13, f. 18v.

[24] BAT. Inventário de Francisca de Paula Fernandes de Oliveira. Cartório do Primeiro Ofício, maço 23.

leather-upholstered divan and storage chests. Some of these objects were most likely also inherited from her mother.[25]

The black woman Jacinta de Siqueira, from Vila do Príncipe, like Chica and the other freedwomen, followed the standards set by the village's white elite when it came to furnishing her residence. Jacinta's furniture, for example, included a sideboard,[26] three large chests, a cupboard, a dining table, and one plain and one carved rosewood cot complete with curtain, silk bedspread, and linen sheets and pillowcases.[27] In Tejuco, the parda Antônia de Oliveira Silva had a cot made of white wood with cotton curtain, three tables, a trunk, a wooden chest, and five leather tabourets.[28]

However, the table utensils and ornaments in the houses of Tejuco were much more sophisticated than the few items of furniture scattered about their rooms. Meals were frequently served in blue, white, and glazed English and Indian china; brass, gold, silver, and glass cutlery and tableware; glass and crystal bottles and drinking vessels; copper or wooden platters; coffeepots and teapots, as well as tin, earthenware, and silver plates; and silver kettles, soup tureens, and salvers.[29]

Filipe José Correia Lacerda, who died in 1794, left behind twenty-two Indian plates, seven china bowls and plates, some tin plates, seven items of silver cutlery, and a table and glassware set.[30] Manuel Pires de Figueiredo owned eighteen iron tablespoons, knives, and forks; eleven teaspoons; and a glass case with another set of knives, forks, and spoons accompanied by a large supply of English and Macau chinaware.[31] Friar João de Freitas Sampaio's furniture was

[25] BAT. Inventário de Rita Quitéria de São José. Cartório do Primeiro Ofício, maço 63, fls. 9v–10.
[26] According to the electronic dictionary Houaiss, it would be "a kind of wardrobe or table used in dinning rooms to settle the meal."
[27] AFS. Testamento de Jacinta de Siqueira. Livro de testamentos no. 8, fls. 33v–38v.
[28] AEAD. Livro de óbitos do arraial do Tejuco. 1752–1895, caixa 350, fls. 162v–163.
[29] A kind of dish, plate, or tray on which to put glasses or drinking cups, and so forth.
[30] BAT. Inventário de Filipe José Correia Lacerda. Cartório do Primeiro Ofício, maço 21.
[31] BAT. Inventário de Manuel Pires de Figueiredo. Cartório do Primeiro Ofício, maço 60.

sparse and rustic. Among the items the cleric owned were a foldup bed and cover, seventeen tabourets, a six-piece silver cutlery set, two pairs of tin spoons, and an assortment of dishes for his daily use.[32]

At the end of the eighteenth century, the habit of eating with one's hands was still widespread (people used to roll their food into mouth-sized balls), though the recurrent presence of cutlery on inventory lists, often accompanied by the phrase "for his/her use," indicates that table manners were becoming more refined and that the elite was already using knives, forks, and spoons at meals. There was a cutlery set at the Buriti farm, along with a tumbler, a silver salver, an Indian chinaware soup tureen, and various plates.[33] The inventories taken at the Pé do Morro property list silver candlesticks, tin plates, and an array of gold-trimmed white enameled china, which might suggest that some ceramic production was going on inside the captaincy. One of Chica's granddaughters inherited some Indian chinaware and a box of gold-tinted glassware that had belonged to her mother and perhaps even her grandmother before her.[34]

This refinement at the table was not exclusive to the white population. Colored women also owned fine tableware, including silver cutlery and salvers, fine china, and crystal glasses and decanters. The tables and beds of the freedwomen of Tejuco and the surrounding areas did not feature only such common cloths as cotton, but also fine fabrics like linen and silk. Thus the clothes iron was an essential household utensil, and evidence of its use can be found in many houses throughout the village, especially those of the free ladies and the freedwomen who would have used it to provide ironing services. The parda Bernardina Maria da Conceição owned nine tin plates and two of Indian china; two spoons, two forks, and a knife, all in silver; as well as various others in brass. She also had a cot bed of carved

---

[32] BAT. Inventário de João de Freitas Sampaio (padre). Cartório do Primeiro Ofício, maço 29.

[33] BAT. Inventário de Francisca de Paula Fernandes de Oliveira. Cartório do Primeiro Ofício, maço 23.

[34] BAT. Inventário de João Germano de Oliveira. Cartório do Primeiro Ofício, maço 27, f. 45.

wood.[35] Another parda, Antônia de Oliveira e Silva, laid her table with silver spoons and forks and a silver cooler,[36] while the creole Inês Fernandes Neves had three tablecloths with which to adorn her table.[37]

The kitchen was equipped with countless, often very specific utensils. There were chocolate kettles, basins for sponge cake, pots of various shapes and sizes, almost always made of copper or brass and used to prepare breads and desserts, as well as forms for baking flour, pot stands, pestles, skewers, grills, grain pounders, skimming ladles, caldrons, pails, and even alembics. Many of these accoutrements equipped João Fernandes's farmhouses, with inventories listing copper pots and pans of various sizes, caldrons, pestles, basins, skimming ladles, brass candlesticks, and chocolate kettles.[38] Jacinta de Siqueira refined the palate of her guests with sponge cakes and fine chocolate melted in her own kettle. Liquor and juice were served in crystal decanters and glasses;[39] the table was covered in lacework and fine linen tablecloths with matching napkins, topped off with silver cutlery and Indian chinaware.

Local inventories also give an idea of the kinds of food that graced the tables of Tejuco in the late eighteenth century. Between July 1793 and October 1796, Ana Perpétua Marcelina da Fonseca, the widow of José Luís de Figueiredo, kept meticulous records of everything consumed at her house so she could present accounts to her dead husband's executors. According to her records, beef was the staple of the local diet, and bacon and giblets were a frequent presence at meal time, as were corn meal, corn, corn flour, beans, sugar, salt, cheese, rice, and, to a lesser degree, vegetables and

---

[35] AEAD. Livro de óbitos do arraial do Tejuco. 1752–1895, caixa 350, fls. 38v–40.
[36] Large earthenware pots filled with cold water used for cooling foods and beverages.
[37] BAT. Inventário de Inês Fernandes Neves. Cartório do Primeiro Ofício, maço 26.
[38] BAT. Inventário de Francisca de Paula Fernandes de Oliveira. Cartório do Primeiro Ofício, maço 23; inventário de Rita Quitéria de São José. Cartório do Primeiro Ofício, maço 63.
[39] AFS. Testamento de Jacinta de Siqueira. Livro de testamentos no. 8, fls. 33v–38v.

greens, vinegar, sweet olive oil, royal butter, and sun-dried meats. Tea, peanuts, and marmalade were consumed in small quantities, though this certainly does not reflect the consumption of these products in the more affluent households of the village, as the inventory is after all that of a widow trying to control her expenses so that she can prove to her husband's executors that she is capable of running her household. It was probably for this reason that Ana Perpétua did not purchase any chocolate during this period, despite possessing a chocolate kettle, as did many in the village. In terms of special supplies, there were bread and chicken for the ill and fish and cod for holy days. The slaves ate the heads and intestines of the slaughtered animals mixed with maize and washed down with cachaça,[40] a strong white rum. Ordinary olive oil was burned in the brass or copper oil lamps used to light the exterior of the house on feast days.

Gold and silver religious images and oratories were indispensable artifacts that not only indicated the material culture of their owners, but also their devotions. Some freedwomen had expensive and sophisticated small portable oratories, but most were content with plainer iron, brass, or glass versions. The saint that drew the most devotion was Our Lady of the Conception, the very figure that would later adorn the ceiling above the main altar of the São Francisco de Assis church in Tejuco and the tile-decorated façade of the Fernandes de Oliveira family home in Lisbon. Bernardina Maria da Conceição and Joana de Carvalho both hung gilded images of this saint from chains, while Josefa da Costa da Visitação possessed gilded images of both Our Lady of the Conception and the baby Jesus.[41] An image belonging to another of Our Lady of the Conception's devotees, Maria de Azevedo, took the form of a "sheet of glass."[42] Rita Vieira de Matos kept a brass religious image and crucifix in her oratory, while Jacinta de Siqueira boasted five oratories at her house stocked with gold images of Christ, Our Lady of the Mercies and

---

[40] Cachaça – Brazilian typical alcohool drink made by sugarcane.
[41] AEAD. Livro de óbitos do arraial do Tejuco. 1752–1895, caixa 350, fls. 32v, 38v–40, 166–167.
[42] BAT. Cartório do Primeiro Ofício, maço 58.

Saint Anne, another of Our Lady with a golden crown, and finally
Saint Anthony wearing a crown of silver.[43] Among the religious
iconography at the Buriti farmhouse were an image of Our Lady of
the Pains, an inlaid Jerusalem cross, a glass image of Saint Gonçalo,
another of Our Lady at the foot of the cross, and a panel depicting
the Holy Shroud.[44]

In such a hierarchical society as Tejuco, everything external was a
sign of the individual's social standing. It was for precisely this reason
that the freedwomen took great pains to dress luxuriously, whether
to attend a ceremony or to take a simple stroll in the village. After
all, life passed before the eyes of all and contact in public spaces was
always an opportunity to reaffirm the social roles that fell to each
individual. The Count of Galveias, governor of Minas from 1732,
was horrified by the behavior he witnessed from the women of Tejuco
who, "irreverent," dared "enter the House of God clad in pompous
garments entirely unbefitting of their condition."[45] What upset the
governor was that by appropriating the clothes and finery hitherto
exclusive to the white ladies the freed black and mulatto women of
the village were turning the social order on its head.

From time to time the king issued new regulations determining
what fabrics and adornments each social class could use. There were
laws, such as the Pragmatic Legislation of 1748, specifically designed
to pare back exaggerated trends in dress, though these were rarely
obeyed. In 1749, João V issued a law permitting all those holding
posts above the rank of second lieutenant to

> [wear] gold or silver lace on their hats and plain gold or silver but-
> tons on their garments, while on the saddlery of their horses they
> may use golden or silver metals with great moderation and gold or
> silver lace on their saddlecloth and holsters, though only around
> the border and without any patterns.[46]

---

[43] AFS. Testamento de Jacinta de Siqueira. Livro de testamentos no. 8, fls. 33v–38v.
[44] BAT. Inventário de Bento Dias Chaves. Cartório do Primeiro Ofício, maço 13.
[45] Bando do governador de 2 de dezembro de 1933. Apud: Xavier da Veiga.
  Efemérides mineiras. 1998, p. 1026.
[46] Antônio Delgado Silva. *Coleção de legislação portuguesa,* vol. (1750–1762), 1842,
  p. 13.

Sunday mass was the main social forum in which to see and be seen. While on a pastoral visit to Tejuco in 1777, Father José Justino de Oliveira Godim reprimanded the villagers for

> the little respect and great irreverence with which many people behave when in the house of the Lord, where one should keep the profoundest silence and deference; with all present lost in [illicit, scandalous] conversation while celebrating the most sacred mysteries of our redemption.[47]

The spectacle would begin when Chica and the other women of Tejuco, free or emancipated, dressed in lavish and luxurious garb, left for the church in sedan chairs[48] trailed by a retinue of slaves. It was up to the owners to facilitate access to the Catholic sacraments for their slaves, though having them arrive for church service carrying the master's wife was useful in underlining the lady's public position. This was not a privilege exclusive to Chica, but was something practiced throughout the region, much to the displeasure of the governor who lamented that the women of color "[were] not content to travel in sedan-chairs and pole couches" on the way to the chapels.[49] An edict published in Olinda in 1726 by the Bishop Friar José Fialho denounced the indecency with which certain women entered the church, carried in sedan chairs and portable hammocks and dressed in the most diabolical and profane attire.[50]

As the items listed in her inventories would indicate, Chica took the same care as the freewomen when it came to dress. Her wardrobes and clothes chests were replete with dresses, petticoats, capes, shoes, vests, buckles, clothes brushes, and skirts cut from fine, colored fabrics. The merchant Francisco da Cruz, after some time trading in Minas Gerais, made various observations about the particularities of the local market. Concerning the colors of fabrics, for example, he

---

[47] AEAD. Lançamento de pastorais e capítulos de visitas dos bispos da freguesia da Vila do Príncipe do bispado de Mariana. 1745–1844, caixa 557, fls. 32–32v.
[48] BAT. Cartório do Primeiro Ofício, maço 52.
[49] Bando do governador de 2 de dezembro de 1933. Apud: Xavier da Veiga, op. cit., p. 1026.
[50] Gilberto Freyre. *The Masters and the Slaves*, 1946.

remarked that "green and blue were the most common,"[51] a preference he explained by the fact that much of his stock was sold to blacks and slaves who favored strong colors to lighter tones.

Generally speaking, Chica's wardrobe was rich and colorful, featuring matching white stockings and underskirts for volume, ornate silk shoes with silver buckles, and colored gems. The skirts, made from silk or some such material, were always of a vibrant color, either striped or floral, and accompanied by camlet or cotton blouses in tones of green, red, or white. There was an array of accessories, including tall hats, gold earrings studded with precious and sparkling gems, collars, and amulets for protection. In her hands she would have carried a fan of white feathers, which she left to the village hospital.[52] To protect from the mist and morning chill, Chica would have used a golden or colored cape, lending an air of distinction and power to her appearance.

The creole woman Inês Fernandes Neves was sufficiently well decked out to be able to attend Sunday mass in full pomp. Her wardrobe contained two satin skirts, a camlet vest, a tall hat, two capes, one of embroidered baize and the other of duroy, and two pairs of silk shoes adorned with silver buckles. She also had various gold necklaces, with one neck chain bearing a gold image of Our Lady of the Conception. Her earrings were of diamond, as was the ornamental bow she also wore.[53] The black woman Rita Vieira Matos wore a golden cape over a duroy skirt and frilled petticoat, topped off with stockings and a hat. As a finishing touch, she used a set of gold earrings, a silver ring, and various gems.[54] Another black woman, Maria de Azevedo, wore a blue satin cape over a silk skirt, while Ana da Encarnação Amorim, also black, in addition to a single satin skirt, possessed a frilled petticoat, Braga hat, scarlet cape, a pair of gold earrings, and a gold neck chain.[55]

---

[51] Lisboa. Hospital São José. Testamentaria de Francisco Pinheiro. Carta 153, maço 29, f. 149.
[52] Belo Horizonte, AAPAH.
[53] BAT. Cartório do Primeiro Ofício, maço 26.
[54] BAT. Cartório do Primeiro Ofício, maço 65.
[55] Ibidem, maços 58 e 4.

Jewels and items in gold and silver were outward signs of wealth that the women paraded around their necks and waists and in their hair. The black women liked to wear various gold chains around their necks and hips, from which they hung gold rosary beads, precious stones, and other trinkets.[56] Among the most common accessories were chains with gemstones, necklaces, trinkets made from precious gems, and images of saints worn on neck chains. Among the belongings listed in the inventory of Bernardina Maria da Conceição were a gold image of Our Lady of the Conception, two gold collars, two earrings and a diamond neck chain, a string of gold beads, a chain, and a pair of gold earrings that she gave to a priest to sell.[57] The black woman Josefa da Costa da Visitação owned a collar, buttons, rosary beads, and a gold conception medal,[58] as well as a pair of diamond earrings.[59] A priest named Father Antonil expressed dismay that so much of the gold extracted from the mines of Minas Gerais ended up in "necklaces, earrings and other trinkets more often seen today adorning blacks and mulattas of ill-repute than the white ladies of society."[60] In 1773, Chica gave a pair of gold earrings as alms to the Brotherhood of the Rosary, of which she was a sister.[61] In similar fashion, Teresa Feliz left her most valuable gold chain to the same brotherhood.[62]

Rita Quitéria, Chica's daughter, owned a lot of jewelry, probably inherited from her mother. Among the items she is known to have possessed are a silver chain and earrings set with yellow gemstones and studded with small diamonds, two pairs of earrings inlaid with pink stones, two silver flowers with pink and yellow stones, four pairs of gilded silver buttons inset with red stone circles, a silver buckle with white gems, two silver bracelets with gold trimming and set with white gems, and a pair of silver buckles to be worn on the

[56] Gilberto Freyre, op. cit.
[57] AEAD. Livro de óbitos do arraial do Tejuco. 1752/1895, caixa 350, fls. 38v–40.
[58] Gold medal coin that King John IV order to mint in 1650.
[59] AEAD. Livro de óbitos do arraial do Tejuco. 1752–1895, caixa 350, f. 32v.
[60] André João Antonil, op. cit., pp. 194–5.
[61] AEAD. Livro de inventário da Irmandade do Rosário. 1733–1892, caixa 514.
[62] AEAD. Livro de óbitos do arraial do Tejuco. Caixa 521, fls. 48–49.

shoes.[63] At Buriti farm as late as 1833, there are records of a gold-cast medal set with a yellow stone cross,[64] carmine topaz stones topped with yellow stone flowers and cast in silver, a smaller medal cast in French gold, a pair of old white stone buttons cast in silver, and two older buttons in gilded metal with white figures at the center.[65]

In addition to the gold and diamond jewelry, many freedwomen also owned objects made from coral and other stones, considered amulets in African tradition.[66] Bernardina Maria da Conceição[67] possessed an amber ball and thirteen strings of alternated coral and gold beads after the African style, while Antônia de Oliveira Silva had two rings set with Itatiaia stone.[68] Chica da Silva certainly would have carried her bunch of charms, beads, and coral balls and worn a protective amulet around her neck just like the women of color in drawings made by the artist Carlos Julião during his visit to the diamantine region.[69]

Cutlery, accessories, silverware, and jewels all meant investment and price was calculated according to their weight in pure gold and gem-carat value. Often used as pawn, these items constituted an informal system of credit in Minas Gerais. The black woman Ana Maria de Freitas, proprietor of two houses in Tejuco and owner of a stock of jewelry, was a good example of how these artifacts could provide an efficient source of capital, as everything she owned – fourteen buttons, some pure gold, a pair of earrings, and a chain – had been pawned for the sum of fourteen eighths of gold.[70]

According to Joaquim Felício dos Santos, Chica kept her hair cropped and covered in a wig of flowing ringlets.[71] However, the only

---

[63] BAT. Inventário de Rita Quitéria de São José. Cartório do Primeiro Ofício, maço 63, f. 2v.

[64] *Crisólito* is a general name used to describe stones of a golden color.

[65] BAT. Inventário de Bento Dias Chaves. Cartório do Primeiro Ofício, maço 13, fls. 32v–33.

[66] Eduardo Paiva, op. cit., pp. 217–38.

[67] AEAD. Livro de óbitos do arraial do Tejuco. 1752–1895, caixa 350, fls. 38v–40.

[68] AEAD. Livro de óbitos do arraial do Tejuco. 1752–1895, caixa 350, fls. 162v–163.

[69] Carlos Julião. *Riscos iluminados de figurinhos de brancos e negros.* 1960.

[70] AEAD. Livro de óbitos do arraial do Tejuco. Caixa 521, fls. 120–120v.

[71] Joaquim Felício dos Santos. *Memórias do Distrito Diamantino da comarca do Serro do Frio.* 1976, p. 161.

wigs found in inventories from Tejuco did not belong to women, free or freed, but to men – José Pedro de Azevedo; João Vieira Martins, who owned an old wig; and Martinho Alves Chaves, who kept his in a locker.[72] This would indicate that in Tejuco wigs were a piece of eminently male attire. When the merchant Francisco da Cruz arrived in Minas Gerais he was able to sell off the various wigs he had brought over from the Realm with relative ease, save two, one of which was too big while the other was too fair.[73]

Chica would have dressed more simply at home. Women generally wore cotton overalls like those used by Maria Martins Castanheira, Rita Vieira de Matos, and Ana Maria da Encarnação,[74] or cotton skirts like the two listed in Bernardina Maria da Conceição's inventory.[75] Many foreign visitors to Brazil in the eighteenth century expressed their shock at the difference between the women's domestic dress, characterized by its informality and emphasis on comfort, and the garb they used in the streets or at public ceremonies.[76]

The beauty of youthful Brazilian women, whether white, mulatta, or black, enraptured the recently arrived Portuguese, though their sedentary lifestyle and large broods of children quickly undid their shapeliness and stole the luster from their cheeks. The descriptions of Brazilian women given by the European visitors of that century must certainly come close to what Chica would have looked like after bearing thirteen children in the space of fifteen years, even if she did live the life of a lady of the manor, exempt from all manner of manual work.

I did note, however, Mrs. Kindersly, that Brazilian women age rapidly; their faces swiftly turning a sickly yellow. This must

[72] BAT. João Vieira Martins. Cartório do Primeiro Ofício, maço 28; José Pedro de Azevedo. Cartório do Primeiro Ofício, maço 31; Cartório do Primeiro Ofício, maço 53.
[73] Hospital São José. Testamentária de Francisco Pinheiro. Carta 150, maço 29, f. 166.
[74] AEAD. Livro de óbitos do arraial do Tejuco. Caixa 521, fls. 387–388; BAT. Cartório do Primeiro Ofício, maço 65; BAT. Cartório do Primeiro Ofício, maço 4.
[75] AEAD. Livro de óbitos do arraial do Tejuco. 1752–1895, caixa 350, fls. 38v–40.
[76] Maria Graham. *Journal of a voyage to Brazil.* 1824, p. 135.

certainly be the result of the many children they bear their husbands; the sluggish, melancholic, lazy domestic life they lead; and the fact that they only ever go out in sedan-chairs covered with heavy coloured canopies.[77]

During his stay in Rio de Janeiro, John Luccock observed that the girls reached maturity at around the age of eighteen; after which they grew fat, soft, pallid, and double-chinned.[78] Many were shocked by the sluggishness of the ladies' movements. So accustomed were they to spending long hours sitting on mats on the floor, waited on hand and foot by their slaves, that some ladies even developed hip deformities.[79]

Like Chica da Silva and Jacinta de Siqueira, other freedwomen filled their houses with objects that facilitated their insertion into white society. Owning material culture – the furniture, apparel, jewelry, bedclothes, and tableware proper to European society – allowed these women to imitate the behavior, style of dress, and ornamentation of the ladies of the Portuguese elite and thus distance themselves still further from the world of the slave quarters into which they had been born.

SLAVE OWNERSHIP

Donna Francisca da Silva de Oliveira, as Chica is often referred to in the official documents of Tejuco,[80] was not the owner only of a house in the village, but also of a significant number of slaves. This behavior, however strange it may seem to the contemporary eye, was common to all freed people of color who managed to accumulate enough capital. Owning slaves was an essential mechanism in the pursuit of insertion into the world of the free where a disdain for work and for living by one's own graft reigned supreme. Immersed in a society in which the sphere of privacy was restricted and life ran freely

---

[77] Gilberto Freyre, op. cit., p. 345.
[78] John Luccock. *Notas sobre o Rio de Janeiro e partes meridionais do Brasil*. 1975.
[79] Gilberto Freyre, op. cit., pp. 347–8.
[80] AEAD. Livro de batizados do arraial do Tejuco. 1745–1765, caixa 297, f. 77.

through the public space, the freed assumed the values of the whites and sought to emulate them. For Chica, like any other freedwoman, it would have been important to show herself to be the owner of a "grand mansion," which automatically implied possessing "a copious stock of slaves, [allowing her to live] in the light of nobility."[81]

To the modern mind, the thought of a former slave buying other slaves may seem inconceivable, especially when we consider that, as they were mostly Africans, they would have guarded the memory of free life on their home continent, the horror of the slave ships, the separation of families, and their sale like meat at the Brazilian ports; in short, these were women who had themselves suffered all the hardships of slavery. Nevertheless, once living in free society, with no way of going back, their only chance of diminishing the social exclusion and stigma of their origins was to avail of precisely the mechanisms the whites used for their survival and promotion. The first of these mechanisms was to purchase a slave, which enabled the owner to remove herself from the world of work. For the freed-women who registered wills in Tejuco in the eighteenth century, slaves were not only their main source of wealth but also of social affirmation.[82]

Josefa Dias, a black woman from the Coast of Mina and the mother of two captives, used her savings to buy a slave-girl named Quitéria instead of buying the freedom of at least one of her own daughters. Curiously, her daughters' owner was none other than Antônio Fernandes de Oliveira, Chica's son.[83] A look at the last will and testament of Inês Fernandes Neves reveals that many generations of freedmen and women had owned slaves. In her will, Inês – a creole and mistress of four slaves of her own – registers that her parents, João Frutuoso and Joana Fernandes Neves, both Mina blacks, had been the slaves of a pardo and his wife, who was herself a Mina black.[84]

---

[81] ANTT. Habilitações da Ordem de Cristo. Letra s. Maço 5, doc. 5, f. 8.
[82] Ibidem.
[83] AEAD. Livro de óbitos do arraial do Tejuco. Caixa 521, fls. 76v–77.
[84] BAT. Cartório do Primeiro Ofício, maço 26.

Inventories and wills are the prime sources of information that allow us to investigate the number of slaves owned by the gentry. Despite the disappearance of Chica da Silva's will from the Fórum do Serro, we can still ascertain approximately how many slaves she owned.[85] Between 1754 and 1804, many of Chica's slaves were registered in baptismal, death, and marriage records and brotherhood rosters now stored in the Ecclesiastical Archives of the Archdiocese of Diamantina. In spite of some gaps in the information, these records give us a reasonably accurate idea of how many slaves she had, what their occupations were, what their family and social arrangements were like, and how the number of slaves owned would have oscillated over the years.

Chica allowed her slaves to receive all of the Christian sacraments, such as baptism, marriage, last rites, burial on consecrated ground, and participation in local black and mulatto brotherhoods. In the slave society of Portuguese America, one of the obligations of a good master was to guarantee his or her slaves access to the religious sacraments, and the church did its best to punish those who failed to have their slaves baptized, prevented them from attending mass, or denied them the last rites and thus the salvation of their souls.[86] Chica da Silva was therefore a conventional owner, as converting slaves to the Catholic faith was an act of acculturation designed to appropriate the captive into white Portuguese culture.

Baptism marked the slave's insertion into a new religion, though it was a faith to which they were usually converted by force. It was also the rite of passage into a new life in which the adults shipped over from Africa symbolically shed their old name in favor of a new Christian one. Some of Chica da Silva's slaves were baptized as adults, like José, who received the sacrament in 1757, and Manuel one year

---

[85] The historian Xavier da Veiga saw the will, which was unfortunately stolen from the Archives of the Fórum do Serro and has been lost.

[86] "...because there is no reason for ye gentlemen to neglect your obligation to instruct your slaves in [the Catholic doctrine]." *Constituições primeiras do arcebispado da Bahia*, 1853. Capítulo I, título 14, p. 22.

later.[87] In these cases, under canonical law, the slaves had to consent to receiving the sacrament.[88] Slave children like Sotério, son of Ana Mina; Francisca, daughter of Catarina; and Margarida, the daughter of Severina da Costa, were all baptized as newborns.[89]

Some of these slaves formed their own families, which was ideal for the owners, as it meant the slaves adapted more readily to captivity, escaped less frequently, and provided new slaves for the household. Chica's slaves Joaquim pardo and Gertrudes creole, José Mina and Joana Mina, and Francisco Mina and Ana Mina[90] all wed on the same day at the parish church. This last couple had two sons, Sotério and Antônio.[91] Other couples also married, including Rita creole and Antônio creole[92] and Joaquim mina and Clara Maria,[93] whose wedding was conducted and witnessed by Cipriano Pires Sardinha in the presence of Domingos Fernandes de Oliveira.[94]

The mortality rate among slaves, especially children and those employed in the mines, was extremely high. A text titled *Manual do fazendeiro ou tratado doméstico sobre as enfermidades* (*Farmowners' manual or domestic treatise on infirmities*) warned the gentry that many slave women, "almost as soon as the children are born, . . . give [them], from time to time, solid foods from their own plates," a

---

[87] AEAD. Livro de batizados do arraial do Tejuco. 1745–1765, caixa 297, fls. 58, 68.

[88] Luiz Mott. *Rosa Egipcíaca.* 1993, p. 18. ". . . in relation to slaves from Guinea, Angola or the Coast of Mina, or from any other part above the age of seven, even those younger than twelve, we declare that they may not be baptised without their consent, unless so backward that they are found to lack understanding and use of reason." *Constituições primeiras do arcebispado da Bahia,* 1853. Capítulo I, título 14, pp. 22–3.

[89] AEAD. Livro de batizados do arraial do Tejuco. 1745–1765, caixa 297, fls. 53, 53v, 56.

[90] AEAD. Livro de casamentos do arraial do Tejuco. 1746–1811, caixa 335, fls. 33v, 34.

[91] AEAD. Livro de batizados do arraial do Tejuco. 1745–1765, caixa 291, f. 53.

[92] Ibidem, f. 39.

[93] AEAD. Livro de casamentos do arraial do Tejuco. 1746–1811, caixa 335, f. 38.

[94] Ibidem, f. 33v.

practice that resulted in a great many deaths.[95] The slave women generally went back to work after a short period of convalescence, taking their newborns with them wrapped in shawls slung across their backs, thus exposing the infants to bad weather and contagious diseases.

In addition to the dangers connected with birth, children were also more susceptible to epidemics, which always spread with greater ease among slaves from the same household who shared the same cramped and unsanitary slave quarters, generally located in the basement where there was little or no light, hygiene, or ventilation. It was probably an outbreak of this sort that claimed a number of Chica's slaves, mostly those of young age, two years in a row in the late 1770s. The first to die was an adult slave named José *maqui*,[96] buried in March 1778, followed by Manuel, son of Antônia; Agostinho, son of Maria Benguela; and Bernardina, daughter of Antônio and Rita creole. The following year, perhaps victims of the same disease, Vicente, son of Bárbara Mina, and Maria, daughter of Rosa Mina, were also buried,[97] as were two adult slaves, José Mina and Domingos Sabaru.[98] In contrast, in 1782, with the disease apparently under control, the only loss was of Maria, daughter of the slave Ana Gomes.[99] The two-year period 1786–1787, however, saw a new flurry of deaths among Chica's slaves, who is registered as having paid a sum of money to the Santo Antônio church for the burials of twenty-four from her estate in the chapel cemetery.[100]

Many of her slaves were rented out to the diamond contract, but exactly how many cannot be known. As the mining operations required at least six hundred slaves, not to mention the many substitutions made necessary through illness and death, the

[95] J. A. Imbert. *Manual do fazendeiro ou tratado doméstico sobre as enfermidades dos negros*. 1839.

[96] AEAD. Livro de óbitos do arraial do Tejuco. 1785–1810, caixa 351, f. 31v.

[97] Ibidem, fls. 30v, 33, 35v, 66v, 67.

[98] Ibidem, fls. 59v, 76.

[99] Ibidem, f. 129v.

[100] AEAD. Livro da fabriqueira da capela de Santo Antônio. 1780–1838, caixa 509, f. 17.

contractors had to hire slaves from the local owners. It was up to the contractors to choose from whom and the number of slaves to be supplied by each, and Chica undoubtedly took full advantage of João Fernandes's power to guarantee herself a secure and plentiful source of income. After 1771, when diamond extraction was monopolized by the Crown, Chica continued to hire out manpower to the Royal Diamond Extractor, although some of these slaves were confiscated under accusations of diamond smuggling.[101] During the Royal Diamond Extraction, it was the diamond intendant that set the rules (though not always obeyed), chose the suppliers, and limited the number of slaves each could provide to the company.[102]

The slaves employed in the mines usually died from drowning or in accidents caused by the mining operations, which were conducted on the margins of diverted rivers and required complicated systems to shore up the high and steep banks. The slaves usually died right there at the mines without the chance of receiving the last rites needed to commend their souls to heaven. This was the fate of João tapa, a slave belonging to Chica who died in the river mining service,[103] and of the captive João Marques de Carvalho, who "on the 1st of November, 1753, lost his life in the service of the contract." Although it was not registered on the death papers that accompanied the body whether he had confessed and received the last rites, given the fact that he had "come straight from the mines, where there [was] a chaplain," who would have attended the slave in his final moments, João Marques was granted burial in the grounds of the Santo Antônio church.[104]

Those who worked in the rivers where conditions were dreadful and where they were forever wet and never appropriately dressed were exposed to a host of illnesses that generally led to a slow death. In the treatise on practical medicine titled *Erário mineral*, published

---

[101] Belo Horizonte. AAPAH. Livro de seqüestro de escravos da Real Extração.
[102] Júnia Furtado. *O livro da capa verde*. 1996, pp. 121–2.
[103] AEAD. Batizados em Couto Magalhães de Minas. 1760–1774, caixa 331, f. 140v.
[104] AEAD. Livro de óbitos do arraial do Tejuco. 1752–1895, caixa 350, f. 7.

in 1732, Luís Gomes Ferreira wrote that those who suffered the most ailments were:

> the blacks, because they spend their days in the water, as they are miners and mine the lower reaches and watercourses, . . . they work there, eat there and often sleep there . . . when they work, they walk around soaked in sweat, with their feet always on cold earth, rock or in the water; and when they rest, or eat, [this sweat] blocks their pores causing such a chill that it gives rise to various dangerous infirmities, such as pleurisy, profound stupor, paralysis, convulsions, pneumonia and many other sicknesses.[105]

In the village of Tejuco, the slaves that worked in the service of the diamond contract were attended at the Contract Hospital, so-called because the diamond contractors had been responsible for its maintenance and staffing prior to the Crown's monopolization of the exploration. In October 1753, the hospital registered the death of one "Pedro Angola[,] rented to the Company [and] slave to Eugênia Maria,"[106] having first "confessed and received his last rites." Like him, many of Chica's slaves would have died after being admitted to this hospital. The slave João sabaru[107] who died there in 1762 is a case in point, as is João congo, who died in 1764.[108] Neither's death was unexpected, as the records show that they were both assisted in their final moments by a member of the clergy who administered all of the necessary sacraments.

The records concerning Chica da Silva's slaves do not tell us anything about what crafts or tasks they specialized in, as this kind of information was usually noted in the asset inventories made after the owner's death, and no such document has ever been found for Chica. We do know that João Fernandes de Oliveira's stable of slaves included one Antônio pedreiro[109] (stone mason) and a Bernardo

---

[105] Luís Gomes Ferreira. *Erário mineral*, vol. 1, 2002, pp. 229–30.
[106] AEAD. Livro de óbitos do arraial do Tejuco. 1752–1895, caixa 350, f. 6.
[107] Ibidem, f. 100v.
[108] Ibidem, f. 133v.
[109] AEAD. Livro de óbitos em São Gonçalo do Rio Preto/Felisberto Caldeira. 1790–1818, caixa 358, f. 9v.

barbeiro[110] (barber), both of whom worked on the Pé do Morro farm inherited by his sons. The burial register for Chica's slave José mina, dated 1782, contains a reference to his having been a *ladino*,[111] or accultured slave, which basically meant that he had mastered Portuguese, was competent in the practice of some craft, and, as someone already adapted to captivity, could help recent arrivals to face their new lives. *Ladino* slaves fetched high prices on the internal slave market, unlike the *boçais*, a category that included new arrivals and those who resisted acculturation and never learned the local language.

Income slaves were a source of inestimable profit and lived with relative liberty on the streets of the urban centers where they hawked services and merchandise. The slaves of Maria de Sousa da Encarnação all washed clothes about town, while Jacinta de Siqueira owned some slaves who mined for gold. When she died in 1811,[112] the black woman Ana de Glória dos Santos was owed a year and three months worth of arrears on a slave rented to Florência da Cunha.[113] The fact that a trumpet was featured among the belongings of Inês Fernandes Neves and that Rita Vieira de Matos possessed a carpenter's hammer and a pressing iron would suggest that these were probably tools their slaves used to ply a trade. Trumpeters, for example, were used at all religious festivals sponsored by the local brotherhoods, and their average fee ranged from a half to two eighths of gold, making it a profitable line of business for their owners, as the brotherhoods of Tejuco held various celebrations per year – Holy Week, Ash Wednesday, Te Deum,[114] Stations of the Cross, Corpus Christi, not to mention funerals and high masses.

As the chief judge owned various farms throughout the captaincy, with some quite near Tejuco, Chica was able to employ some of her slaves in cattle ranching and farming, probably renting them out to

[110] Ibidem, f. 65.
[111] AEAD. Livro de óbitos do arraial do Tejuco. 1785–1810, caixa 351, f. 122v.
[112] AEAD. Livro de óbitos do arraial do Tejuco. 1793–1811, caixa 521, f. 397v.
[113] BAT. Ana da Glória dos Santos. Cartório do Primeiro Ofício, maço 4.
[114] A feast with a mass celebrated to thank God for any blessing to the Portuguese kingdom.

João Fernandes and later to his sons and daughters in his absence. Many of her slaves worked and were buried at the Pé do Morro farm, situated within the Diamantine Demarcation in the vicinity of the village of Rio Vermelho. In 1778, a young boy, a natural son of Maria *cabra*,[115] whose name the chaplain forgot to note, and another unnamed slave woman were both laid to rest at the farm cemetery,[116] followed by the children Agostinho, Maximo, and Procópio and an unnamed adult two years later.[117]

Death, baptism, and marriage records and brotherhood affiliation registers for Tejuco in the second half of the eighteenth century show that Chica da Silva owned at least 104 slaves at different times throughout her life – a large number by local standards. Thirteen of these died at a tender age, which brings the total down to 91. It was possible to determine the gender of fifty-eight of these slaves: twenty-four were women and thirty-four were men. As was normal for the region, where most slaves were employed in the mining operations, the majority of her slaves were men.

Most of Chica's slaves came from Africa. The terrible work and living conditions kept mortality rates extremely high, making it perpetually necessary to bring in fresh manpower from the external slave market. The origins of thirty-three of Chica's slaves have been identified: twenty-one from Africa and twelve Brazilians, of which five were mulatto or pardo, four were cabra, and three creole.[118] The Africans belonged to different ethnicities, tribes, or "nations" – mina, timbu, xambá, angola, congo, sabaru, tapa, and maqui.[119] This

---

[115] AEAD. Livro de óbitos São Gonçalo do Rio Preto/Felisberto Caldeira. 1775–1789, caixa 358, f. 55.

[116] Ibidem, f. 59.

[117] Ibidem, fls. 62, 63v, 65v.

[118] To slave holders, mulatto or pardo was a blood mixture of black and white; pardos had lighter skin; cabra was a mixture of black and Indian; and creoles were sons or daughters of two African blacks.

[119] The denominations of the slaves' African origins are recorded on Minas Gerais' documents in a very imprecise, uncertain, and less than specific way. The terms, which are a mix of names of ethnic groups, nations, place names, dialects, and ports of slave shipment, reflected how the Portuguese understood their African origin from an outside point of view.

mixture was a strategy the owners employed in order to prevent any sense of shared identity developing within the slave community that could lead to the formation of alliances on escape attempts or revolts. As far as Chica was concerned, they were all equal; skin color and place of birth did not make her favor the Brazilians over the Africans, for example.

To form an idea of the extent of Chica da Silva's wealth it will be necessary to compare her assets against those of other figures from the region. Between 1787 and 1822, at the height of the diamond economy and thus also the period in which most large fortunes were made, sixty-six inventories were drawn up, of which forty-two listed the assets of members of the gentry. Among those inventoried, 16.7 percent did not possess any slaves, while 33.3 percent owned a maximum of three, with a mere 6.1 percent registering a slave stock of more than twenty captives.[120] The functionaries of the Royal Diamond Extraction Company, who owned the most slaves, had the privilege of renting a higher and fixed number of slaves to the mining operations. Brigadier Manuel Pires de Figueiredo owned forty-eight slaves,[121] while Filipe José Correia de Lacerda, the general diamond administrator, owned thirty.[122] Sergeant Major José da Silva de Oliveira, who held important posts in the diamantine administration, such as first cashier of the Royal Extraction Company, had twenty-one slaves,[123] as did the physician Luís José de Figueiredo.[124] It must be remembered that the inventories only give the total number of slaves those individuals owned at the moment of their deaths and not over their entire lifetimes.

---

[120] Júnia Furtado. O livro da capa verde. 1996, p. 52.
[121] BAT. Inventário de. Manuel Pires de Figueiredo. Cartório do Primeiro Ofício, maço 60.
[122] BAT. Inventário de Filipe José Correia Lacerda. Cartório do Primeiro Ofício, maço 21.
[123] BAT. Inventário de José da Silva de Oliveira. 1796–1797. Cartório do Primeiro Ofício, maço 28.
[124] BAT. Inventário de Luís José de Figueiredo. Cartório do Primeiro Ofício, maço 52.

Like Chica da Silva, the black freedwoman Jacinta de Siqueira also experienced some numerical oscillations in her slave ownership. In her will, she made a point of detailing all the slaves she had given to her daughters, granddaughters, and great-granddaughters in life so that these could be taken into consideration in the final distribution. When the slaves already passed on to her descendants were added to the twenty-seven slaves she possessed at the time of her death, Jacinta's total slave stock reached sixty-two captives, a considerable number for the mining society. She left twenty to her daughter Bernarda, of which ten had already died, while three had been given as a dowry and one was recovered from pawning. Each of her three other daughters received three slaves each, at least two serving as marriage dowry. Her granddaughters and great-granddaughters received one or two mulattos each. The captives she left to her surviving family were important insofar as they were guaranteed sources of income and helped position them better on the village marriage market, which obviously worked, as they were all married off to white men.

Chica da Silva and João Fernandes's slaves were inherited by their sons and daughters. Despite the significant difference in size between each of their slave stocks, they all did their best to hold on to their captives. Rita Quitéria owned thirty-five slaves at the time of her death, most of whom worked on the Pé do Morro farm. The eldest among them, such as João Coelho, João Barundó, Joaquim Mina, Manuel creole, Lourenço *carapina*, Miguel cafuzo, Ana Mina, and Feliz Mina, all in their seventies,[125] were possibly inherited from her parents. Some of her slaves practiced specific crafts and trades, such as the tailor Aleixo pardo, the shoemaker Dosidério mulatto, the hairdresser Damaso *cabra*, and the carpenter Lourenço.[126] The women mostly worked in the fields and the cotton mill and as clothes

---

[125] BAT. Inventário de Rita Quitéria de São José. Cartório do Primeiro Ofício, maço 63, fls. 4v–6v.
[126] BAT. Inventário de Francisca de Paula Fernandes de Oliveira. Cartório do Primeiro Ofício, maço 23.

makers working the looms. One such seamstress was Claudina parda, who was twenty-two years old in 1808.

Francisca de Paula was the owner of forty-three captives employed on the Buriti farm.[127] Of this stock, only Francisca creole, the shoe-maker Manuel pardo, Manuel creole, Reginaldo creole, and Antônio Rebolo were old enough to have been inherited from her parents. Most of her captives were young, with a quarter of the total under the age of seven (eleven creole children and one pardo); in contrast with Pé do Morro, where there were only three children (two little girls and one boy). Rita Quitéria died in 1808 and Francisca de Paula in 1839, so the age difference between their slave holdings could be explained by a change in behavior among the slave owners of Minas in the face of the steady decline of the slave trade, with an attempt to balance out the high mortality rates with more births of home-grown slaves.[128] Proof of this decline is that only two of Francisca de Paula's slaves, a woman named Francisca and a man named Antônio Rebolo, were natives of Africa, while all the other adult captives had been born in Brazil.[129]

Regardless of the existing lacunas and the fact that the content of her will is not known, the image of Chica da Silva as a redeemer of slaves, as she has so often been romanticized in the historiography, does not hold up in the light of the documentation consulted. In fact, there is only one clear reference to her granting manumission, to Francisca, the daughter of her slave Catarina,[130] who received her freedom at the baptismal font and whose name was clearly a reference to her own. This was Chica's repayment for the services rendered by

[127] Ibidem.
[128] Laird W. Bergad. *Slavery and demographic and economic history of Minas Gerais, Brazil, 1720–1888.* 1999, p. 151. Based on the analysis of inventories and wills from Minas Gerais, this author argues that the increase in the number of births as the chief means of increasing the slave demographic occurred throughout all of the counties of the captaincy of Minas Gerais from the beginning of the nine-teenth century and a little later in the Diamantine District.
[129] BAT. Inventário de Francisca de Paula Fernandes de Oliveira. Cartório do Primeiro Ofício, maço 23.
[130] AEAD. Livro de batizados do arraial do Tejuco. 1745–1765, caixa 297, f. 53v.

her slave, mainly as wet nurse to her children with João Fernandes. While the mother was kept in captivity so as not to lose the money invested in her acquisition, her freed descendants were taken into Chica's protection and favor.

As was typical of the slave owners of Minas Gerais, including the twenty-three colored freedwomen from the region whose wills have been preserved, Chica sought at all costs to maintain the patrimony she had accumulated and that included her slave stock. Perhaps as a throwback to matriarchal African traditions, the freedwomen of Minas Gerais all presented a common strategy of accumulating patrimony with the objective of handing it down to their descendants. As such, while the children of trusted slaves were occasionally given manumission, usually at baptism and sometimes by the agency of their godparents, most adult slaves had to buy their liberty through *coartation*, with very few being freed in recompense for the services rendered and loyalty shown over long years of captivity.[131]

A freed black woman named Maria Fernandes de Oliveira passed away in 1778, lucky enough to have made her last confession given the almost sudden nature of her death. She was buried in the chapel of the freed slaves.[132] Her surname is an evident reference to either Chica or João Fernandes, and she was probably a former slave from one of their households. In the year of Maria Fernandes' death, Chica was still living in Tejuco, though the contractor had already departed for the Realm from where he continued to administer his Brazilian patrimony, of which his slaves were the most valuable assets. These records, however, cannot tell us if she was manumitted or if she bought her own liberty – the latter being more likely.

Other scattered references have been found to Chica da Silva's former slaves being freed, although all of these date to after her death. These documents likewise cannot clarify how the slaves came to be freed. In 1797, the year after Chica's death, Tomásia da Silva

---

[131] For the region of Sabará, see Kathleen J. Higgins. *Licentious liberty, in a Brazilian gold-mining region*. 1999. For Bahia, see Stuart B. Schwartz. "The manumission of slaves in colonial Brazil: Bahia, 1684–1745." *Hispanic American Historical Review*, vol. 54, 1974, pp. 603–35.

[132] AEAD. Livro de óbitos do arraial do Tejuco. 1785–1810, caixa 351, f. 35v.

de Oliveira Fernandes, a cabra who belonged to Chica's household and was inherited by her children, joined the Brotherhood of the Mercies. Though she was still a slave of Chica's upon admittance, she soon attained the status of freedwoman.[133] Tomásia had married in captivity to Antônio pardo, another of Chica's slaves, with whom she had a son named Valeriano who died while still little.[134] Another of Chica's former slaves joined the same brotherhood that year – a creole named Gertrudes, who had married Chica's slave Joaquim pardo. Their daughter, named after the mother, also died at a tender age.[135] Once freed, she went by the name of Gertrudes Maria de Jesus de São José, as it was common practice in the late eighteenth century for freed slaves to assume the surnames of their former masters – and it must be remembered that São José was the surname of all of Chica da Silva's daughters. The same went for the former captives Donata Fernandes de Oliveira cabra[136] and Davi Fernandes de Oliveira pardo, who also became a member of the Brotherhood of the Mercies.[137]

The lives of Tomásia cabra and Gertrudes creole took similar courses and evoke various considerations. Both married slaves from the same household, had babies who died soon after birth, and probably served as nursemaids to Chica's children, earning the owner's gratitude for their services and loyalty. The fact that both joined the Brotherhood of the Mercies one year after Chica's death is significant. In line with the standard practice of the day, the manumission of these women was possibly determined in Chica's will and executed by her children, who would probably have respected the conditions their mother set for this, such as the provision of services to her

---

[133] AEAD. Livro segundo de grades da Irmandade de Nossa Senhora das Mercês. 1793–1837, caixa 521, f. 16v.

[134] AEAD. Livro de óbitos do arraial do Tejuco. 1785–1810, caixa 351, f. 145v.

[135] AEAD. Livro de casamentos do arraial do Tejuco. 1746–1811, f. 33v; Livro de óbitos do arraial do Tejuco. 1785–1810, caixa 351, f. 162v.

[136] AEAD. Livro de certidões de missas da Irmandade de Nossa Senhora das Mercês. 1776, caixa 520, f. 37; Livro segundo de grades da Irmandade de Nossa Senhora das Mercês. 1793–1837, caixa 521, f. 16v.

[137] AEAD. Livro segundo de grades da Irmandade de Nossa Senhora das Mercês. 1793–1837, caixa 521, f. 99v.

heirs or the payment of some sum at a later date when both were in liberty.

Her children were just as parsimonious when it came to granting manumission. Francisca de Paula, for example, freed only four slaves in her will – Joana Mina, Joaquina *parda*, Fabiana, and Inácio *cabra*[138] – without requesting compensation in the form of specie or work. For her part, the will of Ana Quitéria leaves her niece, Antônia Vicência, a slave named Serafina, daughter of Policena *parda*, also her slave, while freeing another, Joaquim *pardo*, without asking for anything in return.[139] However, in order to free Leonor mina, Mariana de Jesus followed the more common line of requesting in exchange a "lad named Antônio, of the benguela *nation*, with whom I am quite satisfied."[140]

The twenty-three freedwomen who lived in Tejuco in Chica's day followed the standard behavior of the free whites when it came to granting manumission. Freeing loyal and trusted slaves was one way these women could show their gratitude for the services received during life and to enable other women to penetrate the world of the free. Granting liberty was also a form of charity to the poor, considered an essential mechanism at the moment of death in ensuring the salvation of the soul. The mulatta Inês de Santa Luzia, single, left her entire wardrobe to her slave, Marina de Santa Luzia, "for having served and accompanied me so loyally to this day."[141] Inês Fernandes Neves manumitted two of her four slaves, one of whom was João angola, "as he is now elderly, and for having served me loyally."[142] Jacinta de Siqueira freed the slave Ângela Mina "for the good services she provided, for having served me well and for having given

---

[138] BAT. Inventário de Francisca de Paula Fernandes de Oliveira. Cartório do Primeiro Ofício, maço 23, fls. 3v–4.

[139] BAT. Testamento de Ana Quitéria de São José. Cartório do Primeiro Ofício, maço 92.

[140] AFS. Livro de notas no. 99. 1793–1794, f. 196v.

[141] BAT. Testamento de Inês de Santa Luzia. Cartório do Primeiro Ofício, maço 26.

[142] BAT. Testamento de Inês Fernandes Neves. Cartório do Primeiro Ofício, maço 26.

me her offspring."[143] A benguela black named Maria de Azevedo, also single, instructed her executors to issue manumission papers to her slave Maria "for the good service she has given me and the good company she has been to me."[144]

According to the domestic census of 1774, for Chica and her descendants, as for all the freedwomen of Tejuco, the main source of income was the services provided by their slaves. More than half of the colored male family heads were skilled in a trade they continued to practice after manumission, though among the freedwomen, only the innkeeper Joana Gertrudes continued to work from her house on Rua do Amparo. The fact that almost all of the freedwomen did not ply a trade or craft would indicate that they, like Chica, managed to achieve what they wanted, namely release from labor, just like the whites they sought to imitate in pursuit of social equality.

---

[143] AFS. Testamento de Jacinta de Siqueira. Livro de testamentos no. 8, fls. 33v–38v.
[144] BAT. Testamento de Maria de Azevedo. Cartório do Primeiro Ofício, maço 58.

Figure 1. Partial view of Diamantina city, old Tejuco village.

Figure 2. Chica da Silva's house in Diamantina.

Figure 3. Diamond exploration. Carlos Julião, Acervo da Fundação Biblioteca Nacional.

Figure 4. Mulattas in Tejuco village.

Figure 5. Black woman in Tejuco village. Carlos Julião, Acervo da Fundação Biblioteca Nacional.

Figure 6. Macaúbas convent where Chica's daughters studied.

Figure 7. João Fernandes's house in Lisbon (Lapa House).

Figure 8. Figure of an Indian, in the tiles that were displayed in the main stairs of João Fernandes's house in Lisbon.

Figure 9. São Francisco church in Tejuco where Chica was buried.

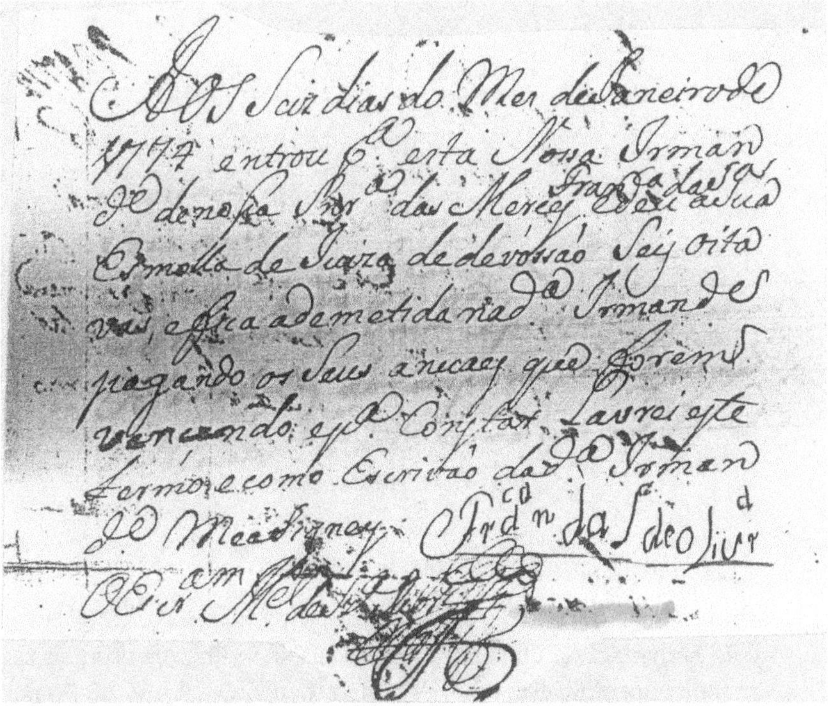

Figure 10. Chica da Silva's signature in the Book of Sisterhood, Confraternity of Brotherhood of Mercês. 1774/1779. Livro s.n.

CHAPTER SIX

Life in the Village

> But the men and the women
> live in this imbroglio...
> There's no fever like the fever
> that pierces Serro do Frio...

Social Networks

On November 24, 1753, soon after arriving in Tejuco, Chief Judge João Fernandes de Oliveira attended his first village baptism as the godfather of Angélica, the legitimate daughter of José de Araújo Guimarães and Inês Maria da Conceição, both white.[1] He thus began to establish the necessary connections with the local elite so often forged through relationships of godparentage.

The young chief judge had to impress the villagers and impose the respect demanded by his presence and the important position of diamond contractor he had come to occupy. He dressed in the European style typical of the village's white elite. The first item of the ritual garb was a pair of long johns, followed by a white linen shirt with frilled cuffs, long or short trousers, and fine silk stockings. On top of this went a black, red, or blue duroy swallow-tailed coat, or a baize, velvet, or satin tailcoat. Finally, an overcoat or sleeved cape was worn in a manner almost wrapped around the body. The trimmings were various: a removable collar,[2] a frilly silk pocket handkerchief and another blue handkerchief for tobacco; a feathered hat with a

---

[1]   AEAD. Livro de batizados do arraial do Tejuco. Caixa 297, fls. 38–39v.
[2]   A white collar as the ones used by catholic priests.

buckled strap; a cross of the Order of Christ worn about the neck; shoes with gold or silver buckles; and a tortoise cane with a gold or silver head and bands set with precious stones. A knife and sword with silver hilts were worn on the belt, along with the customary pistols.[3]

Depending on the situation, he might have worn the habit of the Order of Christ, or the habit and cloak of the Third Carmelite Order of which he was also a member. As a judge of the Exchequer of Minas Gerais, he could also have donned his magistrate's gown, further underlining his importance among his fellow residents.[4]

Circulating in the city was always a studied affair, conducted with the purpose of impressing the passers-by and parading one's prestige. As a show of authority, the chief judge would have gone outdoors in a sedan chair carried by slaves or mounted on horseback in an embroidered velvet or crimson saddle, like those belonging to the physician Luís José de Figueiredo.[5]

Public ceremonies, especially Sunday mass, were unparalleled opportunities to flaunt one's social standing in the village. Attention was paid not only to the individual's dress, but also to the place he or she was allocated at events. Sitting in the front rows at church, at the table of the officer of the highest rank, or marching in the most important block of a religious procession were all clear signs of distinction. As contractor and judge of the Porto Court of Appeal, João Fernandes enjoyed many privileges and a great deal of deference at the public solemnities held at the village. In 1763 he was extended "the honour of appointment to the Exchequer of Minas Gerais, [with] rights to wear the magistrate's gown."[6] From

---

[3] BAT. Inventário de João de Azevedo Pereira (capitão). Cartório do Primeiro Ofício, maço 27, e inventário de José Francisco de Lima. Cartório do Segundo Ofício, maço 206. BAT. Cartório do Primeiro Ofício, maços 21, 52, 60.

[4] ANTT. Ministério do Reino. Livro 214, fls. 43v, 44; Chancelaria de dom José I. Livro 86, fls. 101v–102.

[5] BAT. Inventário de Luís José de Figueiredo. Cartório do Primeiro Ofício, maço 52.

[6] ANTT. Ministério do Reino. Livro 214, fls. 43v, 44; APM. Seção Colonial. 131, fls. 53v–54v; ANTT. Chancelaria de dom José I. Livro 86, fls. 101v, 102.

that moment on he was entitled to sit in the front row at any ceremony,[7] the place closest to the governor,[8] not only in Tejuco but
throughout the captaincy as well.

Besides presenting an opportunity to rub shoulders with the powerful, being in the company of the king's highest representative in the
region also conferred distinction, which is why such placings were so
hotly disputed. In 1725, when the governor Lourenço de Almeida
had to choose who should join him at his table he thought it best
to let the king decide, as the government secretary was complaining
that it was his right to sit "up in the sanctuary, on the left side, facing
the governor, . . . immediately behind the lieutenant general."[9]

While living in Tejuco, João Fernandes often served as sponsor at
the weddings of the children of the white elite and as godfather to
legitimate children, abandoned children, adults, and freed children,
most of whom were born of illegitimate unions. By accepting these
requests he showed charity to the poor and deference to his peers,
thus bringing them into his sphere of influence through gratitude.[10]
The bonds of godparentage and sponsorship – the prime social mechanisms of the day – created clientele networks and interdependencies
between different social segments. An efficient strategy, it inserted
both the godchild and his or her parents within the orbit of someone
more powerful whose protection could be drawn upon when necessary. The godparent or sponsor became at once someone close to the
family and a figure deserving of respect.

The words of a small-scale merchant Francisco da Cruz, then based
in Sabará, written to the businessman Francisco Pinheiro in Portugal
give a good idea of the importance of these relationships. Thanking
his patron for the letters of recommendation he had sent to the local
powerbrokers on his behalf, the merchant adds that the news was
spreading that he, Francisco da Cruz, was related to his patron, which

---

[7] ANTT. Ministério do Reino. Livro 209, f. 184.
[8] Ibidem.
[9] APM. Seção Colonial. 20, f. 145. Apud: Júnia Furtado. *Homens de negócio.* 1999,
     pp. 183–4.
[10] Kathleen J. Higgins. *Licentious liberty in a Brazilian gold-mining region.* 1999. See
     also Joseph Lynch. *Godparents and kinship in early medieval Europe.* 1986.

he says was not entirely untrue, "as we know there are no relatives quite as close as *compadres* (those chosen to be godparents or sponsors)" and, this being so, "these gentlemen will now know that there is someone on this earth who would do me certain kindnesses."[11]

In 1754, for the first time, Chief Judge João Fernandes was chosen as a wedding sponsor, alongside Sergeant Major José da Silva de Oliveira, an old friend of his father's, at a ceremony held at Santo Antônio parish church. The bride and groom were Maria de Oliveira Costa and Manuel da Fonseca, both white. It was thus, accompanied by one of the most important figures in the village, that the young diamond contractor, recently arrived from Portugal, was presented to the local society.[12]

It was to be the first of many marriages between members of the white elite of Tejuco sponsored by João Fernandes during his stay in the village. Others included the unions of João da Costa Marques and Maria Mendes de Azevedo in 1755, José Francisco da Silva and Gertrude Pereira do Sacramento in 1756, and José Ferreira and Joana Caetana de Oliveira. In 1759, he was a sponsor at the wedding of Tomás Pereira Cabral, followed by Vieira da Fonseca and Laureana Maria Vieira a year later, an honor he shared with the diamond intendant Francisco José Pinto de Mendonça. As a matter of strategy, the couple had chosen the two most powerful men in the region to bless them in their new life.[13]

At ten o'clock on the morning of April 20, 1766, Manuel de Soto Gouveia took Inácia da Silva de Oliveira as his wife in a ceremony at which João Fernandes was not only a sponsor but also the host, as the wedding took place at the chapel he had built on the grounds of the Palha farmhouse near Tejuco. It was the first time the farmhouse was used for this purpose, which would suggest that the chapel had only recently been built.[14] Many weddings and other rites of social importance were celebrated on this property in the stretch between

[11] Hospital São José. Testamentaria de Francisco Pinheiro. Carta 149, maço 29, f. 180.
[12] AEAD. Livro de casamentos do arraial do Tejuco. Caixa 335, f. 12.
[13] Ibidem, fls. 13v, 15, 19, 21v.
[14] Ibidem, f. 34v.

the chapel and the garden. In 1768, the Palha farmhouse was the venue for the marriages of Romão de Oliveira Jacome and Ana Maria de Todos os Santos, with the chief judge as a witness,[15] and of Manuel Lopes Falcão and Ana Maria da Conceição.[16]

These occasions could always rely on the presence of the diamond intendant and the most distinguished members of the village community.[17]

Many of Chica's slaves also wed at the Palha farmhouse chapel. In allowing the locale to be used for these ceremonies, the couple demonstrated benevolence towards their captives and contributed to the spread of Catholicism and the European family institutions, thus fulfilling their roles as faithful masters and good Christians. In 1768, Chica's creole slaves Antônio and Rita married there, as did the couples Cláudio and Maria and Francisco pardo and Ana cabra in 1769.[18]

Like the contractor, Chica da Silva also sponsored various newborns and newlyweds in Tejuco. However, her list of godchildren indicates that her condition as a parda and freedwoman limited her selection as godmother to children of equal or lesser status to her own.[19] In 1749, while still a slave, she and Sergeant Major Antônio de Araújo Freitas served as godparents to Ana, the infant daughter of Rita, slave of Antônio Vieira Balverde.[20] Once freed, she

---

[15] Ibidem.

[16] Ibidem, f. 38v.

[17] "... the witnesses present were the chief judge and diamond intendant Francisco José Pinto de Mendonça and the chief judge of the exchequer João Fernandes de Oliveira and other members of the congregation." AEAD. Livro de casamentos do arraial do Tejuco. Caixa 335, f. 34v.

[18] Ibidem, f. 41v.

[19] This and the affirmations that follow refer to baptisms conducted in Tejuco up to 1765. It was not possible to continue the research into the period 1766 to 1795, as the baptismal records for this interval are badly damaged. For other villages and Vila do Príncipe, the research covers all of the dates available in the baptismal record books.

[20] "[Of] Ana, infant daughter of Rita, slave of Antônio Vieira Balverde, the godparents were the Sergeant Major Antônio de Araújo Freitas and *Francisca, the mulatta of Manuel Pires Sardinha*." AEAD. Baptismal records for the village of Tejuco. 1745–1765, box 291, f. 22.

joined Manuel Jacome Soeiro as the baptismal sponsors of Miguel, the legitimate son of Manuel Liam and Donna Joana Antônia, both white and residents of the district of Gouveia.[21] However, unlike João Fernandes, even after manumission, those who called on Chica to be godmother or sponsor were generally not among the village's white elite but were mostly slaves or former slaves. Despite this and having to face other obstacles in her attempt to place herself shoulder to shoulder with the whites of Tejuco, Chica was in a higher social position than her affiliates, for whom it would have been a privilege to have her as the godmother of their children. In any event, her example indicates the role these bonds played in the society, as godparents and sponsors were always more powerful people – individuals who belonged to a higher social station and could therefore offer protection in times of difficulty. It also indicates how hard it was to find two godparents of good standing for slaves and illegitimate children. The baptisms held in Tejuco followed the customs of those of Bahia where there was a better chance of legitimate children, even those of color, having a godfather and a godmother, while the illegitimate generally only had one or the other.[22]

In 1756, Francisca da Silva de Oliveira, accompanied by Manuel Caetano dos Santos, godmothered Maria, the legitimate daughter of a freed black woman named Inácia Maria de Jesus.[23] More godchildren came that year: Francisca parda, named in her honor, the daughter of the slave Inácia, baptized in the company of Manuel Pereira da Cunha; and Vicente, son of Bernarda Lopes and an unknown father,[24] baptized with Manuel Vieira da Fonseca. In the years that followed, she baptized Maria, the illegitimate daughter of a single[25] white woman named Teodora Maria da Concepção, and Joana, daughter of the freed creole Rosa Maria.[26] In 1760, she was

[21] Ibidem, f. 44.
[22] Stuart Schwartz. "Opening the circle: Godparentage in Brazilian slavery." *Slaves, peasants, and rebels: Reconsidering Brazilian slavery.* 1992, p. 142.
[23] AEAD. Livro de batizados do arraial do Tejuco. 1745–1765, caixa 291, f. 46.
[24] Ibidem, f. 47.
[25] Ibidem, f. 65.
[26] Ibidem, f. 69.

godmother to Vitória, the legitimate daughter of the pardo Roberto Antônio da Cruz and his wife, Severina da Silva.[27]

These ceremonies show that Chica walked tall among the local elite, a fact borne out by the men selected to accompany her in most of the baptisms, all of whom were white, occasionally of military rank, and always recognizedly important names in the village, such as Manuel Jacome Soeiro, Manuel Vieira da Fonseca, Heitor de Sá, and José Antônio Ferreira de Melo.[28]

In May 1762, for example, Chief Judge José Pinto de Mendonça, then diamond intendant, and Donna Francisca da Silva de Oliveira, as registered by the notary, served as the godparents of Maria, the legitimate daughter of a white couple, Luís Antônio da Silva and Micaela Arcângela da Silva. However, as she was in convalescence after the birth of her own daughter Ana, Chica could not attend the ceremony and sent Captain Francisco Malheiro de Araújo as her representative.[29] Although João Fernandes never sponsored a captive, Chica was godmother to the children of various slaves, though none from her own household, as was the rule among Brazilian owners. Godparentage was never used to reinforce ties between master and slave; indeed, it was considered antithetical to what was clearly a relationship based on authority rather than fellowship.[30]

In 1756, Chica godmothered Francisca parda, daughter of Inácia parda, slave of Giraldo de Melo dos Santos. A few years later she and a white man named Heitor de Sá[31] baptized Antônio, the legitimate son of the slave Inácia de Melo. Some of Chica and João Fernandes's children godparented slaves from their parents' households, a common practice in the village as exemplified by Chica's eldest daughter, Francisca de Paula, who baptized Margarida, daughter of Severina da Costa, her mother's slave.[32]

---

[27] Ibidem, f. 85.
[28] Ibidem, fls. 44, 47, 80v, 86v.
[29] Ibidem, f. 86.
[30] Stuart Schwartz, op. cit., 1992, pp. 137–60.
[31] AEAD. Livro de batizados do arraial do Tejuco. 1745–1765, caixa 297, f. 80v.
[32] Ibidem, f. 56.

On the other hand, there were also cases of godparents being chosen on the basis of affection or bonds of friendship dating back to the slave days. The relationship between Chica da Silva and Maria parda, slave and concubine to the surgeon José Gomes Ferreira, was a perfect example. In 1756, Francisca da Silva de Oliveira, by now already the chief judge's companion, was chosen as godmother to Rosa, this couple's first child.[33] Two years later Simão Pires Sardinha and Maria Gomes[34] (the same Maria parda, but now going by the surname of her companion, José Gomes) godparented Maria, daughter of Rita parda, Chica's slave. The following year Maria Gomes gave birth to Matilde, baptized by João Fernandes,[35] followed by Francisca in 1754, named after her godmother, Chica da Silva.[36]

Also honored in the world of the free was the friendship she had developed during enslavement with Francisca Pires, mother of Cipriano, Simão Pires Sardinha's half brother. Her daughter Barbara was baptized by Chica da Silva, while her sister, Helena, born in 1762, likewise of an unknown father, was baptized by João Fernandes and their daughter Rita Quitéria.[37] The only time Chica and João Fernandes godparented a child together was in 1760 at the baptism of João, son of Severina creole, held at the Santo Antônio parish church.[38] As they were not married and because concubinage was condemned by the church, they rarely attended these religious ceremonies together. But the fact that Chica continued to be invited to be a godmother even after João Fernandes's return to the Realm shows that the society recognized the position she occupied, regardless of her companion's absence.

From 1759 on, the contractor started to attend many of these ceremonies in the company of his eldest daughter, Francisca de Paula, then only five years of age. In that year alone they godparented an

[33] Ibidem, f. 49.
[34] Ibidem, f. 53v.
[35] Ibidem, f. 76v.
[36] Ibidem, f. 96v.
[37] Ibidem, fls. 50, 86.
[38] Ibidem, f. 77.

abandoned child named Maria and Francisco, son of Páscoa Maria da Costa,[39] followed by the creole Maria, daughter of Joana Roiz and an unknown father,[40] in 1760. As far as the church was concerned, having fathers and their children at these ceremonies, even if illegitimate, was a lesser evil in comparison with concubines, which is why Simão, Francisca de Paula, João, José Agostinho, and Rita Quitéria participated as godparents from very early on, long before the minimum age of fourteen required by canonical law. In 1757, Simão and Francisca de Paula served as godparents to Jacinta, daughter of Escolástica, slave of Ventura Carneiro.[41] In 1764, at the tender age of seven, Rita Quitéria godmothered Maria, daughter of Inácia Pereira, a freed parda.[42] In this manner they learned the importance of the Catholic rites, charity to the poor and to slaves, and the need to protect the white elite and its place in society, while showing themselves to be good Christians and worthy subjects of the empire.

As João Fernandes's consort, Chica da Silva reaped the benefits of the connections the chief judge established with the village's white elite. Permanently bound to him in the name of gratitude, the powerful repaid the diamond contractor's protection and favors with their varied services. During the *de genere* processes through which Chica's bastard sons sought to attain honorable status, important figures in the village made public demonstration of their loyalty to the contractor by the half-truths contained in their testimonies, which proved essential in consolidating the alternative versions of the lives of Simão Pires Sardinha and his maternal line upon which the success of his candidature rested. The deponents therefore aided him in the task of definitively erasing the unfavorable conditions of his birth.

Among the deponents conscripted in Tejuco were Captain Luís de Mendonça Cabral, a knight of the Order of Christ and notary of the Diamond Intendancy; the Captain-Major Francisco

---

[39] Ibidem, f. 71.
[40] Ibidem, fls. 77, 79.
[41] Ibidem, f. 55.
[42] Ibidem.

Malheiros de Araújo, also a member of the order, who made his living from mining operations; the surgeon José Gomes Ferreira; Sergeant-Major Antônio de Araújo de Freitas; Captain Luís Lopes da Costa, a businessman from the village; Sergeant-Major Manuel Batista Landim, later tutor to João Fernandes' younger sons after his return to Portugal; the clergymen Manuel Álvares Ferreira, José Ribeiro Aldonço, and José Marques Ribeiro; and Simão Pacheco, the parson of Santo Antônio church.[43]

João Fernandes's grandeur and importance had to be continuously demonstrated. Being part of the clique of the powerful was not enough if one was to be honored and respected by society. An essential means toward aggrandizement, charity to the poor was not merely a Christian act but an obligation of the rich and an important form of conviviality. Practiced under the guise of selfless generosity, charity was really an effective strategy for garnering prestige. The unwritten social rules dictated that an act of charity had to be public and directed toward members of the lower social classes with the purpose of ensnaring them in inerasable, inextinguishable debt. Material charity, always rewarded in moral gains, was one way of bringing the giver's magnanimity and power to the fore. The recipient was expected to repay the charity done to him by beholding himself eternally to the benefactor or through the provision of small services. Enclosed within an unending circle of compensations, the beneficiary was to forever publicly declare his indebtedness, even on his deathbed.

Pedro Álvares de Araújo, sergeant major of Vila do Príncipe, was one example of the clientele networks João Fernandes established in the demarcation. His will affirms that he basically made his living from renting slaves to the diamond contracts, on which there were still some payments in arrears, and that this was a benefit that depended on the good will of the contractor. Though the owner of some "land for planting and mining," he had not amassed any liquid patrimony and survived off loans from the chief judge. As João

---

43 AEAM. *Auto de genere et moribus de Simão Pires Sardinha.* 1768, armário 10, pasta 1782.

Fernandes was already dead when Pedro Álvares drafted his will, the hundred eighths of gold earmarked for the former contractor went directly to his heirs.[44]

The sick were also the recipients of a great deal of charity. Among the duties and obligations that went with the diamond contracts was the upkeep of a hospital set up mainly to treat the black miners who suffered frequent accidents and from various ailments. During João Fernandes's time, one of the doctors at this hospital was José Antônio Mendes, the author of a medical treatise titled *Governo de mineiros*. . . . In his book, the doctor describes the curing of patients suffering from the canker, including various poor from Tejuco, "who, out of the love of God, the chief judge João Fernandes de Oliveira ordered us to cure, such that many got better with great admiration for the man, who saw them when he had them sent [to the hospital] and when they went to him to give thanks once healed." With this ritual of visiting the sick he had sent to the hospital to be cured free of charge and of having them return favors to him once healed, the chief judge made public show of his grandeur and magnanimity to the less fortunate.

Another public show of charity was the protection of abandoned children, also called "exposed" children, as they were usually left in the streets. In general, these children ended up being baptized and brought up by the villager on whose doorstep they had happened to be left. Sergeant Major José da Silva de Oliveira raised a girl named Dalila, who had been abandoned outside his home.[45] In 1753, Donna Ana Joaquina Rosa, his wife, godmothered Eduarda, another girl abandoned in the same place.[46] A few months later it was João Fernandes's turn to show his pity for these children by serving as the godfather to the orphan Rosa, abandoned outside the house of Pedro

---

[44] AFS. Livro de testamentos no. 34. 1789, fls. 135v–144. Apud: José Newton C. Meneses. *O continente rústico*. 2001, p. 163.

[45] BAT. Inventário de José da Silva de Oliveira. 1796–1797. Cartório do Primeiro Ofício, maço 28.

[46] AEAD. Livro de batizados do arraial do Tejuco. 1745–1765, caixa 297, f. 38.

de Oliveira.⁴⁷ In 1759, the contractor and his daughter Francisca de Paula were the godparents of another abandoned girl called Maria.⁴⁸

Like his father before him, João Fernandes arranged business positions in the village for his extended family. Captain Domingos Fernandes de Oliveira, who served as administrator on the diamond contract working the Manso River, earned the rank of captain and held various prestigious posts in Tejuco, including a seat on the Board of the Brotherhood of the Most Holy Sacrament.⁴⁹

Alongside other local power brokers, the contractor's charitable spirit was once more made manifest to the village through his sponsorship of the construction of the Nossa Senhora do Carmo church. In the edict in which Her Majesty Maria I confirmed the establishment of the brotherhood in 1788, the notary wrote that "they would presently possess a chapel by donation of the chief judge João Fernandes de Oliveira, built by him under license from the ordinary of the respective diocese."⁵⁰ In addition to this, he also left the brotherhood two lodgings he kept in houses located at the back of another house directly facing the chapel, all of which belonged to the order.⁵¹

Although João Fernandes de Oliveira once remarked somewhat offhand that "like my father, by nature and religion, I not only love the poor, but spend lavish sums in the service of the Church,"⁵² the true reward of charity, a virtue reserved only for the grand, was good publicity. In proportion to her social condition, less privileged than others in the village but certainly superior to that of most, Chica also made public displays of charity, albeit less frequently than the chief

---

⁴⁷ Ibidem, f. 42.

⁴⁸ Ibidem, f. 71.

⁴⁹ AEAD. Livro da Irmandade do Santíssimo Sacramento. 1759–1764. Caixa sem identificação, f. 4v.

⁵⁰ Iphan/BH. Pasta de tombamento da igreja do Carmo de Diamantina. Cópia do documento com que Sua Majestade foi servida....

⁵¹ The houses were sold to one Jacome but ended up returning to the patrimony of the Third Order of Carmo. Government trust file of Carmo de Diamantina church. Arquivo do Iphan/BH. Inventário dos bens da Ordem Terceira do Carmo. Pasta de tombamento da igreja do Carmo de Diamantina.

⁵² ANTT. Desembargo do Paço. Ilhas. Maço 1342, doc. 7

judge. In 1787, for example, many years after he had left Tejuco, she paid the Brotherhood of the Most Holy to have a destitute captive buried in the cemetery of the order.[53] At around the same time, forever the zealous mother, she financed the burial of two captives, one belonging to her daughter Francisca de Paula and another to Luísa,[54] in the brotherhood's tombs in the Santo Antônio church in Tejuco.

Charity could even defy death by perpetuating the memory of the giver and his descendants in the world of the living. In 1786, the chief judge's son Antônio Caetano paid for the burial of an indigent in the Santo Antônio church in the name of his father, who had passed away in Portugal seven years earlier.

BROTHERHOODS

In the village of Tejuco, as throughout the captaincy, the construction of churches, the worship of saints, and the organization of Catholic masses and rites fell to the lay brotherhoods, which filled the vacuum left by the religious orders that were barred from installing themselves in the captaincy. Belonging to a brotherhood was essential to the organization and identity of the urban centers that were beginning to form, as the Catholic religion was a fundamental part of daily life. It was for this reason that they were not exclusive to whites, but also admitted blacks and mulattos and in all senses reflected the existing racial and social stratifications.

In Minas Gerais, it was practically impossible not to participate in these brotherhoods. They were the venues for the Catholic rites of baptism, marriage, last rites, and burial, as they owned and administrated the tombs, which were located inside the churches. Among the privileges reserved for the brothers was the guarantee of a series of alms and acts of piety to ensure the salvation of the soul at the hour of death, including the celebration of masses, the payment of funeral expenses, and the right to be buried in the habit of the

---

[53] AEAD. Livro da fabriqueira da capela de Santo Antônio. 1780–1838. Caixa 509, fls. 17–17v.

[54] Ibidem, f. 17v.

order – all essential preparations for death according to the religious beliefs of the day.

The brotherhoods arose out of the invocation of the saints, to whom altars were erected in the churches. As they mirrored the social and racial organization of the day, a distinction can be seen between those that predominated in Minas Gerais in the first and second halves of the eighteenth century, given the greater complexity and stratification of the latter period. In the beginning, white brotherhoods were more common, especially those of the Most Holy in which the most illustrious villagers tended to congregate, though little by little black brotherhoods began to appear, such as Our Lady of the Rosary[55] and those of saints Benedict and Ifigênia.

The mechanisms for the exteriorization of the social standing of each individual, the brotherhoods were intended to be the very portrait of the hierarchical society of the eighteenth century. In Sabará, for example, regardless of how much property they happened to own, freedwomen of color could only belong to black or mulatto brotherhoods, a clear sign of the difficulty they faced in finding their place in the world of the free, monopolized as it was by the whites.[56] In Minas, on the other hand, where miscegenation was much more prevalent, this rule was not always observed. In Tejuco, contrary to the custom in Rio de Janeiro, Salvador, and Sabará, the freed and their descendants often joined the less exclusive of the white brotherhoods, which leads us to conclude that colored women could find more effective opportunities for social reinsertion in the Diamantine Demarcation than they could elsewhere.

João Fernandes, Chica da Silva, and their children were members of the principal brotherhoods of Tejuco in which they even held directorial posts, a privilege in terms of social recognition. They were involved in almost every brotherhood, whether of whites, mulattos, or blacks. However, the fact that Chica and her mulatto offspring

---

[55] Julita Scarano. "Black brotherhoods: Integration or contradiction?" *Luso-Brazilian Review*, 1979, pp. 1–17. See also Patricia Mulvey. "Black brothers and sisters: Membership in the black lay brotherhoods of colonial Brazil." *Luso-Brazilian Review*, 1980, pp. 252–79.

[56] Kathleen J. Higgins, op. cit., pp. 89–120.

were members of brotherhoods that were supposedly reserved for whites is by no means an isolated occurrence, much less constitutes a special privilege. Many colored freedwomen moved among the brotherhoods of Tejuco without encountering the slightest resistance from society. The presence of many of these women on the directorial boards of these institutions conferred protection and distinction upon the brotherhoods, especially true of those that directed the Brotherhood of the Rosary of the Blacks in the second half of the eighteenth century.

The first church built in Tejuco was dedicated to Saint Anthony and later became the parish church as the village grew around it. Nothing remains of the old church, as it was built in loam. Already in ruins in 1822, it was finally demolished in 1940. The brotherhoods used to erect side altars along the flanks of the church in the honor of their respective patron saints. The Santo Antônio church housed altars to Our Lord of the Stations, Our Lady of the Rosary,[57] the Most Holy Sacrament, and Saint Michael of the Souls.

Both the contractor and Chica da Silva and her descendants had free run of the various white brotherhoods, especially those of the Most Holy Sacrament, Saint Michael of the Souls, the Carmelite brotherhoods in Tejuco and in Vila do Príncipe, Saint Francis, and the Holy Land. Chica joined most of these after João Fernandes had returned to the Realm and in the period shortly after his death. This would show that her insertion within the village elite, and that of her descendants after her, was not merely the result of the chief judge's presence, but that she had in fact achieved, at least in part, the social ascension she craved for herself and her kin.

The "core objective" of the Brotherhood of the Most Holy Sacrament was "to promote, to the best possible degree, reverence, devotion and the cult of Our Lord Jesus Christ of the sacraments."[58] In the early colonial years, the cult of the Most Holy was intended to

[57] FBN. Memória histórica da capitania de Minas Gerais, 1693, no. 6524 do CEHB.
[58] Compromisso da Irmandade do Santíssimo Sacramento da capela de Santo Antônio do arraial do Tejuco, filial de Nossa Senhora da Conceição da Vila do Príncipe desta comarca do Serro Frio. Lisboa: Régia Oficina Tipográfica, 1785, capítulo 1.

congregate the white elites of all of the mining villages, but miscegenation among the races led to many mulattos becoming members,
which directly contravened the statutes and demonstrated that the
society no longer regulated itself by, nor behaved in accordance with,
the strict letter of the written rules. Approved by Her Majesty Maria
I, paragraph nine of the statutes of the Brotherhood of the Most Holy
of Tejuco, which speaks of the admittance of members, states the
following: "ye shall take care, however, that the people accepted be
honoured individuals of approved customs." These general directives
not only excluded people of wrong conduct, but principally those
of "suspect" origin – namely mulattos and bastards. For this reason,
members were forbidden to attend the funerals of those who "had
fallen into infamy for their conduct, having affairs with pardos and
giving birth to their children."[59]

Each year, the brothers elected the board of directors from the
ranks of the brotherhood's administrators. The board consisted of a
superintendent – the most important post in the entity – a treasurer,
a notary, an attorney, a messenger, and twenty-four other brothers.
According to the Constitution of the Brotherhood of the Most Holy:

> the post of superintendent is the most noble, and the most hon-
> oured of the brotherhood; which is why only worthy individuals
> should be proposed [for this post; people with] capacity, intelli-
> gence and sound intentions. [The superintendent's] obligations
> include ensuring that the statutes are faithfully obeyed; that there
> is precise economy in the brotherhood's expenses; [handling] the
> preservation, increase and intake of its assets; overseeing the rou-
> tine events and convening the Board in the event of the extra-
> ordinary; maintaining harmony and peace among the brothers
> and, finally, soliciting the general good of the brotherhood.[60]

In the year 1759, Manuel Pires Sardinha was elected superintendent of the brotherhood, and João Fernandes de Oliveira was

[59] Ibidem, capítulo 9.
[60] Ibidem, capítulo 2.

appointed to the board.[61] While based in Tejuco, the chief judge actively participated in the fraternity. During the years 1765–1766 he occupied the position of notary, the post of superintendent in 1768, and sat on the board of directors in 1770.[62]

This brotherhood commemorated Corpus Christi by "displaying the Host on the throne, celebrating a high mass complete with sermon, followed by a procession through the most public streets of the village."[63] During the procession, which was the high point of the event, the most important figures in Tejuco, all members of the brotherhood, marched before God and the rest of the community, reaffirming their social standing and prestige. The illustrious were positioned in the procession according to a strict order that exalted one over the other. The superintendent walked at the head of the procession while the most important brothers, those who had exercised some position within the entity, like Manuel Pires Sardinha and João Fernandes de Oliveira, were invited to carry the poles of the canopy used to cover the image of the Blessed Sacrament.[64] Whenever there were sufficient funds, Holy Week was celebrated in similar fashion.

As a sister of the Most Holy Sacrament, Chica and her slaves had the privilege of being buried in the brotherhood's tombs in the Santo Antônio church. The occupants of directorial positions could be entombed at the altar, while all other brothers and sisters were laid to rest in the nave of the church and their slaves in the grounds.[65]

---

[61] "Election of the superintendent, other officials and brothers of the board to serve the Brotherhood of the Most Holy Sacrament, for the year 1759–60. Attorney Dr. Manuel Pires Sardinha/brother of the board – Dr. João Frz. de Olivr . . ." Compromisso da Irmandade do Santíssimo Sacramento, 1785. AEAD. Livro de termos da Irmandade do Santíssimo Sacramento. 1759, caixa 508, f. 36.

[62] AEAD. Livro da Irmandade do Santíssimo Sacramento. 1759–1764, Box with no identification, fls. 4v, 6, 7.

[63] Compromisso da Irmandade do Santíssimo Sacramento, 1785, Chapter 15. Still today, the Divine Feast is celebrated in Diamantina and the city streets are adorned with painted carpets.

[64] Compromisso da Irmandade do Santíssimo Sacramento, 1785, Chapters 2 and 9.

[65] "This brotherhood has, in the chapel, long and peaceful possession of twelve sepulchres: eight outside the rails, and four inside. In these, only brothers

The books of the Santo Antônio parish church of Tejuco, which administrated the tombs of the Brotherhood of the Most Holy Sacrament, registered various contributions Chica made in payment for the burial of slaves, both her own and those of her daughters. Between 1764 and 1784, João sabaru, João congo, Miguel angola, José maqui, José mina, Domingos sabaru, Antônio xambá, José sabaru, João mina, Francisco rebolo, Matias, Manuel [maçangum], and others whose names could not be identified, as well as some of her slaves' children, were all buried there.[66] Chica's sons and daughters were also members of this brotherhood. The first to join was Simão Pires Sardinha;[67] followed by Antônio,[68] who was notary in 1799;[69] João, who was a member of the board in 1795;[70] Francisca de Paula; and Luísa.[71]

Donna Francisca da Silva de Oliveira, as she was respectfully referred to, joined the Brotherhood of the Holy Land, otherwise known as the Bull of the Holy Crusade in October 1766, an entity to which she would continue to make contributions right up to the year before her death.[72] An old and traditional society in Portugal, belonging to its ranks was a sign of prestige. Although it did not have a temple in the village, it collected donations from its brothers and sisters in the name of its chosen cause – the delivery of the holy lands of Palestine from the hands of the infidels. In addition to

---

who served as superintendents shall be buried." Compromisso da Irmandade do Santíssimo Sacramento, 1785, Chapter 28.

[66] AEAD. Livro de óbitos do arraial do Tejuco. 1752–1895, caixa 350, fls. 100v, 133v, e Livro de óbitos do arraial do Tejuco. 1785–1810, caixa 351, fls. 8, 31v, 59v, 76, 84v, 94v, 122v, 144v, 145v, 156.

[67] AEAD. Livro da fabriqueira da capela de Santo Antônio. 1780–1838, caixa 509, f. 5v.

[68] AEAD. Livro de termos da Irmandade do Santíssimo Sacramento. 1759, caixa 508, f. 98v.

[69] AEAD. Livro da Irmandade do Santíssimo Sacramento. 1759–1764, caixa sem identificação, f. 25v.

[70] Ibidem, f. 23v.

[71] AEAD. Livro da fabriqueira da capela de Santo Antônio. 1780–1838, caixa 509, f. 17v.

[72] AEAD. Livros dos irmãos da Terra Santa no Tejuco. Caixa 509, f. 119.

Chica, Antônia, Luísa, and Ana were all members of this fraternity, the latter having joined while a boarder in Macaúbas.[73] In 1800, now living in Portugal, Simão Pires Sardinha, in the capacity of chief treasurer of the Bull, had the privilege of being able to appoint the attorneys in charge of collecting donations in each of the captaincies of Brazil. During his term of office, Ventura Fernandes de Oliveira, his stepfather's cousin, held the post in Vila Rica.[74]

Another very well-known brotherhood in the mining villages of the first half of the eighteenth century was that of Saint Michael of the Souls whose cult was connected with the belief in this saint as the protector of the souls in purgatory over whom he stood guard and ushered to and fro. Always invoked at the hour of death, this saint was the recipient of many offered masses. In Tejuco, the brotherhood mounted an altar in the Santo Antônio parish church, as it had not built a chapel of its own. We know that João Fernandes de Oliveira was a member of the Brotherhood of Michael of the Souls, as his signature appears on the affiliation papers of one Rosa Pereira in 1756.[75] Chica may have been a sister, but this cannot be verified, as the pages that precede those containing the names of her children in the roster and on which her own name would probably be found have been torn out. Simão Pires Sardinha joined the entity in 1762[76] and João in 1769.[77] Francisca de Paula, Rita Quitéria, Antônio Caetano, Ana Quitéria, Antônia, and Mariana all entered the brotherhood in 1791.[78] Maria also belonged to this order, but the date of her affiliation is unknown.[79]

---

[73] Ibidem, fls. 2, 8, 23.
[74] *Autos da devassa da Inconfidência Mineira.* Belo Horizonte: Imprensa Nacional, vol. 3, 1978, p. 455.
[75] AEAD. Livro de irmãos professos na Irmandade de São Miguel das Almas. 1756, caixa 519, f. 13.
[76] Ibidem, fls. 48v, 87v.
[77] Ibidem, f. 87v.
[78] Ibidem, fls. 248–248v.
[79] AEAD. Livro de óbitos do arraial do Tejuco. 1785–1810, caixa 351, f. 279. In her will, Maria declared she was sister of Michael of the Souls Brotherhood.

The growth of Tejuco and the resulting stratification of its society, which became more complex, the enrichment of the brotherhoods and the increase in membership all led to these entities eventually constructing their own temples. The Rosário church, located in the square of the same name, was initially where all the blacks and mulattos in the village congregated. Originally built as a small chapel starting in 1731, it underwent a series of remodelings throughout the century and was enlarged in 1771. The gilding of the altars and the painting of the ceiling were executed between 1779 and 1802 by Customs Inspector José Soares de Araújo, who was not only the treasurer of the brotherhood at the time but also the best known local artist. The painted ceiling, executed in tones of sepia and a bluish gray, depicted the Virgin of the Rosary surrounded by angels and clouds. Statues of the patron saints of the blacks – Elesbão, Benedict, Anthony Catagerona, and Our Lady of the Rosary – were installed on the altars.

However, whites also joined the Brotherhood of the Rosary and other fraternities that had black and mulatto membership. In this case, what attracted them were not the bonds of identity, but the prestige that came with admittance. Important members of the community were invited to fill directorial positions, as it was believed that in this way the brotherhoods would be protected, as the more powerful brothers often lent money to finance construction work and festivities.

Each year the Brotherhood of the Rosary elected a king, queen, treasurer, notary, members of the board, and four male and four female presidents in charge of devotions to the saints Our Lady of the Rosary, Benedict, Antônio, and Elesbão.[80] The king and queen were generally selected from among the colored members, while the other posts were usually filled by whites or occasionally freed blacks

---

[80] It was an obligation to the members of the board to pay alms to the brotherhood. AEAD. Livro de inventário da Irmandade de Nossa Senhora do Rosário. 1733–1892, caixa 514, f. 49; AEAD. Livro de receita e despesa da Irmandade de Nossa Senhora do Rosário. 1787, caixa 525, f. 30v.

or mulattos who had made their fortunes. In 1749, for example, the Sergeant Major João Fernandes de Oliveira was one of the presidents of the devotions.[81] His son also joined the Rosary, and the records show that his annuity was paid up to February 1773, three years after he had departed for Portugal.[82] In 1793, the Brotherhood of the Rosary's ledgers registered the payment of a sum owed to the chief judge, most likely from loans he had made to the fraternity, but as the contractor had died in 1779, this money was paid to his heirs.[83]

Chica da Silva and other freedwomen were notable benefactors of the Brotherhood of the Rosary and often held directorial positions, thus standing out among the other members, especially the slaves. Chica's participation on the board of directors of this entity only began after João Fernandes' departure, as did her two stints as president of devotions, 1772–3 and 1788–9, a term in which she was also a board member, all of which evidences her role and standing in society.

Maria Martins Castanheira, a black Benguela woman from Angola and wife of the Blackman Francisco Pereira Lima, twice held the post of president of devotions.[84] During the two-year period 1754–5, Francisca Pires, mother of Cipriano Pires Sardinha, was elected sister of the board in honor of Saint Francis.[85] In 1763, Francisca da Silva de Oliveira offered a pair of gold earrings as alms to the Rosary.[86]

Her children also joined the brotherhood and came to occupy positions of note. Her eldest daughter, Francisca de Paula, joined in 1788 and was appointed sister of the board in 1793, the same year

---

[81] AEAD. Livro de inventário da Irmandade de Nossa Senhora do Rosário. 1733–1892, caixa 514, f. 38.

[82] AEAD. Livro de receita e despesa da Irmandade de Nossa Senhora do Rosário. 1787, caixa 525, f. 23v.

[83] AEAD. Livro de receita e despesa da Irmandade de Nossa Senhora do Rosário. 1788, caixa 525, f. 34v.

[84] AEAD. Livro de óbitos do arraial do Tejuco. Caixa 521, fls. 387–388.

[85] AEAD. Livro de inventário da Irmandade de Nossa Senhora do Rosário. 1733–1892, caixa 514, f. 43.

[86] Ibidem, f. 47v.

she donated a gem to the entity.[87] Also in 1793, Quitéria made a donation that earned her the right to carry one of the poles of the canopy used to cover the image of Our Lady during the procession.[88] For the two-year period 1783–4, João and José Agostinho were both board members, the latter having previously served the same function in 1780.[89] João was appointed to the directorate again in 1787–8 and served as president of devotions to Saint Benedict for the period 1793–4.[90] Antônio sat on the board in 1795, and Ana was president of devotions to Saint Benedict in 1801.[91]

For each Rosary festival, celebrated annually, the brotherhood chose a King Congo and Queen Ginga, the former also being elected Emperor of the Divine.[92] The celebration consisted of religious ceremonies and the *congado* (or *reinado*), which involved a reconstruction of the battle between the black and white monarchies and various dances, such as the marujada, the catopê, and caboclos. Throughout the duration of the festival, the emperor exercised real power over his "subjects," even going so far as to free the village prisoners, which really scandalized the imperial officials.[93] In 1771, the parish priest Mariana Leonardo de Azevedo Castro remarked that, in Tejuco:

> this is a custom and every year the king has them free whomsoever he pleases, among a thousand other follies[;] they are

[87] AEAD. Livro de entrada de irmãos professos na Irmandade de Nossa Senhora do Rosário 1782–1808, caixa 514, fls. 26v, 44v.

[88] AEAD. Livro de receita e despesa da Irmandade de Nossa Senhora do Rosário. 1787, caixa 525, f. 24.

[89] AEAD. Livro de inventário da Irmandade de Nossa Senhora do Rosário. 1750–1794, caixa 514, fls. 74, 76v.

[90] AEAD. Livro de inventário da Irmandade de Nossa Senhora do Rosário 1733–1892, caixa 514, fls. 76v, 82, 83v, 92; Livro de inventário da Irmandade de Nossa Senhora do Rosário. 1750–1794, caixa 514, f. 82, e Livro de receita e despesa da Irmandade de Nossa Senhora do Rosário. 1787, caixa 525, fls. 5v, 29v.

[91] AEAD. Livro de inventário da Irmandade de Nossa Senhora do Rosário. 1750–1794, caixa 514, fls. 95, 101v.

[92] Carlos Drummond de Andrade. "Rosário dos homens pretos." *Obra completa.* 1967, p. 642.

[93] Carlos Drummond de Andrade, op. cit., pp. 643–4.

venerated like real kings and even the white men must bow to them as they pass. They make them a throne bedecked with dossal, where they sit with crown and mitre, dispatching petitions, giving audience to whites and blacks alike and dispensing them all.[94]

In 1756, misunderstandings between slaves and freedmen made it necessary to create an exclusive form of representation for freed mulattos and pardos who sought to set themselves apart from the black slaves and increase their social standing, resulting in the emergence of new brotherhoods to accommodate them. In Tejuco, these new entities built the Amparo church and erected an altar to Our Lord of the Stations at Bonfim chapel. In 1771, they met at the Brotherhood of Our Lady of the Mercies, which began the construction of its own church some years later. In that same year, the Brotherhood of the Rosary decided to no longer concede the use of an altar in its church to the Brotherhood of the Mercies, as its brothers now had a "church or chapel and altar [of their own], and had made its separation in the most indecorous manner, with indecent words, saying that this was a brotherhood of Negroes in which they wanted no part."[95] Work began on the Mercês church on the street of the same name in 1778 and continued into the beginning of the next century. On Easter Sunday 1784, the day of the resurrection, the statue of the patron saint, also depicted on the painted ceiling in the company of angels, was placed on the main altar of the chapel where the brotherhood came to meet from that moment on.

Chica was a member of the Brotherhood of the Mercies,[96] where she served as president of devotions in 1770[97] and 1774 when she

---

94 Apud: Carlos Drummond de Andrade, op. cit., p. 644.
95 AEAD. Livro de inventário da Irmandade de Nossa Senhora do Rosário. 1750–1794, caixa 514, fls. 22v–23v.
96 AEAD. Livro de entradas da Irmandade de Nossa Senhora das Mercês. Caixa 520, f. 20.
97 AEAD. Livro de eleição de juízes e juízas da Irmandade Nossa Senhora das Mercês. 1771–1847, caixa 510, fls. 3v, 20; Livro de receita da Irmandade de Nossa Senhora das Mercês. 1770–1772, caixa 510, f. 3.

paid six eighths of gold for her admittance and signed the register.[98] When she died, forty masses were said for her soul,[99] with another ten celebrated the following year.[100]

Simão Pires Sardinha, Francisca de Paula,[101] José Agostinho,[102] Rita Quitéria,[103] Antônio Caetano, Ana Quitéria,[104] Helena,[105] Maria,[106] Antônia,[107] and a protégé of Chica's named Luciana Perpétua[108] were all brothers and sisters of the Mercies, where members of her family held various important posts. Rita Quitéria was a board member on two occasions,[109] while Luciana Perpétua de Oliveira sat on the board in 1778.[110] Francisca de Paula was appointed to the same position in 1791 and Maria in 1804. In 1790

[98] AEAD. Livro de registro de irmãos professos na Irmandade de Nossa Senhora das Mercês. 1774–1799, caixa sem identificação, f. 88.

[99] AEAD. Livros de missas para falecidos da Irmandade Nossa Senhora das Mercês. Caixa 520, f. 10.

[100] Ibidem, f. 20.

[101] In 1774, Francisca de Paula paid alms in gold to enter in the brotherhood. AEAD. Livro de registro de irmãos professos na Irmandade de Nossa Senhora das Mercês. 1774–1799, caixa sem identificação, f. 88.

[102] Admittance on April 20, 1795. AEAD. Livro segundo de grades da Irmandade de Nossa Senhora das Mercês. 1793–1837, caixa 521, f. 9v.

[103] AEAD. Livro de registro de irmãos professos na Irmandade de Nossa Senhora das Mercês. 1774–1793, caixa 557, f. 27.

[104] Admittance on August 15, 1798. AEAD. Livro segundo de grades da Irmandade de Nossa Senhora das Mercês. 1793–1837, caixa 521, f. 2v.

[105] AEAD. Livro de certidões de missas da Irmandade de Nossa Senhora das Mercês. 1776, caixa 520, f. 36.

[106] Admittance on December 21, 1801. AEAD. Livro de entradas da Irmandade de Nossa Senhora das Mercês. 1799, caixa 520, f. 15v.

[107] On January 22, 1788, paid alms in gold. AEAD. Livro de registro de irmãos professos na Irmandade de Nossa Senhora das Mercês. 1774–1799, caixa sem identificação.

[108] As we will see in Chapter 7, Luciana, who entered in Macaúbas with Chica's daughters, were related or protégée of the couple. AEAD. Livro de entradas da Irmandade de Nossa Senhora das Mercês. 1801, caixa 520, fls. 5, 15v; Livro de receita da Irmandade de Nossa Senhora das Mercês. 1770–1772, caixa 510, f. 17v, e Livro de receita da Irmandade de Nossa Senhora das Mercês. 1770–1803, caixa 510, fls. 31, 41v, 45, 48, 50v.

[109] AEAD. Livro de eleição de juízes e juízas da Irmandade Nossa Senhora das Mercês. 1771–1847, caixa 510, fls. 12, 45.

[110] Ibidem, f. 25.

and 1801, Chica's eldest daughter exercised the function of president of devotions to Our Lady of the Mercies,[111] as did Antônia in 1788,[112] Luciana Perpétua[113] in 1798, and Rita Quitéria[114] in 1811, all of whom were registered with the title Donna (Lady) in the brotherhood's records. In 1803, three of Chica's children simultaneously held directorial posts: Maria was president of devotions to Our Lady of the Mercies, Antônio to Saint Ifigênia, while Francisca de Paula was a member of the board.[115]

Chica's slaves also participated in the Brotherhood of the Mercies. The records show that Laureana, a black woman from the Gold Coast of Mina, was admitted to the fraternity in 1789. There are two interesting facts about this: First, she was registered as Laureana da Silva de Oliveira, that is, she had acquired her owner's surnames, and, second, she was able to sign the papers herself, firmly and confidently, which shows that she was literate in Portuguese.[116] Two more of Chica's slaves, Tomásio and Donata Fernandes de Oliveira, both cabras, joined in 1797 and 1804, respectively.[117] As Chica had died in 1796, they were registered as property of her estate. Gertrudes Maria de Jesus de São José, a creole, and Davi Fernandes de Oliveira, a pardo, both former slaves of Chica, were also members of the Mercies.[118]

The Brotherhood of Amparo was started in 1756, but the construction of its chapel dates to the 1770s. The ceiling painting in the nave depicted the Holy Spirit and the various altars were all adorned with images of the protectors of the pardos – Our Lady of Amparo,

---

[111] Ibidem, fls. 20, 26.
[112] Ibidem, f. 26.
[113] AEAD. Livro de entradas da Irmandade de Nossa Senhora das Mercês do Tejuco. Caixa 510, f. 161.
[114] AEAD. Livro de eleição de juízes e juízas da Irmandade de Nossa Senhora das Mercês. 1771–1847, caixa 510, f. 36v.
[115] Ibidem, fls. 28v–29.
[116] AEAD. Livro de registro de irmãos professos na Irmandade de Nossa Senhora das Mercês. 1774–1799, caixa sem identificação, f. 67v.
[117] AEAD. Livro de certidões de missas da Irmandade de Nossa Senhora das Mercês. 1776, caixa 520, f. 37; Livro segundo de grades da Irmandade de Nossa Senhora das Mercês. 1793–1837, caixa 521, f. 16v.
[118] AEAD. Livro segundo de grades da Irmandade de Nossa Senhora das Mercês. 1793–1837, caixa 521, fls. 17v, 99v.

Our Lady of the Rosary, Our Lady of the Birth, Saint Anne, Saint Barbara, Saint Luzia, and Saint Rita.[119] Maria was the only one of Chica's children who became a member of this brotherhood.[120]

In the second half of the eighteenth century differences also began to emerge among the white population of Minas Gerais, which gave rise to a proliferation of brotherhoods constructing their own churches. In Tejuco, the wealthier villagers congregated in brotherhoods devoted to Saint Francis of Assisi and Our Lady of Mount Carmel.

The Carmelite Brotherhood appeared in Tejuco in 1758 when the brothers erected an altar at the parish church. In 1760, sponsored by João Fernandes de Oliveira, work began on a church consecrated in the honor of Saint Francis de Paul, to whom the chief judge and his father were devotees and whose image graced the façade of the family manor in Lisbon.[121] A small chapel dedicated to this saint already stood at the chosen site on Rua do Contrato and the brotherhood continued to hold ceremonies there.

Architectonically speaking, the church stood out among the others in the village because its tower was erected at the back of the building. Customs Inspector José Soares de Araújo carried out a lot of gilding and painting work inside this church, including the ceiling painting in the central nave, which depicts, in perspective, the prophet Elijah blazing through the sky in a chariot of fire. In 1765, once the masonry work was complete, João Fernandes donated the church to the brotherhood, which registered it as having been "built at his own expense."[122] As a condition of the donation, João

---

[119] This feast is still celebrated.
[120] AEAD. Livro segundo de grades da Irmandade de Nossa Senhora das Mercês. 1793–1837, caixa 521, f. 43; Livro de certidões de missas da Irmandade de Nossa Senhora das Mercês. 1776, caixa 520, f. 15v.
[121] Iphan/BH. Pasta de tombamento da igreja do Carmo de Diamantina. Cópia do documento com que Sua Majestade foi servida... VF. GRAFIA.
[122] Walter Almeida. "Igreja de Nossa Senhora do Carmo." Voz do Carmelo, no. 1147, 1998, pp. 325–6. The constitution of the order, approved in 1785, states that "the chapel the [Carmelite brothers] presently possess was donated and built by the chief judge João Fernandes de Oliveira, with the license of the diocesan officials." Iphan/BH. Pasta de tombamento da igreja do Carmo. Documentos avulsos. Cópia do livro de registro desta chancelaria da Ordem, f. 141.

Fernandes stipulated that a mass be said for his soul every Saturday, even after his death.[123]

The chief judge took the habit of the Third Order of Our Lady of the Mount Carmel at a ceremony held at the parish church in April 1764.[124] A year later, the images of Saint Francis de Paul, Our Lady of Mount Carmel, and the Sacred Heart were transferred to the brotherhood's new chapel in a grand procession.[125] In 1766, the congregation organized another party to receive images of the saints Elijah and Teresa, the dead Christ, and Our Lady of Solitude it had acquired in Portugal.[126]

There is nothing in the brotherhood's records to indicate that there were disputes between the chief judge and other members of the order concerning the site chosen for the construction of the church as Joaquim Felício dos Santos asserts in his book.[127] Quite the contrary: as a sign of gratitude for having sponsored the church, João Fernandes was elected first prior, the most important post in the entity, which he held until 1767.[128] In 1798 and 1799, many years after his death, in return for his services to the order, the brotherhood celebrated posthumous masses in his honor, as requested in his will.[129]

In the first years after its foundation, the Carmelite Brotherhood[130] was the most elitist in the village. The membership roll features one Francisca da Silva, but as the name is not complete, we

---

[123] Ordem Terceira de Diamantina. *Mensageiro do Carmelo*, ano 30, pp. 85–6.

[124] AEAD. Livro de registro de irmãos na Ordem Terceira do Carmo. 1763–1808, caixa 541, f. 10.

[125] Ordem Terceira de Diamantina. *Mensageiro do Carmelo*, ano 30, pp. 85–6.

[126] Assis Horta. "Carmo ano 2000." *Estrela polar*. 1959.

[127] Joaquim Felício dos Santos. *Memórias do Distrito Diamantino*. 1976, pp. 123–4.

[128] AEAD. Livro de ordenações da Irmandade de Nossa Senhora do Carmo. 1763–1808, caixa 541, f. 10. Ver Assis Horta, op. cit.

[129] Iphan/BH. Pasta de tombamento da igreja do Carmo. Documentos avulsos. Livro de missas celebradas aos irmãos do Carmo. In 1798, forty-three masses were said in his honor, whereas sixty-two were prayed for his soul in 1799, as attested by João Correia de Sales Oliveira, the commissary of the Order.

[130] An entry dating to 1766 registers the admittance of one Francisca de Sales Oliveira, a name that is not found in any other documents from Tejuco. It is possible that the notary made a mistake when noting the name Francisca da

cannot be sure this was our Chica da Silva.[131] However, it is certain that she belonged to the Brotherhood of Our Lady of Mount Carmel in Vila do Príncipe.[132] Though initially extremely selective, the Carmelite Brotherhood in Tejuco started admitting free, freed, and even captive men and women of color as the years wore on. In 1782 alone, five slaves and four creole women joined the brotherhood,[133] while two former slaves of Chica, Tomásio and Laureana, joined in 1805.[134]

Following in their father's footsteps, Chica's children all actively participated in the Third Carmelite Order. Francisca de Paula,[135] João,[136] Quitéria,[137] Antônia,[138] Mariana,[139] Ana,[140] Rita, Maria,[141] Luísa,[142] and Helena[143] were all members of the brotherhood, while

Silva de Oliveira. AEAD. Livro de ordenações da Irmandade de Nossa Senhora do Carmo. 1763–1808, Caixa 541, f. 15.

[131] Diamantina, Igreja do Carmo. Livro contendo todos os nomes dos membros Ordem Terceira de Nossa Senhora do Carmo. 1788–..., s.n.

[132] AEAD. Livro de ordenações da Irmandade de Nossa Senhora do Carmo do Serro. 1780, box 528.

[133] Ibidem. Admitted on October 15, 1782 (João, Silvana, Josefa, and Ana, slaves, and Cândida creole, belonging to Luís Coelho); October 16, 1782 (Maria, slave, and the creoles Luísa, Custódia, and Ursula).

[134] Ibidem. Admitted on July 16, 1805.

[135] Ibidem. Admitted on July 16, 1798.

[136] Ibidem. Admitted on July 16, 1798.

[137] AEAD. Livro de ordenações da Irmandade de Nossa Senhora do Carmo. 1763–1808, caixa 541, f. 53.

[138] BAT. Documentos avulsos. Ordem Terceira de Nossa Senhora do Carmo. Caixa 478, f. 233.

[139] AEAD. Livro de registro de irmãos na Ordem Terceira de Nossa Senhora do Carmo. 1763–1808, caixa 541, no. 616.

[140] AEAD. Livro de ordenações da Irmandade de Nossa Senhora do Carmo. 1763–1808, caixa 541, f. 53, e Livro de registro de irmãos na Ordem Terceira de Nossa Senhora do Carmo. 1763–1808, caixa 541, no. 629.

[141] AEAD. Livro de registro de irmãos na Ordem Terceira de Nossa Senhora do Carmo. 1763–1808, caixa 541, no. 615.

[142] BAT. Documentos avulsos. Ordem Terceira de Nossa Senhora do Carmo. Caixa 478, f. 233.

[143] AEAD. Livro de ordenações da Irmandade de Nossa Senhora do Carmo. 1763–1808, caixa 541; BAT. Documentos avulsos. Ordem Terceira de Nossa Senhora do Carmo. Caixa 478, f. 233.

Antônio was secretary of the board in 1777, 1781, and 1788,[144] years in which his signature features on the registers.[145]

The brotherhood of Saint Francis was established in 1762 and began work on the construction of a church dedicated to Our Lady of the Conception situated in the expanding eastern side of the village four years later. Built on the corner of Rua Macau, at the top of a flight of stone steps, a single tower was constructed in front of the building. An image of Saint Francis of Assisi hung above the throne in the sanctuary whose painted ceiling bore an image of the Virgin surrounded by angels and clouds, once more by the hand of José Soares de Araújo. Although it was founded as a white brotherhood, in addition to the chief judge,[146] Chica,[147] Antônio Caetano,[148] Francisca de Paula,[149] and Ana Quitéria[150] were all members. In 1782, Maria, also a member,[151] made a donation to the collection for the gilding of the church in Tejuco.[152]

Chica was no exception in Tejuco. Other freedwomen also participated widely in both black and mulatto brotherhoods and those that were supposed to be exclusively for the village's white elite. In 1766, a parda named Antônia de Oliveira Silva was a member of the Souls and Holy Land in Tejuco. She was also a sister of the Carmelite

[144] Igreja do Carmo. Livro contendo todos os nomes dos membros Ordem Terceira de Nossa Senhora do Carmo. 1788–..., s.n. (The keeping of these books began in 1788 when Antônio Fernandes de Oliveira was secretary of the board.)

[145] Iphan/BH. Pasta de tombamento da igreja do Carmo. Documentos avulsos. Ata de 1777: "Termo a respeito das duas imagens de Christo."

[146] AEAD. Documentos avulsos da Ordem Terceira de São Francisco. 1787, caixa 503.

[147] AEAD. Livro de óbitos da Ordem Terceira de São Francisco, f. 55.

[148] AEAD. Documentos avulsos da Ordem Terceira de São Francisco. 1781–1782, caixa 503.

[149] AEAD. Livro de óbitos da Ordem Terceira de São Francisco. 1772–1857, caixa 350, f. 96.

[150] AEAD. Livro de óbitos de irmãos da Irmandade de São Francisco. 1772–1857. Caixa 350. Letra A.

[151] AEAD. Documentos avulsos da Ordem Terceira de São Francisco. 1763–1769, caixa 501.

[152] AEAD. Documentos avulsos da Ordem Terceira de São Francisco. 1783, caixa 503.

and Franciscan brotherhoods in her native Bahia and left payment at their respective convents in Salvador to have two hundred masses said for her soul.[153] At the end of the eighteenth century, the creole Rita Pais Gouveia was a sister of the Souls,[154] while at the beginning of the nineteenth century, the black woman Ana da Encarnação Amorim was registered as a sister of the Brotherhoods of the Rosary, the Mercies, and Saint Francis of Assisi,[155] which shows the level of social ascension the condition of freedwoman allowed.

The black woman Jacinta de Siqueira sought to have her status in life reaffirmed and publicly paraded in death. Her corpse was draped in the Franciscan habit and buried in the parish church of Vila do Príncipe after the celebration of a funeral mass. She was escorted to her final resting place by the Brotherhood of the Souls, which, in the mining towns of the first half of the eighteenth century, was exclusive to the local elites, and by the Brotherhood of Our Lady of the Rosary, of which she was also a member.[156] The purpose of this outward display of honor was to show that she had succeeded in extricating herself from the social limbo to which her color and enslavement had consigned her.

Chica da Silva was an assiduous churchgoer who "contributed with many offerings and in any other way she could to pious works and [to] the divine cult," "attending all of the feast days, processions and acts of piety and devotion with all the demeanour of a Christian of old."[157] Father José Ribeiro Aldonço said of Chica that she "attended all the services with devotion and [all the] demonstrations of a good Christian."[158] In the religious education she gave her children, her orientation was always that they attend mass, help in the

---

[153] AEAD. Testamento de Antônia de Oliveira Silva. Livro de óbitos do arraial do Tejuco. Caixa 350, fls. 162v–163.

[154] AEAD. Testamento de Rita Pais de Gouveia. Livro de Óbitos do arraial do Tejuco. Caixa 521, fls. 35–35v.

[155] BAT. Inventário e testamento de Ana da Encarnação Amorim. Cartório do Primeiro Ofício, maço 4.

[156] AFS. Testamento de Jacinta de Siqueira. Livro de testamentos no. 8, fls. 33v–38v.

[157] AEAM. *Auto de genere et moribus de Simão Pires Sardinha*. 1768, armário 10, pasta 1782. Testimony of Custódio Vieira da Costa and Manuel Francisco Cruz.

[158] Ibidem. Testemunho do reverendo José Ribeiro Aldonço.

celebration of the rites, godparent the newly born (especially the children of slaves), participate in the brotherhoods, observe the feast days and processions, and give alms. Captain Luís Lopes da Costa claimed to know Simão Pires Sardinha very well and described him as a young man who, like his mother and grandmother before him, was

> applied and correct in proper behaviour, always living in the fear of God and with good habits . . . , contributing with many donations for the construction of the church and . . . to the divine cult as a whole, with special zeal and devotion, which he has learned from seeing and beholding, as he himself has occasionally received alms in the capacity of official witness for certain brotherhoods.[159]

According to Father Aldonço, Chica's children were well behaved, the result of the "good education their mother gives and has given them, cautiously and with singular doctrine."[160]

Chica followed the Christian models of devotion to the letter and instructed her children in the teachings on the essential acts of the faith, those indispensable to the soul's ascension into heaven after death. Her motives, however, were not strictly religious. Making public show of her unreserved acceptance of Catholicism was one way she and her descendants could achieve good social standing among the white and Catholic village elite.

---

[159] Ibidem. Testemunho de Luís Lopes da Costa.
[160] Ibidem. Testemunho do reverendo José Ribeiro Aldonço.

CHAPTER SEVEN

Mines of Splendor

Ah, such swollen rivers,
and mountains so high!
. . .
Ah, such biting whips,
Such golden chapels!
Ah, such haughty manners,
And decisions so false . . .
Ah, such happy dreams . . .
Such miserable lives!

The Patron

In 1753, when Chica da Silva and Francisca Pires appeared before the ecclesiastical visit in Tejuco to sign their admission to the crime of concubinage with Manuel Pires Sardinha, "as neither knew how to write, the reverend inquisitor signed on their behalf."[1] Chica, like most of the slaves scattered throughout Brazil, was illiterate. Nevertheless, during her relationship with João Fernandes de Oliveira, she had access to a refined culture and was before long a lady "occupied with the service of her house [and] living off her slaves."[2] The chief judge was a cultured man, educated at Coimbra and possessed of a refined musical and theatrical taste. Chica started to attend the soirées, plays, and musical recitals he promoted, especially the operas,

---

[1] AEAD. Livro de termos do Serro do Frio. 1750, box 557, f. 102v.
[2] AEAM. *Auto de genere et moribus de Simão Pires Sardinha.* 1768, cabinet 10, file 1782. Testimony of Reverend Leonardo da Costa Amado.

the preferred style of the day. She also received some formal education, which at least enabled her to sign her own name and distance herself from her past of enslavement and illiteracy.

The following annotation can be found on various papers registering her daughters' movements to and from Macaúbas nunnery: "So signed she, [Francisca da Silva de Oliveira], the mother of the charge,"[3] is incontrovertible proof that she possessed this ability. In 1774, the abridged form of her name – "Fran^ca. da S. de Olivr^a"[4] appears in expectedly shaky lettering on her admittance papers to the Brotherhood of Our Lady of the Mercies. Among her personal possessions was a portable lacquered writing table with oriental motifs, which she would have used for writing and reading.[5]

At João Fernandes's side, Chica helped promote culture among the village society. While a student at the São Patrício seminary, the future judge learned to appreciate theatre, a core element of Jesuit pedagogy. According to Joaquim Felício dos Santos, the Palha farmhouse, which he left to his eldest son upon his return to Portugal, served as a stage for balls and theatre pieces.[6] Situated on the road to Itambé Peak, at the meeting of the Grande and Piruruca rivers, the farmhouse had a chapel and spacious salon where various plays were staged, such as *Porfiar amando* (*Porfiar in Love*), *Xiquinha por amor de Deus* (*Xiquinha for the Love of God*), *Os encantos de Medéia* (*The Enchantments of Medea*), and *O anfitrião* (*Amphitryon*).[7] Generally jocular in tone, the operas, with their mix of text and music, were experiences designed to at once entertain and enthrall the audience with the richness of the costumery and the harmony of the

[3] ARM. Livro de registro de saídas do recolhimento. 1781.
[4] AEAD. Livro de registro de irmãos professos na Irmandade de Nossa Senhora das Mercês. 1774–1799, unidentified box, f. 88.
[5] Belo Horizonte. AAPAH.
[6] Although until today in Diamantina it is said that the farmhouse belonged to Chica da Silva, it was João Fernandes's property, and several marriages were performed in the gardens. AEAD. Casamentos no Tejuco. Caixa. 335, f. 38. Later on the farmhouse was inherited by João Fernandes's elder son and then to his grandson João Germano de Oliveira Grijó. Biblioteca Antônio Torres. João Germano de Oliveira Grijó. Cartório do Primeiro Ofício, box 27.
[7] Joaquim Felício dos Santos. *Memórias do Distrito Diamantino*, 1976. p. 124.

instruments and voices. The pieces *Porfiar amando* and *O anfitrião* were staged at Santo Amaro da Purificação in Bahia in 1760 during the wedding festivities for the future queen Maria I.[8] The descriptions of these pieces give us an idea of the kind of spectacles Chica and João Fernandes would have presented to their select and enraptured audience in Tejuco. *Porfiar amando*, which was bankrolled by the village merchants, was accompanied by actors and "musicians...richly dressed in tragedian garb who sang the arias to the sound of harmonious instruments, elevating the senses of the numerous throng."[9] In the staging of this piece in Bahia, the director, Gregório de Sousa e Gouveia, added an introduction in the form of a poem celebrating the princes and recited by four figures representing earth, air, fire, and water. He also composed two additional ballroom pieces and a short farce, though the plot and text are not known.

O anfitrião was performed by the students of João Pinheiro de Lemos, and firsthand accounts relate that "there was much in this opera to please the eye in the precious costumes and excellent scenery, and to please the ear, given the properties of the voices, the harmony of the arias and the consonance of the instruments."[10] Both this piece and *Os encantos de Medéia* were written by Antônio José da Silva,[11] "the Jew," and were performed for the first time by the Spaniard Antônio Rodrigues[12] and company at the Public Theatre in Bairro Alto in Lisbon between 1733 and 1738. Born in Rio de Janeiro, Antônio da Silva was burned to death by the Inquisition in Lisbon in 1739 under accusations of Judaic heresy. His playful operas suited the tastes of the day and were hugely successful in the Portuguese capital, where they were published in small books that enabled them to reach stages all across the Empire.

Both pieces were adapted from Greek myths, with heroes for protagonists and tragic love as their theme. In *Os encantos de Medéia*, Jason travels to the kingdom of Colchis in search of the Golden

---

[8] Francisco Calmon. *Relação das faustíssimas festas*. 1762.
[9] Ibidem, p. 24.
[10] Ibidem, p. 25.
[11] Antônio José da Silva (the Jew). *Theatro cômico português*. 1788.
[12] Ibidem, p. 213.

Fleece, where he meets Medea, daughter of King Etas, who falls in love with him and helps him steal the fleece. However, finding herself tricked and abandoned by Jason, she assails his ship, the *Argos*, with a terrible storm, forcing him back to Colchis. Enraged by her behavior, the king marries Jason to his niece Creusa and gives him his kingdom. A despairing Medea disappears into the air.[13]

O anfitrião or *Júpiter e Alcmena* speaks of Jupiter's passion for Alcmene, the wife of Amphitryon. With the help of Mercury, Jupiter, the husband of Juno, takes advantage of Amphitryon's absence to assume his guise and seduce the desired Alcmene. On his return to Thebes, Juno avenges herself upon Amphitryon and Alcmene by having them arrested and condemned to death, though they are acquitted and escape their sentence. From the illicit tryst between Jupiter and Alcmene is born the powerful and undefeatable Hercules.[14]

The staging of these librettos at the Palha farmhouse shows that the village accompanied the theatrical successes of the Realm, with which it maintained a constant and fertile cultural interchange. These performances would have required mastery of the scenic arts as well as groups of musicians and choirs, varied and elegant costumery, and sometimes even fireworks displays and other entertainments with which to close the performances.

João Fernandes and Chica da Silva also promoted musical soirées of reputedly good quality. Feeling the lack of the chief judge's concerts, which he was no longer able to attend, Antônio da Mota e Magalhães, a notary of the Royal Revenue Commission in Vila Rica, tried to emulate them by organizing a band of slave musicians along the lines of the mulatto bands the contractor put together in Tejuco. The notary remarked that "at night I have seven slaves play, and they are not bad, [in fact] they are tolerable[;] with two trumpets, two flutes, two fiddles and a double bass." However, as he was looking for diversity, he asked João Fernandes to send him some sheet music, adding that it "has to be lovely stuff." The notary also complained

---

[13] Antônio José da Silva (the Jew). Op. cit. 1788, p. 214.
[14] Ibidem, p. 213.

that he would have liked to have singers like those he used to hear in his friend's ensemble, but "only one wants to be [a singer], though blacks from Africa are never a real treat, which is good for the creoles and mulattos."[15]

The *modinha*, a type of popular tune invented in Brazil, was the most often requested and played at the soirées. The lyrics, laden with erotic undertones, evoked impossible loves, often between white gentlemen and their black or mulatto slaves.[16] The sensual atmosphere that gripped the listeners was difficult to resist. The music "seized the heart before one could protect oneself against the malevolent influence; one finds oneself drinking of its milk and admitting the venom of voluptuousness into the most secret recesses of one's existence."[17] Reminiscent of the affair between the ex-slave and the white contractor and a host of other mixed couples, one of these tunes goes as follows:

> *My little white charmer,*
> *Sweet master my brother,*
> *I adore your bondage,*
> *My sweet-hearted whitey.*
> *Coz you call little sister*
> *A poor black lass like me,*
> *who trembles with pleasure.*[18]

According to Joaquim Felício dos Santos, the farmhouse was a refined place, with many exotic plants, trees brought over from Europe, and waterfalls and fountains trickling over crystals and shells. The taste for building closed gardens harked back to the Renaissance, and this, with its tree-lined walkways, benches, flowers, and groves, was a propitious venue for encounters, whether amorous, social, or religious. The farmhouse seems to have been a setting for

---

[15] AHU, MAMG. Caixa 99, doc. 17. Attached letters from Antônio da Mota Magalhães.
[16] Gilberto Freyre. *The Masters and the Slaves.* 1946, p. 355.
[17] William Beckford. "Italy, with sketches from Spain and Portugal." Apud: Gilberto Freyre, op. cit., pp. 340–1.
[18] Gilberto Freyre, op. cit., pp. 341.

social get-togethers of all types – a space for conviviality rather than reclusion and even for the weddings of the local elite. It was also a place of distinction, as few in the village society possessed the means to build something similar. This was somewhere Chica could leave the condition of her birth behind her and revel in the world of the whites.

With its fragrances and odors, nature of an altogether superior order to the dry ruggedness that surrounded the village, the gardens underlined the importance of the hosts before their guests, reminding all of how they should be celebrated in the daily life of the village society. The imported European trees made it a kind of remembrance, an invocation of the Realm and its codes of conduct. The carefully tended orchard blended tropical fruit trees,[19] such as mango, banana, and jaboticaba, with an assortment of the "thorny"[20] pine trees that dominated the region's vegetation, while the garden abounded with flowers and vegetables.[21]

However, as with any colonial society, the image the garden and its ceremonies intended to reflect was somewhat blurred and skewed. Nature inverted the order of things, as the species – like the people – had to adapt to the local conditions. Unlike in Portugal, the peach, pear, apple, and plum trees only partly shed their leaves in September.[22] In similar fashion, however much they sought to mirror the gestures and habits of the white elite in those gardens, at their core was always a mestizo woman who had been born a slave.

MACAÚBAS

The household education that Chica da Silva had as an ex-slave elevated to a higher social standing as the concubine of a white man

---

[19] Auguste de Saint-Hilare. *Viagem pelo Distrito dos Diamantes e litoral do Brasil.* 1974, p. 27–8.

[20] BAT. Inventory of Caetano Miguel da Costa. Cartório do Segundo Ofício, box 175; AEAM. *Auto de genere de Cipriano Pires Sardinha.* 1785, cabinet 3, drawer 34. Testimonies of Reverend Leonardo da Costa Amado and Manuel Antônio dos Santos Rocha.

[21] Alcide D'Orbigney. *Viagem pitoresca através do Brasil.* 1974, p. 135.

[22] Ibidem, p. 136.

from Portugal would have been very different to that she wanted for her children. The chance of positioning them on a much higher social level than her own made her opt for the most refined education available in Minas at the time.

The boys initially studied in Tejuco under the local curates and tutors before joining João Fernandes in the Realm, though it was not possible to determine exactly what university courses they took there.[23] It is certain that Simão Pires Sardinha first attended "school, where he learned to read and write, and then continued . . . his studies in grammar." He also studied Latin, necessary to get an ecclesiastical degree.[24] He graduated in Arts at the School of Arts in Portugal[25] and became a wise and learned naturalist.[26]

Chica's nine daughters were all sent to the retreat of Our Lady of the Conception of Monte Alegre de Macaúbas, the best educational establishment in the captaincy, where they would be assured a devout and honorable life.[27]

A mix between a convent and a school, Macaúbas was basically intended for the daughters of the white elite, though it also accommodated widows; married women in search of asylum, refuge, and peace[28]; and women interned by their husbands for committing adultery. It was one of the few places in Minas Gerais where women had

---

[23] They certainly did not study in Rome, nor at Coimbra, like their father, as there is no record of their presence there. They may have studied in France, as had their paternal grandfather's illegitimate son, but this could not be verified.

[24] AEAM. Auto de genere et moribus de Simão Pires Sardinha. 1768. Armário 10. Pasta 1782.

[25] AHU, MAMG. Caixa 140, doc. 49. Simão did not study at the Sapienza Institute in Rome as some authors granted but in Portugal at the School of Arts.

[26] AHU, MAMG. Caixa 123, doc. 89.

[27] Macaúbas was an institution entirely independent of the religious orders, which were prohibited in Minas Gerais. It functioned as a form of convent, as women could prepare to take vows as nuns, but also as an elementary school and general retreat. Macaúbas is a kind of palm tree, typical of the region.

[28] In 1768, the mother superior of Macaúbas filed a suit against Manuel Rodrigues Lima, resident of Bananal da Passagem in Mariana, as he had been obliged by public writ to pay "4 thousand cruzados, with interest . . . should his wife, d. Rosa Maria Varela de Mendonça, enter said retreat, which she did, many years [before], and remains to this very day." ACS. Notificações. Códice 171, Auto 4148.

access to formal education, as the families tended to be far more concerned with educating the males. There was a chronic lack of women in the colony, especially white women, and in such a recently populated region turned over to the generally male activity of mining for gold and diamonds, the situation was even worse. Women were far outnumbered by men, and the predominance of black and mulatta women reduced the supply of husband material and hindered the establishment of stable relationships legalized in Catholic matrimony. The Crown found itself obliged to limit the number of women allowed to enter convents and even prohibited their installation in the captaincy,[29] which is why Macaúbas functioned more or less unofficially throughout most of the eighteenth century despite coming under the supervision of the bishopric of Rio de Janeiro.

Macaúbas was not the only option at the time. There was also another retreat in Minas Novas village, much closer to Tejuco, known as Casa das Lágrimas[30] (The House of Tears). Dedicated to Saint Anne, the institution was built on the rural property of one of its inmates and was renowned for its poverty. Nonetheless, in the hope of providing her daughters with a more polished education, Chica preferred to send them further afield to Macaúbas, halfway between Tejuco and Vila Rica, beside the Velhas River in the environs of Jaboticatubas in Sabará County.

This building of somber architecture stood upon a knoll in a narrow valley walled in by mountains. The imposing structure, ringed by the palm and macaúba trees from which it took its name, was at once integrated with the surrounding landscape and removed from it, lending it an air of the peace and quietude necessary for the elevation of the soul. The chapel, which was the center of the spiritual life of the retreat, was located at the front of the ground floor in the middle of the façade. The sides of the building contained glass windows, some of which were closed with shutters. Internally, the building consisted of cloisters and cells built around a central garden patio. A trellised belvedere, in similar style to the muxarabis in the

29 AHU, MAMG. Caixa 18, doc. 40.
30 AHU, MAMG. Caixa 116, doc. 39.

town houses of Tejuco, allowed the interns to view the world outside without being seen.[31]

Providing a polished education for women meant, above all, preparing them for a virtuous life. The convent walls had to function as an unbreakable barrier to the mundane life that ran riot outside. Pure, untouched, and well instructed, these women found themselves at the crossroads between a religious vocation and an honored marriage. Situated in a delightful though distant and secluded location, Macaúbas was the ideal space in which Chica's children could prepare to assume their place among the village elite.

Chica da Silva's priority in sending her daughters to the convent was that they receive a formal, virtuous, and quality education, and of them all, only Francisca de Paula, Helena, Rita Quitéria, Ana Quitéria, and Antônia took vows and became nuns.[32] All but Antônia later abandoned the habit in order to marry. Macaúbas followed the rules of the Franciscan Conceptionists, according to which education was to be based on Christian values and demand a severing of connections with the outside world. Cloistered in simple individual cells, the interns were expected to shed the values to which they were accustomed back home. The duration of their retreat was to be entirely devoted to God and the convent environment, which, adrift somewhere between heaven and earth, lent itself well to the formation of charitable and pure Christian souls.

As soon as they entered the convent, they were obliged to adopt standards of behavior that marked the beginning of a new life. They abandoned their old names, clothes, and manners as a rite of passage and, having chosen a new name, donned the habit of the patron saint Our Lady of the Conception, which consisted of white vestments and blue veil. Their behavior conveyed humility, their gestures were expected to be contained, and they were to "speak only when necessary, and always modestly"[33] in a hushed voice. Upon entering the

[31] As we shall see, the belvedere was built with money donated by Chief Judge João Fernandes de Oliveira.

[32] ARM. . . . Termo de paga dos dotes das três sobreditas . . .

[33] AN. Mesa do Desembargo do Paço. Estatutos do recolhimento de Macaúbas. Caixa 130, pac. 2, doc. 57.

convent, all of Chica's daughters took the name São José, that of their paternal grandmother and the saint to which she was devoted (Saint Joseph was the patron of the church and the protector of Christian homes and possessed an unshakable faith). One daughter, Helena, added "Leocádia da Cruz"; while Francisca de Paula[34] and Mariana took the appendage "de Jesus."[35]

The daily routine at the convent consisted of various spiritual exercises that filled the time and molded and elevated the spirit, as "the practice of mental prayer dissolves the doubts of the interns and . . . moves them stridently and fervently along the path towards perfection."[36] Chapter 4 of the Macaúbas statute extolled the virtue of poverty, as had Christ and His Apostles, and exhorted the interns to "detach their hearts from temporal things, applying themselves exclusively to the eternal, setting aside worldly possessions, be they many or few, as well as all wish or desire to have and to acquire . . . so as to devote themselves entirely to the love of God, the reason for which they had left the outside world."[37] The convent demanded strict obedience to the rules, as therein resided virtue and sanctity, values for which they were to continuously strive.

The rigid discipline that reigned at the convent was designed to sculpt body and soul in accordance with Christian principles. However, there was an enormous gulf between the theory and the practice, the statutes and the reality. In the early decades of the eighteenth century, for example, the chaplains Manuel Pinheiro de Oliveira, João da Costa, and Antônio Álvares Pugas wound up in the dungeons of the Inquisition accused of the crime of solicitation, that is, of abusing of the intimacy created at the moment of confession to attempt to seduce the interns. The investigation revealed a convent completely at variance with the expected standards of morality, a place where all the young interns could do was confide in one

---

[34] ARM. Termo de paga dos dotes das três sobreditas. . . .
[35] ARM. Livro de registros do recolhimento. 1781, s.n.
[36] AN. Mesa do Desembargo do Paço. Estatutos do recolhimento de Macaúbas. Caixa 130, pac. 2, doc. 57.
[37] Ibidem.

another the indecent proposals received in the confessional, along with "illicit molestations [and] obscene words."

In 1741, an inquisitional visit to Macaúbas laid bare the disorder that reigned there. The mother superior, who ought to be the first person to guard and preserve the rigid internal norms, was accused of not tending to the sick and of failing to conduct the nocturnal cell inspections. There were interns who shared the same bed, suggesting a libertine and unchaste environment far removed from the ideal. The situation was further aggravated by the lack of confessional boxes, which increased proximity with the confessors. In the years following the inquisitional visit, many denunciations from interns alleging harassment by these priests reached the Inquisition. The last visit took place in 1763, just four years before the arrival of Chica's oldest daughters at the institution. On this occasion, three young interns denounced Father Custódio Bernardo Fernandes for soliciting "embraces and kisses, breasts to fondle and garter belts to serve as mementos, summoning them for furtive encounters in his room."

Finding a suitable confessor to "administer their spiritual needs" was always a challenge for the interns at Macaúbas. In 1783, the mother superior tried to sway the choice of the parish priest against one Friar José Lopes da Cruz, who had been appointed by the vicar of Roça Grande, the parish under whose jurisdiction the convent fell, as the cleric responsible for administering the sacraments there.[38]

The convent routine was designed to avoid free time, considered the cradle of vice and perversion. In addition to the spiritual exercises, prayer, penitence, choir practice, and confession, the interns were expected to fill all remaining idle moments with manual tasks. Prior to 1743, the courses available were limited to first letters, Christian doctrine, needlework and Gregorian chanting. Contrary to the statutes, the outside world did manage to penetrate the convent walls and reproduce itself inside. As the young ladies had an aversion to any form of manual labor, which was considered highly degrading, they were permitted to bring slaves inside the convent, a practice that readily subverted the reigning order and made a mundane

38 AHU, MAMG. Caixa 199, doc. 66.

environment of what was supposed to be a sanctuary for the edification of spirit and elevation of the soul. In 1749, there were seventy interns served by fourteen slaves at the convent.[39] By the beginning of the nineteenth century, 1806 to be precise, the opulence of Macaúbas had become impossible to conceal, with 86 interns and students served by 185 slaves, most of whom were employed in mining and agriculture in addition to their normal duties.[40]

Such laxity of order was not exclusive to Macaúbas. In Bahia, Desterro convent was known for the idle lifestyle of its interns, the richness of their dress, and the ample cash flow they enjoyed, as they often lent money at rates of interest on the financial market of Salvador.[41] It was also renowned for the illicit romances of its lascivious nuns,[42] satirized in the poems of Gregório de Matos, such as:

> Mother abbess, sacristan, door women, Discreet women of the Abbey and the scoundrels, That as they are already in the confusion, Would like to get profits as anyone, Haughty old women, indecent nuns.[43]

The internal environment of Macaúbas was never as degenerate as that of the Desterro convent. Even though Chica took advantage of the institution's laxity to come and go as she pleased, visiting her daughters whenever she liked and bringing them special foods, such as chicken for the sick and other treats.[44] João Fernandes had a small cottage built just outside the convent, where he and Chica often spent extended spells, as in September and October of 1770 when the chief judge stayed there for a number of days.[45] He also paid for the construction of a new wing so that his daughters could be accommodated in more comfortable cells and funded the

---

[39] Códice Costa Matoso, vol. 1, 1999, p. 707.

[40] AN. Mesa do Desembargo do Paço. Caixa 130, pac. 2, doc. 57

[41] Susan Soeiro. "The social and economic role of the convent: Women and nuns in colonial Bahia (1677–1800)." *Hispanic Historical American Review*, 1974, p. 230.

[42] Ibidem, p. 226.

[43] Gregório de Matos. *Obras completas*, vol. 1, 1945, p. 237.

[44] AAPAH. Documents of Macaúbas convent. List of foods sent to the daughters of Francisca da Silva.

[45] AHU, MAMG. Caixa 99, doc. 17.

construction of the trellised belvedere and the chapel dedicated to
Our Lady of the Pains.[46] The main altar, painted in sky blue and dec-
orated with spring flowers, was reminiscent of the chapel in Our Lady
of the Conception on the Vargem farm near Mariana, a property João
Fernandes inherited from his father.

In 1767, Francisca da Silva de Oliveira enrolled her eldest daughters at Macaúbas. Francisca de Paula was eleven, Rita Quitéria
ten, and Ana Quitéria five,[47] the ages at which most girls were
immured.[48] With them, she sent three pardo slave girls and a couple
who stayed on the outside to serve them in any way they needed.
They received an allowance of 60,000 reis per year, a sum João
Fernandes paid upfront in the first year.[49] In 1768, while visiting his
daughters, the chief judge personally paid 900,000 reis in gold bars
for each to receive her vows, with a 300,000 reis discount per daughter for donations previously made to the institution.[50]

In that same year, Helena, then aged five, also entered Macaúbas,
where she joined her sisters in taking the habit of Our Lady of the
Conception.[51] Helena was accompanied by Francisca Romana da
Conceição, daughter of Ventura Fernandes de Oliveira, and Maria
Teresa de Jesus, daughter of Antônio Martins Guerra, both of whose
dowries of 900,000 reis and 4,000 cruzados were paid by João Fernandes.[52] Also in 1768, Chica escorted Luciana Perpétua do Amor
de Jesus to the convent and settled her dowry of 900,000 reis in
the contractor's name.[53] According to Leila Algranti, the girl was
Chica's niece, a parda, and the natural daughter of someone important from the village. When writing her will at the beginning of the

---

[46] ARM. Livro de termos de paga dos dotes, f. 53v
[47] ARM. Livro de termos de entradas no recolhimento. 1767, f. 50.
[48] At the convent of Our Lady of the Humble in Bahia, 35 percent of the interns
were between the ages of four and fifteen.
[49] ARM. Registro de entrada no recolhimento, pp. 85–6.
[50] ARM. Termo de paga dos dotes das três sobreditas ...
[51] ARM. Livro de termos de entradas no recolhimento. 1768, s.n.
[52] ARM. Livro de termos de entradas no recolhimento. 1768, f. 53v, e Livro de
receita do recolhimento. 1768, f. 57.
[53] ARM. Livro de termos de entradas no recolhimento. 1768, f. 53v, e Livro de
receita do recolhimento. 1768, f. 57.

nineteenth century, Francisca de Paula referred to Ana Angélica, daughter of Luciana and Tomás Francisco de Aquino, as her niece.[54] However, it is also very possible that she was a child abandoned on Chica and the contractor's doorstep, who was taken in and raised as a daughter. In 1774, Luciana, now a fully fledged nun at the convent, joined the village branch of the Brotherhood of the Holy Land.[55] Though she took her vows at Macaúbas, she later left the convent along with the couple's daughters. Four years later Luciana became a sister of the board of the Brotherhood of the Mercies in Tejuco[56] and, in 1798 as president of devotions, paid the endowment for her daughter Ana Angélica Fernandes de Oliveira and endorsed her admittance into that same society.[57] In 1806, when the Brotherhood of the Holy Land produced a roll of its members, Luciana was registered as deceased.[58]

Macaúbas's income came from the annuities paid by the interns, the dowries of those taking vows, the labor of the institution's slaves, and donations collected from the people of Minas Gerais by hermits the convent was authorized to send from place to place on its behalf.[59] The Lei de Mão Morta (Dead Hand Law), which prohibited religious institutes from possessing landed property, proved an inconvenience when it came to donations in the form of plots.[60] Many mother superiors lobbied the Crown to open exceptions that would at least allow them to legalize the allotments on which the convent was built and other lands in the vicinity that were used to supply provisions for the interns.[61]

[54] BAT. Inventory of Francisca de Paula Fernandes de Oliveira. Cartório do Primeiro Ofício, maço 23.

[55] AEAD. Livro de irmãos da Terra Santa. 1806, caixa 509, f. 212.

[56] AEAD. Livro de eleição de juízes e juízas da Irmandade Nossa Senhora das Mercês. 1771–1847, caixa 510, f. 25.

[57] AEAD. Livro de entradas da Irmandade de Nossa Senhora das Mercês do Tejuco. Caixa 510, f. 161.

[58] AEAD. Livro de irmãos da Terra Santa. 1806, caixa 509, f. 212.

[59] AHU, MAMG. Caixa 132, doc. 27 and caixa 140, doc. 47.

[60] AHU, MAMG. Caixa 182, doc. 69 and caixa 180, doc. 23.

[61] AHU, MAMG. Caixa 128, doc. 40; caixa 128, doc. 41 and caixa 136, doc. 1.

While the installations at Macaúbas were more adequate than those at Minas Novas, conditions inside the cells cannot have been all that good; and various illnesses thrived in this precariousness. One source tells us that "because of the accommodation therein," many interns at Vale das Lágrimas convent, "suffered from a serious illness for which there is presently no cure." The doctor assigned to treat the sick at Macaúbas revealed that the interns' ailments were aggravated by "the mental nature of which they [women] are possessed."[62] While at Macaúbas, Chica's daughters endured countless infirmities that their mother sought to abate by bringing them substantial meals and, if their condition deteriorated, by securing authorization to have them treated at home. In 1776, Rita Quitéria received treatment at home throughout a period of six months,[63] having been stricken with a "serious malady," "with sores on her throat and nose that have survived for seven months without comfortable cure."[64] The year 1780, with Luísa, Maria, and Quitéria now also at Macaúbas,[65] was a decisive year in the destinies of all of Chica's daughters interned at the convent. As João Fernandes had died at the end of 1779, it was necessary to take certain steps in relation to the girls' futures. Almost all of the girls returned to Tejuco definitively, though there is no evidence that the family was experiencing any financial difficulties. Before returning to Portugal, João Fernandes had appointed a guardian for the children, Chica was well provided for with assets he had left to her, and there were attorneys handling his affairs and patrimony in Brazil. In his will, the chief judge left a third of his fortune to be divided among twelve of his thirteen children, all of whom received slaves and properties, though the execution of the will undoubtedly dragged on for years.

Chica probably thought it better to prepare her girls for marriage than to keep investing in those who clearly had no inclination

---

[62] AHU, MAMG. Caixa 116, doc. 39.
[63] ARM. Registro de saídas do recolhimento. 1776, s.n.
[64] ARM. Livro de registros de petições ao recolhimento. 1776, s.n.
[65] ARM. Livro de termos, s.n.

toward the monastic life. Then again, perhaps she simply wanted to have her daughters around her. The reforms implemented by Friar Domingos da Encarnação Pontevel, which prohibited free entry into the house in the interests of moral rectitude, may have led to Chica's decision to call them home from Macaúbas. While these changes undeniably carried a lot of weight, the absence of support and parental will must have also been decisive, not to mention the need to set a direction for her daughters' lives. As permanence at the convent was subject to the payment of a dowry, Chica declared in a petition sent to the mother superior that Luísa, Maria, and Quitéria had "only entered [Macaúbas] to receive instruction in the rudiments and in the virtues so laudably practiced at said convent"[66] and that the reason she had not settled their dowries was because she never actually decided whether they would stay there perpetually. Her request was witnessed by Sergeant-Major Manuel Batista Landim, the guardian appointed by João Fernandes to tend to his daughters' education after his departure.[67]

In 1781, in response to Chica's requests, Francisca de Paula, having taken ill, was authorized to spend a year at home to receive treatment, though she would nonetheless "be ordered to return to the convent . . . and [while home] was obliged to wear the habit, like a nun in retreat, and in all things observe the determinations."[68] At the same time, Ana Quitéria, also unwell, was remanded into her mother's care "despite the fact that the convent possessed [sufficient] assets, was ready to assist her in anything necessary to her cure" and that she had already taken her vows.[69] The three younger daughters all left the convent soon afterward,[70] while Helena and Rita Quitéria, already fully fledged nuns, decided to abandon the habit and return to their mother's home, the former having fallen seriously

[66] ARM. Livro de registros de petições ao recolhimento. 1780, s.n.
[67] ARM. Livro de registros de saídas do recolhimento. 1781, s.n.
[68] Ibidem.
[69] Ibidem.
[70] Ibidem.

ill.[71] Antônia entered the convent "of her own free will"[72] that same year, proof that Chica continued to esteem the institution despite Pontevel's reforms. Antônia was still at Macaúbas in 1806, where she was served by a slave woman named Edvirges, on loan from her sister Maria.[73]

As a benefactor of the convent, João Fernandes helped enlarge its installations in the hope of improving the treatment offered to his daughters. We have seen that his construction of new cells to accommodate the young ladies, among other improvements he sponsored, earned him a discount on their annuities.[74] Years later, when Quitéria went to immure her daughters Mariana Vicência and Maria dos Prazeres, not only was no dowry charged, but she presented a receipt for the settlement of outstanding debts to her father "for the cells constructed by the chief judge, in lieu of which [the convent] is obliged to accept the two interns." Both girls took the habit, and Maria remained at Macaúbas until her death in 1832.[75]

The lives of Chica's daughters were permanently linked to the convent. Many reentered its walls in search of refuge in times of affliction and in old age. Quitéria[76] returned to Macaúbas in 1786 and remained there until her death in 1855. Ana Quitéria and Mariana de Jesus, although both married, also returned, as did Francisca de Paula upon being widowed.[77]

Mirroring the outside world, the Macaúbas retreat was not only for the daughters of the white elite of Minas Gerais, but also for those

---

[71] Ibidem.

[72] ARM. Livro de termos de entradas no recolhimento. 1781, s.n.

[73] AFS. Livro avulso de testamentos.

[74] ARM. Livro de receita do recolhimento, s.d., s.n., f. 53v.

[75] ARM. Livro de receita do recolhimento, s.d., s.n.

[76] In the *Autos da devassa da Inconfidência Mineira*, Antônio Coelho Peres de França affirms that Father Rolim (companion of Rita Quitéria) had "some items in gold and precious stones, including jewellery, gold buckles, chains of the same metal, buttons, rings and other such things, which he had given to a woman today in retreat at Macaúbas." *Autos da devassa da Inconfidência Mineira*, vol. 6, 1978, p. 299. This demonstrates that Quitéria was already in Macaúbas when the failed uprising Inconfidência Mineira happened in 1789.

[77] BAT. Documentos avulsos. Caixa 478, f. 233.

born from consensual relationships with colored women. For Chica's daughters and other eighteenth-century women, such institutions provided a place for prayer and contemplation, but also access to education, the guaranteed preservation of a girl's honor, and preparation for marriage. It was in this manner that Chica sought to open up new possibilities for her daughters' insertion into the society of the day, a goal that was paradoxically not always reached.

CHAPTER EIGHT

Separation

*And from there proceeded to the Court
The owner of Serro do Frio.*

The House in Lapa

After sealing the fourth diamond contract, the father, Sergeant Major João Fernandes de Oliveira, settled definitively in the Realm where, thanks to the friendship he had zealously woven with the governor of Minas Gerais, Gomes Freire de Andrade, he began to frequent the higher echelons of the court and won the confidence of the powerful Sebastião José de Carvalho e Melo, the Count of Oeiras and future Marquis of Pombal. In the meantime, his son, the chief judge, having been carefully educated in Portugal, established himself in Tejuco where he was to manage the diamond contract.

The strategy employed by the Fernandes de Oliveira family was common among the wealthy men of business. As relations of power in the Portuguese Empire were of a private nature, success in one's endeavours relied upon close and daily contact with the powerful and especially with the king. Based on the same premises, business relations intermingled with family, and it was not unusual to have various members of a family occupying positions in the same company. In general, while one or two looked after business, another had to frequent the court to canvass for favors, concessions, and privileges.

Similar behavior could be observed among some of the most important Portuguese corporations and business families of the eighteenth century, such as the Pinto de Miranda and Pinheiro families.

The Pinto de Mirandas were wine producers who exported this and other products to Brazil. One of the brothers, named Baltazar, remained in Portugal as a liaison at court and ended up being appointed administrator of the Alto Douro Winery Company, created by Pombal to organize the production and sale of port wine. In the meantime, the other brothers set themselves up in Brazil, with Antônio arriving in Rio de Janeiro in 1739 and João settling in Vila Rica. Another important Portuguese businessman of the century was Francisco Pinheiro, who enjoyed sufficient intimacy with King João V to have the liberty to ask favors directly on visits to Mafra Castle. Such an approach was fundamental to the proper running of his business, and it was thus that he obtained posts for the agents he had spread throughout the empire, many of whom were members of his family, like Antônio Pinheiro Neto, who settled first in Rio and later in Minas, and his brother-in-law and compadre Francisco da Cruz, who established himself in Sabará.[1]

When Sergeant Major João Fernandes de Oliveira returned to Portugal in August 1751, significant political transformations were under way, with more still to come. The powerful monarch João V had died the previous year, and his son José I had ascended to the throne. The new king installed his cabinet, to which he appointed three secretaries of state: Pedro da Mota e Silva, home secretary; Diogo de Mendonça Corte Real, secretary of the seas and overseas colonies; and Sebastião José de Carvalho e Melo, secretary of war and international relations.[2] With time, Sebastião José de Carvalho e Melo, the future Marquis of Pombal, won the king's trust and swept aside his peers to become Dom José's right-hand man, coordinating and centralizing the politics of the Realm.

In Lisbon, Sergeant Major João Fernandes de Oliveira moved into a house near Horta Seca, directly facing the residence of the Count of Vila Nova.[3] He later acquired and moved into a mansion on Rua

---

[1]   *Compadrio* is the relation between someone and the godmother or godfather of someone's child.

[2]   Charles Brooks. *Disaster at Lisbon.* 1994, p. 105.

[3]   ANTT. Índice de leitura de bacharéis. João Fernandes de Oliveira. Maço 22, doc. 37. Certidões de José Carlos Castelo e Antônio Velho da Costa.

do Guarda-mor[4] in the borough of Santos Velho.[5] Like the thousands of other residents of Lisbon, his peace was shattered by the violent earthquake that devastated the capital on Saturday, November 1, 1755 – All Saints' Day. It was shortly after nine o' clock on a clear morning, with blue skies overhead, that the tremors began. The residents of the city were either already in the churches or were on their way to attend holy day mass.[6] Corralled inside the churches or in the narrow streets, many were crushed to death beneath the rubble to which the once gleaming city was reduced in minutes. Aftershocks followed and a terrible fire spread through the city gutting the buildings that had managed to withstand the initial onslaught. It must have been terrifying to behold; "the work of a thousand years destroyed in two minutes." "Lisbon had been razed, burned and turned to ash: Lisbon had collapsed upon Lisbon."[7]

The Sergeant Major and his wife Isabel survived unscathed, with their house sustaining only minor damage. However, for fear of further quakes, like all of the city's residents including the royal family, they took shelter in wooden huts assembled in the gardens.[8] A family friend from São Paulo, one Pedro Taques de Almeida Pais Leme, moved into the Fernandes de Oliveira residence to recover from his injuries and from a liver complaint, remaining in their hospitality for two years. In thanksgiving for divine protection during the earthquake, the couple spent the entire year of 1756 on a pilgrimage to Santiago de Compostela, though preceded by a brief stop in the province of Minho where the Sergeant Major wished to revisit the landscape of his childhood. He also visited his daughters enclosed at the convent of Madre de Deus de Monchique in Porto, giving alms to the poor he encountered along the way.

The experience was traumatic for the survivors, many of whom offered thanks or implored protection for themselves and their families by making promises to the saints of their devotion. For instance, Teresa de Jesus Perpétua Corte Real beseeched the protection of

4   ANTT. Cartórios notariais. 5B. Caixa 15, livro 78. Notas. Atual 12, f. 48.
5   ANTT. Cartórios notariais. Notas. Cartório 2, livro 8, fls. 70v–74v.
6   Charles Brooks, op. cit., p. 3.
7   Apud: Charles Brooks, op. cit., p. 24.
8   Ibidem, p. 125.

Our Lady of the Light, whose image was displayed on the altar of a local church during the earthquake. When she and her husband did indeed survive the tragedy, they moved to Tejuco, where he assumed a post at the Diamond Intendancy. Teresa brought the image of the miracle-working saint with her to Brazil and paid her promise by having a church built in the name of the Virgin of the Light, complete with an addendum to shelter orphaned girls, all of whom received a cash dowry, trousseau, and silver cutlery set when they married.[9]

Lisbon underwent fundamental urban transformation and enlargement after the earthquake. While the Marquis of Pombal struggled to rebuild the lower and central zones of the city, the wealthier families in search of new lands on which to settle began to occupy the airier, more salubrious areas farthest from the ruins, such as the borough of Lapa where the ascendant bourgeois elite built beautiful mansions.

Among its many consequences, the earthquake brought about a redistribution of the city's wealth. While, on the one hand, it decimated the patrimonies of many noble families who could only watch as their properties and treasures were destroyed,[10] it did not curb the rise of the merchant class buoyed by its business overseas. Effectively, the riches of Brazil, particularly its gold, were largely responsible for the recuperation of the imperial capital. The colony across the oceans contributed with its "voluntary subsidy," a tax set up by Pombal to finance the reconstruction of Lisbon, for far longer than the period of ten years initially prescribed. Furthermore, the big businessmen and powerful financiers connected to Pombal were quite happy to capitalize the Realm, lending money at interest to the state and to the struggling nobility and allying themselves with the marquis to win a hand in the reconstruction of the lower city. The diamond contractor was no different. He lent a sum of money to Pombal himself[11] and purchased a tract of land on Rua Augusta in the

---

9   AEAD. "Artigo de José Augusto Neves." Dom Joaquim de Souza. Documentos diversos. 1920–1929, caixa 58.
10 Various valuable paintings, including work by Rubens, as well as Persian rugs and tapestries were destroyed during the earthquake.
11 ANTT. Desembargo do Paço. Ilhas. Maço 1342, doc. 7.

"Pombalian" lower city where he built a block of high-grade houses that soon became one of the most valuable areas of real estate in the capital.[12]

Two years after the earthquake, having returned from Santiago de Compostela, João Fernandes and Isabel decided to build a new house that could more appropriately reflect the considerable power and patrimony of the much-enriched contractor. The site they chose was the delightful Buenos Aires farm in the borough of Lapa, which, from its privileged position on the upper tagus, enjoyed a beautifully scenic view and the breeze that swept in off the river.[13] The house went up near the cross on Rua Buenos Aires, and the Sergeant Major subinfeudated another plot on the same land tract in August 1757 from Count Redondo, Fernando de Sousa Coutinho Castelo Branco e Meneses, a knight of the Order of Santiago,

> [for] the sum of 6 thousand reis, ... on which to build houses 170 palms in width on the northern face and the same on the southern face, and 785 palms in length facing the sunrise and 705 palms towards the setting sun.[14]

The deeds João Fernandes signed stipulated that the house had to be constructed within a two-year timeframe; otherwise he would have to return the land.

In the years that followed, the couple concentrated on building a sumptuous mansion, an undertaking in which they spared no expense. The Marquis of Pombal would later testify that the time came when there was no alternative but to cap the Sergeant Major's withdrawals from the coffers of the diamond contract, as he was spending out of control "on some real estate project [that was] dissipating all his assets."[15]

---

[12] ANTT. Cartórios notariais. 5B. Caixa 15, livro 78. Atual 12, fls. 48–49.
[13] For a good study on the house and the occupation of the borough of Lapa, see Sarmento Matos. Uma casa na Lapa. 1994. See also Pedro Taques de A. Paes Leme, "Nobiliarquia ...," op. cit., p. 208.
[14] ANTT. Cartórios notariais. Notas. Cartório 2, livro 8, fls. 70v–74v.
[15] ANTT. Desembargo do Paço. Ilhas. Maço 1342, doc. 7.

It was a magnificent construction, an imposing two-story manor complete with mansard that took up an entire block on the narrow Buenos Aires street. Simple, rectilinear, and symmetrical, with a touch of the colonial architecture of Minas Gerais, the house with its majestic external appearance followed the civil architectural style in vogue in the Lisbon of the day. The sloping rectangular plot made it possible to construct a wine cellar beneath floor level at the back of the mansion. The first floor façade, which was entirely symmetrical, consisted of two doors (a main entrance and a service entrance) and nine windows, matched on the second floor by eleven windows enframed in an undulating stuccoed gable (like the windows in Tejuco[16]) and opening onto balconies of wrought iron. As was customary at the time, the first floor, with its eleven rooms and facilities, entrance included, was the functional part of the house comprising the store, kitchen (with its black stone paving), and stables.[17]

The noble quarters of the house were located on the second floor, which was subdivided into nine compartments.[18] A large two-tier staircase led up to this floor, which the chief judge, when master of the house years later, was to have adorned with tile panels (specially produced by the Rato factory in Lisbon) expressing the close intertwinement between the contractors' personal lives and their business in Minas Gerais. These tiles depicted Indians taking aim with bow and arrow, palm trees, and oriental figures, representations of his connections with Brazil and India, the sources of the precious diamonds. This staircase led into a room with four window balconies overlooking the rear gardens, and it was here that the more illustrious visitors were received.[19] There were other rooms besides this at the back of

---

[16] José Sarmento Matos, op. cit., p. 100.

[17] ANTT. Avaliação dos bens de José Joaquim de Barros Mesquita. Estremadura. Desembargo do Paço. Maço 115, no. 19. Apud: José Sarmento Matos, op. cit., p. 102.

[18] ANTT. Avaliação dos bens de José Joaquim de Barros Mesquita. Estremadura. Desembargo do Paço. Maço 115, no. 19.

[19] ANTT. Avaliação dos bens de José Joaquim de Barros Mesquita. Estremadura. Desembargo do Paço. Maço 1152, no. 19.

the house, each with its own fireplace and delicately stuccoed ceiling, while the bedrooms all ran along the front, facing onto the street. The third floor, or mansard, was reserved for the household staff and slaves.

The magnificent view to be had from the rear of the mansion was a privilege reserved for only the most select visitors. One of the balconies opened onto a stairwell, with a built-in fountain of crystalline waters, that gave access to the rectangular grounds, which sloped gently down against a backdrop of the Tagus river into a spread of splendorous gardens where there was "an excellent orchard, [complete] with even fruits of Brazil,"[20] including jaboticaba, watermelon, and maracuja. Speaking of the landscape that could be seen from the borough of Lapa, a nineteenth century English visitor wrote: "It seems to me extraordinary that anyone could contemplate the majesty of the Tagus . . . and not be impressed by the grandeur of the sight."[21]

In a play of mirrors, the garden at Lapa recalled Brazil and would have boosted the host's stock before his guests, as planting and maintaining a tropical garden in Portugal was both costly and complicated. It was, effectively, a show of power and wealth, as it was the sort of thing reserved for the Portuguese kings whose palaces, especially in Belém, had aviaries and greenhouses with Brazilian birds and plants, some of which had been collected in Tejuco.[22] Especially appreciated were "the tropical plants that produced beautiful and fragrant flowers."[23] The seeding and upkeep of these gardens required the work of a gardener with vast experience of Brazil, and this was perhaps the source of João Fernandes's close relationship with the

---

[20] Pedro Taques de A. Paes Leme, "Nobiliarquia . . . ," op. cit., p. 208.

[21] S. A. "Sketches of Portuguese life," 1826. Apud: José Sarmento Matos, op. cit., p. 95.

[22] APM. Seção Colonial. 290, fls. 249, 254. Order for the shipment "to this realm of all species so as to fill the tree nurseries of the Royal Gardens at Belém" with "the utmost quality of plant seeds that can be gathered, with tags bearing their native names, collecting in particular all those that produce beautiful and fragrant flowers."

[23] APM. Seção Colonial. 290, f. 249.

official gardener Baltazar Gonçalves de Carvalho, who had lived in the colonies and was in charge of the royal gardens.[24]

Mounted on the upper rear façade of the mansion, a tile medallion bearing the images of the saints to which, according to the Sergeant Major's will, the family was most devoted and after whom the chief judge named all his sons and daughters, stood guard over the residents. At the center of this piece, nestled among a choir of angels, was the chalice of the Most Holy Sacrament, with the Holy Trinity depicted directly above it. Below the chalice, Our Lady of the Conception, the patron saint of the Realm and most important devotion in Minas Gerais, took pride of place. It was precisely this saint that was depicted in the chapel the Sergeant Major constructed on the Vargem farm in Mariana and that featured on the painted ceiling of the nave of the Saint Francis of Assisi church in Tejuco. The likeness the Sergeant Major chose for the tile resembled the slightly mulatto figure he would have been used to seeing in the temples of Minas Gerais. This saint adorned and protected the house, guaranteeing that no evil could ever prevail upon those who placed their trust in her.

The side panels represented the saints of particular significance to João Fernandes de Oliveira, with the peregrine monk Saint Francis de Paul, the Virgin Mary, and Saint Rita of Cascia, the patron of lost causes, portrayed on one side; and the Franciscan monk Saint Anthony of Pádua, the patron saint of Lisbon, carrying the baby Jesus in one hand and a cross in the other; Saint Joseph, the protector of the home and saint of particular devotion for Maria de São José, the Sergeant Major's first wife; and Saint Quitéria with a cross and a palm sprig in her hands as signs of her martyrdom,[25] all depicted on the other. At the bottom of the fronton read the following phrase in Latin: "Holy God, Holy Strong One, Holy Immortal One, have mercy upon us."[26]

---

[24]   ANTT. Habilitações da Ordem de Cristo. Letra s. Maço 5, doc. 5, f. 11.
[25]   Pierre Pierrard. *Dictionnaire des prénoms et des saints*. 1987. See also Donald Attwater. *The Penguin dictionary of saints*. 1983.
[26]   "Sanctus Deus, Sanctus fortis, sanctus Immortalis, Miserere nobis."

One of the details that best demonstrate the elevated status of the Fernandes de Oliveira family was its construction of an exclusive water channel. In the eighteenth century, the scarce water supply was the cause of an undeclared war between the rich and the poor in the streets of Lisbon. The city's chronic water shortage would only be resolved at the end of the century with the construction of an aqueduct by Maria I. A clear example of the tensions generated by this dispute over water was the terrible accusation lodged against Pombal that he had constructed a secret duct to channel water directly into his new house from a water fountain he had ordered to be built right in front of the residence – already a handy location in itself. The existence of a tunnel hundreds of meters long supplying water to João Fernandes's manor and irrigating his tropical orchard clearly demonstrates the extent of the power the diamond contractors enjoyed.[27]

In addition to the slaves they had brought home with them from Brazil, the staff of the old Sergeant Major João Fernandes and his wife also included the servant João José, a kind of butler whose salary was 2,440 reis, and Antônio José who earned about a tenth as much. In 1766, they hired João Bolieiro who drove the household carriage,[28] and Luís Galego and Domingos Caseiro, who served the family for less than a year. In 1767, João Moço, Vicente Moço, and Luís Moço[29] were all admitted to the household staff at a salary of a mere 800 reis. The couple lived luxuriously; circulating about town in elegant carriages and adorning their house with carefully chosen objects of decoration, such as silver and gold ornaments, fine

[27] In the first half of the nineteenth century, the waters of the river Tejo were channelled into many houses, supplying families with one of the greatest commodities one could enjoy in a hot climate. It is not known exactly when this system was installed, but it was certainly after the public duct opened in 1752 to channel water from the Tejo stream to the fountain erected in the city center. It is not improbable that the construction of the duct feeding the contractor's house was inspired on the system previously installed in Tejuco.

[28] The word bolieiro seems to derive from boléia (driver's seat), as the individual in question here was a carriage driver.

[29] AHTCL. Livros da décima da cidade. Arruamentos, freguesia de Santos e Lapa. 1762–1834. Apud: José Sarmento Matos, op. cit., p. 116. Moço in Portuguese means groom or page.

furniture, tableware, and tapestries.[30] Isabel dressed sumptuously to impress her guests and wore delicate jewelry, "such as a diamond necklace ... and many other precious pieces for her adornment."[31] "Peacefully slumbering in indolence,"[32] João Fernandes and Isabel passed their time at court displaying the fortune and authority the contractor had acquired and that the imposing mansion house monumentalized for Portuguese society.

THE DIAMOND CONTRACT

The business dealings of the son were permanently intertwined with those of the father. Every year the chief judge sent the ample profits from his diamond operations back to the Realm where his father lived like a noble. Close relations with the powers that be were essential to the success of the financial interests of a contractor, which is why the elder João Fernandes sought to establish important connections, such as those he maintained with Sebastião José de Carvalho e Melo. There is also evidence to suggest that he had close ties with the secretary of state. In an exchange of favors in 1770 during the negotiations for the renewal of the sixth diamond contract, the Sergeant Major paid the then Count of Oeiras the sum of "eight contos de reis, or twenty thousand cruzados, so that [he] could complete work on some houses under construction near the dilapidated parish church of São Paulo," which the future marquis had inherited from his brother, Cardinal Paulo de Carvalho e Mendonça.[33] The ties between the two João Fernandes de Oliveira, father and son, and the Marquis of Pombal extended far beyond the death of the three. As such, in 1825, the attorney Lourenço João de Oliveira Grijó, grandson of the chief judge, was promoted to the post of judge of the town of Oeiras near Lisbon, home to the Marquis of Pombal's

---

[30] ANTT. Desembargo do Paço. Ilhas. Maço 1342, doc. 7.
[31] Ibidem.
[32] Ibidem.
[33] José Sarmento Matos, op. cit., p. 71.

castle. The nomination was secured thanks to a letter from Pombal promising the post to the Chief Judge's descendants.[34]

Attention was drawn to the son's sound performance at the head of the family's business in Tejuco on various occasions, but it was with obvious exaggeration that the chief judge complained of "the fruit of the harshest exile, copious sweating and incessant fatigue" he had to suffer in Brazil. As soon as he assumed the function of contractor in Tejuco, João Fernandes set about organizing the diamond exploration and making the profits grow, both for himself and for the king, as he possessed "the intelligence and probity required for such an important business."[35] He therefore joined his father in Sebastião José de Carvalho e Melo's sphere of trust. Father and son were among the businessmen that ascended in Portuguese society during Pombal's administration, in which the marquis looked to unite the interests of the Realm with those of the emerging merchant class.[36]

At the core of the Pombaline approach was the development of a merchant class enriched and ennobled through admittance to the Order of Christ and appointment to administrative positions. In the case of Brazil, "Pombal used the contract system to concentrate the wealth within the hands of a new class"[37] of which the elder and younger João Fernandes were classic examples.

The chief judge's presence at the helm of the diamond business in Tejuco directly overlaps with the growth and success the village enjoyed in terms of its diamond production. Shortly after his arrival, the new contractor replaced the representative José Álvares Maciel, who was removed from the post under accusations of bad management. In his first report to the shareholders, João Fernandes

---

[34] ANTT. Mercês. Registro Geral. Provisão. D. João VI, Lv. 20, f. 266, 266v.
[35] ANTT. Desembargo do Paço. Ilhas. Maço 1342, doc. 71; Ministério do Reino. Livro 212, fls. 6–6v.
[36] Kenneth Maxwell. "Pombal and the nationalization of the Luzo-Brazilian economy." *Hispanic American Historical Review*, 1968, pp. 608–31.
[37] Kenneth Maxwell. *Pombal: Paradox of the enlightenment.*

Table 8.1. *Official Diamond*
Production (1765–1771)

Year	Carats
1765	84,862
1766	91,382
1767	70,942
1768	74,450
1769	76,689
1770	55,414
1771	35,369

Source: Torre do Tombo National Archive.
Extracted from the Revenue Board. Gen-
eral directory of the diamond commission.
Book 3, p. 6v.

de Oliveira stressed the success and mounting profits resulting from
his performance:

There can be no doubt, as the ledgers of the contract and of the
administrators both confirm, that the diggings of Jequitinhonha
proved most useful, rich and of considerable interest to the present
contract, which currently finds itself enjoying large profits, according to the calculations I have made of the expenses and of the diamonds so far extracted and forwarded to the cashiers in the city of
Lisbon.[38]

Diamond production plummeted (see Table 8.1) after his departure for Lisbon in 1770, especially from the end of the second
semester and all throughout 1771, despite the business having been
entrusted to one of the contractor's men of confidence, the general
administrator Caetano José de Sousa.[39] Given the sheer volume of
wealth he generated, João Fernandes must have been much more
than a notorious smuggler in the eyes of the Crown. In fact, the

[38] Report presented to the shareholders and stakeholders in the diamond company
by Chief Judge João Fernandes de Oliveira. Apud: Joaquim Felício dos Santos.
Memórias do Distrito Diamantino. 1956, p. 149.
[39] ANTT. Núcleos extraídos do Conselho da Fazenda. Junta de direção-geral dos
diamantes. Livro 3, p. 1.

private and public interests involved in diamond production became a closed circle that gave rise to mutual benefit. As Pombal well knew, the chief judge was a fundamental piece in the intricate web of relations that united the captains of business and the Crown.

The contract system effectively pitted the interests of the contractors, the sole bearers of the right to exploit the mines, against the interests of the local population, deprived of access to the riches found in the diamond-bearing deposits. The locals could get around this difficulty by securing the right to mine rivers they could prove were exclusively auriferous, by renting slaves to the contractors, and by illegally extracting diamonds from the demarcation.

The Crown attended various requests to have local rivers liberated and the gold mines distributed.[40] The locals regularly sent consignments of gold to the General Diamond Administration to have the fifth removed in tax. On December 31, 1771, a freed black named Francisco Gomes registered sixteen eighths, three quarters, and four vinténs of gold.[41] In 1793, the physician Luís José de Figueiredo died in Tejuco and left three gold mines to his wife.[42]

The contractors rented a considerable number of slaves to carry out the heaviest tasks of diamond mining. The death records for Tejuco and the surrounding areas register long lists of slaves rented out to the contracted company who were killed in almost always work-related accidents. In 1753, among others, "Manuel angola, slave of Francisco Afonso do Rego" and "Antônio Sabaru, leased to the company and slave of João Homem, of Rio de Janeiro"[43] died quick deaths at the Inferno mining site.

João Fernandes fought long and hard to ensure that illegal mining of precious gems was severely repressed. In the early years, he

---

[40] AHU, MAMG. Caixa 64, doc. 86. Carta de Tomás Roby de Barros Barreto informando com o seu parecer acerca da pretensão dos mineiros do distrito do Tejuco em pretenderem mais lavras. APM. Seção Colonial. 192, fls. 183–185; AHU, MAMG. Caixa 97, doc. 65.

[41] MO. Registro de entradas de ouro na administração-geral dos diamantes (1771–1777–1779). Livro avulso sem número, registro no. 1219.

[42] BAT. Cartório do Primeiro Ofício, maço 52.

[43] AEAD. Livros de óbitos do arraial do Tejuco. 1752–1895, caixa 350, f. 1.

was able to rely on the support of the diamond intendant Tomás Robi de Barros Barreto, who opened investigations as soon as he assumed the post and took measures to curb the practice, especially against the runaway slaves that were rife in the demarcation.[44] In later years he was assisted by the governors, who ordered the confiscation of debtors' assets, informed the contract of the discovery of new mining fields, and guaranteed the steady running of the exploration by promptly covering the growing financial costs and by sending soldiers to patrol the diamondiferous region.[45] In return, the contractor positioned himself as a loyal subject willing to fulfil the whims and desires of the king. When the Crown decided to extend the voluntary subsidy for another ten years, João Fernandes was called upon to convince the councilmen of the inevitability of the confiscations.[46]

The chief judge was quick to realize that the interests of the locals ran counter to his own. Felisberto Caldeira Brant, the previous contractor, had won local favor by defraying the rent of 1,500 to 2,000 slaves over and above the 600 permitted under the contract. All told, Brant managed to siphon off thirty times the legally permitted exploitation total during his administration. However, when the rental ledgers fell into the hands of the authorities, they provided damning evidence against the ex-contractor, who was already in custody at the time.[47]

---

[44] AHU, MAMG. Caixa 63, doc. 38. Letter of Tomás Robi de Barros Barreto, . . . informing the general magistrate of Tejuco, Francisco Moreira de Matos, of the measures taken to avoid the extraction of diamonds. In caixa 66, doc. 12 of the same archive, letter from Tomás Robi de Barros Barreto informing of the precautions he took in Serro do Frio to purge the region of thieves and runaway slaves. Caixa 67, doc. 32. Letter from Tomás Robi de Barros Barreto giving news of the diamond theft practiced by smugglers on the Jequitinhonha River.

[45] On debt-related confiscations, see APM. Seção Colonial. 135, fls. 118–122v. On the discovery of the deposits in the Periguasû and Parimarim mountains, see the same file and section 143, fls. 197–197v, 201v. On the necessary assistance, idem, 137, f. 1. On prompt financial aid, idem, fls. 55–57, and 143, fls. 124, 179v. On military assistance, idem, 143, f. 197.

[46] APM. Seção Colonial. 143, fls. 165v, 172–172v.

[47] AHU, MAMG. Caixa 63, doc. 29.

The fact that João Fernandes was so important to the success of a business that was fundamental to the Realm does not mean that he did not reap his share of the profits – some of them illicit. Individual benefits and lack of administrative control were inherent characteristics of the Portuguese administrative machine that helped keep the sources of power private.

The expedient João Fernandes found to resolve the conflict of interests surrounding access to the rich diamond mines did not leave nearly as many traces as that of the careless Caldeira Brant:

> [He sent] his blacks to buy the very diamonds they stole from him by day, in full surety that the thieves would not be unmasked, and there were weeks when he invested more than a thousand eighths in the purchase of his own yield. This made the black rob his master more diligently during the day so as to have more to sell back to him by night, without risk of punishment, and the whites judged attributable the crime of contraband, as they saw the contractor engaged in his usual exercise, thus making trafficking common, for others out of vice, for the contract, out of necessity.[48]

On at least one occasion, evidence surfaced that João Fernandes was buying diamonds illegally from third parties. In 1770, the Count of Valadares informed Sebastião José de Carvalho e Melo, then still Count of Oeiras, of the investigation he had opened into the misappropriation of a massive diamond of many carats, which he hoped to recover. According to the evidence, the contractor had attempted to acquire the enormous gem, then in the hands of Manuel Pacheco Ferreira, bailiff of the Royal Revenue in Vila Rica, who in turn contacted Antônio da Mota Magalhães, notary of the Royal Revenue Commission in Vila Rica, who then approached the contractor in Tejuco with the proposal of brokering the sale.

João Fernandes was scheduled to leave for Macaúbas to visit his daughters and decided to stop at Vila Rica on his way back to examine the stone and close the deal. However, his letters were

---

[48] BNL. Notícias das minas dos diamantes. Seção de Reservados. Avulsos. Cód. 7167.

intercepted by the authorities and an investigation was opened into
the incident, leading to the arrest of Manuel Pacheco Ferreira and
Antônio da Mota Magalhães and their suspension from their posts.
At no time whatsoever was João Fernandes accused of committing
any crime. He was merely called as an expert witness to attest to
the preciousness of the gem, which he dismissed as a simple crystal.
No suspicion was cast upon João Fernandes's behavior in either the
reports of the investigation or in the letters of the Count of Valadares,
which agree that he had acted in defense of his own interests and
those of the Crown. According to the official version, the contractor made contact with the seller simply to ascertain if he was being
robbed by some third party in a business in which he was supposed
to have a monopoly.[49]

An analysis of the relations between the contractors and the
authorities in Brazil and Portugal reveals mutual trust with no trace of
bad feeling in the years leading up to the royal monopoly, decreed in
1771 and installed in 1772. As we shall see, João Fernandes's return
to Lisbon owed itself to contingencies in his private life as opposed
to any eventualities in the public sphere. He was not suspended from
the contract under accusations of smuggling, nor was he summoned
back to the Realm by Pombal or obliged to pay hefty fines into the
public coffers.[50] As the marquis could no longer count on someone
he trusted in Tejuco, the state followed the tendency it had so often
manifested elsewhere and restored its control over the Realm's riches
by decreeing the monopoly.

In 1768, João Fernandes was granted his request to appoint
Caetano José de Sousa as his representative in the administration
of the diamond contract.[51] Everything would indicate that he made
this request because he wished to travel to Portugal to help his father
negotiate the renewal of the sixth diamond contract, in place since
1762, and its extension for four more years starting from 1770.[52]

[49] AHU, MAMG. Caixa 99, doc. 17.
[50] Joaquim Felício dos Santos, op. cit., pp. 125–7.
[51] ANTT. Ministério do Reino. Livro 212, fls. 6–6v
[52] ANTT. Desembargo do Paço. Ilhas. Maço 1342, doc. 7.

A further motivation was that father and son had fallen out over the withdrawals the Sergeant Major was making to finance the construction of the house in Lapa and to bankroll the high standard of living he and Isabel were enjoying in Lisbon.[53] In relation to these withdrawals, the chief judge managed to obtain authorization from José I to not only limit the sums his father could withdraw, but render them subject to approval from the cashiers in Lisbon.[54] At the beginning of the following year, João Fernandes was informed by the Count of Valadares that the king had granted him license "to return to court at his earliest convenience,"[55] but he chose to stay in Tejuco and the negotiations were conducted by the old Sergeant Major.

At much the same time, Chief Judge João Fernandes complained to the Count of Oeiras (later Marquis of Pombal) about the credit limits Valadares, then governor of Minas Gerais, was imposing on the withdrawals he was entitled to make from the Royal Revenue to cover the costs of the diamond operations,[56] which, from 1765 on, ran to 500,000 cruzados a year.[57] The Count of Oeiras took the chief judge's side and ordered the governor to verify the amounts loaned and to meet the contractor's requests; otherwise they risked a slump in diamond production.[58] Following the orders from the Realm, Valadares had the Royal Revenue of Minas prepare a statement of all of the contractor's withdrawals between 1753 and 1769.[59] The data revealed that the sums lent to the contractor had been cut by almost half since the new governor had taken office two years earlier in August 1768. Valadares's justification for this was that "[he had] satisfied the debts [his] predecessors had failed to satisfy and [was] still waiting to pay the rest owed to João Fernandes."[60]

---

53 Ibidem.
54 Ibidem.
55 AHU, MAMG. Caixa 96, doc. 46.
56 AHU, MAMG. Caixa 97, doc. 65.
57 AHU, MAMG. Caixa 96, doc. 57.
58 Ibidem.
59 AHU, MAMG. Caixa 93, doc. 11.
60 Ibidem.

In the years 1769 and 1770 Valadares was deeply concerned about diamond smuggling in Tejuco and surrounding areas, but João Fernandes was not the suspect. In fact, the contractor and the court were considered the injured parties in the illicit dealings of locals, prospectors, and runaway slaves. The governor, contractor, and diamond intendant joined forces on this occasion to stamp out illegal prospecting, especially in the region of Santo Antônio do Itucambirussu, near Minas Novas, where there was news of fresh diamond finds.[61]

Throughout the year 1769, Commander José Luís Saião, who was under the governor's orders to find out what was going on in the mountains, sent back various reports informing that he had found operational mines and makeshift encampments, which indicated diamond smuggling on the part of the locals. The inquest Valadares set up to investigate the commander's leads identified Sergeant Major José de Abreu Guimarães Mota, Manuel Roiz de Araújo, and a pardo named Jerônimo as the culprits. In November of the following year, Valadares informed Sebastião José de Carvalho e Melo of his findings and that he had entrusted the task of assessing the mountains' hidden riches to João Fernandes de Oliveira and his administrator Caetano José de Sousa, a mission of extreme confidence. Their report pointed toward the existence of deposits of gold, diamonds, and other precious stones.[62] At the end of the process, the diamonds confiscated from José de Abreu Guimarães were turned over to the chief judge to be deposited in the coffers of the contract, as they belonged to him and the Crown.[63]

João Fernandes frequented the governor's palace in Vila Rica where he liaised with the Count of Valadares's intimate circle, which included many of his own friends. In two letters from Antônio da Mota Magalhães about the negotiations for the purchase of the supposedly illicitly extracted diamond, he mentions that he was greatly

---

[61] AHU, MAMG. Caixa 99, doc. 15.
[62] Ibidem.
[63] Ibidem.

missed by his friends at the palace and that they sent him their regards.[64]

Far from revealing any animosity, the correspondence the governor exchanged with the contractor during 1770 expresses only trust and gives no indication whatsoever that the contract was about to be rescinded or that the chief judge was likely to be arrested on suspicion. At the beginning of that year, Valadares informed João Fernandes that he had received his petition to have new rivers opened up for diamond exploration.[65] In October, he informed the diamond intendant, Francisco Pinto de Mendonça, that the Crown had decided in favor of "conceding to João Fernandes and his son, the contractors, the right to mine the Pequeno and Grande rivers," effective immediately.[66] The chief judge had affirmed that His Majesty thought him "so capable of continuing and completing the business of his house, chief amongst which was the contract for the extraction of diamonds," that he had already signed a document, dated the eleventh of September 1770, extending his representation, "as he had seen fit to order the continuation of the aforesaid contract and his partnership with the supplicant [Chief Judge João Fernandes de Oliveira]."[67] This was not just empty rhetoric, as other documents also mention the renewal of the contract.[68]

The correspondence between the Marquis of Lavradio, the viceroy of Brazil, and Caetano José de Sousa, the contract administrator, are likewise characterized by friendship and even camaraderie. In August 1770, the former congratulated the latter not only for having taken the initiative to set up a postal service between Tejuco and Rio de Janeiro but for not having forgotten to seek his advice and authorization on the matter, given its "usefulness in the

---

[64] AHU, MAMG. Caixa 99, doc. 17. Contain letters from Antônio da Mota Magalhães.

[65] APM. Seção Colonial. 176, f. 45. João Fernandes' request in AHU, MAMG. Caixa 97, doc. 65

[66] APM. Seção Colonial. 176, f. 82v.

[67] ANTT. Desembargo do Paço. Ilhas. Maço 1342, doc. 7, fls. 46–46v.

[68] Ibidem, f. 62.

establishment of this kind of postal service, so important, and, in my view, indispensable, to greater facility in commerce."[69]

The fleet that arrived in Rio de Janeiro in mid-October 1770[70] brought news of old João Fernandes de Oliveira's death in the Realm on September 8 of that year.[71] As if presaging the irreversible changes this event would announce, part of the fleet almost sank on October 4 during a violent day-long storm off the island of Madeira.[72]

The Sergeant Major was bedridden for the last month of his life after suffering a stroke that left him paralyzed on his left side. Taking turns at his bedside were the Discalced (shoeless) Carmelites from the Remédios Monastery, especially Friar Francisco da Visitação,[73] who provided spiritual aid; Father Nuno Henriques Dorta, parish priest of Lapa, who administered the last rites; and his physicians, who tried to minimize the effects of the devastating convulsion.[74] Despite the suffering he endured, he remained lucid until the very end and passed away peacefully thanks to the comfort and consolation of the monks. He was buried in the convent of Our Lady of Jesus.[75]

---

[69] Marquês do Lavradio. *Cartas do Rio de Janeiro*. 1978, p. 43 (carta 244).

[70] Ibidem, p. 60 (carta 271).

[71] ANTT. Registros paroquiais, no. 1, caixa 7, microfilme 1019.

[72] *Primeira exposição nacional de painéis votivos do rio, do mar e do além-mar*. 1983, p. 52. "Miracle worked by Our Lady of the Conception of Porto Seguro unto Jorge de Lima, who departed the city of Lisbon for Rio de Janeiro aboard the ships *Bom Jesus de Além* and *Nossa Senhora da Esperança*. After fifteen days at sea, on the 4th of October, at approximately seven o'clock in the morning, with the island of Madeira within sight, he was assailed by a storm of southeasterly winds that he could but run astern with foremast alone throughout that entire day, without hope of surviving, and beseeching the aforesaid Lady. At around two o'clock in the morning the storm abandoned him, this in the year 1770."

[73] Besides Friar Francisco da Visitação, the definitor general of the shoeless Carmelites, also present were the Carmelite friars José do Menino Jesus and Antônio de São José. ANTT. Desembargo do Paço. Ilhas. Box 1342, doc. 7.

[74] The doctors were Baltazar Lara, doctor in philosophy and medicine who worked at the Hospital Militar de Lisboa, and Inácio Lamagnini, Gualter Wade e Antônio Martins Vidigal, surgeon. ANTT. Desembargo do Paço. Ilhas. Maço 1342, doc. 7

[75] ANTT. Registros paroquiais, no. 1, caixa 7, microfilme 1019.

Only days before the old contractor's death, his second wife, Isabel Pires Monteiro, induced him to alter his will, entitling her to half of his assets as opposed to the amount initially agreed in their pre-nuptial pact. She even managed to get him to sign a writ through which she would recover the sums she had spent on the endowment and marriage of her grandson. As the Sergeant Major was incapable of writing, "given the tremendous shaking in his arms," and since his wife was illiterate, the documents had to be signed on his behalf by one Dr. José Pires Monteiro de Oliveira, Isabel's cousin.[76]

On September 24 of that year, the chief judge and Chica da Silva left Tejuco to visit his daughters at Macaúbas convent. While Chica remained at Macaúbas, he proceeded to Vila Rica to settle the business of the purloining of the supposed diamond.[77] It was there that he received the letter apprising him of his father's death and decided to return to the Realm as quickly as possible to fight for the annul-ment of the rewritten will, which would have been a mortal blow to his interests. The signing of the diamond contracts in partner-ship rendered the economic interests of father and son completely indissociable. In the years preceding his death, the chief judge had made a considerable contribution to the Sergeant Major's enrich-ment and he saw his inheritance as his recompense for the success of the diamond contracts, on which he had initially served as an administrative partner and later, between 1753 and 1770, as a full partner.[78]

Without delay, João Fernandes set about "putting his house in order" so that he could travel.[79] On November 12, back from Macaúbas, Chica wrote her last will and testament, which she registered in Vila do Príncipe. Unfortunately, the document has since been lost to us.

As he foresaw a prolonged stay in Lisbon – in fact, he feared he would never return – good-byes were inevitable. Leaving Chica

---

[76] ANTT. Desembargo do Paço. Ilhas. Maço 1342, doc. 7.
[77] AHU, MAMG. Caixa 99, doc. 17.
[78] ANTT. Desembargo do Paço. Ilhas. Maço 1342, doc. 7.
[79] Ibidem, f. 45v.

behind in Tejuco, with little José in her arms or still on the way, João Fernandes left for Vila Rica, where he would make the final legal arrangements for his voyage to the Realm. On November 28, in the presence of the notary of that same county, Patrício Pereira da Cunha, the chief judge registered his last will and testament,[80] in which he divided his assets among the thirteen natural children born of his relationship with Chica. He also availed of the occasion to appoint Sergeant Major Manuel Batista Landim as tutor to the younger kids.[81]

Appointing a tutor to one's illegitimate offspring was by no means common practice. When a couple was legally recognized, the husband automatically assumed the tutelage of the younger children and the administration of their inheritance upon their mother's death, though not vice versa. The wife had to file a petition requesting appointment as tutor to her own children and, depending on the patrimony in question, the requisition had to be made to the king himself. Single women with illegitimate kin did not suffer such probation. As the ladies of their houses and patrimonies, they were free to manage their own business and family affairs. By designating a tutor for their children, Chica da Silva and João Fernandes were acting as if they were legally married, once again imitating the habits of the elite.

While the chief judge set about finalizing his travel preparations, the Count of Valadares and Caetano José de Sousa both wrote to the viceroy in Rio de Janeiro requesting that the fleet be held beyond the customary seventy days. The former argued that he had not yet managed to organize his remissions, while the latter alleged that he was late with the annual diamond shipment. Both hoped to buy the contractor enough time to reach the fleet scheduled to leave from Rio de Janeiro at the end of December. On November 21, the viceroy sent word telling them not to worry, that he would hold the fleet at port until mid-January.[82]

---

[80]   ANTT. Registro geral de testamentos. Livro 312.
[81]   ARM. Livro de registros de saídas do recolhimento. 1781, s.n.
[82]   Marquês do Lavradio, op. cit., p. 60 (cartas 270, 271).

From Vila Rica, the chief judge made his way as swiftly as possible to Rio de Janeiro, crossing the Serra do Mar for the last time. As he found himself in the city as early as December 6, "whiling away the hours" as he waited for the fleet to set sail and take him back to the Realm,[83] it was no longer necessary to hold up the ships. The viceroy took pains to becalm the Count of Valadares, his cousin, and the administrator Caetano José de Sousa, "his bosom friend," telling them not to be apprehensive, as another ship would be leaving in January and that "they could make their diamond shipment then."[84] After all, so long as the private matters of the wealthy contractor were resolved, those of the state could wait just a little longer.

On December 24, "on the last of those seventy unpostponable days," the warship *Nossa Senhora de Belém*, under the command of Bernardo Ramires Esquivel, set sail from Rio de Janeiro. In addition to the anxious contractor,[85] other illustrious passengers were the magistrate of Goiás and the brother of the diamond contract cashier.[86] The fleet made a stopover in Bahia where it received two more chief judges, both magistrates from the Appeals Court of Bahia whose terms of office had just expired.[87] While at port, the captain ordered some repairs and the ship was loaded with a cargo of native woods.[88] Though the ship was already overcrowded, the Marquis of Lavradio had obliged Esquivel to take João Fernandes on board,[89] as the warships were more comfortable than the heavy merchant vessels, unless the passenger could secure the captain's favors.[90] The marquis also wrote to Valadares informing him of the chief judge's departure on what he "believe[d] would be a good journey" despite the excess passengers, which, "being so numerous, I am sure will

---

[83] Ibidem, p. 61 (carta 274).
[84] Ibidem, p. 62 (carta 277).
[85] Ibidem, p. 62 (carta 278), p. 63 (carta 280).
[86] Ibidem, p. 65 (carta 282).
[87] They were Rodrigo Coelho Machado Torres and José Gomes Ribeiro, judges of High Court of Bahia. AMU. Documentos relativos ao Brasil – Bahia, nos. 8401, 8402, 8403, 8404, 8405, 8406.
[88] AMU. Documentos relativos ao Brasil – Bahia, no. 8407, 8408, 8409, 8410.
[89] Marquês do Lavradio, op. cit., p. 65 (carta 282).
[90] Ibidem, p. 126 (carta 436).

be of some use to him."[91] The fleet finally left Brazilian shores on January 29.[92]

And so we see the real reason behind João Fernandes de Oliveira's return to Lisbon. The establishment of the royal diamond monopoly and the creation of the Royal Extractor were not retaliations against the contractor. Nor is there any truth in the story that the Count of Valadares traveled to Tejuco with the secret purpose of investigating irregularities on the part of the chief judge, nor of any ruse on the governor's behalf to compromise him. There is not a single reference in any of the documentation to suggest that Valadares was in any way involved in or influential in the Crown's decision to assume control of the diamond operations, a decision taken long after João Fernandes's arrival in Portugal. Any suggestion to the contrary is readily undermined by the behavior of the Marquis of Lavradio and the Count of Valadares during the preparations for the Sergeant Major's son's voyage to Lisbon, in which both were considerate and helpful.[93]

There is nothing in the political career of the governor of Minas Gerais that could raise any doubts about his honor. Some historians have suggested that Valadares blackmailed João Fernandes, receiving a vast sum of money not to denounce the contractor to the Crown, something he ended up doing anyway. José Luís de Meneses Abranches Castelo Branco e Noronha, the sixth Count of Valadares,[94] hailed from a family that belonged to the high nobility of Portugal. Francisco Varnhagen wrote that "[d]espite his young age, being not yet 25 when he took the bar, he always knew how to instil respect for authority [by] persecuting wrongdoers." Appointed governor at the age of 26, it was his first designation of note and the only post he ever held overseas. Upon his return to the Realm in 1774,

[91] Ibidem, p. 65 (carta 282).
[92] AMU. Documentos relativos ao Brasil – Bahia, no. 8400.
[93] Marquês do Lavradio, op. cit., pp. 62–5.
[94] Francisco Varnhagen, in *História geral do Brasil*, written between 1854 and 1857, merely registers that the Crown began to conduct the mining operations through its Public Revenue Service after the death of Sergeant Major João Fernandes de Oliveira. Francisco Adolfo Varnhagen. *História geral do Brasil, antes da sua separação e independência de Portugal*, vol. 4, 1948, p. 114, nota 107.

in recompense for his services rendered to the Crown, he enjoyed a long career as a gentleman of the royal court.

The dates also confirm that the decision to monopolize the diamonds was motivated by the fact that Pombal could no longer count on João Fernandes in Brazil, as the ex-contractor found himself obliged to remain in Portugal to oversee the litigation surrounding his inheritance. He arrived in the Realm in early 1771 and the royal monopoly was only decreed in August of that year, some months later, when it was already clear that the chief judge's stay in Lisbon would be prolonged. The sixth contract did not terminate at the end of 1770 as one would expect in the case of rescission, but saw itself through until December of the following year. The royal monopoly only came into effect in January 1772 with the announcement of the constitution of the Royal Extractor, which gave João Fernandes's administrator time to organize his accounts and close the year. This decision permitted the contract to continue exploiting the mines throughout the dry season of 1771, the winter months between May and September, the period in which low water levels made the riverbeds more readily accessible.

In July 1771, José I justified his decision to terminate the contract at the end of that year, declaring that

> with the death of João Fernandes de Oliveira, contractor of the Royal Diamond Extractor for the mines of Brazil[,] so expired [the tenure of] the leasing contract celebrated in his name. As such, the said contract must now cease to trade so that it can settle all accounts with its partners, and to this effect, avail of the time remaining on that contract in conformity with all others pertaining to My Royal Revenue. I hereby declare terminated the present leasing of the abovementioned late contractor and his partnership as of the last day of the coming December ... the current general administrator Caetano José de Sousa will be maintained in the village of Tejuco for as long as he is judged to be properly executing the duties to which he is beholden.[95]

[95] ANTT. Núcleos extraídos do Conselho da Fazenda. Junta de direção-geral dos diamantes. Livro 3, f. 1. Copy in AHU, MAMG. Caixa 97, doc. 65. "Decreto de 1771 sobre se não arrematar o contrato dos diamantes e se administrar."

There is nothing in this to indicate the suspicion of smuggling or other irregularities, and Caetano José de Sousa, the chief judge's right-hand man, did in fact continue to represent the contract in Tejuco up to the total closure of its accounts some years later. When the Royal Extractor took charge of the exploration, de Sousa was taken on as a functionary of the Diamond Intendancy, where he remained until 1773.[96]

News of the recently decreed monopoly reached Brazil amid rumors that Caetano José de Sousa, as opposed to João Fernandes, absent from the village since the previous year, had been involved in smuggling. On September 23, 1771, the viceroy, the Marquis of Lavradio, wrote to his friend the administrator in order to assuage his fears, affirming that there was no suspicion surrounding his conduct and no ulterior motives behind the administrative measure. According to the viceroy, "the reform and new method your good self sought to implement [served] of greater utility to the interests of my Lord the King."[97] He offered further consolation, saying:

> Just as I do not admire the rumour that has spread about this captaincy, [so do I disdain] the slander that has also reached it, ... the slander and falsehoods with which they hope to denigrate the disposition of a vassal who has only ever employed himself with loyalty, honour and without self-interest. . . . All who eschew the ill-trodden path and make their way in truth and honour are subject to such falsehoods and afflictions . . . I, who have endured such tempests, can speak on the matter as from experience.[98]

In December 1771, now deeply concerned about the situation in Tejuco, though he was still able to count on the support of the contractor and his representative in Brazil, the Count of Valadares sent the second lieutenant Francisco José de Aguilar on a secret mission around the demarcation to verify that the new intendant was carrying out his orders to stamp out smuggling. Nonetheless, he warned his

---

[96] AHU, MAMG. Caixa 97, doc. 65.
[97] Marquês do Lavradio, op. cit., pp. 83–4 (carta 324).
[98] Ibidem.

scout that he should "provide assistance and the amounts [of money] and in no way interfere with the contractor's disposition. First determine that there is no partiality and give him everything he asks for, making sure that all keep their peace with the aforesaid, and inform me of anything that disturbs the general harmony."[99] The preamble to the law by which the royal monopoly was decreed justified the decision in the face of the "certain awareness of the intolerable abuses being practiced, the disorganized manner in which the lands are mined and the streams exhausted, and the number of slaves introduced under fraudulent pretexts to extract diamonds."[100] The statement quoted above is taken from a letter Pombal attached to the Diamantine Directive he sent to the new diamond intendant in Tejuco, the chief judge Francisco José Pinto de Mendonça, on July 12, 1771. Though it does not directly level any accusations against the contractors – merely stating the occurrence of abuses, which the royal monopoly would presumably manage to avoid – it is highly likely that this missive was the spark that sent rumours spreading throughout the captaincy. The Marquis of Pombal's text, in which he makes clear the intention to accentuate the rigor with which the new method was to be implemented, reads:

> The abuses necessarily introduced into this administration while in the hands of private individuals and the badly crafted system by which this contract was established have made this reform urgently necessary, given the impossibility of continuing under the existing terms, [only] Royal authority [will be able] to avoid disorder, curb the abuses and keep all within the limits of the permitted.[101]

Under the Pombaline administration, responsible for the promotion and ennoblement of an elite merchant class, the strategic matters of the Realm were constantly entrusted to figures in the minister's confidence and inner circle. The only way he could remedy

---

[99] APM. Seção Colonial. 183, fls. 5–6.
[100] Robert Southey. *História do Brasil*, vol. 3, 1977, p. 342.
[101] ANTT. Núcleos extraídos do Conselho da Fazenda. Junta de direção-geral dos diamantes. Livro 3, p. 2v.

the absence of a vital component of the diamond contract, which was the case with the two repatriated João Fernandes de Oliveira – father and son – was by decreeing a royal monopoly, a measure perfectly in keeping with the Crown's wish to restore its direct control over the wealth of the empire. In this case, however, the measure was not the culmination of any long-term strategy on Pombal's part, but an inevitable reaction to a specific set of circumstances that were difficult to resolve.[102] Without the valuable contractors, the best alternative was to deliver the business into the hands of public administrators, who, after all, were being prepared for precisely this end.[103]

[102] Camilo Castelo Branco defended the thesis that the Pombaline reforms were not the result of a long-term strategy, but were defined by chance and drawn up by others as opposed to by the marquis himself. Camilo Castelo Branco. *Perfil do marquês de Pombal*. 1982, pp. 114–15, 131, 134, 274–5.

[103] Pombal created the College of the Nobles in order to prepare the sons of the nobility for public administration and the Commercial Lessons to keep the merchant class up to date with knowledge important to their trade.

CHAPTER NINE

DISPUTES

Some, there, in the rugged pits,
rot away in the rivers,
while others, far off, reap the profits
of these mines of martyrdom.

THE GRIJÓ ESTATE

As was customary, Chief Judge João Fernandes de Oliveira embarked for the Realm with a retinue of personal slaves to serve him and make his long voyage more comfortable. He left behind the cliffs of Tejuco, which he would never set eyes on again, along with the mountain ranges and rivers of Minas. From the decks of his ship he bade farewell to the tropical heat, to the fresh Brazilian mornings, and the sweltering afternoons with their lazy siestas. Upon arrival in Lisbon, he settled comfortably into the house his father had constructed in Lapa, where he saw fit to make some additions,[1] including the installation of a tile panel along the main staircase depicting Brazilian scenes.

The staff that served him at the mansion included slaves, six servants with varied skills and crafts, and other trusted aides, some of whom had been brought over from Brazil.[2] In 1776, he is known to have had a butler, Maurício Pedro de Araújo; a buyer, Bartolomeu Vaz Lourenço, the contractor's longest-serving charge; and a coach

[1] ANTT. Desembargo do Paço. Estremadura. Maço 1049, doc. 10.
[2] AHTCL. Livros da Décima da Cidade. Arruamentos, freguesia de Santos e Lapa. 1762–1834. Apud: José Sarmento Matos. *Uma casa na Lapa*. 1994, p. 116.

driver, bodyguard, and cook, named José Gomes Dias, Luís José de Sousa, and Manuel do Nascimento.[3] The house must have had a total staff of about twenty, including employees and slaves,[4] of whom six were of the former contractor's strictest confidence and personal service.[5]

Chica da Silva remained on Ópera street, where she tended to the futures of her daughters and little José Agostinho,[6] still too young to join his elder brothers João, Joaquim, and Antônio Caetano and half brother Simão Pires Sardinha at his father's side in Lisbon, as he later would.[7]

Soon after his arrival, João Fernandes directly entreated the king not to allow any legal action to be brought over the inheritance of his father's estate, as "the supplicant has no wish to take recourse to legal measures, nor would these be necessary in a matter so easily decided"; adding that such a long drawn-out process would be of "irreparable damage to the supplicant and to those merchants with interests in the large contracts of his house."[8] He was afraid that a prolonged stay in the Realm would prevent him from continuing at the head of the diamond contract. In his own words, he was legally "the sole heir to his father's estate and just as capable of continuing and completing the business of his house, most importantly the diamond extraction contract."[9]

João Fernandes was in a hurry to have this dispute resolved. Continuously calling attention to the royal interests in his family's business and trusting in "royal and paternal protection," he urged that proceedings be "carried forth summarily, or as His Majesty sees

---

[3] ANTT. Testamento de João Fernandes de Oliveira. Registro Geral de Testamentos. Livro 312, fls. 170, 171v.

[4] José Sarmento Matos, op. cit., p. 116.

[5] In his will, João Fernandes left alms for six house servants. ANTT. Chancelaria de dona Maria I. Livro 20, f.11

[6] The census held in Tejuco in 1774 registers Francisca da Silva e Oliveira as a resident on Rua da Ópera in the company of a son. This son must certainly have been José Agostinho. AHU, MAMG. Caixa 108, doc. 9, f. 2.

[7] ANTT. Desembargo do Paço. Estremadura. Maço 1078, doc. 11.

[8] ANTT. Desembargo do Paço. Ilhas. Maço 1342, doc. 7, f. 47

[9] Ibidem, fls. 46v–47.

fit, to ascertain whether or not the stepmother should be equal heir to the couple's assets."[10] However, the days were gone when royal justice was dispensed so directly without going through the legal institutions, which, at least in theory, were supposed to provide more objective decisions in the light of the abiding legislation.

When the contractor arrived in the Realm, Minister Sebastião José de Carvalho e Melo was reaching the height of his power, having been conferred the title of Marquis of Pombal in 1769.[11] João Fernandes knew that he enjoyed the favor and the recognition of the marquis and of the king himself, as "His Highness, King José, sleeps peacefully in the knowledge that in João Fernandes de Oliveira he has an honoured and useful vassal, so much so that he appointed him to that administration."[12] Indeed, Pombal clearly took the chief judge's side in his dispute with the widow Isabel Pires Monteiro, issuing royal decrees that always favored the contractor's interests.

Even before he made port at Lisbon, João Fernandes's lawyers at the court filed a petition to have all exactions against the Sergeant Major's estate suspended pending his arrival. In granting this request, His Majesty ordered the promulgation of a decree dated September 11, 1770, in which he declared that

> faced with the great encumbrance in which we find the house of João Fernandes de Oliveira, the recently deceased diamond extraction contractor, given the various interests that remain to be settled among his heirs and partners, and in the absence of any member of that house apt enough to remove said encumbrance, [though] also aware of the imminent arrival at court of dr. João Fernandes de Oliveira, son and partner of the deceased, and bearing in mind the turmoil this couple, the interested parties and all

[10] ANTT. Ministério do Reino. Livro 212, f. 236.

[11] AMU. Documentos relativos ao Brasil – Bahia, no. 8353. In: Eduardo de Castro Almeida. "Inventário dos existentes..." *Anais da Biblioteca Nacional*, vol. 32, 1910, p. 249. Private letter from the Count of Povolide to the Marquis of Pombal in which he congratulates the latter on the conferral of the title. Bahia, November 28, 1770.

[12] ANTT. Desembargo do Paço. Ilhas. Maço 1342, doc.7. Defense of Chief Judge João Fernandes de Oliveira.

those who depend upon their charges and the adjustments of their accounts would face in the event of legal proceedings and disputes through the ordinary means and the inevitable delays therein[,] I hereby bar[,] for the time being[,] any legal action against said house until the arrival of the abovementioned heir and partner[,] should his present state be preserved.[13]

This privilege, originally conceded for a three-year period, was successively renewed in 1772[14] and 1775.[15] The king's protection was once more made evident through the concession of the "privilege of summary court and process in the judicial decision," which would have accelerated proceedings despite the embargoes the stepmother tried to obtain. Nevertheless, with João Fernandes embroiled in a protracted legal battle in the Realm, the contract system was abolished and substituted by a royal monopoly.[16]

The stepmother's defense was consistent: the doctors who accompanied the Sergeant Major on his deathbed and the clerics that gave him the last rites all attested to his sound mind at the final hour and fit state to change his testament of his own free will. Faced with the prospect of losing the case, João Fernandes had no choice but to remain in Portugal in order to pull some strings. He managed to have Fernando José da Cunha Pereira, a member of the Marquis of Pombal's inner circle, appointed as the judge who would oversee the inventory of the Sergeant Major's assets.[17]

All throughout the dispute between the chief judge and his father's widow, the Marquis of Pombal somewhat overdid the rhetoric in lauding the virtues of the former over the inept Sergeant Major who, he claimed, spurred by his wife's greed, had spent his last years at court chipping away at the family estate with his excessive spending, especially on the construction of the new house. Pombal

---

[13] ANTT. Ministério do Reino. Livro 212, fls. 143–145; Desembargo do Paço. Ilhas. Maço 1342, doc. 7, fls. 45v–46.
[14] ANTT. Ministério do Reino. Livro 213, fls. 40v–41.
[15] ANTT. Ministério do Reino. Livro 214, f. 43v.
[16] ANTT. Ministério do Reino. Livro 212, f. 236; livro 213, f. 41.
[17] ANTT. Ministério do Reino. Livro 212, f. 212; Desembargo do Paço. Ilhas. Maço 1342, doc. 7.

even went so far as to write an attestation in which he stated that the Sergeant Major was unfit to manage his patrimony, "showing himself to be increasingly more inapt, plummeting to the deplorable state of being wholly incapable of any act or negotiation whatsoever." In reference to the diamond contract, he declared that "[Sergeant Major] João Fernandes de Oliveira's incapacity to run and govern a business of such importance was notorious."[18]

The powerful minister maligned his old friend and ally in the name of the family's interests, which now centered on the figure of his son. The marquis's attestation was nothing more than an artifice of rhetoric designed to strengthen the chief judge's case that his father had been unfit to take a decision of such magnitude. While Pombal damned the Sergeant Major for giving, spending, and lending "without contract or caution,"[19] he had himself taken out loans with the old contractor only days before his death. If the marquis's allegations were true, this act, granted in return for all the favors the minister had done him over the years, would have been just as invalid.

Despite all the evidence that the Sergeant Major had been of sound mind in the days leading up to his death, the appeals court ruled in João Fernandes' favor in January 1773, citing the *Lei da Boa Razão* (Law of Good Reason)[20] and determining that "she [Isabel] should not be equal heir to her husband's estate, nor to any acquired [assets], being entitled to no more than her dowry repaid in full."[21] Pombal's attestation proved crucial, as, "being a minister of the State and Financial Secretary of the Realm, his credibility [wa]s unquestionable," even if his testimony contradicted all the sworn evidence the stepmother had collected from the clerics and doctors who had witnessed the events firsthand.[22]

The widow claimed that the friendship Pombal bore the Sergeant Major, and which extended also to his son, was decisive in turning

---

[18] ANTT. Desembargo do Paço. Ilhas. Maço 1342, doc. 7, fls. 60–60v.
[19] Ibidem, f. 60.
[20] Pombal's legal reforms instituted the Law of Good Reason as a substitute for citation from the classical jurists of antiquity, like Cicero.
[21] Ibidem, fls. 54v–65.
[22] Ibidem, f. 63v.

the case in the chief judge's favor, given her "stepson's opulence and
the protection of the Ministers of State."[23] She mentioned various
favors the enriched diamond contractors had exchanged with the
minister, his wife the marchioness, his brothers, and other powerful
figures at Court.

João Fernandes defended himself against these accusations as best
he could, implying that it was a question of commercial interests,
geared toward profit rather than the establishment of client networks, always invoked in times of need. As for the cash loans made to
Pombal and his uncle, chancellor Paulo de Carvalho,[24] the contractor alleged that, friendship aside, the loans were a matter of business,
just "profit without risk," adding that "a minister's lot would be hard
indeed if he could not sell, buy, give or receive loans without fear of
offence to his honour and to justice, either for himself and for his
relatives."[25]

He used a similar argument to justify his purchase of the
Portela Farmhouse from Francisco Xavier de Mendonça Furtado, the
Marquis of Pombal's brother, which he declared was "assessed by
experts and assured by such a trustworthy seller."[26] The contractor
also refuted the suspicions Isabel raised as to the impartiality of the
court reporter, claiming that only a few months earlier the very same
judge had ruled against "the illustrious José de Menezes[,] a man just
as closely connected to the Marquis of Pombal."[27]

As soon as she learned of the ruling, Isabel Pires Monteiro took
refuge at the house of her grandson, Luís de Sousa. João Fernandes
accused her of having stolen "all of the inventoried jewellery, trinkets
and adornments, 11 thousand and something cruzados, [as well as]

---

[23] Ibidem, f. 101.
[24] "Sebastião José de Carvalho e Mendonça, nephew of Chancellor Paulo de
Carvalho, from whom he inherited properties and a palace on Rua Formosa."
Jacome Ratton. *Recordações de Jacome Ratton sobre ocorrências do seu tempo em
Portugal.* 1992, p. 149.
[25] ANTT. Desembargo do Paço. Ilhas. Maço 1342, doc. 7.
[26] Ibidem.
[27] Ibidem.

silver, gold and tapestries."[28] Two months later, though her where-
abouts was still unknown, the stepmother filed an appeal against the
ruling[29] and João Fernandes found himself once more bound to the
Realm, caught in another web of litigation. Livid, the contractor discovered his stepmother's hideout and – with a little further help from
Pombal – secured a court order to have her locked up in the Convent
of Our Lady of the Powers in Vialonga just outside Lisbon.[30]

In the early hours of October 3, 1773, the criminal judge of
the borough of Santa Catarina, armed with a note written by the
Marquis de Pombal, turned up unannounced at the Sapataria farmhouse, the property of Isabel's grandson, where the widow was in
hiding. Caught unaware, a precariously dressed Isabel was dragged
out of bed and handed over to the mother superior of the convent,
Sister Maria Antônia Xavier, along with her chamber slave. By five
o'clock that morning she was immured in a cell with nothing of her
own except the slave to serve her.

Vialonga was located north of the capital, near the Tagus River,
on the junction of two roads that connected Lisbon with the north of
Portugal. Founded by Brites de Castelo Branco in 1561 on the Santa
Maria farm, the convent of the Powers was run by the Clarist nuns.[31]
It was there that Isabel Pires Monteiro lived for the next years
years at the Clarists' expense, despite João Fernandes' promise to
send her an allowance as demanded by the court ruling. Though
the insistent mother superior wrote to the Marquis de Pombal on
three occasions informing him of her charge's precarious situation,
it was only in 1776 that João Fernandes began to contribute with

[28] ANTT. Desembargo do Paço. Ilhas. Maço 1342, doc. 7. Defesa do desembargador
João Fernandes de Oliveira.
[29] Ibidem, fls. 66–67.
[30] Ibidem, f. 77.
[31] Practically nothing remains of the old building today, "which was intact up to
the 1980s. All that one can find of it today are some of the small constructions that surrounded the convent, among them one that is located behind
the Brioso wine-cellar which used to be the nuns' cells. The convent heraldic
shield is located today in front of Vialonga Main church." http://vialonga.no.
sapo.pt/locaisquintas.htm

a monthly stipend of 30,000 reis.[32] The contractor justified this by saying that he had not acted out of malignancy, but had genuinely believed that his stepmother required no subsistence, especially as she had fled with the coffer containing the family money and jewelry, some of which had never been returned, and that all throughout her marriage she had swindled large sums of money on behalf of members of her family who, it was only right, should now shoulder the costs of her upkeep.[33]

Anxious about the possibility of losing the appeal and counting on Pombal's help once again, João Fernandes managed to sway the appointment of the judge who would preside over the second hearing. As he was still well regarded by the powers that be and by the Marquis in particular, he promptly got his wish. In 1774, Dr. José Luis França was designated "the new minister in charge of the inventory of his father's estate."[34]

In 1775 the contractor fell seriously ill with "a dangerous ailment."[35] Fearing for the integrity of his patrimony, as the legal dispute with his stepmother was still dragging on, he decided to give a new destiny to the family estate and eternalize the power he possessed by establishing an entail (morgado[36]). In so doing he could perpetuate the Sergeant Major's project of aggrandizement of the Fernandes de Oliveira family and erase the dishonorable origins of his children with Chica. The chief judge was looking ahead; his decisions regarding his estate were taken with the future in mind and clarified his wishes for his descendants. In the twilight of his life, sensing the proximity of death, he wrote an adjunct to his will that was of a more pious nature, as was common practice, seen as one's final act

---

[32] ANTT. Desembargo do Paço. Ilhas. Maço 1342, doc. 7. Defesa do desembargador João Fernandes de Oliveira.

[33] Ibidem.

[34] ANTT. Ministério do Reino. Livro 213, f. 168.

[35] ANTT. Cartórios notariais. 5B. Caixa 15, livro 75. Notas. Atual 12, f. 77v.

[36] As in the Portuguese legislation, the wife had the right of half of the inheritance and the children – male or female – had the right of equal amounts. It was possible for the noble to decide that part of their inheritance could not be split, inherited normally by the elder son over the generations. It was done by the morgado institution.

of charity that is decisive to the fate of the soul. Wills tended to be a way of settling with the past, with those one ended up owing along the way, while all thoughts of the future turned toward the beyond and to ensuring a good place for the soul within it.

Regulated by various clauses, an entail consisted of an agreement between the institutor and the king. It was basically a repayment "for the good services rendered unto the kings by our predecessors, for which they deserve to be honoured and increased,"[37] a reward to loyal and honored subjects, forever understood as a royal concession and subject to Portuguese law. It was for this reason that "His most loyal majesty, through his royal grandeur and beneficence, deigned to grant to . . . the chief judge João Fernandes de Oliveira, the faculties and licences required for the establishment of an entail in the form of a Royal Provision."[38]

Thus he preserved his name and his achievements, eternalized through his male successors and with the full sanction of the Crown. The entail created a mosaic of assets that could not be divided or alienated and which would pass to the firstborn son of each grantee upon his death. In the preamble to the document that instituted the Grijó entail, João Fernandes de Oliveira declared his goal to be "the establishment of an Estate in which[,] conserving the perennial memory of the privileged benefits and honours it owes to your Lord-ship [the king], its successors shall distinguish themselves for their zeal and devotion in royal service."[39] According to the *Ordenações filipinas* (Philipine Code), which regulated such acts, the entail as an institution was the prerogative of the powerful and characterized by the founder's wish to preserve and ennoble his name: "the inten-tion of the grand and aristocratic, and the noblemen of our king-doms and domains, who establish entails . . . is the conservation and memory of their names and the increment of their estates, houses and nobility."[40]

---

[37] *Ordenações filipinas*. Livro IV, tít. 100, § 5.
[38] ANTT. Cartórios notariais. 5B. Caixa. 15, livro 75. Notas. Atual 12, f. 75.
[39] Ibidem.
[40] *Ordenações filipinas*. Livro IV, tít. 100, § 5.

The *morgadio* system was based on land assets, which were regulated and rendered indivisible, as land was a source of wealth and social prestige. In order to have their patrimonies entailed, businessmen like the diamond contractor, whose wealth was derived from the mercantile sector, were obliged to convert a considerable part of this patrimony into real estate. However, as most of João Fernandes' rural properties were in Brazil and still embroiled in the legal dispute with Isabel Pires Monteiro, he started acquiring new properties as soon as he arrived in the Realm. His first purchase was the Grijó farmhouse, which the state had sequestered from the Augustinian monks.[41] This property, which he purchased at the price of 36 contos de réis, was chosen as the seat of the "Grijó" entail, a title adopted as a surname by all of the contractor's male descendants.[42] Located in Vila Nova de Gaia, in the Porto district of northern Portugal, the property housed a convent and a church built in the first half of the sixteenth century. In addition to this and the Portela farmhouse located on the road to Sacavém, which we have already mentioned was purchased from Pombal's brother, João Fernandes also acquired the Enxara do Bispo (Bishop's Woods) in Leiria County, which came with an estate of seven houses.[43]

The contract declared that João Fernandes de Oliveira hereby "instituted, ordered and established . . . a perpetual, ordinary and regular entailing of all of the lands, real estate and other such assets that would become free upon his death."[44] The diamond business had enriched him and enabled him to accumulate a vast patrimony spread throughout Minas Gerais, Rio de Janeiro, and Portugal – he, who having "moved to the States of America in the year 1753, applied his laudable industry to acquiring a decent patrimony through commerce, with which he established his House."[45]

---

[41] Recent images of the *mosteiro* can be found at http://www.apel-arquitectura. pt/obras/mosteiro_de_grijo.htm

[42] ANTT. Cartórios notariais. 5B. Caixa 15, livro 78. Atual 12, fls. 48–49.

[43] Ibidem, f. 48.

[44] ANTT. Cartórios notariais. 5B. Caixa 15, livro 75, f. 75.

[45] Ibidem, f .77v.

Back in the captaincy he owned a house in Vila Rica and another in Pitangui, where he also had some land at Ponte Alta, and thirteen cattle and horse ranches, namely Santa Rita in Paraná, Riacho das Areias, Jenipapo, São Domingos, Povoação and Paracatu (both on the São Francisco River), Jequitaí, Rio Formoso, Santo Tomás, Santo Estêvão, Santa Clara, Ilha, and Formiga. Some of these farms had come down to him through the incorporation of Isabel Pires Monteiro's assets with those of the Fernandes de Oliveira family through her marriage to the Sergeant Major.[46]

The chief judge's estate also included the Palha farmhouse on the outskirts of the village of Tejuco and the Santa Bárbara farm near the Curamataí River, which included plantations, a cattle, horse and donkey farm, and a "one-story house, completely tile-covered, ..., an ox-driven sugar mill, also covered with tiles, a tile-covered chaff house, ... [and] a good water channel." The demesne was so large that it was divided into two separate units – Cavagaldura and São Miguel – each with its own lath-and-plaster corral.[47]

We are told that he was the proprietor of some *"noble* houses" in Rio de Janeiro, probably a reference to his grandparents' house in Rosário Square. In addition to the farmhouses he acquired in Portugal, his properties in Lisbon included a block of houses on Rua Augusta, an upmarket address in Pombal's lower city with twenty-two front windows and eleven overlooking Rua da Sapataria, plus the mansion built by his father on Rua Buenos Aires in the borough of Lapa, another at the end of Rua Bela Vista, two facing the Estrela convent, and another smaller house on Rua Guarda-Mor.[48] His coffers contained 96,000 cruzados in cash, which he ordered to be lent out at interest to the benefit of his heirs.[49] Without counting

---

[46] ANTT. Cartórios notariais. 5B. Caixa 15, livro 78. Atual 12, f. 48v. The farms of Santo Tomás, Santo Estêvão, Ilha, Rio Formoso, Jequitaí, and Paracatu belonged to Isabel Pires Monteiro. ANTT. Desembargo do Paço. Ilhas. Maço 1342, doc. 7, fls. 3–4.

[47] BAT. João Germano de Oliveira Grijó. Cartório do Primeiro Ofício, maço 27.

[48] ANTT. Cartórios notariais. 5B. Caixa 15, livro 78. Atual 12, fls. 48–49.

[49] ANTT. Desembargo do Paço. Estremadura. Maço 2112, doc. 37.

the son's contribution, the Sergeant Major's fortune alone was calculated at around 2 million cruzados, making him the richest man in Portugal in his day.

The Buriti and Pé do Morro farms, both in Serro do Frio near the villages of São Gonçalo do Rio Preto and Rio Vermelho in the Diamantine Demarcation, were posthumously donated to the contractor's children through the will he registered in Vila Rica shortly before his departure.[50] The Buriti farm, located fourteen leagues from Tejuco, included some two-story or more houses with tiled roofs and a corral, two mills, two hydraulic pestles, a sugar cane mill, and two barns. The farm was used to grow corn and beans, and to raise sheep, cattle, pigs, and donkeys. There were also some weaver's looms and a site for spinning and threading cotton to produce fabrics and clothing, such as lacework dresses.[51] The Pé do Morro farm housed a small horse and cattle ranch and plantations of corn, cassava, sugarcane, bean, and castor bean, from which oil was extracted. In terms of machinery, there were two mills, one ox-driven and the other for grinding cassava.[52]

Lineage was the structuring characteristic of an entail, the purpose of which was not merely to regulate the destination and administration of land assets but also to crystallize and preserve the achievements of one's predecessors by creating a chain of commitment between generations and imposing a code of conduct upon one's successors. Continued possession and clan leadership was conditional upon strict obedience to these norms. According to João Fernandes, his intention was that "his sons and descendants should walk in conformity with the clauses of which the institution was made and ordered," proof that he firmly followed these precepts himself.[53]

In a hierarchical society based on estates, the individual's pedigree, and consequently also that of his family, was fundamentally

---

[50] ANTT. Registro geral de testamento. Livro 312, f. 170.
[51] BAT. Inventário de Rita Quitéria de São José. Cartório do Primeiro Ofício, maço 63.
[52] BAT. Inventário de Francisca de Paula de Oliveira. Cartório do Primeiro Ofício, maço 23.
[53] *Ordenações Filipinas*. Livro IV, tít. 100, § 5.

important in defining the place a person occupied, and though the chief judge ranked among the grandees of the Realm, neither his genealogy nor that of his descendents justified such an entitlement and therefore had to be either concealed or redeemed. Through entails, not only stigmas such as illegitimacy could be transmitted from generation to generation, but also nobility and the memories of grandiose achievements. With the destination of his assets decided, João Fernandes began to declare the wishes by which his successors were expected to abide. He determined that his successive heirs should put themselves entirely in the service of His Majesty, to which end he set aside two thirds of the entailed patrimony, which he considered was "more than sufficient income for them to be educated and treated as noblemen." He also hoped that his initiative would "equally serve as a perpetual awakening to their obligations."[54]

Among the demands he made upon them was that they be true to the laws of God and obedient to the Catholic Church, as well as to the "substitute of God on earth, the king and natural lord of this monarchy, . . . all of which they shall love and fear, which are the two poles around which the nobility and happiness of a family should be amassed." He exhorted them to be esteemed, a state they should be able to attain through affability and honor, serving and benefiting as many as possible and seeking friendship with the powerful.[55] He did not forget to mention the important client networks by which the Portuguese Empire was both united and hierarchized from the king down to even the least of his subjects and of which both father and son had equally and wisely availed to the aggrandizement of their house.

Furthermore, he sought to diminish the stigmas of miscegenation and illegitimacy that tarnished his descendants by advising them to always pursue "the best possible marriages and to increment the income of the house as they honestly can."[56] An adjunct stipulated

---

[54] ANTT. Cartórios notariais. 5B. Caixa 15, livro 75. Notas. Atual 12, f. 75v.
[55] Ibidem.
[56] Ibidem, f. 76.

that his successors were not free to marry before the age of thirty, unless with the legal consent of their father, mother, grandparents, or tutors.[57]

He instituted as his successor any legitimate son or daughter he might still come to have, though in the event that no such child be born, his immediate heir was to be his eldest natural son, João Fernandes de Oliveira Grijó, legitimized by José I, followed by his legitimate male line.[58] In the absence of his namesake, the grantee was to be Antônio Caetano, his third-born natural son, followed by his paternal cousins Lieutenant Colonel Ventura Fernandes de Oliveira and José Dias de Oliveira, the maternal cousin Pedro da Silva Pimentel, and their legitimate descendants.[59]

While his other natural children were not appointed heirs to the entail, the chief judge set aside the remaining third of his fortune to be divided among them, with the exception of José Agostinho, who was allotted an annual stipend of 400,000 reis in payment for his services as head priest at the chapel of Grijó monastery. He also left 30,000 reis per year to each of his five sisters, all still alive and immured at Monchique convent in Porto.

The only permanent incumbency he left was the payment of an annual donation of one-hundredth of the entailed estate's returns to a pious cause, be it to serve as "a marriage dowry for a lady, orphan or otherwise . . . or as alms in favour of a prisoner, . . . or as ransom for captives."[60]

With his will now done and his name immortalized, the chief judge spent the last years of his life tending to the business of his estate, endeavoring to receive his father's inheritance, and preparing his sons for succession. He was suffering from a terminal illness and knew that death was drawing near. From the balcony of the house in Lapa he watched as the ships entered the Tagus estuary, having crossed the ocean that separated him from the Minas of his glory, from the "mines of all delirium."

[57] ANTT. Cartórios notariais. 5B. Caixa 15, livro 78, f. 48v.
[58] ANTT. Cartórios notariais. 5B. Caixa. 15, livro 75. Notas. Atual 12, f. 77.
[59] Ibidem, fls. 76v–77.
[60] Ibidem, f. 76.

The Marian Era

The death of José I in 1777 and the ascension of his daughter Maria I to the throne brought disturbing changes to bear on the Realm that had direct reflections upon the house of João Fernandes, especially on the plans he had so carefully traced for the eternalization of his name and assets. The setbacks the former contractor faced during the first years of the young queen's reign and the various royal decisions that went in his favor in his disputes with his stepmother were clear proof that he was always able to count on the Marquis de Pombal's special protection and therefore, by extension, also that of the monarch herself.

Under Maria I, the political landscape of the Realm suffered a wave of inversions that came to be known as the *Viradeira*, and Pombal's protégés found themselves under threat. In 1778, in the wake of the Marian reforms, João Fernandes saw his luck begin to change. Isabel Pires Monteiro, his father's widow, somehow managed to get a petition to the queen in which she described the misfortune into which she had fallen, affirming that she had been treacherously locked up in a convent under Pombal's orders, where she had to live off the charity of the nuns because the chief judge had failed to honor his commitment to pay the annual stipend she was due.[61]

The petition was the result of the stepmother's continued efforts to secure her part of her husband's inheritance. Taking advantage of the political upheaval, Pombal's incarceration, and the persecution of his old allies, Isabel succeeded in winning the queen's sympathy and reopening her claim for the distribution of the Sergeant Major's assets.[62]

On December 21, 1779, a seriously ill João Fernandes passed away at his mansion in the Buenos Aires neighborhood.[63] His condition must certainly have been aggravated by the tribulations of the Marian era and the persecution of Pombal's partisans. After a brief funeral he was laid to rest near his father's tomb at Our Lady of

---

[61] ANTT. Desembargo do Paço. Ilhas. Maço 1342, doc. 7.

[62] Ibidem.

[63] He was sick since at least 1775. ANTT. Cartórios notariais. 5B. Caixa 15, livro 75. Notas. Atual 12, f. 78.

Jesus convent.[64] So weakened was he by his illness that he was even unable to sign a final adjunct to his will written three days before his death.[65] Many years later, in 1795, the Brotherhood of the Most Holy Sacrament in Tejuco celebrated four masses in his honor as requested by the board of directors in thanks for the services he had rendered to the entity.[66]

The chief judge wrote a last will and testament and two complements. The first will was registered in Vila Rica in November 1770 only days before his return to the Realm and approved by the court in 1774. In 1775 he established the Grijó entail, in which he laid out his concerns over what would become of his patrimony.[67] The first adjunct, made two years later, in which he minutely described a significant portion of his accumulated wealth, was couched in a clear businesslike language.[68] The second and last alteration, hurriedly made at the final hour and revealing a Christian fearful of the fate awaiting his soul, adopted a manner more typical of his time. All pious in nature, his final instructions stipulated the provision of alms:

> To his religious sisters; to the six slaves, of various trades, that served and accompanied him; to the Lapa convent; to the Brotherhood of the Most Holy Sacrament of said parish; to Friar Antônio das Angústias, cleric of the Third Order of the Penitence; to a widow and her five children; orphans and minors under the age of fourteen; to two ladies for their dowries.[69]

Unhappy about the loss of the patrimony his father had destined for charity, his principal heir, João Fernandes de Oliveira Grijó, filed a suit at the high court contesting his father's will – an act that horrified Father Nuno Henriques Dorta, the executor of the late

[64] ANTT. Registros paroquiais, no. 1, caixa 7, microfilme 1019.

[65] ANTT. Registro geral de testamentos. Livro 312, fls. 170–170v.

[66] AEAD. Certidão da capela das quintas-feiras pelas almas dos irmãos falecidos da Irmandade do Santíssimo Sacramento. 1760–1849, caixa 519.

[67] AEAD. Certidão da capela das quintas-feiras pelas almas dos irmãos falecidos da Irmandade do Santíssimo Sacramento. 1760–1849, caixa 519.

[68] ANTT. Cartórios notariais. 5B. Caixa 15, livro 75. Notas. Atual 12, fls. 75–78v.

[69] ANTT. Chancelaria de dona Maria I. Livro 20, f. 11.

contractor's will and the man entrusted with carrying out his final wishes, especially those for the remission of his sins and for the good of the poor. According to the priest:

> Either the age or inconsiderateness of that lad prevents him from contemplating debts of gratitude, as, taking advantage of his father's extraordinary complaisance, his disposition and the royal beneficence to constitute an entail [,] and lord of such a vast inheritance, [he has] contested, trampled upon and defamed his father's arrangements, which envisaged the good of others.[70]

After various appeals, the will was still inconclusive five years later, as João Fernandes's firstborn heir continued to enter with recourses that prevented the settlement of accounts and the finalization of the process.[71]

With the ascension of Maria I, the heirs of the once powerful contractor suffered a series of major setbacks. In 1780, granting a solicitation from the Augustinian monks, the queen ordered

> that the Congregation of the Observing Canons of Saint Augustine be revested of the monastery of São Salvador de Grijó in Feira county, in the bishopric of Porto, and all its belongings exactly as sold to the chief judge João Fernandes de Oliveira, also revesting his son and successor João Fernandes de Oliveira Grijó of the sum of 36 contos, this being the purchase price paid by his father, ... with these reciprocal restitutions made, the abovementioned sale shall be undone, as if it had never indeed been celebrated, and the farms and assets of said monastery shall be returned to exactly the state in which they were found when in the possession of the aforementioned observing canons[,] and shall be once more peopled by the clerics.[72]

This royal decision was a severe blow to the Grijó entail, which, divested of its rural seat, lost all reason for its existence. Upon the restitution of the monastery to the religious order in 1783,

---

[70] ANTT. Chancelaria de dona Maria I. Livro 22, f. 294v.
[71] ANTT. Casa da Suplicação. Juízos diversos. Inventários. Maço 375, caixa 2093.
[72] ANTT. Chancelaria de dona Maria I. Livro 15, fls. 335–335v.

João Fernandes Grijó used the returned cash to buy a "farmhouse called Casal Novo, located in Requengo do Gradil in Torres Vedras county," which was to become the entail's new seat.[73] He acquired another property, Mata do Requengo, at the same time. A few years later he requested "all the privileges, exemptions, imperial edicts and commissions conferred upon residents of Requengo do Gradil, among other privileges in benefit of the chapels of his lordship, king Afonso IV."[74]

The death of the chief judge and the end of the Pombaline era, along with the changes at court, gave fresh encouragement to Isabel Pires Monteiro, who continued to sue his heirs in the figure of the eldest son and spared no effort to ensure that the dispute over the Sergeant Major's inheritance was brought to its conclusion. Isabel left the convent on the orders of Maria I and returned to Lisbon where she lived in rented houses. Her appeal was still in its second instance, though the announcement of the ruling was being held up by the contractor's influence and the sluggishness of the legal system. Grijó, on the other hand, deprived of the royal protection that used to sway justice in the family's favor, continued with his father's policy of dragging the decision out for as long as possible.

Upon Chief Judge João Fernandes de Oliveira's death, his estate was annexed to the dispute surrounding the Sergeant Major's patrimony and both suits ran concurrently. As the administrator appointed to the inheritances of both his father and grandfather, possession of the assets went to Grijó.[75] In 1783, with the process at a standstill since the death of the presiding judge in 1779, Isabel entered with a request for the appointment of a new judge.[76] The nomination of José Fernando Nunes in 1785 was not in Isabel's favor, as he was a partisan of Grijó. The widow managed to have

---

[73] ANTT. Desembargo do Paço. Estremadura. Maço 2116, doc. 95.

[74] ANTT. Desembargo do Paço. Ilhas. Maço 968, doc. 96.

[75] ANTT. Desembargo do Paço. Estremadura. Maço 694, doc. 125.

[76] ANTT. Desembargo do Paço. Estremadura. Maço 692, doc. 32. Pedro Taques, in his book, says that Isabel granted a favorable decision in 1783. But at this moment she was still trying to move the lawsuit. Pedro Taques de A. Paes Leme, "Nobiliarquia...," op. cit., p. 213.

him declared suspect[77] and requested that Marcelino Xavier da Fonseca Pinto be recommended as a replacement, though to no avail.[78] Isabel had to appeal to the Crown, alleging that she had "delivered the provision of said nomination to João Fernandes [Grijó], the defendant against the plaintiff, and . . . the defendant has so far not given the right to proceed, [causing] a delay that is prejudicial to the plaintiff."[79] That same year João Fernandes Grijó had his own chance to try to sway the nomination of a new judge, claiming that the process was at a halt because of the ill health of the presiding arbiter. The queen granted Grijó's request and appointed Chief Judge José Antônio Pinto Boto, though as he too died soon afterward, Isabel managed to have Antônio Álvares do Vale nominated as his replacement.[80]

The power play between the two parties began to reach some definition with Isabel's death from a stroke on November 12, 1788. Grijó tried to put the ruling off for as long as possible, as in his capacity as administrator of his father's and grandfather's fortunes, their assets were already at his disposal anyway, in deed even if not by right. In 1793, Caetana Maria Brandão, Isabel Pires Monteiro's daughter, pressured for the completion of her mother's inventory and João Fernandes Grijó was forced to request the conclusion of the dispute surrounding his grandfather's inheritance. The queen ordered the process to be brought to a close once and for all, and a ruling was passed in Grijó's favor. The estates could now finally be divided among the chief judge's heirs.[81]

News reached Tejuco at the beginning of 1794, and the surviving heirs registered powers of attorney in Vila Rica requesting the inheritances due to them from their father's and grandfather's estates.[82] Ana Quitéria appointed a lawyer to sue against her brother

[77] ANTT. Desembargo do Paço. Estremadura. Maço 694, doc. 125.
[78] ANTT. Desembargo do Paço. Ilhas. Maço 693, doc. 27.
[79] ANTT. Desembargo do Paço. Estremadura. Maço 692, doc. 32.
[80] ANTT. Desembargo do Paço. Estremadura. Maço 694, doc. 125.
[81] ANTT. Desembargo do Paço. Estremadura. Maço 707, doc. 10; maço 706, doc. 32.
[82] AFS. Livro de notas. 1793–1794, no. 99, fls. 29–29v.

and contest the sum he planned to pay them.[83] Antônio Caetano chose his half-brother Simão Pires Sardinha as court attorney to file civil and criminal proceedings on his behalf.[84] The disputes over the inheritance soured relations between the descendants living in Tejuco and their eldest brother. With the Atlantic Ocean between them, the children of Chica da Silva and the powerful contractor locked into a protracted battle over their father's estate.

[83] Ibidem. Procuração de Ana Quitéria de São José em 1° de janeiro de 1794 para receber a herança do pai.

[84] AFS. Livro de notas. 1793–1794, no. 99, fls. 10v–11.

Destinies

Fortune is always blind,
and varied is the luck of men.

The Donna of Serro do Frio

Everything would indicate that the only reason Chica da Silva's relationship with João Fernandes was not completely conventional was
that the hierarchical society of the period impeded legal matrimony
between individuals from such different backgrounds or social conditions. Though omitted from the contractor's entail and wills, Chica
was never far from his thoughts after his return to Portugal, as can be
seen from the zealous care he dispensed to their children, for whom
he strove to establish the best possible footing in life. Eager to introduce his sons at court, the chief judge knew he would have to hide
their origins, which his contemporaries would have considered illegitimate and ignoble. It was therefore essential that he push his relationship with the former slave to the back of his memory and hide it
from future generations, as proved the case in Simão Pires Sardinha's
de genere process for admittance into the Order of Christ. Leaving
Chica out of his legacy was in no way a sign that she had slipped
from his thoughts or his gratitude; indeed, by endeavoring to ennoble
their children before the elitist society of the Realm, João Fernandes
was, from a distance, also indirectly protecting Chica, whom he had
left in Tejuco with a considerable patrimony.

Donna Francisca da Silva de Oliveira died at her home in the
village of Tejuco on February 16, 1796. Accompanying her at her

deathbed was the parish priest, who administered the last rites, absolved her sins, and consoled her in her final agony.[1] She was no longer a parda slave girl with nothing to call her own; she was now the lady of a "large house," the owner of real estate and a stock of slaves. The social status she had attained in life was demonstrated in the manner of her burial: Chica was laid to rest in tomb number sixteen in the nave of the church of the Brotherhood of Saint Francis of Assisi, theoretically reserved for the local white elite, having received all of the privileges, funeral rites, and sacraments that distinguished the brothers.[2]

With all the pomp and ceremony she was due as a sister of the Most Holy Sacrament, Saint Francis of Assisi, the Souls, the Holy Land, the Mercies, and the Rosary brotherhoods, her funeral included an open-casket vigil by the entire sacerdotal corps of the village regaled in vestments and purple stoles. At the end of the ceremony, the church bells tolled and the corpse was accompanied to the tomb by a procession of the memberships of the brotherhoods of which she was a sister and by the parish clergy bearing lighted candles.[3] As a member of the Brotherhood of the Most Holy Sacrament,[4] she was entitled to twenty-four masses prayed for her soul at the Santo Antônio church in the month following her death. Also in 1796, as instructed in her will, a further forty masses were said in her honor at the church of the Mercies.[5]

In the mid-nineteenth century, the bodies entombed inside the Saint Francis of Assisi church were exhumed and transferred to the

---

[1] On the last ceremonies, see *Constituições primeiras do arcebispado da Bahia*, pp. 81–2.

[2] AEAD. Livro de óbitos de São Francisco. Caixa 350, f. 55.

[3] AEAD. Livro de óbitos do arraial do Tejuco, f. 73v.

[4] "In case of a brother's death, the body shall be accompanied to the tomb by the Brotherhood, which will be obliged to provide a grave, and which will have 24 masses said. . . . The offering up of 24 masses for the soul of the deceased brothers must not delay under any reason, title or pretext; but must be executed within the period of one month, including the day of the passing." Compromisso da Irmandade do Santíssimo Sacramento . . . , 1785, capítulos 11 e 13.

[5] AEAD. Livro de missas para falecidos da Irmandade de Nossa Senhora das Mercês, caixa 520.

grounds where they were deposited in ossuaries. The reform was conducted in order to adapt the construction to the new sanitary norms. The remains of Chica da Silva and João Lopes Cardoso, both buried in tomb sixteen, were moved to ossuary number twenty-four.[6] Even then at the time of her death, the villagers already knew her by the nickname Chica and as the Donna of the Palha estate. The use of a nickname reveals a certain familiarity and is proof of the former slave's inclusion in the diamantine society, both during her lifetime and perpetuated in death by her many descendants.

Descendants

Throughout the course of their lives, Chica da Silva and João Fernandes de Oliveira sought to offer their children the best possible footing in society. The boys joined their father in the Realm, where he tried to prepare them for succession, while Chica dedicated herself mainly to her daughters' education, all of whom remained under her care in Tejuco. With the contractor's return to Portugal in 1770, Chica had to fend for herself just like the other freedwomen of Tejuco and find mechanisms by which she could maintain the social status she had achieved in the village.

The destinies of her children were somewhat paradoxical. While the fortune they inherited and the importance of their father and paternal forebears were decisive at times, on other occasions it was the skin color inherited from their mother that weighed most upon their lives. However mobile the society they lived in may have appeared, it still put great store on birth, a stigma that was passed down through various generations.

Above all, the course of Chica's life reveals an attempt to whiten her way into a more favorable position within the prejudiced society that took hold in Brazil, which, far from being a racial democracy, possessed various exclusion mechanisms based on color, race, and conditions of birth. In establishing the Grijó entail, João Fernandes

---

[6] AEAD. Livro de óbitos da Ordem Terceira de São Francisco. 1772–1857, caixa 350, f. 55. For funeral ceremonies, see Constituições primeiras do arcebispado da Bahia, pp. 289–93.

managed to have José I legitimize all of his sons, but their mulatto complexion and the slave origins of their mother proved barriers far more difficult to overcome or to forget.

João Fernandes de Oliveira Grijó, the firstborn son, was nominated as the chief judge's immediate heir. As such, he received two-thirds of the entire fortune entailed under the title Grijó,[7] thus becoming the rightful administrator of the considerable sums deposited with the Tribunal for Orphans and Absentees in Lisbon,[8] the organ responsible for accruing interest to the funds by issuing loans.[9] The death of his father in 1779 saw the heir return to Tejuco, certainly to convey the sad tidings to his mother and also to organize matters of the house.[10] It was there that he was caught broadside by Maria I's order issued in 1780 for the restitution of the Grijó monastery to the Augustinians.[11]

He remained in Tejuco for some time, where he took posts in the local brotherhoods, though he was forced to return to the Realm when Isabel Pires Monteiro reopened the dispute for the Sergeant Major's inheritance. He took up permanent residence at the house in Lapa, though he sojourned at the entail's rural properties.

Back in Lisbon, Grijó married at the age of twenty-eight to Donna Ana Maria da Silva Fernandes de Oliveira, from Guimarães, who bore him two sons, João Germano and Lourenço João.[12] Given his father's goal of continuing with the process of the family's aggrandizement, the clauses of the Grijó entail removed all natural sons from the line of succession and barred his successive heirs from marrying by free choice before the age of thirty, urging them to "take care with how they increased their line, always seeking the best possible marriages."[13] This was not the case with João Fernandes de Oliveira

7   ANTT. Cartórios notariais. 5B. Caixa 15, livro 75. Notas. Atual 12, fls. 75–78v.
8   ANTT. Desembargo do Paço. Ilhas. Maço 1405, doc. 5.
9   ANTT. Desembargo do Paço. Ilhas. Maço 1390, doc. 8.
10 ANTT. Desembargo do Paço. Estremadura. Maço 1078, doc. 11.
11 ANTT. Chancelaria de dona Maria I. Livro 15, fls. 335–335v.
12 ANTT. Leitura de Bacharéis. Letra L. Maço A, doc.24.
13 ANTT. Cartórios notariais. 5B. Caixa 15, livro 75. Notas. Atual 12, fls. 75–78v.

Grijó's intended bride, a landowner's daughter.[14] As his guardian opposed the marriage, he appealed to Maria I for permission to honor his commitment to his beloved. Analysis of the process indicates that the girl must have been pregnant, as he requested the queen's permission to "redeem through marriage the honour and reputation he had caused her to lose."[15]

The queen granted him the right to marry whomsoever he pleased without losing his right of succession. As the public interests of the royal state were to be held above those of its subjects, João Fernandes's prohibition that his descendants marry below their station ran counter to the state's preference that its subjects formalize their emotional ties in matrimony.[16]

Another argument Grijó availed of in his bid to convince the queen to sanction his marriage reveals the paradoxical position of João Fernandes's heirs in relation to the color they had inherited from their mother. The supplicant complained that it was practically impossible for him to meet the requirement of marrying someone above his own station, as such was the prejudice against miscegenation that it would be no easy task to "find anyone among the nobility willing to grant him a daughter's hand and call him son-in-law." Though his enormous wealth was well known, he had never received any proposal of marriage. He said that he believed the noble families "would rather see their daughters live in mediocre decency than allow into their families a blemish so patent to the eyes of all."[17] Father Nuno Henriques Dorta, responsible for seeing through the contractor's last wishes as expressed in his will, made the prejudice of the day manifestly clear when he recalled that the heir was a natural son of the chief judge born to a "black woman."[18]

Throughout his life the contractor's son administered the entailed assets, particularly the loan fund run by the Tribunal for

---

[14] ANTT. Chancelaria de dona Maria I. Livro 22, f. 294v; Ministério do Reino. Decretos. Maço 37, doc. 41.
[15] ANTT. Ministério do Reino. Decretos. Maço 37, doc. 41.
[16] ANTT. Chancelaria de dona Maria I. Livro 22, f. 294v.
[17] ANTT. Ministério do Reino. Decretos. Maço 37, doc. 41.
[18] ANTT. Chancelaria de dona Maria I. Livro 20, f. 11.

Orphans and Absentees, a resource many in the Realm availed of, including noble families in financial difficulty.[19] The Marquis de Penalva, finding himself in debt since the demise of his father, the Marquis de Algrete, requested a loan of 25,000 cruzados, so as not to "fall short with the obligations of his house and large family."[20] The chief judge Antônio de Campos Figueiredo Melo took a loan of 6,000 cruzados in order to carry out repairs on a property whose buildings had lain in ruins since the earthquake of 1755.[21] Rodrigo de Noronha borrowed money from João Fernandes to cover the costs of the marriage of his son, Francisco Xavier da Costa e Noronha, the immediate heir to the Pancas Estate, to Lady Mariana da Arrábida.[22]

Some of the borrowers put up real estate as a guarantee on their loans. One example was Father João Antônio de Siqueira, who offered a farm as security,[23] while Luís Francisco Paliarte and his wife Luciana Joaquina remortgaged the Manteigas farmhouse.[24] Viscount Asseca borrowed the 24,000 cruzados he needed to pay for his wedding at 5 percent interest,[25] while Chief Judge João Gualberto Pinto de Morais Sarmento offered his ownership of the Sal Court as surety on a loan to cover his travel expenses to Sabará, where he would take up the position of county magistrate.[26]

João Grijó died in or around 1821 and was succeeded at the head of the entail by his eldest son, João Germano. As his immediate heir was not yet of age, he gave power of attorney in Brazil to the second

[19] ANTT. Desembargo do Paço. Ilhas. Maço 1123, doc. 8. ANTT. Desembargo do Paço. Estremadura. Maço 2124, doc. 44; Desembargo do Paço. Ilhas. Maço 1405, doc. 5. ANTT. Desembargo do Paço. Estremadura. Maço 1078, doc. 11.

[20] ANTT. Desembargo do Paço. Estremadura. Maço 2112, doc. 37.

[21] ANTT. Desembargo do Paço. Estremadura. Maço 2121, doc. 75; Desembargo do Paço. Ilhas. Maço 1390, doc. 8.

[22] ANTT. Desembargo do Paço. Ilhas. Maço 1374, doc. 6.

[23] ANTT. Desembargo do Paço. Estremadura. Maço 2133, doc. 43.

[24] ANTT. Desembargo do Paço. Estremadura. Maço 2125, doc. 97; Desembargo do Paço. Ilhas. Maço 1420, doc. 9.

[25] ANTT. Desembargo do Paço. Estremadura e Ilhas. Maço 1364, doc. 1; Desembargo do Paço. Estremadura. Maço 2116, doc. 47.

[26] ANTT. Desembargo do Paço. Estremadura. Maço 2120, doc. 17; AHU, MAMG. Caixa 125, doc. 40.

lieutenant Bento Dias Chaves, husband of Rita Quitéria, Bento Dias de Moura, and his uncle José Agostinho Fernandes de Oliveira.[27] Following in the footsteps of his magistrate grandfather, the youngest son, Lourenço João, graduated in law from Coimbra.[28] At the age of twenty-three he entered the Superior Royal Court and embarked on a legal career[29] that would see him assume the post of appeals judge at a commercial court in the Portuguese capital.[30] Unmarried, he resided at the Colégio dos Nobres (College of the Nobles), founded by Pombal to prepare the nobles of the Realm for posts in the imperial administration.[31] In 1825, he became town judge for Oeiras, a post Pombal had granted to his grandfather.[32]

The second eldest son, Joaquim José, settled in Brazil, where he obtained the rank of colonel in the cavalry of Minas Gerais. Little is known about him, other than that he was still alive in 1840 and living in Vila Rica.[33]

After the chief judge's death, Antônio Caetano moved to the Realm, where he worked as a businessman and administrated the entail during his elder brother's stay in Brazil.[34] In 1781, most likely fleeing the adverse political climate at court, he too returned to Tejuco, where he received the ranks of second lieutenant,[35] sergeant major, and finally captain of the militias of Minas Gerais.[36] Ten years later he was living in the village of Paraúna. He held various

---

[27] BAT. João Germano de Oliveira. Cartório do Primeiro Ofício, maço 27, f. 32.

[28] ANTT. Casa da Suplicação. Juízos diversos. Inventários. Maço 375, caixa 2093.

[29] ANTT. Índice de leitura de bacharéis. Letra L. Maço A, doc. 24.

[30] Manoel da Silveira Cardozo. O desembargador João Fernandes de Oliveira. 1979, p. 313.

[31] With the Colégio dos Nobres, Pombal sought to discipline the noble young while instructing them in the knowledge required to occupy positions of note within the nation. ANTT. Índice de leitura de bacharéis. Letter L. Pack A, doc. 24.

[32] ANTT. Mercês. Registro Geral. Provisão. D. João VI, Lv. 20, f. 266, 266v.

[33] BAT. Inventário de João Germano de Oliveira. Cartório do Primeiro Ofício, maço 27.

[34] ANTT. Desembargo do Paço. Estremadura. Maço 1078, doc. 11.

[35] AFS. Livro de notas no. 95, 1791, fls. 71–71v.

[36] AHU, MAMG. Caixa 159, doc. 22. Simão Pires Sardinha said that his half-brothers was enlisted in the troops like him. Autos da devassa da Inconfidência Mineira, vol. 3, p. 458.

directorial posts in the guilds of Tejuco, principally in the Carmelite Brotherhood, whose church had been sponsored by his father. In 1794, he appointed lawyers in Brazil and in Portugal to launch civil proceedings to sue for his share of his father's and grandfather's inheritances.[37]

Antônio Caetano held various positions in the local administration. From 1786 to 1821 he was the administrator of the São Gonçalo ferry service. From 1800 to 1803 he exercised the function of court notary in Tejuco, receiving direct instructions from the Prince Regent João himself.[38] As the squadron commander Diogo José Paiva held tenure in this position, Antônio Caetano felt his recompense was too low and applied for a tenure of his own in 1805 in the equivalent position at the Tribunal of Orphans and Absentees of Vila do Príncipe.[39]

It becomes more difficult to keep track of Antônio Caetano from this date on. Given the sheer volume of homonyms and incomplete names, the chances of corroborating anything in the existing documentation are extremely remote.

José Agostinho did not fulfill his father's wishes that he be ordained a priest, despite the annual ecclesiastical revenue[40] of 400,000 reis set aside for him in the entail to cover his proposed services at the head of the Grijó monastery.[41] The restitution of the property to the Augustinian monks must have weighed in his decision to bow out of an ecclesiastical career. José Agostinho, like his other brothers, was in Lisbon when his father died, but returned to Tejuco along with Antônio Caetano in 1781, where he settled

---

[37] AFS. Livro de notas no. 99, 1793–1794, fls. 10v–11.
[38] AHU, MAMG. Caixa 159; doc. 22; caixa 175, doc. 17.
[39] AHU, MAMG. Caixa 175, doc. 16.
[40] The annual ecclesiastical revenue was payment received by the lay priests from the Royal Exchequer. In this case, concerned for his son's well-being, the chief judge took it upon himself to guarantee this payment.
[41] The monastery had been sequestered by Pombal from observing the canons of Saint Augustine and sold to Chief Judge João Fernandes de Oliveira for 36 contos. ANTT. Chancelaria de dona Maria I. Livro 15, fls. 335–335v.

definitively and also obtained the rank of captain of the militias of Minas Gerais.[42]

In 1788, José Agostinho asked the governor to have Manuel Ferreira Pinto, husband to his sister Luísa, arrested for the havoc he was causing in Tejuco.[43] The brother-in-law, an important local figure who even held a military post, left an inheritance of two houses, forty-nine slaves, and objects in gold and silver.[44]

In 1795, he joined the Brotherhood of Our Lady of the Mercies in Tejuco, an entity directed toward the parda population.[45] In 1800, attending the request of Simão Pires Sardinha, whom he held in high regard,[46] the Prince Regent had the governor of Minas Gerais, Bernardo José de Lorena, appoint José Agostinho to the position of notary of the Magistracy of Vila do Príncipe. Five years later, José Agostinho requested tenure in this position in honor of his half-brother Simão and his father, "who was an attentive vassal and deserved a lot of attention for the relevant services he rendered and which are still remembered."[47] However, the official pronouncement of the Overseas Council on the matter declared against his request, alleging that he was not apt for the position and that he did not have antecessors "of greater influence in Brazil," which "has been, is and will be fatal to the service of Your Royal Highness and could even cause the people to lose their belief in and respect for the authority public officials must have."[48]

José Agostinho died in Tejuco a few years later in December 1808. His death was so sudden that there was not enough time to send for

---

[42] AEAD. Livro de inventário da Irmandade do Rosário. 1750–1794, Box 514; AHU, MAMG. Box159, doc. 22.

[43] APM. Seção Colonial. 253, f. 83.

[44] BAT. Inventário de Manuel Ferreira Pinto. Cartório do Segundo Ofício, maço 66.

[45] AEAD. Livro segundo de grades da Irmandade de Nossa Senhora das Mercês. 1793–1837, caixa 521, f. 9v.

[46] AHU, MAMG. Caixa 159, doc. 22; caixa 175, doc. 17; caixa 175, doc. 16.

[47] AHU, MAMG. Caixa 175, doc. 16.

[48] AHU, MAMG. Caixa 175, doc. 17.

a priest to administer the last rites. He was buried in the chapel of the village branch of the Amparo.[49]

Simão Pires Sardinha received total support from his stepfather in his pursuit of more noble status. In 1768, at the age of seventeen while still living in Tejuco under the protection of his mother and the contractor, he embarked upon an ecclesiastical career. He was accepted into the four lower orders, which allowed him to assist in religious services, and committed himself to pursuing a life of vocation.[50] He argued that there was a shortage of priests in the region and that he was requesting the habit so he could celebrate mass in the local chapels. However, despite his early enthusiasm, Simão gave up on an ecclesiastical career upon joining his stepfather in Portugal.

He learned his first letters and Latin while still in Tejuco, as these were prerequisites for an ecclesiastical career or superior education, both fundamental means of access to administrative posts and noble honors. He completed his studies in Lisbon[51] where he graduated in the arts.[52] While still in Portugal he obtained the rank of sergeant major of the armed forces of Minas Novas in Minas Gerais.[53] He was also admitted into the Order of Christ, where he later became a commissary.[54] In addition to this, he received various annuities as a superintendent of the Realm.[55] He returned to Brazil in 1784 as part of the entourage of the new governor of Minas Gerais, Luís da Cunha Meneses, who he greatly admired.[56] It was Meneses who entrusted

---

[49] AEAD. Livro de óbitos do arraial do Tejuco. 1785–1810, caixa 351, f. 316v.

[50] AEAM. *Auto de genere et moribus de Simão Pires Sardinha.* 1768. Armário 10, pasta 1782.

[51] There is a certain unanimity among historiographers that Simão Pires Sardinha studied at the Sapienza Institute in Rome. However, research conducted in the institution's archives found no record of his presence there as a student. Roma. Archivio Centrale dello Stato. Fondo Archivio della Universitá di Roma – siglo XIV–XIX. Série seconda: studenti. Livro 103, Dottorado, 1759–1782. Tomo IV e livro 104, Dottorado, 1783–1797. Tomo V.

[52] AHU, MAMG. Caixa 140, doc. 49.

[53] APM. Seção Colonial. 238, f. 179v.

[54] AHU, MAMG. Caixa 125, doc. 7.

[55] ANTT. Chancelaria de dona Maria I. Livro 6, f. 314; livro 23, fls. 23v, 24v, 25.

[56] In Simão's own words: "As this Lord [Luís da Cunha Meneses] is possessed of vast erudition, full of the most ardent zeal for the sciences, which he has proved

Simão with the study of the region's first fossil find made on the farm of Father José Lopes in Prados, declaring that the sergeant major was "one of the most able naturalists and mineralogists presently to be found in the captaincy."[57]

Like many other illustrious individuals of the time, Simão Pires Sardinha was an associate member of the Royal Academy of the Sciences in Lisbon.[58] In August 1785, he submitted his "analysis or report on the physical state and condition in which he found the aforementioned bones of said skeleton" to Luís Cunha Meneses, who sent the report to Portugal along with some of the bones.[59] The colossal skeleton measured fifty-six palms in length and forty-six in height. The slaves mining the locale started to hack at the bones with levers and hoes, as they thought they were dealing with tree roots. Despite the destruction of the bones, which meant "there was no way of knowing to which part of the animal they belonged," two teeth remained intact from which the wise naturalist was able to conclude that "they are not from any animal known in Brazil, but perhaps belong to some animal that, through the revolutions of time, has lost its species." He was, however, deeply shocked to discover what was undoubtedly human hair. From his analysis of the teeth and the size of the bones, he could only conclude that the animal in question was a giant.[60]

In 1786, the governor handed him another delicate mission: the arrest of the ex-diamond intendant José Antônio de Meireles, otherwise known to the locals as "Iron Head." The intendant had

through the rigorous orders he has issued in his captaincy that he be apprised each day of everything unusual that happens in the captaincy, so that he can make the most perfect Geography and veridical history of this as yet unknown country." AHU, MAMG. Box 140, doc. 49.

[57] AHU, MAMG. Caixa 123, doc. 89. *Revista do Arquivo Público Mineiro*, 1925, p. 612.

[58] AHU, MAMG. Caixa 140, doc. 49. The Royal Academy was created by Queen Maria I in 1779 to encourage the study of the sciences in the Portuguese Empire and put the intellectuals in the service of the state.

[59] AHU, MAMG. Caixa 123, doc. 89.

[60] Simão Pires Sardinha's report can be seen in AHU, MAMG. Caixa 123, doc. 89.

set off for Rio de Janeiro, where he planned to await the fleet sailing for Lisbon. He was intercepted near Matias Barbosa, close to the border between the two captaincies, and the gold he was carrying was confiscated under the allegation that it belonged to the Royal Revenue Commission. On fresh orders from the governor,[61] however, Meireles was not actually arrested and proceeded to Rio de Janeiro, where he filed a complaint against Simão Pires Sardinha, the officer in charge of the operation. In his defense, the sergeant major claimed that he had always been "an exact observer of the law, pleasant and civil with the people, from whom he had never received any complaint, whether personally or juridically, nor had he ever committed any crime."[62]

In 1788, when Luís da Cunha Meneses returned to Portugal, Simão spent a year and a month in the Brazilian capital where he began to frequent the Literary Society. The Literary Society was a meeting place for illustrious nonconformists, some of whom were dissatisfied with Brazil's dependence upon Portugal.[63] He thus became involved in the Inconfidência Mineira, though the nature and extent of this involvement has never been fully clarified. Tiradentes is known to have called on him at his house in Rio de Janeiro to have him translate the *Compilation of the constitutional laws of the English colonies, confederated under the title of the United States of North America*. It is also known that it was Simão who sent word to the second lieutenant that he was under surveillance and that his arrest was imminent.[64]

Shielded by the viceroy, Luís de Vasconcelos, Simão withdrew to Portugal in August 1789. He was only summoned to give account of his participation in the Minas uprising the following year, though as a witness rather than as a respondent. The story that he received direct protection from his stepfather João Fernandes in order to escape is patently untrue, as the contractor had already been dead for more than ten years at the time. In order to exonerate himself, Simão

---

[61] AHU, MAMG. Caixa 125, doc. 7.
[62] AHU, MAMG. Caixa 125, doc. 7.
[63] *Autos da devassa da Inconfidência Mineira*, vol. 2, 1978, p. 75.
[64] Ibidem, vol. 3, p. 462.

argued that he had thought Tiradentes insane and therefore indulged him, but without ever paying him any real attention. He justified his hurried return to Lisbon on the grounds that he had urgent family matters to attend to and that he was responding to a request from João Fernandes de Oliveira Grijó, who lived at court.[65]

Wise and learned, Simão Pires Sardinha sought to minimize his involvement in the Inconfidência Mineira, but without losing contact with the rebels. Once newly settled in Portugal, he began to purchase and send books to a fellow suspect in Tejuco, the physician and naturalist José Vieira Couto, for resale. The content of these books, some of which expounded claims like "there is no hell, because when a creature dies its soul goes walking in Elysian Fields,"[66] reveals that Simão remained sympathetic to less-than-orthodox ideas. While in Portugal he managed to obtain the rank of lieutenant colonel of the militia of the Bambuí Cavalry back in Minas Gerais,[67] and held the position of treasurer for the Brazilian branch of the Brotherhood of the Bull of the Holy Crusade, appointing Ventura Fernandes Rodrigues administrator of the entity in Vila Rica. In 1803, now a little over fifty years of age and basking in nobility, Simão was still in the Realm.[68] He once remarked of himself that he had forever "acted in accordance with the law of nobility . . . and always communicated with the most important people in Minas Gerais, Rio de Janeiro and even at the Court."[69] He enjoyed great prestige in the eyes of the Prince Regent João, and he used this to secure administrative posts for his half-brothers back in Brazil.

As for the future of her daughters, Chica's main concern was to arrange good marriages. Marriage and convent life were the only honorable alternatives available to women. Those that did not remain at Macaúbas as nuns returned to their mother's house, and though they were all mulatto, many were married off to young Portuguese. The inheritance from their father would certainly have

---

[65] Ibidem, vol. 3, pp. 457–65.

[66] ANTT. Inquisição de Lisboa. Maço 1076, processo 12 957.

[67] AFS. Livro de notas no. 99, 1793–1794, fls. 10v-11. AHU, MAMG. Caixa 138, doc. 16; caixa 141, doc. 11; caixa 142, doc. 32; caixa 140, doc. 49.

[68] ANTT. Chancelaria de dona Maria I. Caixa 23, f. 124v.

[69] AHU, MAMG. Caixa 125, doc. 7.

given them a reasonable dowry, which was essential if a woman was to entice a consort of higher standing. However, the twists of fate they suffered along the way reveal something of the difficulty the descendants of freed slaves faced when it came to integrating with the mining society. Some of Chica's daughters ended up having natural children, while others never managed to have their relationships legitimized. There were moments when the only place they could find refuge and protection was within the convent walls.

Francisca de Paula took the habit and spent many years at Macaúbas as a nun, though she later abandoned convent life. On August 12, 1796, at the small chapel dedicated to Saint Quitéria on the grounds of her mother's house, she married José Pereira da Silva e Sousa, the legitimate son of the Custodian José Pereira e Maria da Silva de Jesus, from Porto.[70] As she wed at the age of forty-one, the marriage bore no children.[71] In 1808, she was living in a house of her own overlooking the São Francisco River on a laneway leading to the village cemetery, next door to the mansion of Martinho Alves Chaves.[72] She inherited part of the Buriti farm from her father, where she grew sugarcane, cassava, corn, and beans and raised animals. She died on July 6, 1839, on the Pé do Morro farm, where she had been living for some time. She left money for the confection of a richly crafted gold frontispiece dedicated to the Most Holy Sacrament for the altar of the São Gonçalo do Rio Preto parish church and provisions for two hundred masses to be said for her parents' souls.[73] She was buried at the farm chapel after an open casket vigil presided by the vicar João Floriano do Santos Correia e Sá.[74]

The course of Rita Quitéria's life is a perfect example of the paradoxical nature of the social insertion obtained by colored women

---

[70] AEAD. Livro de casamentos do arraial do Tejuco. 1746–1811, caixa 335, f. 203.
[71] BAT. Francisca de Paula de Oliveira. Cartório do Primeiro Ofício, maço 23.
[72] BAT. Cartório do Primeiro Ofício, maço 53.
[73] BAT. Francisca de Paula de Oliveira. (Last will and testament), Cartório do Primeiro Ofício, maço 23, fls. 3v–4v.
[74] BAT. Francisca de Paula de Oliveira. Cartório do Primeiro Ofício, maço 23, fls. 5v–6.

and their offspring. As a reflection of her father's power and her mother's social rise, she was married to second lieutenant Bento Dias Chaves, from Braga in Portugal, with whom she had already been living consensually. In 1799, she was imprisoned for the crime of concubinage by the visiting Inquisition and remained incarcerated in the Conceição do Mato Dentro jail for more than a year.[75] The couple had two natural children, João and Manuel,[76] though the latter died during childhood before his parents' marriage and was buried at the Our Lady of the Mercies chapel.[77] Once officially a wife, Rita had a daughter named Frutuosa Batista de Oliveira, who became her sole heir, as she outlived both her sons. The second lieutenant had also fathered three natural children with other women: Bernardina, Bento, and Rodrigo. João Fernandes de Oliveira Grijó appointed one of these children, Bento Afonso Dias, as his administrative representative for the entail's assets in Brazil.

The couple owned a dry goods business in Tejuco and a house on Rua do Bonfim, which Rita inherited from her mother, and part of the Pé do Morro farm, left to her by Chief Judge João Fernandes. The Pé do Morro property, located between the Jequitinhonha and Araçuaí rivers, included living quarters, a sugar cane mill, a chapel, various barns, and a staff of thirty-five slaves. The farm cultivated and processed cotton, which was used to produce rough material and clothes,[78] to which end there were two looms for weaving fustian and cotton cloth, another for making garments, a workshop for carding and spinning the cotton, and three spinning wheels. The farm was also used to grow corn, beans, and sugarcane and raise pigs, sheep, horses, mules, cows, and bullocks.[79]

---

[75] ACO. Livro de assento dos presos da cadeia. 1796, f. 27v.

[76] Baptized March 2, 1811. AEAD. Livro de óbitos do arraial do Tejuco. 1808–1812, caixa 298, f. 78.

[77] AEAD. Livro de óbitos da Irmandade de Nossa Senhora das Mercês. 1793–1811, caixa 521, f. 121.

[78] This Brazilian cotton-plant variety, with its brown-colored fibers, is common in the São Francisco region; blue or yellow Indian fabric.

[79] BAT. Inventário de Rita Quitéria de São José. Cartório do Primeiro Ofício, maço 63.

Upon Rita Quitéria's death in 1808, three masses were said for
her soul at the Mercies church where she had been a member.[80] She
was buried at the Santo Antônio parish church, a privilege reserved
for members of the Brotherhood of the Most Holy Sacrament.[81] She
left thirty-five slaves, ranch hands, and domestic staff at the farm
and more in the village, including her own hairdresser. As Frutuosa was only eleven years old at the time, the second lieutenant
took charge as her guardian.[82] The dry goods business was mired in
debt, as the couple used to buy stock from large merchants in Rio de
Janeiro and had taken out loans with the Grijó entail, so the inventory took years to complete. Bento Dias Chaves negotiated deadlines
with the Tribunal of Orphans and Absentees for the settlement of
the debts, alleging that the assets he received as joint heir were inferior to the sums owed. Throughout this period he rushed all over the
captaincy in search of business, "both in Registro Velho near Vila
de Barbacena, and in Jaguará, in Sabará County."[83] He ended up
going to Vila Rica "at the behest of the governor of the captaincy
to put the spinning jennies to work, ... a machine so much to His
Majesty's interest and approval."[84] The machine in question was for
carding cotton and was powered by mules, which was a considerable
technological advance for the day.[85] Bento Dias Chaves brought the
technology over from Portugal and installed an experimental system
at the Jaguara farm in Sabará.[86] A widower, Bento Dias Chaves had

[80] AEAD. Livro de certidões de missas da Irmandade de Nossa Senhora das Mercês.
      1776, caixa 520, f. 17.
[81] AEAD. Livro de óbitos do arraial do Tejuco. 1785–1810, caixa 352, f. 30.
[82] BAT. Inventário de Rita Quitéria de São José. Cartório do Primeiro Ofício, maço
      63.
[83] Jaguara Farm cosntituted an important entail in Minas Gerais in the eighteenth
      century.
[84] BAT. Inventário de Rita Quitéria de São José. Cartório do Primeiro Ofício, maço
      63.
[85] Also called the mule system, invented in 1799 by the Englishman Samuel
      Crompton.
[86] " ... would say to Y. Exc. that there is a fellow near the Diamantine Demar-
      cation, one Bento Dias Chaves, who studied this subject in Portugal and has
      only just told me that he has set up a mule-driven jenny in Jaguara, with
      its competent carding mechanism." Apud: A indústria filatória na demarcação

one more natural child named Antônia Vicência, who was raised by his half aunt, Ana Quitéria.[87]

In order to tend to Frutuosa's education while her father was off trying to make a living, Ana moved with her to Buriti farm. In 1823, the young lady married lieutenant Feliciano Atanásio dos Santos[88] in a ceremony held at the Pé do Morro chapel. Shortly after the wedding, the lieutenant began to demand the completion of Rita Quitéria's still pending inventory so that he could lay his hands on his bride's dowry.

Frutuosa was also nominated heir to her aunt Francisca de Paula, along with two boys, Antônio Caetano Fernandes de Oliveira and Luís Pereira da Silva, for whom she had developed an affection and raised in her own house. As Luís was still a minor, she had to appoint a guardian, a role that fell to Feliciano Atanásio.[89] As his father-in-law had done with Rita's assets, the lieutenant sought to delay the division of Francisca de Paula's patrimony for as long as possible, which he justified on the grounds that he had to shoulder the costs of raising the two boys. In the end, Antônio and Luís managed to have him stripped of the guardianship, claiming that they were living in penury.

Relations between Frutuosa and Feliciano deteriorated, and the marriage ended in divorce. At the time, the Catholic Church permitted the dissolution of a marriage if public, notorious, and scandalous concubinage by either party could be proved, resulting in risk to the family patrimony. While divorce physically and financially separated a couple, it did not invalidate the matrimonial bond sealed by God. This meant that divorcees could not remarry in the eyes of the church. The divorce was authorized on January 20, 1853, by the archpriest of the cathedral, Father Rodrigues de Paula, officer

diamantina. Letter from the naturalist Bithencourt to the Chamber of Governor Count de Palma, *Revista do Arquivo Público Mineiro*, Belo Horizonte, year 2, 1897, pp. 755–6.

[87] BAT. Inventário de Rita Quitéria de São José. Cartório do Primeiro Ofício, maço 63.

[88] Ibidem.

[89] BAT. Cartório do Primeiro Ofício, maço 53, f. 4.

of *de genere* justifications and matrimonial dispensations.[90] Frutuosa requested the separation on the grounds that she had always behaved "with total honesty and absolute fidelity, fulfilling to a tee her duties as a consort and the mother of a family and treating her [husband] with love and affection, while he, on the contrary, showed only indifference to his wife's deeds, indifference and antipathy to her person and disregard for his conjugal duties, constantly living in public and scandalous concubinage with Tomásia Dias Chaves, with whom he had had various children." Frutuosa and her son Joaquim[91] were expelled from the house to make way for her husband's lover and natural children.[92] Feliciano moved to Paraná some years later.

Frutuosa died in 1873 at Buriti farm, leaving five children and two grandchildren. No mention is made of Joaquim in her will, so he was probably already dead at the time.[93] As Joaquim was her only child when she divorced Feliciano Atanásio, we can conclude that she had another relationship afterward, from which were born Antônio Augusto dos Santos; José Amador dos Santos, who became a priest; Rita Umbelina de Gouveia; Franklin Amador dos Santos; and Felicíssimo Pereira dos Santos, who died before his mother, leaving behind two children: Mariano Pereira dos Santos and Genoína Pereira dos Santos, aged twelve and thirteen, respectively.[94]

In February 1807, at the Pé do Morro chapel,[95] Ana Quitéria married João Barbosa, the brother-in-law of her sister Mariana.[96] Her

---

90 BAT. João Germano de Oliveira. Cartório do Primeiro Ofício, maço 27 (contém arrecadação dos bens do morgado do Grijó).

91 BAT. Testamento de Ana Quitéria de São José. Cartório do Primeiro Ofício, maço 92.

92 BAT. Inventário de Francisca de Paula de Oliveira. Cartório do Primeiro Ofício, maço 23.

93 In 1837, Ana Quitéria nominated Joaquim as one of her heirs, which proves that the boy was still alive at the time. BAT. Testamento de Ana Quitéria de São José. Cartório do Primeiro Ofício, maço 92.

94 BAT. Testamento de Frutuosa Batista Fernandes de Oliveira. Cartório do Primeiro Ofício, maço 23. Felicíssimo was married to Maria. As the parents died while the children were under age, Antônio Augusto de Oliveira Costa was nominated their tutor.

95 Dom frei José da Santíssima Trindade. *Visitas pastorais*. 1998, p. 102.

96 AEAD. Casamentos em São Gonçalo do Rio Preto. 1789–1916, caixa 318, f. 117.

wedding sponsors were Bento Dias Chaves, her brother-in-law, and José Pereira de Sousa. The couple did not have children of their own, but did raise Antônio Vicência, the natural son of Rita Quitéria's widower.[97] According to the registers of the Brotherhood of the Mercies, Ana Quitéria died at the Pé do Morro farm in January 1846[98] and was buried in the habit of the Our Lady of the Conception at the village chapel in São Gonçalo do Rio Preto.[99] She left provisions for the celebration of a hundred masses for her soul and fifty for Chica and João Fernandes.

Little is known about Helena. When she returned from Macaúbas in 1781 she was suffering from a serious illness from which she probably did not recover.[100] Records show that she was dead at the beginning of the nineteenth century[101] and that three masses were said for her soul by the Brotherhood of the Mercies in 1815.[102]

Luísa married Manuel Ferreira Pinto, but left no offspring. Little is known about her other than that she and her husband owned two houses near the Amparo chapel in Tejuco, one of which served as her home.[103] In 1779, her slave Joaquim Mozambique was buried at the Rosário chapel,[104] while the following year Chica paid the Brotherhood of the Most Holy in her name for the burial of another slave.[105] When Manuel Ferreira Pinto died in his seventies in 1817 he was already a widower.[106] His inventory shows that he owned "a farm with a sugar cane mill and all belongings, dependencies and

---

[97] BAT. Documentos avulsos. Caixa 478, f. 233.
[98] AEAD. Livro segundo de grades da Irmandade de Nossa Senhora das Mercês. 1793–1837, caixa 521, f. 20v.
[99] AEAD. Livro de óbitos de irmãos da Irmandade de São Francisco. Caixa 350. Letra A.
[100] ARM. Livro de registros de saídas do recolhimento. 1781, s.n.
[101] BAT. Ordem Terceira de Nossa Senhora do Carmo. Caixa 478, f. 233.
[102] AEAD. Livro de certidões de missas da Irmandade de Nossa Senhora das Mercês. 1776, caixa 520, f. 36.
[103] BAT. Inventário de Manuel Ferreira Pinto. Cartório do Segundo Ofício.
[104] AEAD. Livro de óbitos do arraial do Tejuco. 1777, caixa 351, f. 56v.
[105] AEAD. Livro da fabriqueira da capela de Santo Antônio. 1780–1838, caixa 509, f. 17v.
[106] AEAD. Livro de óbitos do arraial do Tejuco. 1785–1810, caixa 351, fls. 88–88v. Testamento de Manuel Ferreira Pinto.

slaves," the fruits of his own labor. Among the assets he left behind
him were forty-nine slaves, various items of furniture, bedclothes,
cutlery and silverware, images and oratories of the saints, and some
Indian china, as well as a pair of gold earrings and a gold chain, which
must have belonged to Luísa.[107]

Maria declared that "I never married and lived my entire life as
a single woman, in which condition I had a daughter named Maria,
left as a foundling at the house of my sister, Donna Ana Quitéria,"
by whom she was raised.[108] In 1804, the girl's baptismal certificate was altered and the child was registered as the natural daughter of Maria and Lieutenant Agostinho José, with whom she maintained a long-term relationship, though they never wed.[109] Maria
died during childbirth on September 4, 1806, at the age of forty. In
accordance with her will, she was buried in the Franciscan habit[110]
the day after her death at the church of the Brotherhood of Saint
Francis de Assisi.[111] Her corpse was accompanied to the grave by
the memberships of the brotherhoods of the Souls, Amparo, and
Mercies, of which she was a sister.[112] On April 24 of the same year,
as we have already seen was the entitlement of every member of the
Mercies,[113] masses were said for her soul at the brotherhood's church.
Maria declared that she owned twenty-five slaves, including the runaway Francisco Angola and Edvirges creole, on loan to her sister
Antônia, interned at Macaúbas convent.[114] Maria lived in Chica's
house in Tejuco, part of which she inherited, as did her brothers and
sisters. At the Pé do Morro farm, where she raised cattle and horses,
she kept some items of furniture and "some pieces made of gold, silver

---

[107] BAT. Inventário de Manuel Ferreira Pinto. Cartório do Segundo Ofício.

[108] AFS. Livro avulso de testamentos.

[109] AEAD. Livro de batizados do arraial do Tejuco. 1806–1812, caixa 298, f. 11.

[110] AFS. Livro avulso de testamentos.

[111] AEAD. Livro de óbitos da Ordem Terceira de São Francisco. 1772–1857, caixa
350, f. 57.

[112] AEAD. Livro de óbitos do arraial do Tejuco. 1785–1810, caixa 351, fls. 279–280.
Testamento de Maria de São José.

[113] AEAD. Livro de certidões de missas da Irmandade de Nossa Senhora das Mercês.
1776, caixa 520, f. 21.

[114] AFS. Livro avulso de testamentos.

and precious stones" that she had inherited from her mother.[115] Like her brothers and sisters, Maria was also due her share of a third of the Grijó revenues, a sum never actually paid by her eldest brother, the administrator of the entail, a fact of which she constantly complained.[116]

Her daughter, Maria Joaquina, inherited all of her assets, including a slave named Catarina Mina, who was buried at the church of the Mercies.[117] Maria Joaquina married sergeant major Agostinho Gomes de Oliveira and had two sons, Antônio de Oliveira Costa and Antônio Augusto de Oliveira Costa.[118]

On August 25, 1796, Mariana married second lieutenant José Barbosa da Fonseca, from the bishopric of Porto and legitimate son of João Barbosa da Fonseca and Maria Josefa da Fonseca. She was a sponsor at the wedding of the intendant João Inácio do Amaral Silveira, which shows that Chica was capable of establishing relations with the most distinguished local figures even after João Fernandes had returned to the Realm. In 1806, Mariana lost a newborn child named Luís. The cause of death was registered as "malino,"[119] a popular name for a fulminant infectious disease similar to typhoid[120] that caused high fevers and did not respond to medication.[121] Mariana de Jesus returned to Macaúbas some years later. It is not known precisely why, though it is possible she had been widowed.[122] It was not possible to identify the exact date and place of her death, though she may have passed away at the convent. She left one son, João Fernandes de Oliveira Fonseca,[123] and two daughters,

---

[115] Ibidem.
[116] AEAD. Livro de óbitos do arraial do Tejuco. 1785–1810, caixa 351, fls. 279–280.
[117] Ibidem, f. 30.
[118] BAT. Justificantes: netas de João Fernandes de Oliveira. Cartório do Primeiro Ofício, maço 150B.
[119] AEAD. Livro de óbitos do arraial do Tejuco. 1785–1810, Caixa 351, f. 213.
[120] Laudelino Freire, op. cit., p. 3280.
[121] Rafael Bluteau, op. cit., p. 271.
[122] BAT. Documentos avulsos. Caixa 478, f. 233.
[123] BAT. Testamento de Ana Quitéria de São José. Cartório do Primeiro Ofício, maço 92.

Francisca Joaquina de Oliveira Fonseca and Maria de São José de Oliveira Fonseca. Francisca married Jacinto Rodrigues Costa, while Maria wed second lieutenant Joaquim Quintiliano dos Santos.[124] In 1846, Maria, then pregnant, was already the mother of two daughters, Mariana and Feliciana.[125]

Quitéria Rita became the concubine of Father Rolim, with whom she had five children: José da Silva de Oliveira Rolim Jr., Tadeu José da Silva de Oliveira Rolim, Domingos José Augusto, Mariana Vicência da Silva de Oliveira, and Maria dos Prazeres da Silva de Oliveira.[126] Father Rolim was the son of José da Silva de Oliveira, an old friend of Sergeant Major João Fernandes de Oliveira. In 1789, when he was arrested for his involvement in the Inconfidência Mineira, Rolim, who was ugly and of medium stature, was around thirty-five years of age.[127] According to descriptions from the time, Rolim's long face bore a scar down the right cheek, his nose was a little upturned, his mouth large and wide with badly stacked teeth, had brown eyes and hair, and a grizzled beard.[128] A witness at the inquest that followed the uprising claimed that Father Rolim had deflowered Quitéria and then forced her to marry another white man,[129] though no record of such a marriage has been found in Tejuco. Accused and convicted of the crime of disloyalty to the Realm, Rolim spent twelve years imprisoned in a convent in Lisbon and only returned to Brazil in or around 1808. It seems his relationship with Quitéria had ended shortly before he became involved in the movement. In 1786,

[124] BAT. Justificantes: netos of João Fernandes de Oliveira. Cartório do Primeiro Ofício, maço 150B.

[125] BAT. Testamento de Ana Quitéria de São José. Cartório do Primeiro Ofício, maço 92.

[126] BAT. Testamento de José da Silva de Oliveira Rolim. Cartório do Primeiro Ofício, maço 39, f. 21v.

[127] On December 29, 1747, "at the Santo Antônio chapel of Tejuco, Joseph, the legitimate son of Joseph da Silva de Oliveira and Donna Ana Joaquina Rosa Batista [was baptised], the godparents were João Fernandes de Oliveira and his wife, Donna Isabel Pires." AEAD. Baptismal records of the village of Tejuco – 1745–1765. Box 297, p. 11.

[128] *Autos de devassa da Inconfidência Mineira*, vol. 8, pp. 213–14.

[129] *Autos de devassa da Inconfidência Mineira*, vol. 4, p. 46.

Quitéria entered Macaúbas convent with her daughters, where she joined the Carmelite Brotherhood of Tejuco.[130]

Mariana Vicência and Maria dos Prazeres took their vows at Macaúbas and became nuns.[131] José Rolim Jr. died at a young age and was buried at the church of Saint Francis.[132] Quitéria probably died at the convent in 1885, where she spent sixty-eight out of her eighty-eight years of life.[133] Father Rolim died on September 21, 1835, in his early eighties. He was buried the following day at the Church of Our Lady of Mount Carmel.[134] Tadeu José died before his father and was survived by one son, Antônio José da Silva.[135]

Maria dos Prazeres died in Macaúbas in 1832, though Mariana Vicência abandoned her vows and married Floriano Martins Pereira, who she later divorced. In the ensuing division of assets, Floriano ended up keeping Jacinta and Tomásia, slaves Mariana had inherited from her deceased mother, Quitéria. Mariana Vicência settled on a plot she owned in Lagoa Santa, where she died in 1859.[136] On one of his travels, the Bishop of Mariana, Joaquim Silvério de Sousa, passed by her lands and was shocked to see the poverty in which she lived.[137] Nevertheless, Mariana's will listed a cash deposit of 1 conto, 384,000 reis in the city of Ouro Preto, a sum she had inherited from her parents.[138]

---

[130] BAT. Ordem Terceira de Nossa Senhora do Carmo. Caixa 478, f. 233.

[131] ARM. Livros avulsos, s.d., s.n.

[132] AEAD. Livro de óbitos da Ordem Terceira de São Francisco. 1772–1857, caixa 350, letra J.

[133] Joaquim Silvério de Sousa. *Sítios e personagens históricos de Minas Gerais*, 1980, p. 365. See also Roberto Wagner de Almeida. *Entre a cruz e a espada*. 2002, p. 45.

[134] AEAD. Livro de óbitos da Ordem Terceira de São Francisco. 1772–1857, caixa 350, letra J.

[135] BAT. Testamento de José da Silva de Oliveira Rolim. Cartório do Primeiro Ofício, maço 39, f. 21v.

[136] Arquivo da Cúria Metropolitana de Belo Horizonte. Livro de testamentos da freguesia de Nossa Senhora da Lagoa Santa. 1824. Testamento de Mariana Vicência de Oliveira Rolim.

[137] Joaquim Silvério de Sousa, op. cit.

[138] Arquivo da Cúria Metropolitana de Belo Horizonte. Livro de testamentos da freguesia de Nossa Senhora da Lagoa Santa. 1824. Testamento de Mariana Vicência de Oliveira Rolim.

In 1806, Antônia was still studying at Macaúbas, where she took her vows. She had only the borrowed slave Edvirges to serve her, though she did own some other slaves in Tejuco, such as the creole Josefa Maria Fernandes de Oliveira and mina João Antônio Fernandes de Oliveira, who both joined the Brotherhood of the Mercies.[139] She was the only daughter of Chica da Silva and João Fernandes de Oliveira who spent her entire adult life at Macaúbas convent, where she died at an unknown date.

Many years after Chica's death, between 1835 and 1840, her heirs started a lawsuit to disassociate the assets of the Grijó entail in Brazil. The prevailing legislation after independence permitted Brazilian descendants to take possession of properties belonging to Portuguese citizens either dead or disappeared for a period of at least ten years. Chica's descendants claimed to have heard nothing from João Germano for more than eleven years. It seemed he had been killed in the devastating civil war that raged between the Miguelites and forces loyal to Pedro and his daughter Maria de Glória.[140] The assets in question were the Santa Bárbara farm in Curral Grande, the farm at Ribeirão da Areia in Curamataí, and the Palha farmhouse on the outskirts of Tejuco. The heirs accused Bento Dias Chaves, the administrator appointed by João Germano, of spending what was not his to spend.[141]

The loss of some of the patrimony of the once formidable contractor contravened one of the main objectives of the institution of the Grijó entail, namely the preservation of its indivisibility. Despite João Fernandes' best efforts, his heirs stubbornly disregarded his instructions and haggled over their slice of the spoils. Emblematically, the Palha farmhouse, whose exotic gardens had once hosted the local society, now lay in ruins. At the time, the property was known locally as "Chica's farmhouse,"[142] and her heirs could only lament

---

[139] AEAD. Livro segundo de grades da Irmandade Nossa Senhora das Mercês. 1793–1837, caixa 521, ps. 27v and 39.

[140] Pedro IV of Portugal was known by the title of Pedro I in Brazil. BAT. João Germano de Oliveira. Cartório do Primeiro Ofício, maço 27.

[141] BAT. João Germano de Oliveira. Cartório do Primeiro Ofício, maço 27.

[142] Ibidem, p. 14.

the fact that the administrator had torn it down little by little and sold it to scrap, as with the half-fallen gateway peddled in 1839.[143]

If the Grijó entail was incapable of preserving the name of its founder and his past achievements, time certainly perpetuated the memory of the mestizo Chica da Silva and her relationship with the powerful diamond contractor. Her remains lay forgotten in the ossuary of the São Francisco church, but what sets her apart from the various other colored women who filled the streets of eighteenth-century Tejuco and who have faded from memory over the years and centuries is that her life has been immortalized in the legend of *Chica-que-manda* – Chica the boss.

---

[143] Tradition has it, and it would appear to be true, that the best part of the wooden framework was used in the construction of Casa da Glória, a building that now houses the Eschwege Institute in Diamantina. Aires da M. Machado Filho. *Arraial do Tejuco, cidade Diamantina.* 1980, p. 264.

CHAPTER ELEVEN

CHICA-QUE-MANDA

Swirl the night, swirl,
golden sifter
of Chica da Silva,
of Chica-que-manda.

HISTORICAL MEMORY

In 1853, Joaquim Felício dos Santos, a lawyer from Diamantina, was appointed attorney on the amicable division of assets that followed the divorce[1] of Lieutenant Feliciano Atanásio dos Santos, the lawyer's uncle,[2] and Frutuosa Batista de Oliveira, Francisca da Silva de Oliveira's granddaughter. Seven years later, Chica's heirs appointed this same lawyer as their attorney on a lawsuit demanding possession of the Brazilian assets of Chief Judge João Fernandes de Oliveira.[3]

These legal proceedings provided him with an unusual source of material from which to compose his colonial chronicles, as in his spare time Joaquim Felício compiled a history of the region, which he published in chapters between 1862 and 1864 in the local newspaper, *O Jequitinhonha.* After all, here was a family descended from slaves, heirs to a vast patrimony that included farms, a considerable number

---

[1] BAT. Inventário de Francisca de Paula de Oliveira. Cartório do Primeiro Ofício, maço 23.
[2] José Teixeira Neves. "Estudo biográfico." In Joaquim Felício dos Santos. *Memórias do Distrito Diamantino.* 1956.
[3] BAT. Primeiro Ofício, maço 150 b.

of slaves, urban properties, and various nonfixed assets. As he had access to all the documents relevant to his case in the dispute over the diamond contractor's assets, the lawyer was able to include in his chronicle a transcription of the will in which João Fernandes meticulously listed his various properties in Portugal, Rio de Janeiro, and Minas Gerais.

It was in the pages of O Jequitinhonha, and later in book form under the title Memórias do Distrito Diamantino, published in 1868, that Chica da Silva first emerged as an historical figure from the mists that erased and obscured the region's past.[4] This author's take on the history of the Diamantine District ensured its immortalization far beyond the pages of his book, crammed as it was with heroes and villains locked in the eternal struggle between imperial domination and colonial resistance.

Chica da Silva was the only eighteenth-century woman Joaquim Felício deigned to elevate to the status of historical personage. All of the men born in terra brasilis – whether free or slave – were featured in Memórias as martyrs who belong in the pantheon of national heroes. The same could not be said of Chica. A man of the nineteenth century, the author shaped her character in accordance with the dominant view of his time, much of which he projected upon the preceding century. He worked from his own everyday social reality, in which women and their families were expected to regulate their behavior by Christian morality and in which prejudice against ex-slaves, colored women, and consensual unions reigned supreme.

Since the thirteenth century, the Catholic Church had enforced the notion of a monogamous family united in the bonds of holy matrimony. This process, with its many oscillations, came at the price of repression and a standardization of behavior. Its consolidation in Brazilian lands came late, occurring in or around the second half of the nineteenth century, after the transferral of the Portuguese court to Brazil. In the 1700s, especially in Minas Gerais, the population

---

4   Joaquim Felício dos Santos, op. cit., Chapter 15, 1868.

was far from fitting the moral bill the church intended to install, as there was a proliferation of heterodox family models based around concubinage and short-lived relationships. The role of women was also far more dynamic than the prim and home-loving ideal they hoped to impose.

It should be no surprise that Joaquim Silvério dos Reis, in the testimony he gave at the inquest into the Inconfidência Mineira held at Ilha das Cobras, referred to Chica with respect in his account of how Father Rolim had deflowered one of her daughters. He called Chica by her full name, put no store whatsoever on her color or on the fact that she was a former slave, and made it clear that he considered the priest's behavior to have been an insult to the honor of both women.[5]

Not even at the dawn of the nineteenth century did the travelers who visited and wrote about the region, such as Auguste de Saint-Hilare, Spix, and Martius, make any mention of the existence of Chica da Silva, the ex-slave who became the diamond contractor's consort.[6] Their travel writings do contain versions of accounts by locals that they felt were somehow part of the region's history – but Chica's life, just like those of an untold number of freed black women who lived in concubinage with white men, would have struck them as neither unique nor particularly romantic.

It was only in the mid-nineteenth century, when the patriarchal family took hold in Minas Gerais, that the existence of a Chica da Silva became in any way noteworthy. For the men of the time, the slave women were sensual and licentious wenches with whom it was impossible to maintain any stable bonds of affection. With the publication of *Memórias do Distrito Diamantino*, Chica da Silva became the incarnation of the stereotype of the black slave woman, which, however negative, gave rise to her legend. As a member of a prejudiced nineteenth-century white elite, the author was incapable of understanding the power of attraction these women of colour wielded. Joaquim Felício describes Chica as a low-born mulatta

---

[5]   *Autos de devassa da Inconfidência Mineira*, vol. 4, 1978, p. 46.
[6]   A. de Saint-Hilare. *Viagem pelo Distrito dos Diamantes e litoral do Brasil.* 1974.

of crude features, tall, fleshy, whose shaven head was covered in a wig of flowing curls, as was commonly used at the time; she possessed no grace, no beauty, no spirit, no education, in short, she possessed not one attraction that could justify such ardent passion.[7]

In Felício's book, João Fernandes de Oliveira is portrayed as having become a little sovereign who oppressed the population of Tejuco in order to satisfy his lover's every whim. He built her a marvelous farmhouse surrounded by paradisiacal gardens and obliged the local elite to bow before his oppressive and domineering slave, who dressed luxuriously and had everything that money and power could buy.[8]

Various misconceptions took hold concerning the figure of Chica da Silva. According to Felício's version, Chica was a slave of José da Silva de Oliveira, from whom she inherited her surname and who may have even been her father. José da Silva de Oliveira was the father of Father Rolim, which would have made Chica the half-sister of this famous rebel of the Inconfidência. Prior to becoming the contractor's concubine, Chica reputedly had two sons by Manuel Pires Sardinha, named Simão and Cipriano. She ruled over the village and had the powerful João Fernandes wrapped round her little finger. She owned a house with its own chapel and a dream farmhouse – the Palha farmhouse – where theater pieces were staged and bands of musicians played. It was on the Palha property that the chief judge ordered the construction of an artificial lake in which he installed a ship, all because she wanted to be able to enjoy the delights of a fake sea in the backwoods of Minas Gerais. At church, the best pew was always reserved for Chica da Silva and her entourage of twelve sumptuously dressed mulattas.

João Fernandes – the version goes – was a despot who flouted the imperial authorities and subjugated the local elite. As an example of his blind use of power, Joaquim Felício dos Santos mentions the events that surrounded the construction of the Carmelite church.

---

[7] Joaquim Felício dos Santos, op. cit., 1976, pp. 123–4.
[8] Ibidem.

The contractor was to decide the site at which the church would be built and went against the wishes of the rest of the membership by choosing a peripheral and cramped spot simply because it was close to his house. Most of the brotherhood refused to cooperate out of protest, so he shouldered the costs alone. As his wealth grew, so too did his greed, and he began to breech the clauses of the diamond contract, using far more slaves than was permitted and exploring a greater number of streams, eventually provoking the ire of the celebrated minister of the Portuguese state, the Marquis de Pombal.

For the author of *Memórias do Distrito Diamantino*, the situation in Tejuco had spun so far out of control and the contractor's abuse of power was so great that Pombal sent Count Valadares, the governor of the captaincy, directly to Tejuco with the task of ordering João Fernandes back to the Realm where he was to present himself before Pombal. Should the contractor refuse, Valadares was authorized to use force and take him into custody. The chief judge is said to have deployed certain ruses in order to gain time. He received the governor like a king, smothered him in gifts, put him up at Chica's farmhouse and, finally, tried to bribe him by offering to settle all his debts. However, after a period of indecision, during which he seemed to have been won over, Valadares delivered the orders from the Realm, which the contractor duly obeyed. João Fernandes set sail for Portugal under arrest and was never able to return. After paying a fine of 11 million cruzados into the Royal Exchequer, João Fernandes assembled all of his assets and instituted the Grijó entail, leaving all of his patrimony to his eldest son, also named João Fernandes de Oliveira. The entail amounted to a considerable fortune and, content that he had assured the future of his line, João Fernandes passed away in 1799 (twenty years after the true date of the contractor's death).[9]

The historiography that came after Joaquim Felício dos Santos did little to change Chica's image; in fact, it served only to augment her reputation with the added traits of lavish spendthrift, witch,

[9]   Ibidem, pp. 123–30.

and shrew. In 1896, Joaquim Silvério de Sousa, the bishop of Mariana, published a book titled *Sítios e personagens históricos de Minas Gerais*,[10] in which he revealed Chica's nickname – "*Quemanda*" – meaning "the boss," apparently in reference to the power she had over the contractor, which left her free to issue orders and counter orders about the house while reveling in his vast patrimony. The bishop flatly states that João Fernandes had not been a benefactor of Macaúbas convent, as was commonly believed, having paid no more than the fees due for his daughters' enrollment there. The bishop also relates that while traveling to Macaúbas he once passed by some apparently fertile lands that were nonetheless completely abandoned. Curious, he inquired after the owner and was impressed to discover that they belonged to one Mariana Vicência, who, having been robbed by her husband, now whittled away her final days in total misery like an indigent. When he found out later that she was the granddaughter of Chica da Silva and João Fernandes de Oliveira, he concluded that the fortune must have been lost without even reaching the third generation, most likely as divine retribution for their lack of charity and transgression of the moral laws of the Catholic Church. Mariana Vicência bore the stigma of being the natural child of a clergyman, a matter the bishop was careful to omit, though he must have secretly thought this an aggravating factor in her unhappy fate.

One year after the publication of the bishop's book, Xavier da Veiga completed his *Efemérides mineiras*, initially published in various issues of *Revistas do Arquivo Público Mineiro*, and later in book form.[11] Chica is cited twice in this work: First, in an entry for January 1, 1740, when briefly announcing the establishment of the diamond contract, the author emulates Joaquim Felício dos Santos and suggests that João Fernandes and Chica da Silva's life together was like "a page from *A Thousand and One Nights*."[12] Another entry, for November 12, 1770, refers to the drafting of Chica's will. This

---

[10] Joaquim Silvério de Sousa. *Sítios e personagens históricos de Minas Gerais.* 1980.
[11] João Pedro Xavier da Veiga. *Efemérides mineiras.* 1998, 2 vols.
[12] João Pedro Xavier Da Veiga, op. cit., Efeméride 1/1/1740, vol. 1, p. 119.

long text offers impressions similar to those previously expressed by Joaquim Felício and Joaquim Silvério de Sousa, and the author even cites their works.[13]

By the twentieth century Chica was already a myth. She featured among the few individuals from the eighteenth century who had become historical figures, despite not having belonged to the Portuguese white elite. After all, besides being a former slave, she was also a woman, and it was precisely in the light of these exceptions that she was understood. She became a legend in Diamantina, the subject of countless bedtime stories that fueled the dreams and nightmares of the children of what was once Tejuco.

In the second edition of *Memórias*, published in 1924, Nazaré Meneses, the author of the explanatory notes that accompanied the volume, sparked a controversy about Chica's appearance. She effectively rehabilitated the mulatta, claiming that she must have been "rough round the edges, but never odious or loathsome... Otherwise, she could never have inspired in a man as opulent, noble [and] gallant as chief judge João Fernandes de Oliveira, such an ardent and lasting passion."[14] With no empirical base whatsoever – much like almost everything that was said about Chica – one woman singlehandedly managed to revitalize the slave-girl's image, working purely from the notion of romantic love in vogue at the time, which could only be understood as physical attraction, as being grounded in the physical attributes of the lovers.

In 1940, a doctor from Diamantina named Juscelino Kubitschek was elected mayor of Belo Horizonte, followed by governor of Minas Gerais in 1950 and president of the Republic just a few years later. His meteoric rise drew a lot of attention to his hometown, which fast became an important commercial center and service provider for the northeast of the state. Tourism grew and became a substantial segment of the local economy, with its typically *mineiro* historical

---

[13] João Pedro Xavier Da Veiga, op. cit., Efeméride 12/12/1770, vol. 2, pp. 968–70.
[14] Nazaré Meneses. Note 1, Chapter 15, 1924. In Joaquim Felício dos Santos, op. cit., 1976, p. 124.

heritage as its most precious asset. Iphan – the Instituto do Patrimônio Histórico e Artístico Nacional (National Institute for Historical and Artistic Heritage) – was the organ responsible for selecting and determining the nation's heritage sites. Reflecting upon the constitution of memory in the urban spaces of Minas, the modernist poet Carlos Drummond de Andrade, a native of Minas Gerais and Iphan employee for many years, wrote of Vila Rica that "the houses remain, but the loves do not."[15]

In Diamantina, the house in which Chica da Silva lived, in what was then the village of Tejuco, was declared part of the national heritage in 1950, the decade in which the ex-slave began to attract renewed attention and fill up the pages of books by local historians eager to pepper the old lanes and alleyways with figures from the 1700s. The intellectual elite of the town, whose parameters lay in the work of Joaquim Felício dos Santos drew upon the oral tradition and re-read in the light of new values, in order to reconstruct and propagate its myths.

In 1945, another native of Diamantina, Aires da Mata Machado Filho, published a book titled *Arraial do Tejuco, cidade Diamantina*.[16] The work begins with a summary of the local history, in which the author accentuates the more picturesque, little known, and unusual elements, and ends with a description of the town's main colonial monuments of civil and religious architecture. It is an historical and tourist guide typical of the tastes of the day, meeting the demands of visitors avid for references to the past in which to anchor a fast-emerging modern Brazil.

Like the town's other historical figures, the memory of Chica da Silva's presence and existence was always associated with a building, a tourist attraction. The guide makes special mention of her house and its appurtenant chapel on the junction of Ruas Bonfim and Lalau Pires and of the Palha farmhouse, built for her on the outskirts of

---

[15] Carlos Drummond de Andrade. "Estampas de Vila Rica." In *Antologia poética*. 1992.
[16] Aires da M. Machado Filho. *Arraial do Tejuco, cidade Diamantina*. 1980.

the town. Because of a lack of research on specific documentation that could have revealed the true owners of the town's properties in the eighteenth century, Aires de Mata Machado Filho settles for the "old tradition, the near-certain presumption, . . . this general conviction"[17] – in short, the repository of village memory that says that this was the house where the slave lived with the contractor.

For Aires Machado, the house did not belong to Chica da Silva, but to the contractor, an assumption he hoped the discovery of João Fernandes's inventory in Lisbon would confirm. While Joaquim Felício states that Chica always occupied the best places at church, Aires Machado affirms that it was precisely because the former slave was unable to frequent the Carmelite church, where the white elite attended mass, that the chapel was annexed to her house.[18] In relation to the Palha farmhouse, the author was even more emphatic. Based on the writings of Joaquim Felício dos Santos and the canon of Joaquim Silvério de Sousa, Aires Machado speaks of a feudal castle of Asian splendor, adorned with golden roofs, but which served as the stage for "tragic dramas and inhuman acts of bestial cruelty best left unmentioned."[19] Here was a Chica da Silva that still bore the stigmas of the nineteenth century, wrapped in a negative myth that nevertheless continued to bring in the tourists.

It was with Soter Couto, author of *Vultos e fatos de Diamantina*, written in 1954, that Chica began to acquire a more positive image.[20] Couto exalts her beauty – the only way to explain her romances, first with Manuel Pires Sardinha and later with the wealthy contractor. Her luxuries, hitherto considered excessive and wasteful, were now interpreted as refinements, akin to the "aristocratic fare of the grand courts," as she had encouraged theater and the formation of musical groups.[21]

---

[17] Ibidem, p. 252.
[18] Ibidem.
[19] Cônego Antônio dos Santos Rocha. Apud: Aires da M. Machado Filho, op. cit., p. 265.
[20] Soter Couto. *Vultos e fatos de Diamantina*. 1954.
[21] Ibidem, p. 46.

Unable to shake off Chica's reputation as a petulant shrew and witch, Soter Couto splits her personality, portraying her as a woman with "good and bad attributes." To the Portuguese she showed only the deepest hatred, which would explain the legend, already circulating in Joaquim Felício's day, that she put some newly arrived courtiers to work like slaves in the mines. For Couto, the "African blood coursing through her veins made her maltreat them, exacting revenge for the torment inflicted upon her brothers, hunted down and shackled to be sold like animals in other lands." This approach would later be turned on its head, as Chica became the first heroine of a nascent Brazilian nationality, the redeemer of her race. Thus closed the first cycle of the myth, which modernized and adapted to mid-twentieth-century values, acquiring fresh dimensions and sophistications and gaining in psychological complexity. It was only in this new context that a woman could step out of a secondary role. Prior to this, her power over her male partner had to be veiled, indirect, and, above all, deceitful, especially as it was based in sex. An active character, with a firm hold over her own destiny, Chica da Silva was the first Brazilian woman to reign in a truly matriarchal system, thus making hers "one of the golden ages of our land."[22]

José Teixeira Neves, who compiled the explanatory notes for the third edition of *Memórias do Distrito Diamantino*, published in 1956, disagreed with Nazaré Meneses and Soter Couto and became a fresh advocate of Chica's ugliness. Neves reminds us that the former slave died in 1796, only "thirty-two years before the birth" of Joaquim Felício dos Santos, who probably based his account on first-hand information from people who would have known her in life, thus making him the most qualified to speak on Chica's true appearance.[23] However, Teixeira Neves forgot that countless cultural filters had separated the author from the people of the previous century. The concept of beauty and the things that attracted a man to a woman and that brought the sexes together were no longer the same. Besides,

[22] Ibidem, p. 47.
[23] José Teixeira Neves. Note 25, Chapter 15. In Joaquim Felício dos Santos, op. cit., 1956, p. 161.

in her twilight years, Chica would certainly have looked rather different from when she first met the young contractor.

José Teixeira Neves ratified almost everything Joaquim Felício dos Santos said about Chica, claiming that all the information upon which the book was based had come down to the author via the oral tradition of the lawyer's own family and from old residents of Diamantina he had interviewed, including a supposed granddaughter of Chica's, a centenarian named Inês Vicência da Silva, still completely lucid[24] despite her advanced years. Teixeira Neves guarantees the veracity of the claim that João Fernandes was persecuted by Pombal for involvement in diamond smuggling on the grounds that "we know [this] from tradition and from the testimonies of respectable and trustworthy individuals, who we took the trouble to consult, who heard as such from contemporaries of João Fernandes, [people] who knew him and witnessed events first hand." To reinforce his argument he claims that his information had been corroborated by "an old fellow from the time, who can confirm everything we have said."[25] For Teixeira Neves, oral memory, which he held to be the prime source of information, was a counterweight to historical discourse, toward which he harbored a prudent distrust, given that in his *História geral do Brasil*, Francisco Varnhagen had mistakenly lauded the zeal and probity of Count Valadares, a description clearly refuted by the oral tradition of the city.[26]

Also adopting the tone and style of the historical tourist guide, Lúcia Machado de Almeida published *Passeio a Diamantina* in 1960, a work dedicated to the memory of President Juscelino Kubitschek de Oliveira, whom she says "revealed an unknown Brazil to the world."[27] Kubitschek is renowned for having moved the Brazilian capital from Rio de Janeiro to Brasília, a purpose-built city in the

---

[24] José Teixeira Neves. "Estudo biográfico." In Joaquim Felício dos Santos, op. cit., 1956, p. 23.

[25] José Teixeira Neves. Note 28, Chapter 15. In Joaquim Felício dos Santos, op. cit., 1956, p. 166.

[26] Francisco Adolfo Varnhagen. *História geral do Brasil, antes da sua separação e independência de Portugal.* 1948, vol. 4, p. 257.

[27] Lúcia Machado de Almeida. *Passeio a Diamantina.* 1960, p. 5.

geographical center of the nation designed by the modernist archi-
tect Oscar Niemeyer. From the very introduction, the author evinces
the privileged position of the city and its past in the general imaginary repertoire of the time:

> Welcome to the land of diamonds, my friend! As soon as you
> arrive, you will notice, here and there, scattered blocks of stone.
> ... When you open the pores of your sensibility, you will sense
> that there is something imponderable in the air, as if events from
> bygone times have marked these parts forever: the lashing of whips
> tearing at the black flesh of rebellious slaves ... The muffled sighs
> of couples in love ... The whispers of intrigue and betrayal ... [28]

The streets were silent witnesses to the comings and goings of this
parda ex-slave and all her dangerous femininity, as she paraded, covered in diamonds, with her entourage of mestizas, just as described
by Joaquim Felício. João Fernandes was seduced by the demoniacal
arts of Chica da Silva, a woman undoubtedly beautiful and of strong
personality and magnetism. The tales the author tells about Chica,
heard on a visit to Diamantina, made the very stones of Tejuco tremble, as her wickedness knew no bounds. One story, for example, tells
of how she had a slave woman's teeth pulled out.[29] Lúcia Machado
de Almeida transforms this visit into an unforgettable experience,
worthy of being set down in a book, almost, indeed, a novel.

This author was the first to take the trouble to research documents that could confirm Joaquim Felício dos Santos' affirmations.
In her footnotes, Lúcia Machado de Almeida includes information
garnered by Rodrigues Lapa in 1946 when he researched sundry documents on Minas Gerais contained in the Overseas Archives in
Lisbon. The historian's efforts shed light on what had become of
Simão Pires Sardinha, revealing that, having received noble rank
in Lisbon, he returned to Brazil as part of the entourage of Governor Luís da Cunha Meneses. However, the ephemeral nature of this
gesture and the discontinuation of any systematic and scientifically

[28] Ibidem, p. 9.
[29] Ibidem, pp. 10, 41–7.

rigorous research prevented the initiative from resulting in a mean-
ingful contribution toward debunking the myth that was enveloping
Chica. In addition to citing the documents obtained by Rodrigues
Lapa, the author also followed the advice of Bishop Raimundo
Trindade, then director of the Museu da Inconfidência in Ouro Preto,
and consulted the ordination papers of Cipriano Pires Sardinha, who
was believed to have been Chica's second son. Though she duly
noted the inconsistency of the information, as the young priest's
mother is registered as Francisca Pires, Lúcia Machado de Almeida
went no further than to ask herself if this Francisca Pires might be
Chica da Silva. Without reaching any conclusion of her own, she
was content to leave it to the historians to unveil the mystery.[30]

In their publication of the minutes of the inquiry into the Inconfidência Mineira, *Autos de devassa da Inconfidência Mineira*, Tarquínio
de Oliveira and Herculano Mathias included various explanatory
notes, some of which, given Simão Pires Sardinha's involvement in
the seditious plans, mention Chica da Silva and her descendants.[31]

In the absence of a real historiography, Tarquínio de Oliveira,
who wrote most of the notes and all of those that mention Chica
da Silva, based himself upon the writings of Joaquim Felício and
on documents collected from the archives during complementary
research on the minutes. The historian affirms that one of Chica's
daughters had been the companion of Father Rolim, with whom she
had five children. During the rebel's imprisonment, Rita Quitéria
and her children remained at Macaúbas convent, where she had
studied with her sisters. According to the research carried out at
Macaúbas, Chica signed the admission papers for her daughters at
the institution and had beautiful handwriting. Tarquínio conjectures
as to whether Chica had not studied there herself. Analysis of the *de
genere* process for Simão Pires Sardinha's admission into the Order
of Christ revealed that Chica da Silva, daughter of Captain Antônio
Caetano de Sá and the mulatta Maria da Costa, had only a quarter

---

[30] Ibidem, pp. 43–4.
[31] Tarquínio J. B. Oliveira and Herculano Mathias. Notes and organization. *Autos
de devassa da Inconfidência Mineira*, vols. 1–9, 1978.

of African blood.[32] The historian also claims that Chief Judge João Fernandes de Oliveira had left three natural children back in the Realm, one of whom was his namesake. Upon arriving in Minas Gerais and falling for Chica da Silva, he asked her owner, José da Silva de Oliveira, Father Rolim's father, to grant her manumission. The historian corroborates the story that Chica was therefore not only the priest's half-sister, but also later his mother-in-law.[33]

The historiography sedimented the view of Chica da Silva as having been somehow unique. Slavery ensnared the black population in a state of social abandonment, so the prevailing idea was that the women lived like recluses in the slave quarters, endlessly giving birth to illegitimate and mostly mulatto children. Chica stood out for having escaped the fate reserved for the women of her race; she was therefore one of a kind, a figure that could only awaken the most contradictory sentiments in her chroniclers, for whom she was a witch, seductress, lavish spendthrift, and shrew, but also a redeemer and liberator of her people.

SPREADING THE MYTH

Up to the second half of the twentieth century, works on Chica da Silva had been dominated by a more historical approach. Based on oral sources, though without the necessary critical thought or filtering, these works were basically limited by respect for tradition. Most of the information they contained came from Joaquim Felício dos Santos, who, despite often being the object of diverging interpretations, nonetheless became the sole source of the facts.

The literature on Chica da Silva broke through the limits that restrained the historical accounts, based as they were on adherence to the facts, to the empirically verifiable. Literature's freedom to reconstruct reality meant the gaps in the history could be filled with imagination, the novel's own stylistic resource, thus aggregating further qualities to the myth. The boundaries separating fact from

[32] Ibidem, vol. 3, p. 349.
[33] Ibidem, vol. 3, pp. 138, 452–3.

fiction became increasingly blurred, as the historical substratum upon which the plot was based embarrassed the uninformed reader incapable of unbraiding the strands of history and imagination. The confusion was exacerbated by the fact that there was no consistent historical research on this woman and the eighteenth-century mining society in which she lived.

In 1953, after a trip to Minas Gerais left deep impressions upon her, Cecília Meireles wrote *Romanceiro da Inconfidência*,[34] in which the region's historical figures came to life in delicate verses couched in intricate plots:

> *This is a time of gold.*
> *That of blood soon follows.*
> *Soon come chains, soon come sentences,*
> *Soon come nooses and the gallows.*[35]

What drove the *Romanceiro* and guided the memory was the modernist spirit – so dominant in the 1950s – of understanding the urban space of Minas in the 1700s in the light of the figures that peopled it. This long poem, subdivided into numbered shorter poems, deals with the main themes of the colonial history of Minas, especially the Inconfidência of 1789. Sections XIII to XIX tell the story of the diamond contractor and his slave Chica da Silva, and here too the pages of Joaquim Felício guide Cecília Meireles' pen.[36] Her Chica is a seductress who has her lover in the palm of her hand. Her time, a time of riches, would end in suffering, like the history of Minas Gerais itself, written in blood and tears.

> Romance XIV or
> OF CHICA DA SILVA
> *What saint is on show*
> *on that veranda?*
> *It's Chica da Silva:*
> *it's Chica-que-manda!*

---

[34] Cecília Meireles. *Romanceiro da Inconfidência*. 1965.
[35] Ibidem, p. 40.
[36] Ibidem, pp. 40–53.

Face the colour of night
Eyes the colour of stars.
People come from afar
Just to meet her.
(Under the wig,
her shaven head,
and some even say she was ugly)
. . .
Look on her, white ladies,
out on her veranda,
Chica da Silva,
Chica-que-manda!

In 1959, Antônio Callado brought the character to the stage in the play O *tesouro de Chica da Silva* (*Chica da Silva's Treasure*).[37] The plot centers on a visit from Count Valadares, then governor of Minas Gerais, who has traveled to Tejuco at the Marquis de Pombal's behest to investigate suspected irregularities in the diamond contract, thus endangering the couple's bubble of luxury and wealth. Callado accentuated the intelligence and cunning of Chica-que-manda, who contrasts sharply with the "meek and mild" João Fernandes, incapable of preventing the execution of the count's threatening plan. In this play, it is not the contractor's presents that save the two lovers from ruin, but Chica's astuteness in engineering a Machiavellian plan to ensnare the governor. Chica coaxes Valadares's bastard son, who has fallen head over heels in love with her, to murder the chief guard. The deed done, she agrees to protect the lad in return for the count's silence. Valadares declares that Chica da Silva is a witch who casts her spell over all.

Chica que manda,[38] a novel by Agripa de Vasconcelos written in 1966, became the main source of information on Chica da Silva. In the six novels that comprise the *Sagas do país das Gerais* (*Sagas of the Country of Minas Gerais*), the novelist and member of the IHMG – Instituto Histórico de Minas Gerais (Historical Institute

---

[37] Antonio Callado. *Pedro Mico; o tesouro de Chica da Silva.* 1970, pp. 47–121.
[38] Agripa Vasconcelos. *Chica que manda.* 1966.

of Minas Gerais), sought to highlight the history of the state and its
most important inhabitants. Though based on real facts, imagination
fills the gaps, further blurring the bounds between fact and fiction.

In Agripa's novel, Chica was slave to a jealously that gnawed
at her insides – as both Cecília Meireles and Lúcia Machado de
Almeida had previously noted. She was a person at once capable of
acts of extreme kindness, usually directed toward slaves and natives
of the land, and acts of profound hatred, generally leveled at the
Portuguese authorities and anyone else who happened to provoke
her distrust. She spared no expense in treating the terminally ill, but
took a child allegedly born to the contractor in an extramarital affair
and hurled it into a well. An indomitable woman, she represented
the spirit of rebellion in the colony and in the Negro race.

In 1971, Paulo Amador, a novelist from Diamantina, published
a work of literary fiction in which he gave Chica new qualities and
distanced her from the extreme stereotypes of roughneck and man-
eater to which she had long been subject. In *Rei branco, rainha negra*
(*White King, Black Queen*),[39] the story is narrated by Father Rolim,
who is ultimately responsible for rehabilitating this figure he knew
so well. Chica da Silva is intellectualized and becomes a sensitive
woman, a patron of the slave and the arts. Rolim's decision to join
the Inconfidência is shown as having largely resulted from her influence over him and from the ideas of liberty and equality she planted
in his mind. Her relationship with João Fernandes is painted in a
very romantic light, with none of the erotic contours it would later
acquire in cinema. Paulo Amador's pretense that the story was based
on the contents of a manuscript attributed to Father Rolim and cited
by Joaquim Felício was designed to lend his account an air of veracity
and obscure once again the limits between fact and fiction.

In an article that appeared after the publication of *Rei branco,
rainha negra*, Paulo Amador revealed that he had conferred these
traits upon the character and the plot because he shared the view that
the history of Brazil had been constructed by its people. In his novel,
therefore, Chica da Silva would represent the Brazilian people,

---

[39] Paulo Amador. *Rei branco, rainha negra*. 1971.

hitherto ignored in the history books. Female, black, poor, intelligent, courageous, and extraordinary, she had helped found a new Brazil by seizing control of her own destiny.[40]

João Felício dos Santos wrote *Xica da Silva*[41] as the script for a movie by Cacá Diegues filmed in 1975. The following year he turned the script into a novel of the same name. This author updated the myth and gave it the sensual character so much in vogue in the 1970s, as the sexual revolution freed women from the chains of stereotypes of bashfulness and homeliness. Paradoxically, it was the grandson of a sibling of Joaquim Felício dos Santos who gave the myth of Xica – with an X indeed – the sexual twist that would never leave it. The justification for this radical transformation of the character was the lack of historical documents on the subject, which meant the sensuality of the mestizo woman was the only guiding thread for this "crazy adventure of power and love, lived out amongst the rocks and wilderness of 18th century Brazil."[42]

Cinema[43] democratized the myth, and the dimensions it acquired both in Brazil and abroad were proportional to the size of the silver screen. The film changed the spelling of her name – which became Xica da Silva – and ensured that the former slave would be eternally associated with sensuality and beauty. It therefore broke definitively with the grotesque image presented by Joaquim Felício, which the historiography, as a tributary of oral memory, had never thought to question. Having no compromise whatsoever with this tradition and with the sole aim of winning its audience, cinema, by electing to

---

[40] Paulo Amador. "História e preconceito," *Revista Palmares*, vol. 3, 2000, pp. 72–6.

[41] João Felício dos Santos. *Xica da Silva* (novel). 1976.

[42] Carlos Diegues. Introductory note. In: João Felício dos Santos, op. cit., p. 13.

[43] *Xica da Silva* was filmed in Diamantina between January and March 1975. Directed by Carlos Diegues, who also co-wrote the script with João Felício dos Santos, the film was produced by Jarbas Barbosa, with Jarbas Medeiros as historical advisor. The cast included, among others, Zezé Mota (Xica da Silva), Walmor Chagas (João Fernandes), Elke Maravilha (Donna Hortência), Altair Lima (the intendant), José Wilker (Count Valadares), and Stepan Nercessian (José). *Xica da Silva* won the awards for Best Film, Best Director, and Best Actress at the Brasília Film Festival.

accentuate black feminine sensuality, constructed a myth that was suited to the collective image repertoire of the day.

The interests of the Cinema Novo movement, of which Cacá Diegues was a part, lay in the Brazilian people and its history, but it reserved the right to take poetic license in how it retold that history. For the director, what mattered was understanding and recovering the Afro-American tradition in contemporary Brazilian society and, in pursuit of this objective, he produced celluloid renditions of the stories of two icons of African Brazil: Chica da Silva and Zumbi dos Palmares. Above all, this re-reading aimed to offer the viewer a critical vision of the relationships between the Portuguese and the Brazilian elite on the one hand, and the slaves and outcasts on the other.[44]

While the whites and their customs emerged as awkward, cold, and almost ridiculous, Chica da Silva's sexuality and radiant energy portrayed a rich and complex African culture.[45] As such, it undermined the stereotype of white domination over blacks in Brazilian culture and presented an alternative picture of this relationship. Xica da Silva is the vehicle of redemption in this movie: using her sexuality in her favor, she inverts the mechanism by which the whites ensured their dominance over her race, namely, the use of colored women to satisfy their sexual appetites.[46]

The final scenes of the film show the decline of Chica's power, which owed its existence entirely to the presence of the white dominator, represented by the diamond contractor. If the power amassed by this impudent slave challenged the reigning order, its limits were also prescribed by that same regime. Nevertheless, even stripped of her former glory, she believed that her force would never die, as its crux lay in the interest black sexuality stirred in Brazilian society.[47]

---

[44] Carlos Diegues. "Cinema Novo," *New Latin American Cinema*. 1997, p. 273; see also Amelia O'Neill. *Racial representation in film: Xica da Silva and Quilombo*. 2001, pp. 3–4.

[45] Amelia O'Neill, op. cit., p. 4.

[46] Ibidem, p. 5.

[47] Ibidem, pp. 5–6.

Last, and most recently, Chica's myth was popularized and given mass appeal in a television soap opera produced by the Manchete network in 1997.[48] The price of the democratization of the myth was its total perversion. The eroticism and bad taste were taken beyond all limits and absolutely no attempt was made to reflect the eighteenth-century reality, which historical research was unveiling in all its multiplicity and complexity. The muddled plot, which followed the flow of viewer ratings, incorporated everything from the contemporary Italian porn icon Cicciolina to a rehashing of the Renaissance drama of Romeo and Juliet, set against the mountains of Minas Gerais, complete with poison, intrigue, and the walking dead. The blatant historical distortions betrayed one of television's greatest abilities, if not its prime objective, of educating the general public while providing entertainment.

If the history was based on a metaphorical Chica, the novels, movies, and TV soaps merely created new stereotypes. Nothing was done to lift the veil that concealed the figure behind the myth. Francisca da Silva de Oliveira – the woman of flesh and bone; the former slave who walked the streets and lanes of the village of Tejuco in the 1700s; who lived through the gold and diamond cycle, an important period of Brazilian history; who accumulated wealth, acquired property, slaves, and lands; and who raised fourteen children – remained unknown.

Beyond the individual history of Chica da Silva, the course her life took sheds a great deal of light upon race relationships in the

---

[48] Author: Adamo Angel (pseudonym used by Walcyr Carrasco). Cast: Taís Araujo, Victor Wagner, Drica Moraes, Carlos Alberto, Jayme Periard, Fernando Eiras, Giovanna Anttonelli, Murilo Rosa, Mírian Pires, Ana Cecília, Carla Regina, Terena Sequerra, Eliana Guttman, André Felipe di Mauro, Maurício Gonçalves, Andréa Avancini, Lui Mendes, Maria Clara, Marco Polo, Fernando Vieira, Charles Moeller, Maria Alves, Matheus Petinatti, Luciano Rabelo, Walney Costa, José Steinberg, Lucimara Martins, Haroldo de Oliveira, Guilherme Piva, Alexandre Moreno, Edson Montenegro, Romeu Evaristo, Joana Lima Verde, Alexandre Lippiani, Iléa Ferraz, Rita Ribeiro, Ludmila Dayer, Ingrid Fridman, Octavio Victoriense, Antonio Marques, Lídia Franco, Anabella Teixeira, Rosa Castro André, Adriane Galisteu, Ângela Leal, Zezé Motta, Altair Lima, Eduardo Dusek, Leci Brandão, Sérgio Viotti, Lu Grimaldi, and Cicciolina.

geographical space of Minas Gerais. Under the mantle of a racial democracy, the mestizo society subtly and obliquely sought to whiten itself and masked the cold social and racial exclusion that really went on in Brazil.

This book has tried to reconstruct Chica da Silva in the light of the times in which she lived rather than from the perspective of the present. Like other freed women of the period, she was manumitted, loved, had children, brought them up, and strove to rise in society in the hope of diminishing the stigma her parda complexion and condition of freed slave imposed upon herself and her descendants. Though the social inclusion she sought proved paradoxical, it was the only way women like Chica could wrest back control over their own lives. They all accumulated assets, joined the brotherhoods that were emerging at the time (regardless of the color of the member-ship they purported to congregate), owned slaves, and imitated the behavior of the white elite – that was how they worked their way into white society, in search of recognition and acceptance.

Abbreviations

1. Archives and Libraries

AAPAH   Arquivo e Acervo Particular Assis Horta
ACO   Arquivo da Casa dos Ottoni
ACS   Arquivo da Casa Setecentista
AEAD   Arquivo Eclesiástico da Arquidiocese de Diamantina
AEAM   Arquivo Eclesiástico da Arquidiocese de Mariana
AFS   Arquivo do Fórum do Serro
AHCMM   Arquivo Histórico da Câmara Municipal de Mariana
AHTCL   Arquivo Histórico do Tribunal de Contas de Lisboa
AHU   Arquivo Histórico Ultramarino
AMU   Arquivo de Marinha e Ultramar
AN   Arquivo Nacional
ANTT   Arquivo Nacional da Torre do Tombo
APM   Arquivo Público Mineiro
ARM   Arquivo do Recolhimento de Macaúbas

AUC   Arquivo da Universidade de Coimbra
BAT   Biblioteca Antônio Torres
BNL   Biblioteca Nacional de Lisboa
FBN   Fundação Biblioteca Nacional – Rio de Janeiro
INSC   Igreja de Nossa Senhora do Carmo – Diamantina
IPHAN/BH   Arquivo do Instituto do Patrimônio Histórico e Artístico Nacional/Belo Horizonte
IPHAN/RJ   Arquivo do Instituto do Patrimônio Histórico e Artístico Nacional/Rio de Janeiro
MO/CBG   Museu do Ouro/Casa Borba Gato

2. Document Collections

AHU/MAMG   Manuscritos Avulsos de Minas Gerais. Fundo do Arquivo Histórico Ultramarino

APM/SC   Seção Colonial. Fundo do Arquivo Público Mineiro

HSJ/TFP   Testamentaria de Francisco Pinheiro. Fundo do Hospital São José

SUGGESTED READING

What follows is a list of readings in **English** related to themes discussed in this book, not necessarily only those dealing with slavery as such, but other social and cultural matters (some in French) as well that pertain to the life of Chica da Silva and the world in which she lived. This list is not exhaustive, but rather suggests some possible avenues for further study and research. The Brazilian titles listed are only the ones that were cited (for the complete list see the Brazilian edition).

ALDEN, Dauril. "The population of Brazil in the late eighteenth century: A preliminary survey." *Hispanic American Historical Review,* v. 43, n. 2, pp. 173–205, 1963.

ALEXANDER, Herbert. "Brazilian and United States slavery compared." *Journal of Negro History,* v. 7, n. 4, pp. 349–64, 1922.

ANDERSON, Bonnie, and ZINSSER, Judith. *A history of their own.* London: Penguin Books, 1988.

ANDREWS, G. R. "Black and white workers: São Paulo: Brazil, 1888–1928." *Hispanic American Historical Review,* v. 68, n. 3, pp. 491–524, 1988.

ATTWATER, Donald. *The Penguin dictionary of saints.* London: Penguin Books, 1983.

BEEMAN, Richard R. "Labor forces and race relations: A comparative view of the colonization of Brazil and Virginia. *Political Science Quarterly,* v. 86, pp. 609–36, 1971.

BERGAD, Laird W. "After the mining boom: Demographic and economic aspects of slavery in Mariana, Minas Gerais, 1750–1808." *Latin American Research Review,* v. 31, n. 1, pp. 67–97, 1996.

BERGAD, Laird W. *Slavery and demographic and economic history of Minas Gerais, Brazil, 1720–1888.* Cambridge: Cambridge University Press, 1999.

BLACKBURN, Robin. *The overthrow of colonial slavery, 1776–1848.* London/New York: Verso, 1988.

BOURDIEU, Pierre. "L'illusion biographique." *Actes de la Recherche,* Paris, v. 62–3, pp. 69–72, 1986.

BOXER, Charles Ralph. *Race relations in the Portuguese empire, 1415–1825.* Oxford: Oxford University Press, 1963.

BOXER, Charles Ralph. "Negro slavery in Brazil." *Race*, v. 3, pp. 38–47, 1964.

BOXER, Charles Ralph. *Golden age of Brazil: Growing pains of a colonial society, 1695–1750.* New York: St. Martin's Press, 1995.

BROOKS, Charles. *Disaster at Lisbon: The great earthquake of 1755.* Long Beach: Longley Press, 1994.

BURTON, Richard F. *Explorations of the highlands of Brazil with a full account of the gold and diamond mines.* London, 1869, 2v.

COHEN, David W., and GREENE, Jack P. (orgs.). *Neither slave nor free: The freedmen of African descent in the slave societies of the New World.* Baltimore: Johns Hopkins University Press, 1982.

CONRAD, Robert. *Brazilian slavery: An annotated research bibliography.* Boston: G. K. Hall & Co., 1977.

CONRAD, Robert. *Children of God's fire: A documentary history of black slavery in Brazil.* Princeton: Princeton University Press, 1983.

CARDOSO, Ciro Flamarion S. "The peasant breach in the slave system: New developments in Brazil." *Luso-Brazilian Review*, v. 25, n. 1, pp. 49–57, 1988.

COSTA, Emília Viotti. *The Brazilian empire: Myths and histories.* Chicago: University of Chicago Press, 1985.

CURTO, José C., and LOVEJOY, Paul E. (eds.). *Enslaving connections: Changing cultures of Africa and Brazil during the era of slavery.* New York: Humanity Books, 2004.

DANTAS, Mariana L. R. *Black townsmen: A comparative study of persons of African origin and descent in slavery and freedom in Baltimore, Maryland, and Sabará, Minas Gerais.* Baltimore: Johns Hopkins University, 2003. (PhD, History).

DEGLER, Carl. *Neither black nor white: Slavery and race relations in Brazil and the United States.* Wisconsin: University of Wisconsin Press, 1986.

DE GUIBERT, Joseph. *La spiritualité de la Compagnie de Jésus.* Rome: Institutum Historicum, 1953.

DIAS, Maria Odila Leite da Silva. *Power and everyday life: The lives of working women in nineteenth-century Brazil.* New Brunswick, NJ: Rutgers University Press, 1995.

DIEGUES, Carlos. "Cinema Novo," *New Latin American Cinema.* Detroit: Wayne State University Press, 1997.

DONALD JR, Cleveland. "Slave resistance and abolitionism in Brazil: The Campista case." *Luso-Brazilian Review*, v. 13, n. 2, pp. 182–93, 1976.

DUTRA, Francis A. "Membership in the Order of Christ in the seventeenth century: Its rights, privileges and obligations." *Americas*, v. 27, n. 1, pp. 3–25, 1970.

DUTRA, Francis A. "Blacks and the search for rewards and status in seventeenth-century Brazil." *Proceedings of the Pacific Coast Council on Latin American Studies*, v. 6, pp. 25–35, 1977–9.

ENGERMAN, Stanley L., and GENOVESE, E. *Race and slavery in the Western hemisphere: Quantitative studies*. Princeton: Princeton University Press, 1975.

ENGERMAN, Stanley L. "Studying the black family." *Journal of Family History*, v. 3, n. 1, pp. 78–101, 1979.

FERNANDES, Florestan. *The negro in Brazilian society*. New York: Columbia University Press, 1969.

FLAX, Jane. "Gender as a social problem: In and for feminist theory." *American Studies*, 1986.

FREYRE, Gilberto. *The Masters and the Slaves*. New York: Knopf, 1946.

GANSS, George. *Saint Ignatius, idea of a Jesuit university*. Milwaukee: Marquette University Press, 1954.

GRAHAM, Richard. "Brazilian slavery re-examined: A review article." *Journal of Social History*, v. 3, pp. 431–53, 1970.

GRAHAM, Richard. "Slave families on a rural estate in colonial Brazil." *Journal of Social History*, v. 11, n. 3, pp. 382–402, 1976.

GRAHAM, Sandra Lauderdale. *House and street. The domestic world of servants and masters in nineteenth-century Rio de Janeiro*. Cambridge: Cambridge University Press, 1988.

GRAHAM, Sandra Lauderdale. *Caetana says no: Women's stories from a Brazilian slave society*. Cambridge: Cambridge University Press, 2002.

GRAHAM, Sandra Lauderdale. "Writing from the margins: Brazilian slaves and written culture." *Comparative Studies in Society and History*, v. 49, n. 3, pp. 611–36, 2007.

GUDEMAN, Stephen, and SCHWARTZ, Stuart B. "Cleasing original sin: Godparentage and baptism of slaves in eighteenth century Bahia." In SMITH, Raymond T. (ed.). *Kinship ideology and practice in Latin America*. North Carolina: Chapel Hill, 1984.

HAASE-DUBOSC, Danielle, and VIENNOT, Éliane (ed.). *Femmes et pouvoirs sous l'Ancien Régime*. Col. Histoire. Paris: Rivages, 1991.

HIGGINS, Kathleen J. "Masters and slaves in a mining society: A study of eighteenth-century Sabará, Minas Gerais." *Slavery and Abolition*, v. 11, n. 1, pp. 58–73, 1990.

HIGGINS, Kathleen J. "Gender and the manumission of slaves in colonial Brazil." *Slavery and Abolition*, v. 18, n. 2, pp. 1–29, 1997.

HIGGINS, Kathleen J. *Licentious liberty in a Brazilian gold-mining region*. University Park: Pennsylvania State University Press, 1999.

HUNT, Morton. *The natural history of love*. Londres: Hutchinson and Co., 1960.

KARASCH, Mary. *Slave life in Rio de Janeiro, 1808–1850*. Princeton: Princeton University Press, 1987.

KIDDY, Elizabeth W. "Ethnic and racial identity in the Brotherhoods of the Rosary of Minas Gerais 1700–1830." *Americas*, v. 56, n. 2, pp. 221–52, 1999.

KLEIN, Herbert. "The colored freedmen in Brazilian slave society." *Journal of Social History*, v. 3, n. 1, pp. 30–52, 1969.

KLEIN, Herbert. "Nineteenth-century Brazil." In COHEN, D., and GREENE, J. (eds). *Neither slave nor free: The freedmen of African descent in the slave societies of New World*. Baltimore: Johns Hopkins University Press, 1972, pp. 309–34.

KLEIN, Herbert. "The population of Minas Gerais: New research on colonial Brazil." *Latin American Population History Newsletter*, v. 4, pp. 1–10, 1984.

KLEIN, Herbert. *African Slavery in Latin America and the Caribbean*. New York: Oxford University Press, 1986.

KLEIN, Herbert, and PAIVA, Clotilde A. "Freedmen in a slave economy: Minas Gerais in 1831." *Journal of Social History*, v. 29, n. 4, pp. 935–62, 1996.

KLEIN, Herbert, and LUNA, Francisco Vidal. "Free colored in a slave society: São Paulo and Minas Gerais in the early nineteenth century." *Hispanic American Historical Review*, v. 80, n. 4, pp. 913–41, 2000.

KUZNESOF, Elizabeth. *Household economy and urban development: São Paulo 1765–1836*. Boulder: Westview Press, 1986.

KUZNESOF, Elizabeth. "Household, family and community studies." *Latin American Population History Newsletter*, v. 14, 1988.

LASLETT, Peter (ed.). *Household and family in past time*. London: Cambridge University Press, 1972.

LE GOFF, Jacques. *Saint Louis*. Paris: Gallimard, 1996.

LEVI, Giovanni. "Les usages de la biographie." *Annales*, Paris, v. 44, n. 6, pp. 1325–35, 1989.

LEWIN, Linda. "Natural and spurious children in Brazilian inheritance law from colony to empire: A methodological essay." *Americas*, v. 48, n. 3, pp. 351–96, 1992.

LIBBY, Douglas P. "Proto-industrialization in a slave society: The case of Minas Gerais." *Journal of Latin American studies*, v. 23, pp. 1–35, 1991.

LUCCOCK, John. *Notes on Rio de Janeiro and the southern parts of Brazil*. London: Leigh, 1820.

LUNA, Francisco V., and KLEIN, H. "Slaves and masters in early nineteenth-century Brazil: São Paulo." *Journal of Interdisciplinary History*, v. 21, n. 4, pp. 549–73, 1991.

LUNA, Francisco V., and KLEIN, H. *The slave economy and society of São Paulo, 1750–1850*. Stanford: Stanford University Press, 2003.

LYNCH, Joseph. *Godparents and kinship in early medieval Europe.* Princeton: Princeton University Press, 1986.

MANCHESTER, Alan K. "Racial democracy in Brazil." *South Atlantic Quarterly,* v. 44, n. 1, pp. 27–35, 1965.

MARTINS FILHO, Amilcar, and MARTINS, Roberto B. "Slavery in a nonexport economy: Nineteenth-century Minas Gerais revisited." *Hispanic American Historical Review,* v. 63, n. 3, pp. 537–68, 1983.

MATTOSO, Kátia Q. *To be a slave in Brazil, 1550–1888.* New Brunswick, NJ: Rutgers University Press, 1986.

MATTOSO, Kátia Q. "Slave, free and freed family structures in nineteenth-century Salvador, Bahia." *Luso-Brazilian Review,* v. 25, n. 1, pp. 69–84, 1988.

MAXWELL, Kenneth. "Pombal and the nationalization of the Luzo-Brazilian economy." *Hispanic American Historical Review,* v. 4, n. 48, pp. 608–31, 1968.

MAXWELL, Kenneth. *Conflicts and conspiracies: Brazil and Portugal, 1750–1808.* Cambridge: Cambridge University Press, 1973.

MAXWELL, Kenneth. *Pombal: Paradox of the enlightenment.* Cambridge: Cambridge University Press, 1995.

MAWE, John. *Travels in the interior of Brazil, particularly in the gold and diamond districts.* London: Longman, Hurst, Rees ... , 1812.

METCALF, Alida C. "Searching for the slave family in colonial Brazil: A reconstruction from São Paulo." *Journal of Family History,* v. 16, n. 3, pp. 283–97, 1991.

METCALF, Alida C. *Family and frontier in colonial Brazil: Santana de Parnaíba, 1580–1822.* Berkeley and Los Angeles: University of California Press, 1992.

MULVEY, Patricia. *The black lay brotherhoods of colonial Brazil.* New York: City College of New York, 1976. (PhD, History).

MULVEY, Patricia. "Black brothers and sisters: Membership in the black lay brotherhoods of colonial Brazil." *Luso-Brazilian Review,* v. 2, n. 17, pp. 252–79, 1980.

NABUCO, Joaquim. *Abolitionism: The Brazilian antislavery struggle.* Urbana: University of Illinois Press, 1977.

NARO, Nancy Priscilla. *A slave's place, a master's world: Fashioning dependence in rural Brazil.* London/New York: Continuun, 2000.

NARO, Nancy Priscilla (ed.). *Blacks, coloureds and national identity in nineteenth-century Latin America.* London: ILAS, 2003.

NAZZARI, Muriel. "Concubinage in colonial Brazil: The inequalities of race, class, and gender." *Journal of Family History,* v. 21, pp. 107–23, 1996.

NAZZARI, Muriel. *The disappearance of the dowry: Women, families and social changes in São Paulo, Brazil (1600–1900)*. Palo Alto: Stanford University Press, 1991.

NISHIDA, Mieko. *Slavery and identity: Ethnicity, gender, and race in Salvador, Brazil, 1808–1888*. Bloomington: Indiana University Press, 2003.

O'NEILL, Amelia. *Racial representation in film: Xica da Silva and Quilombo* (mimeo). Princeton: Princeton University, 2001.

PESCATELLO, Ann M. (org.). *The African in Latin America*. New York: Knopf, 1975.

PESCATELLO, Ann M. *Power and pawn, the female in Iberian families, societies, and cultures*. Westport, CT: Greenwood Press, 1976.

PIERRARD, Pierre. *Dictionnaire des prénoms et des saints*. Paris: Larrouse, 1987.

PIERSON, Donald. *Negros in Brazil: A study of race contact at Bahia*. Carbondale/ Edwardsville: Southern Illinois University Press, 1967.

PRADO Jr, Caio. *The colonial background of modern Brazil*. Berkeley/Los Angeles: California University Press, 1967.

RAMOS, Donald. *A social history of Ouro Preto: Stresses of dynamic urbanization in colonial Brazil, 1695–1726*. Miami: University of Florida, 1972, 2v. (PhD, History Department)

RAMOS, Donald. "Marriage and family in colonial Vila Rica." *Hispanic American Historical Review*, v. 55, pp. 200–25, 1975.

RAMOS, Donald. "City and country: The family in Minas Gerais, 1804–1838." *Journal of Family History*, v. 3, n. 4, pp. 361–75, 1975.

RAMOS, Donald. "Vila Rica: Profile of a colonial Brazilian urban center." *Americas*, v. 35, n. 4, pp. 495–526, 1979.

RAMOS, Donald. "Single and married women in Vila Rica, Brazil, 1754–1838." *Journal of Family History*, v. 16, n. 3, pp. 261–81, 1991.

REIS, João José. *Slave rebellion in Brazil: The Muslim uprising of 1835 in Bahia*. Baltimore: Johns Hopkins University Press, 1993.

RUSSELL-WOOD, A. J. R. "Class, creed, and colour in colonial Bahia: A study in prejudice." *Race*, v. 9, n. 2, pp. 133–57, 1967.

RUSSELL-WOOD, A. J. R. "Black and mulatto brotherhoods in colonial Brazil: A study in collective behavior." *Hispanic American Historical Review*, v. 54, n. 4, pp. 567–602, 1974.

RUSSELL-WOOD, A. J. R. "Preconditions and precipitants of the independence movement in Portuguese America." In *From colony to nation: Essays on the independence of Brazil*. Baltimore: Johns Hopkins University Press, 1975.

RUSSELL-WOOD, A. J. R. "Women and society in colonial Brazil." *Latin American Studies*, v. 9, pp. 1–34, 1977.

RUSSELL-WOOD, A. J. R. "Iberian expansion and the issue of black slavery: Changing Portuguese attitudes, 1440–1770." *American Historical Review*, v. 83, n. 1, pp. 16–44, 1978.

RUSSELL-WOOD, A. J. R. Female and family in the economy and society of colonial Brazil. In LAVRIN, Asunción (org.). *Latin American Women, historical perspectives*. Westport: Greenwood Press, 1978, pp. 60–100.

RUSSELL-WOOD, A. J. R. *The black man in slavery and freedom in colonial Brazil*. New York: St. Martin's Press, 1982.

SCARANO, Julita. "Black brotherhoods: Integration or contradiction?" *Luso-Brazilian Review*, v. 1, n. 16, pp. 1–17, 1979.

SCHWARCZ, Lilia. *The spectacle of the races: Scientists, institutions, and the race question in Brazil, 1870–1930*. New York: Hill and Wang, 1999.

SCHWARTZ, Stuart B. "Magistracy and society in colonial Brazil." *Hispanic American Historical Review*, v. 50, n. 4, pp. 715–30, 1970.

SCHWARTZ, Stuart B. "The Mocambo: Slave resistence in colonial Bahia." *Journal of Social History*, v. 3, pp. 313–33, 1970.

SCHWARTZ, Stuart B. "The manumission of slaves in colonial Brazil: Bahia, 1684–1745." *Hispanic American Historical Review*, v. 54, 1974, pp. 603–35.

SCHWARTZ, Stuart B. "Resistance and accommodation in eighteenth-century Brazil: The slave's view of slavery." *Hispanic American Historical Review*, v. 57, n. 1, pp. 69–81, 1977.

SCHWARTZ, Stuart. "The plantations of St. Benedictine sugar mills of colonial Brazil." *Americas*, v. 39, n. 1, pp. 1–22, 1982.

SCHWARTZ, Stuart B. *Sugar plantation in the formation of Brazilian society, 1550–1835*. New York: Cambridge University Press, 1985.

SCHWARTZ, Stuart B. *Slaves, peasants, and rebels: Reconsidering Brazilian slavery*. Urbana: University of Illinois Press, 1992.

SKIDMORE, Thomas E. *Black into white: Race and nationality in Brazilian thought*. Durham, NC: Duke University Press, 1993.

SILVA, Eduardo. *Prince of the people: The life and times of a Brazilian free man of colour*. London/New York: Verso, 1993.

SKIDMORE, Thomas. *Black into white*. New York: Oxford University Press, 1974.

SLENES, Robert et alli. "Coments on 'Slavery in a non-export society.'" *Hispanic American Historical Review*, v. 63, n. 3, pp. 569–91, 1983.

SOEIRO, Susan. "The social and economic role of the convent: Women and nuns in colonial Bahia (1677–1800)." *Hispanic Historical American Review*, Durham, v. 54, n. 2, pp. 209–32, 1974.

SOEIRO, Susan. "Recent work on Latin American women: A review essay." *Journal of Interamerican Studies*, v. 17, pp. 497–517, 1975.

SOUTHEY, Robert. *History of Brazil*. London: Longman, Hurst, Rees and Orme, 1810–19. 3 vols.

SOUZA, Laura de Mello e. *The devil and the land of the holy cross: Witchcraft, slavery, and popular religion in colonial Brazil*. Austin: University of Texas Press, 2003.

STEDMAN, J. G. "Narrative of a five year expedition against the revolted negroes of Surinam." In PRICE, Richard et al. (org.). *Stedman's Surinam*. Baltimore: Johns Hopkins University Press, 1992.

STEIN, Stanley. *Vassouras, a Brazilian coffee county, 1850–1900: The roles of planter and slave in a plantation society*. Princeton: Princeton University Press, 1985.

SWEET, James H. *Recreating Africa: Culture, kinship and religion in the African-Portuguese world, 1441–1770*. Chapel Hill/London: University of North Carolina Press, 2003.

VERGER, Pierre. *Bahia and the West Coast trade, 1549–1851*. Nigeria: Ibadan University Press, 1964.

VOVELLE, Michel. "De la biographie à l'étude de cas." In *Problèmes et méthodes de la biographie*. Paris, 1985.

WILLIAMS, Mary Wilhelmine. "The treatment of negro slaves in the Brazilian empire: A comparison with the United States of America." *Journal of Negro History*, v. 15, n. 3, pp. 315–36, 1930.

INDEX